Human Resources in Organisations

We work with leading authors to develop the
strongest educational materials in human resource
management, bringing cutting-edge thinking and
best learning practice to a global market.

Under a range of well-known imprints, including
Financial Times Prentice Hall we craft high quality print and
electronic publications which help readers to understand
and apply their content, whether studying or at work.

To find out more about the complete range of our
publishing, please visit us on the World Wide Web at:
www.pearsoned.co.uk

Human Resources in Organisations

Edited by

John Leopold

An imprint of **Pearson Education**

Harlow, England · London · New York · Reading, Massachusetts · San Francisco · Toronto · Don Mills, Ontario · Sydney
Tokyo · Singapore · Hong Kong · Seoul · Taipei · Cape Town · Madrid · Mexico City · Amsterdam · Munich · Paris · Milan

Pearson Education Limited
Edinburgh Gate
Harlow
Essex CM20 2JE
England

and Associated Companies throughout the world

Visit us on the World Wide Web at:
www.pearsoned.co.uk

First published 2002

© Pearson Education Limited 2002

The rights of John Leopold, Rachael Hall, Jim Stewart, Yvonne Leverment, Susan Simpson, Hazel Williams and Diannah Lowry to be identified as the authors of this work have been asserted by them in accordance with the Copyright, Designs and Patents Act 1988.

ISBN 0273 64399-1   PPR

British Library Cataloguing-in-Publication Data
A catalogue record for this book is available from the British Library

Library of Congress Cataloging-in-Publication Data
A catalog record for this book is available from the Library of Congress

10 9 8 7 6 5 4 3
08 07 06 05 04

Set in 9.5/12.5pt Stone Serif by 35
Printed by Ashford Colour Press Ltd., Gosport

To our parents

Contents

1 **Introduction**

2 **Employee resourcing**

3 **Employee reward**

4 **Employee development**

5 **Employee relations**

List of Figures

List of Tables

List of Case Studies

Contributing Authors

All contributing authors are members of the Department of Human Resource Management, Nottingham Business School, The Nottingham Trent University.

Rachael Hall is Senior Lecturer in Human Resource Management. After working as a food technologist, a manager with Coats Viyella and a human resource and quality manager with an engineering consultancy, Rachael has taught employee resourcing and development to both undergraduate and postgraduate students at NBS. Currently on secondment with the Corporate Business Unit at Nottingham Business School, Rachael is involved in delivering and designing a wide range of management development programmes in a range of organisations. Particularly involved with the Chartered Institute of Personnel and Development (CIPD) professional programmes, Rachael leads the Department's involvement in teaching on the Lloyds TSB CIPD programme and the Lloyds TSB DMS programme.

John Leopold is Associate Dean of Nottingham Business School and Professor and Head of Department of Human Resource Management. His research interests are the development of HRM in greenfield sites in the United Kingdom and New Zealand and control over working time in the United Kingdom and in the Netherlands. Joint editor of a *Personnel Review* special edition on HRM in greenfield sites, he has published in all the leading HRM and Industrial Relations journals, and is co-editor of *Strategic Human Resourcing: Principles, Perspectives and Practices*, FT Management, 1999. He is a member of the CIPD's Quality Assurance Panel.

Yvonne Leverment has worked for many years in the health service – both as a clinician and as a health manager. As a member of the human resource department in the business school she is Senior Lecturer in Organisational Behaviour and Employee Relations. Her research interests focus on the professions, professional associations and changes in working practice and job redesign. She is currently completing her PhD which examines changes in work practice in the health service.

Diannah Lowry is Senior Lecturer in HRM at Nottingham Business School which she joined from the University of New South Wales in Sydney, Australia. She is module leader of a Level 2 undergraduate module, Human Resources in Organisations, from which the book derives its title. Her academic areas of interest include the impacts of flexible labour forms, ethics and HRM, and the concept of presenteeism. Diannah's research pursuits reflect these academic areas, and she is currently engaged in research that examines improved HRM practices for casualised workers, the ethical implications of flexible work forms, and the impact of managerial presenteeism.

Sue Simpson is a Senior Lecturer in HRM at the Business School. Sue lectures in organisational behaviour, business ethics and HRM, drawing on her previous experience in personnel work in both the public and private sectors, including several years in an industrial relations role in the telecommunications industry. She has taught at undergraduate, postgraduate and professional levels and as a volunteer in a Malay secondary school. She served for five years on the local CIPD committee. Sue has researched both educational initiatives and employees' attitudes to involvement and is currently focusing on human resource impacts in the service sector.

Jim Stewart is Professor of Human Resource Development, Reviews Editor of the *International Journal of Training and Development*, and Chair of the University Forum for HRD. He is author of *Employee Development Practice* (1999: FT Pitman Publishing). He is a National Assessment Moderator and a member of the Quality Assurance Panel of the CIPD. He founded the MSc in Human Resource Development at NBS, is currently joint course Leader of the DBA and teaches Human Resource Development on this and other programmes, drawing upon his prior experience as a management and employee development professional in both local government and the retail sectors.

Hazel Williams is Senior Lecturer in Human Resource Management. Hazel has worked in a range of industries including computing, heavy structural engineering, retail, hospitality and leisure in mainly HR specialist roles. She has taught at both undergraduate and postgraduate level at NBS, particularly on CIPD programmes. Her current research interests focus on the strategic use of human resource information systems. Hazel is also the Principal of *ACE* Consultancy, where the focus is on integrating human resourcing at a corporate level to enable competitive advantage.

Preface

This book is aimed primarily at undergraduate students who aspire to become managers in a general sense rather than those seeking to become human resource specialists (although it also serves as an introduction for them). We recognise that virtually every BA Business Studies degree programme has somewhere at Level 1 or 2 an introductory module that all students, not just those specialising in HRM, must take. This module may also be for students on related accountancy, management, or other specialist degree programmes. Many of these students may not see the immediate relevance of this module to their overall studies. This book is for them. Therefore we try to offer case studies, examples and discussion questions that examine the role of line managers in managing the employment relationship on a day-to-day basis. This material may be supplemented by additional reading that appears as a guide to each chapter.

Each chapter is written around a common structure of learning and teaching features that will assist readers in addressing the issues raised in the chapters. These features include clear student learning objectives, activities to engage students, clearly laid out definitions of key terms, chapter summaries, a major case study, discussion points and a guide to further reading at the end of each chapter. The material in the chapters, especially the activities and case studies, has been piloted, and subsequently refined, in our teaching on introductory HRM modules in undergraduate programmes aimed at a wide range of Business Studies and Management students, as well as on the certificate level of postgraduate programmes. In short, this book is the product of a team experienced in teaching the students at whom it is aimed, and the chapters have been shaped by the authors' pedagogic experience and research work.

We have made a deliberate and conscious decision that as this is an introductory book; we do not have comparative chapters on other countries, or chapters on our own detailed research, or chapters on specialist areas of human resource practice. However, we have sought to integrate international comparisons where relevant, to include examples from small and medium enterprises (SMEs) rather than have a separate chapter, and to integrate equal opportunities and legal issues into appropriate chapters.

Using this book

Each chapter contains a number of common features that will help readers to gain most benefit from it. In addition, there is an accompanying tutor's guide that offers advice and suggestions for using these exercises, case studies and discussion questions in the classroom situation. Each chapter begins with a set of objectives that readers should be able to achieve on completion of the chapter and its associated exercises. Throughout the chapters are activities that can be used in a number of ways depending on the learning context of the reader. At the end of each chapter is a major case study that attempts to draw on the key learning points in the chapter and offers the opportunity to examine and discuss a range of questions around each case. Activities and case studies can be used as either individual or group-work exercises by course members as directed independent learning activities, or as part of tutor-guided workshop discussions. To that end, the case studies are of varying length and the number of questions set for discussion can be varied by tutors to suit the needs of the student group and the time available. Guidance on this is to be found in the accompanying tutor's guide. The-end-of-chapter case studies are ideal for use with a supporting lecture followed by seminar activity. Most chapters conclude with a set of questions that can be used to open up new areas for discussion or as reflective exercises on what has been learned. Lastly, each chapter ends with suggestions for further reading.

In producing the exercises and case studies, we have attempted to draw on a range of organisational contexts, including manufacturing, public sector, SMEs and non-profit-making bodies to reflect the range of settings where the employment relationship is managed. We are mindful of the fact that most students taking introductory HRM modules will have limited work experience, mostly of a part-time and casual nature, to draw upon. But we have tried to use examples that even such students can relate to.

Throughout the book we have tried to analyse the respective role and responsibilities of specialist and line managers.

Authors' Acknowledgements

This book would not have seen the light of day without the dedicated skills of the Departmental Administrator, Debbie Wojtulewicz, who prepared the final manuscript from a motley collection of disks, e-mail attachments and even hand-written notes. We thank her for her efforts.

A number of other colleagues within the Department read draft chapters and offered valuable comments. We are grateful to David Walsh and Tony Watson.

We would also like to thank our Commissioning Editor Catherine Newman, and desk editor Verina Pettigrew, at Pearson Education, for all their support and assistance in bringing this project to fruition.

Publisher's Acknowledgements

We are grateful to the following for permission to reproduce copyright material:

Table 2.11 from *HR Information Systems: Stand and Deliver Report 335* published by the Institute for Employment Studies (Robinson, D.C. 1997); Table 3.1 adapted from *Human Resource Management: A Contemporary Approach*, published by Pitman Publishing Ltd., (Beardwell, I. and Holden, L. 1994); Figure 4.1 adapted from *Employment Resourcing*, published by Financial Times/Pitman Publishing Ltd., (Corbridge, M. and Pilbeam, S. 1998); Figure 5.1 adapted from *Management and Organisational Behaviour*, 4e, published by Pearson Education Ltd., © L. Mullins (Mullins, L. 1999); Figure 5.4 from 'A New Strategy for Job Enrichment' (Hackman, J. Richard *et al.*) Copyright © 1975, by The Regents of the University of California. Reprinted from the *California Management Review*, Vol. 17, No. 4. By permission of The Regents; Figure 6.3 from Kaplan and Norton (1992) 'The balanced scorecard – measures that drive performance' Harvard Business Review, January–February, pp. 71–9; Tables 9.1 and 9.6 from *Employee Development Practice*, published by Pearson Education Ltd., (Stewart, J. 1999); Guardian Newspapers Limited for three extracts by Seamus Milne 'Danish firm's UK staff await equal treatment', 'Tesco embrace of union opens way to "new era"' and 'Question time for press barons', all published in *The Guardian*.

Whilst every effort has been made to trace the owners of copyright material, in a few cases this has proved impossible and we take this opportunity to offer our apologies to any copyright holders whose rights we may have unwittingly infringed.

Part 1 Introduction

Chapter 1 From welfare to human resource management
John Leopold

Chapter **From welfare to human resource management**

John Leopold

Having completed this chapter and its associated activities, readers should be able to:

- appreciate the different phases of development that personnel management has gone through since the origins of welfare work at the beginning of the twentieth century
- understand the weaknesses and limitations of personnel management as a separate management group
- be aware of potential tensions and ambiguities in the relationship between line managers and human resource specialists
- understand that the personnel function has to be fulfilled in all organisations even if there is no separate department
- appreciate the differences between personnel management and human resource management
- outline some of the main models of human resource management available
- appreciate the kaleidoscope as a device to understand the inter-relationship between the organisation, its environment and specific human resource policies and practices.
- appreciate the content, structure and layout of the rest of the book

INTRODUCTION

Personnel management and human resource management have had in the past, indeed may have at the present, an image problem. This affects the way these specialist managers are viewed by employees and more importantly by other managers. This image problem may be thought of by looking at examples of the way both personnel managers and human resource managers have been portrayed in films and television.

Torrington and Hall (1998) cite the 'Dirty Harry' view of Personnel. In the 1970s Clint Eastwood appeared in the role of Harry Callaghan, the fast-shooting, ask-no-questions cop Dirty Harry. His style of policing often landed him in trouble with his superiors and politicians. Following a particularly gruesome shooting spree he is called into the Chief of Police's office and told that as a result of this he is being transferred – to Personnel. There is a moment of electric silence. A nervous tic flickered briefly on Harry Callaghan's right cheek. His jaw locked and those famous cold blue eyes gave the Chief a look that could have penetrated armour plate as he hissed his reply through clenched teeth: 'Personnel is for assholes.'

Thirty years later at the end of the twentieth century many personnel departments had become human resource management departments. A member of such a department was Philippa, a character in the television comedy series *Dinner*

Ladies. Philippa is a rather well-meaning but ineffectual character and introduces herself to the canteen team: 'Gosh, I never know whether to say what it used to be, or what it is now. It's . . . it was Personnel and now it's Human Resources.'

Of course both characters are stereotypes, but even thirty years apart they show that personnel managers are not that highly regarded in society generally. Similar jokes are not confined to personnel: other management groups also have their stereotypes, such as dull, boring accountants, or dubious sales people. The two snap-shots reveal the name change from personnel to human resources, but suggest that this change may not have altered the image. What we therefore intend to do in the remainder of this chapter is outline and explain the origins and development of personnel management as a specialist group of managers, and to consider some of the tensions and ambiguities about the role of personnel specialists and line managers. We consider differences in meaning between personnel management and human resource management, and then establish the tasks that need to be done in organisations as part of the HRM function and demonstrate the importance and significance of these to organisations. Finally, we introduce the framework of the *kaleidoscope* as a way of visualising the relationship between the organisation and the environment in which it operates and the internal relationships between the various policies and practices of the human resource management function. This helps us to frame and outline the content and structure of the rest of the book.

Activity 1.1

1 Think about organisations you have worked in or read about. Did they have a personnel department, or a human resource management department, or perhaps neither?

2 If the department was called human resources do you know when the name was changed and why?

3 Does either the Dirty Harry or Philippa stereotype apply to personnel/human resource managers you have come across in these organisations?

4 Are there other images of the roles these managers played that you could offer?

Overview of the development of personnel management

We can get a snapshot overview of the development of personnel management in the UK by looking at Table 1.1. This shows the various name changes that what is now the Chartered Institute of Personnel and Development, the professional body for personnel and development practitioners, has gone through and its membership at various key points in time. From this we can make comments about both the number of people involved in personnel management and the differing emphasis of the job as reflected in the name of the professional body.

Table 1.1 The origins and development of the Institute of Personnel and Development

Year	Title of Organisation	Number of members
1913	Welfare Workers Association	34
1919	Welfare Workers Institute	700
1928	Institute of Industrial Welfare Workers	(1927) 420
1934	Institute of Labour Management	(1933) 513
1939	Institute of Labour Management	760
1946	Institute of Personnel Management	(1956) 3,979
1987	Institute of Personnel Management	31,444
1991	Institute of Personnel Management	47,000
1994	Institute of Personnel and Development	70,000
2000	Chartered Institute of Personnel and Development	105,000

The welfare origins of personnel management

The first discernible distinct group of professional people engaged in aspects of personnel work were welfare workers employed by leading paternalist Quaker employers such as Cadbury, Fry and Rowntree. Essentially these welfare workers were social workers in industry whose role was to dispense benefits to unfortunate, but deserving, employees. They were overwhelmingly women and their numbers grew markedly during the First World War, especially after Rowntree, responsible for the Industrial Welfare department at the Ministry of Munitions, made it obligatory to have such a staff member in explosives factories. The role of welfare workers extended into recruitment and selection especially as most of the new wartime munitions workers were women. By 1919 the then Welfare Workers Institute had an individual membership of some 700 and, as well as welfare workers, included a group of managers with an industrial relations orientation who had been members of the North Western Area Industrial Association.

However, the numbers employed in this role fell after the end of the war and membership numbers did not reach the 1919 level again until 1939. Moreover during the 1920s and 1930s there was a marked change in both the composition of the Institute and in the role carried out by its members. The focus of work moved away from welfare to the dual roles of control of time-keeping and dealing with trade unions, primarily in large factories in the engineering and metal-bashing industries. The gender composition of the group doing this work changed from being predominately female to predominately male. These changes were reflected in the name change of the Institute to Labour Management.

The Second World War period saw an enormous growth in the numbers of personnel officers and a consequent renaming of the association in 1946 as the Institute of Personnel Management. They were particularly prevalent in munitions factories and had a goal of simultaneously maximising labour productivity and fostering industrial peace.

By the 1960s members of the Institute of Personnel Management were primarily engaged in establishment control, a role that concentrated on maintaining the *status quo* and servicing the needs of line management for staff. A significant amount of time was taken up with 'firefighting' crises in the relationship between unionised employees and managers. In short, the role could be designated as reactive rather than proactive. In 1968 a Royal Commission identified a weakness in UK companies in that they did not give personnel a high enough priority. This had led to a lack of clear policies which meant that there was inconsistency and uncertainty among line managers in the way they managed the people in their sections and departments.

Two developments in the 1970s gave some personnel departments and the managers within them an opportunity to enhance their status and position within management and move away from the mixture of welfare work, establishment control and personnel administration that characterised much of their work. The first was the rise of trade union power and the second the growth of employment legislation. Organisations had to deal with these contingencies and if personnel managers could demonstrate that they had the knowledge and skills to ensure that organisations could deal with them, then there was a possibility of enhancing their status and standing in the managerial hierarchy. This was also the period when concepts and practices derived from behavioural science came to be the basis of the professional qualifications that personnel managers could take.

Yet despite these developments the Dirty Harry view of personnel was still alive. The problem facing personnel managers can be summed up in three words – ambiguity, marginality and trashcan. We can introduce a number of the key issues involved here by examining the following (fictional) dialogue between a personnel manager and a department manager.

Sheila Solo So, you are the new personnel manager. I hope you are going to make a difference to my life, but I doubt it.

Martin Partner I am sorry. You seem to have a poor opinion and experience of personnel management. Would you like to tell me about it?

SS   But how will you be able to help me do my job? If you are anything like the previous personnel people you will always be coming to me to tell me I have got to follow this procedure, or do that because it is in an agreement with the unions.

MP   These things are important. We need to act in a fair way towards our employees.

SS   Yes, but surely I as a manager need to make decisions about motivating, rewarding and disciplining, if necessary, the employees in my department. I need the freedom to act in the way that I think is relevant.

MP   Yes, it is important that you take responsibility for managing the people in your department, but we in personnel can assist you to do this by providing procedural frameworks, advice and guidance.

SS   Well, all your colleagues have seemed to provide in the past is bureaucracy and paperwork. We have to fill in so many forms to be able to do anything. It takes hours to fill in the performance appraisal form, or the form to approve filling of posts.

MP   That may have been what happened in the past. I want to discuss with you how we might do things differently by working together to achieve common goals.

SS   That's all very well, but another problem you personnel people cause us is that you always seem to take the side of the employee. If you are not telling us that we can't make this change or that change because the unions have objected, you want to increase our costs by introducing new employee benefits. When are you going to come off the fence and be on management's side rather than the employees'?

MP I would like to be seen as your business partner, someone you can work with and get support from.

SS Well, you are going to have to be a lot more professional than the people we have had here in the past. By the way are you still organising the annual outing for pensioners?

. . .

Ambiguity relates to the differences between the personnel function, the task connected with employing and managing people, and the personnel department, a separate group of managers carrying out specialist roles. The personnel function includes activities such as:

- Staffing – human resource planning, recruitment and selection
- Rewards – performance management, performance appraisal and rewards systems
- Employee development
- Employee maintenance – health and safety
- Employee relations – individual and collective relationships with employees

However, while these tasks need to be accomplished in most organisations they need not necessarily be undertaken by personnel specialists. Indeed there is an assertion that every manager should have a responsibility for managing those in their charge and this creates an ambiguity as to whether the personnel function is being maintained by line managers or personnel specialists. Armstrong (1992) sought to resolve this ambiguity by arguing that line managers manage people while personnel managers manage people systems. Or as Marchington and Wilkinson (1996: 65) put it, 'line managers are increasingly taking over the *practice* of personnel and development while functional specialists retain responsibility for drawing up *policy* and reviewing procedures'. In many respects this degree of ambiguity is not present in the work of other specialist managers such as finance or marketing and thus potentially there is a difficulty for personnel specialists in pressing their claims for board level representation and equal status with other senior managers.

There is another dimension of ambiguity and that concerns the relationship between personnel specialist and employees. If there is an emphasis on the welfare role of personnel, a role concerned with the well-being of employees, then this might suggest that personnel was situated midway between the interests of employer and employees. On the other hand with an emphasis on the management control role and a concern for efficiency and effectiveness at work, personnel could claim to be a central part of management.

Personnel management has also suffered from a problem of not being at the centre of organisation decision-making. Part of the work of personnel is routine, to do, for example, with organising recruitment adverts, making sure that people are paid on time, or arranging welfare visits, and as such other managers may feel this to be at the margins of the organisation. Senior personnel people on the other hand assert their right to be at the centre of decision-making but had to find a way of turning that assertion into reality.

The trashcan view of personnel management is one attributed to the management writer Peter Drucker who saw it as the place that other managers dropped the tasks and roles that they did not see as important and did not want to do. This view is still cited in personnel management and HRM textbooks and reflects a view held by a number of managers about the role of personnel managers and departments.

The topics and issues that we address in this book are important not just to personnel or human resource specialists but also to all those who have managerial responsibilities. There is a continuing debate as to whether personnel and human resource management should be a specialist function or whether it should be part of every manager's activity. We have deliberately called this book *Human Resources in Organisations* to emphasise that it is written for those who will have some managerial responsibility for staff and this will include knowledge and understanding of what their role might be in, for example, selecting staff, rewarding them, or disciplining and dismissing them. But such potential managers also need to know what their relationship with human resource specialists might be and how such specialists might assist general managerial colleagues to fulfil their role well. This interrelationship is feature of the approach taken in this book.

Addressing the image problem

We now turn to look at ways in which senior personnel people have recognised this image problem that affected their status and standing in organisations not just in relation to employees but more importantly *vis-à-vis* other managers. One way in which this issue has been tackled has been by the adoption of human resource management as a separate and distinct approach to managing the employment relationship; one which sought to overcome the weaknesses of personnel management identified above.

However, as the usage of the term 'human resource management' has developed from the 1980s we can identify a new problem as the term has taken on a number of different meanings. Watson (1999: 20) has summed these up thus:

Table 1.2 Four usages of the term 'human resource management'

'HRM' is variously used:
• As a more fashionable name for personnel management.
• To refer to all managerial activity – beyond as well as within a personnel function – that involves relationships between the organisation and its employees.
• To describe an area of academic study, integrating the 'subjects' of personnel management, industrial relations and elements of organisational behaviour.
• As an umbrella term for 'new management' practices, involving higher commitment from employees and giving them greater task discretion, which have been given increased emphasis in the US and UK in the latter decades of the twentieth century.

The *Dinner Ladies* example is of the relabelling implied in the first definition, but in this book the emphasis is on the second. We prefer to refer to the fourth definition in Table 1.2 as 'HRM-style practices' to distinguish some practices as opposed to all HRM. Indeed a number of different new models called 'HRM' exist and this only serves to underline the danger of using the term 'HRM' in an all-embracing way.

However, in order to highlight the differences between a particular view of a traditional personnel management approach and HRM-style practices we now focus on one example of the fourth definition of HRM. We are using the Guest (1987) model of HRM policy goals. This stresses four key concepts – strategic integration, commitment, flexibility and quality. We will examine these in turn and then look at the contrast between this model and that of traditional personnel management.

Strategic integration has two interrelated meanings. First that there is an internal coherence and integration of employment management policies and practices with each other. For example, if work organisation emphasises teamwork then it would be invidious to have a reward system that stressed individual contribution. The second dimension of integration is of human resourcing strategy with overall business strategy. Indeed there cannot be a human resourcing strategy independent of business strategy, but there needs to be a close interrelationship between the two. The Guest model would also have line managers incorporating HRM-style practices into the way they work.

The second concept, **commitment**, is at the heart of HRM-style policies. The objective is to elicit from employees attitudinal and behavioural commitment that will deliver service to customers and enhance the standing and reputation of the organisation and hence its profits. Thus commitment behaviours should ideally come from within the employees who should through processes of selection, induction and leadership understand what is required of them and deliver it. All this without a constant need for checking and supervising so that layers of supervisors and managers dedicated to such tasks may be removed from organisational structures. Closely connected to commitment is building loyalty to the organisation that employees work for.

Flexibility is also a key word in the HRM lexicon, but here the emphasis is on functional rather than numerical or distancing flexibility. The aim would be to develop workers able to operate over a number of key tasks and to end previous demarcation lines between particular skills and functions. An example of this comes from the Exxon greenfield ethylene plant in Fife. Skills and competencies were required in the areas of electrical, mechanical and instrument engineering. But rather than hire people with those specific skills Exxon preferred to recruit technicians able and willing to be trained across the three areas of competencies and to work flexibly when trained (Leopold and Hallier, 1997).

The final dimension of the Guest model is **quality**. Here there is meant to be an interrelationship between high-quality employees in whom employers are prepared to invest and develop in the belief that such employees will in turn deliver high-quality goods and services that will help distinguish an organisation from its competitors.

If we now contrast the Guest model of HRM-style practices with the picture of traditional personnel management that we built up earlier, we can see clearly in Table 1.3 four points of distinction.

We have seen that a criticism of traditional personnel management is that it is at the margins of organisational life in the importance afforded to both its message and the status of its leading practitioners. Human resource management places its message at the centre of organisational life through the dual meaning

Table 1.3 Personnel management and human resource management contrasted

Personnel management	Human resource management
Marginal	Central
Isolated	Integrated
Compliance	Commitment
Tactical	Strategic

of integration of the policies and practices with each other and of the interrelationship between organisational and human resourcing strategy. So, rather than being separate policy initiatives, human resource policies such as recruitment, appraisal and rewards come to be integrated and form a coherent whole that contributes to organisational success. Moreover, the responsibility for achieving these policies in practice rests firmly with line managers who have to live with them on a day-to-day basis and so they become integrated into the organisation rather than remain isolated at the periphery.

Much of this is to be achieved through the commitment of employees which is gained through inner understanding of the attitudes and behaviours expected rather than gained through compliance measures of time-keeping, strict supervision and repeated quality checks. Finally, through these approaches the tactical reactive fire-fighting weakness of traditional personnel management is meant to be replaced by a proactive forward-looking and strategic contribution from HRM-style policies and the managers associated with them.

Some textbooks (for example, Stredwick, 2000) present the notion of integration by using the metaphor of the jigsaw puzzle in which each piece, whether it be performance management or recruitment and selection, is seen as being part of the whole and fits in to make up the whole in an interlinked way. While this captures the notion of integration, it does so in a way that suggests that the puzzle has a solution, indeed that, as with a jigsaw, there may be only one solution. Others (e.g. Bratton and Gold, 1999) use the HRM cycle (derived from Fombrum, Tichy and Devanna, 1984) to capture the internal coherence of HRM policies and their interactions with each other and to some extent with the organisation's external environment.

One of this text's contributing authors, Diannah Lowry, has for some time been using the image of the *kaleidoscope* as an appropriate visual metaphor in relation to HRM policies and practices, and it is this image that we have adopted in the text. The kaleidoscope captures both the interrelationship and possible integration of specific HRM policies and practices, and the impact of the external environment in limiting and constraining the choices open to management and employees. The boundary of the organisation is represented by a dotted line to indicate that while the organisation may appear to have a permanent shape, this is never final or fixed as economic, legal, political and social factors may all have an impact on the organisation, requiring or forcing a change in shape. For example, changes in exchange rates may affect decisions about future investment in country A or country B. Changes in the law on the Minimum Wage or rights for employees to unionise may impact on companies, or the balance between a

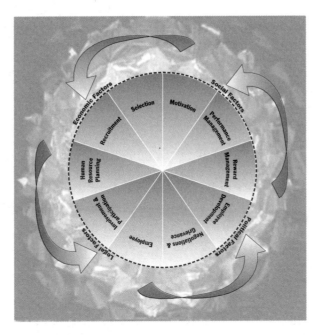

Figure 1.1 The kaleidoscope model of the organisation, its environment and the relationship of internal HRM policies and practices

regulated or deregulated labour market may influence organisational direction. Finally, social factors, such as the idea of 'family friendly' working policies, may influence managers' policies and practice towards working hours and the employment of women. Each of these issues will be addressed later in the book.

The kaleidoscope, therefore, suggests that the external environment can have an impact on internal choices and thus change the overall shape and cause movements in the pattern, but also that a change in any one internal component may simultaneously affect other, seemingly settled, parts. Thus the shape is never fixed but is constantly changing. A change in one component, such as the introduction of a team-based rewards system, may have an impact on employee motivation and in turn require the introduction of a new training programme. Thus the original change can lead to alterations in the internal relationships and also the overall shape of the organisation, but at the same time external changes may require, or even force, internal changes in shape. Thus the notion of integration is never a puzzle to be solved but a problem to be tackled in the best way possible.

We have stressed that there is no single prescriptive model of HRM but a number of different, often competing ones. We have used the Guest model to highlight the contrasts between traditional personnel management and HRM-style prescriptions. We must, however, be careful not to overstate the distinction, as many would argue that best practice of personnel management did seek to achieve the goals that Guest has identified as being the preserve of HRM. Moreover, it is necessary to introduce some distinction and differences that are to be found in the literature about different approaches to human resource management. The most commonly discussed is that between 'hard' and 'soft' HRM.

The 'hard' version of human *resource* management stresses the word 'resource' and sees the human resource on a par with other resources, such as capital or land. It is therefore to be measured and quantified in a calculative, instrumental way with a view to minimising costs and maximising outputs. The main advocates of this view are Fombrum, Tichy and Devanna in *Strategic Human Resource Management* (1984).

The 'soft' version, on the other hand, stresses the *human* dimension of the term and sees human beings as a unique resource available to organisations and one which needs to be led, motivated and communicated with. It is the creativity, commitment and skill of employees that can create real comparative advantage. To achieve this, employers must carefully select, extensively nurture and develop, and reward their employees, even though at first sight they may seem expensive. This model is associated with Beer, Spector, Lawrence, Mills and Walton, *Managing Human Assets* (1984).

Whichever model, if any, an organisation may have adopted, the range of activities undertaken by HR specialists, indeed whether there are specialists at all, will vary from organisation to organisation. Factors that may influence this include the size and structure of the organisation, whether it is foreign owned or not, the presence or not of trade unions and the philosophy of senior management. Larger organisations are more likely to employ specialist HR managers and also to divide the particular aspects of HR such as remuneration, human resource development and employee relations into separate sections or departments. Similarly the relationship between specialist HR managers and line managers is likely to vary from organisation to organisation. In this book we try to focus on that relationship and consider issues from the perspective of the line manager.

A note of caution needs to be entered into this discussion about HRM. Its origins and development are clearly Anglo-American. It is premised on unregulated free market capitalism and advanced as a way for organisations to gain and sustain competitive advantage. While we can find a number of different American and British models, it is much harder to find an equivalent European HRM model. Here we might turn to look at the Rhineland model or *Modell Deutschland*, or its variant the Rhine Delta model. Here we find a different relationship between employers, trade unions and the state and a different approach to the relationship between employers and employees based on social partnership. Many of the concepts and practices of HRM jar with these approaches even though some of the language of HRM is to be found in continental European firms. The position of Britain, between America and the Continent, means that representative bodies of managers and trade unions advocate elements of both approaches. In general terms managers and employers' organisations are wary of the social partnership approach and hostile to the regulation of labour markets, while unions strongly support ideas of social partnership and are wary of, if not hostile to, Human Resource Management.

Other criticisms of HRM-style approaches include, on the one hand, a degree of imprecision, especially given the number of variations and versions of models, but on the other hand also its very prescriptiveness. Some versions of HRM-style policies can be presented as a way of managing the employment relationship, indeed the *only* way to do so. But there is a justifiable case for employers adopting traditional personnel management as an appropriate response to their product and labour market situation. While some advocate HRM-style approaches precisely because they are allegedly different from traditional personnel management, others criticise HRM as just being personnel management in another guise, the 'new wine in old bottles' syndrome (Armstrong, 1987).

There is also some doubt about the extent to which HRM-style practices have been taken up extensively by employers and about the responses to such approaches from employees.

Examination of the way in which HRM-style policies have worked out in practice reveals a number of contradictions: for example, between the HR role as a caring one, perhaps based on the welfare origins of personnel management, or a controlling one with an emphasis on the establishment-control function and seeing people as a cost to be controlled (Legge, 1995). Or between the emphasis on treating people as individuals, individualising the employment relationship, and simultaneously emphasising the collective through teamwork. A further contradiction exists between the philosophy of empowering employees yet at the same time controlling and setting boundaries on that empowerment. There is a contradiction between gaining the commitment of employees and expecting them to be loyal to the organisation while employing some through fixed-term or temporary contracts to gain a flexible response to product market fluctuations. Finally, there is a contradiction between the flexibility and adaptability supposedly required by organisations to be able to respond to a turbulent environment and the emphasis on creating and maintaining a strong culture in an organisation which is meant to reinforce the values and mission of that organisation.

There are a number of implications that flow from the above discussion. First, we prefer to use the term 'human resourcing strategy' rather than HRM strategy. We recognise that a range of human resourcing strategies are possible depending on choice, chance and circumstance, and that what has been discussed above as HRM is better regarded as but one possible approach and therefore should be called HRM-style practices. We do not put forward any single approach in a prescriptive way but seek to illustrate and demonstrate a range of possibilities that managers can adopt to suit their particular circumstances.

The structure of the book

The book is structured in to six parts each containing a number of chapters, each one being a segment of the kaleidoscope. Part 1 summarises the development of personnel management from its welfare origins to the current debate about the meaning of Human Resource Management and introduces the overall concepts used in the book. Parts 2–5 are the substantive parts of the book and cover employee resourcing, employee rewards, employee development and employee relations.

Part 2 examines employee resourcing issues, beginning with an examination of human resource planning in the context of a turbulent and changing environment. The links between business planning and human resource planning are discussed and a distinction is drawn between 'hard' and 'soft' versions of human resource planning. Contrasts between manpower planning and human resource planning are also made. Human resource planning is seen as long term, linked to business strategy and seeking to manage employee behaviour through involvement. It is also very closely linked to the notion of integration, both vertical and horizontal, as discussed in Chapter 1.

A model is presented to assist in understanding the processes of human resource planning. This involves analysis of external and internal labour markets, organisational culture and corporate strategy. To assist with analysis of the external labour market the Atkinson and Meager (1986) model of the flexible firm is presented, along with a critique of this model. Consideration is then given to analysis and investigation, forecasting, planning and resourcing, and implementation and control elements of the HRP model. At all stages the relationship between the parts the human resource specialist and line managers may play in the operation of the model is considered.

The link between human resource planning and recruitment and selection is then made in the next two chapters. Chapter 3 focuses on recruitment and it is pointed out that recruitment is about generating a pool of applicants and selection is about picking the most appropriate person from this pool. They are therefore separate but complementary processes. Different organisational and occupational contexts of recruitment are considered, especially on how formal the process might be and the role of specialists in this.

A stage model for the recruitment process is then presented. The first stage is considering whether or not a vacancy exits. Alternative ways of getting the work done may be through use of overtime or outsourcing the work. This leads on to job analysis which in turn assists in the production of job descriptions and person specifications. Models of these are examined and it is argued that these set objective criteria by which applicants may be assessed. The use of internal promotion as a way of filling vacancies is examined and contrasted with external recruitment. Management may need to consider using recruitment agencies or executive consultancies.

Four rules for recruitment advertising are examined and consideration is given to alternative media, but these should always be linked to the nature of the vacancy. It is argued that line managers have a significant role to play in the recruitment process as ultimately they have to rely on the success or otherwise of the choices made. Finally, it is stressed that recruitment is a two-way process and that success is dependent on agreement by both sides and this depends on a degree of openness and trust.

In Chapter 4 this consideration of recruitment is built on by examining methods of selection. In an overview of selection practice, the practice of merely using application forms, references and interviews is scrutinised. Concepts such as validity and reliability are introduced and used as a way of criticising past practice and moving from *ad hoc* methods to a systematic process. This may involve pre-selection, shortlisting, testing, interviewing, assessment centres, biodata and references. The strengths and limitations of these methods are analysed so that the weaknesses of each may be minimised.

It is stressed that the selection process involves contributions from the HR function, line managers and sometimes outside agencies. The choice of appropriate selection approaches and methods must reflect the organisational and occupational context. Selection can focus on skills, experience, attitude or potential, or a combination of these. Following selection comes the induction process and the importance of this is stressed. Finally, it is argued that selection is a two-way process and that if done well it will contribute to retention of the successful candidate and assist in generating the organisation's competitive advantage, organisational performance and long-term effectiveness.

In Part 3 there is first of all a discussion about motivation to work. You may have covered this in an organisational behaviour module but this self-contained chapter enables you to recap on that learning and relate it directly to the world of work. The chapter is structured round discussing content, or needs, theories of work motivation and process theories. The first set of theories assumes that psychological needs lie behind human behaviour and include Maslow's hierarchy of needs and Herzberg's two-factor theory. The second concentrates on the cognitive process of determining levels of motivation. Theories examined here include expectancy-based models, equity theory and goal-setting theory. Overall it is suggested that issues of fairness and justice are becoming more prominent in organisational life.

The concept of job enrichment is explored through the work of Lawler (1973) and Hackman and Oldham (1975). The concept of the psychological contract between employer and employee is then discussed and its implication for employee behaviour and motivation explored. Finally, there is an examination of three types of organisational commitment. It is pointed out that individuals can have multiple commitments in the workplace but that organisational commitment is encouraged by positive experiences at work.

The links between motivation and performance management are explored in Chapter 6. The tensions between performance management as a controlling/ judgemental process and as a supportive/developmental one are discussed. The case is made that performance management should be a continuous process rather than a rigid and bureaucratic system, and it is argued that both formal and informal processes are appropriate. Performance management can have an effect on other dimensions of management – on rewards, on training and on motivation.

A central process in performance management is performance appraisal and this is examined thoroughly. It is suggested that different appraisers are appropriate according to the situation as the choice of appraiser can impact on the outcome. Trait systems of appraisal are contrasted with objective-based, competency-based and multi-source systems. The pros and cons of each approach are examined.

The management of ineffective performance is discussed and it is suggested that management need to investigate thoroughly the organisational and work context of this. Again this demonstrates the interconnections between the various dimensions of personnel and human resource management. Finally, in considering the ethics of performance management, it is suggested that it is better to regard employees as resourceful humans rather than human resources and therefore demonstrate respect for the individual when carrying out performance management.

Issues of motivation and performance link in to rewards management and this is the subject of Chapter 7. However, as employees and employers may have divergent views about pay and rewards, the design of reward systems is complex. There is a discussion of 'new pay' which involves a focus on linking pay with business strategy and of making some pay contingent on performance. Readers are reminded that for some employees intrinsic (non-financial) rewards are as important as extrinsic (financial) ones. Recapping on individual motivational theories, but also introducing organisational theories of motivation, the links between motivation and rewards are examined. It is suggested that to achieve the motivational impact of a rewards system employees should be involved in the design of the system.

There then follows an examination of pay structures, looking at a number of external and internal pay relationships that might affect the choice of a design. Pay systems are the processes involved in remunerating employees within the pay structure. A number of such systems are discussed. Moving beyond pay, the role of other employee benefits in a reward package is considered. It is suggested that the design of pay and rewards systems is becoming ever more complex, so organisations may wish to use management consultants to do this, but some of the dangers of this approach are pointed out. Finally, taking account of the variety of organisations people may be working in, it is argued that there is no 'one best method' of reward management, but that if employees are involved in the process of designing and implementing the reward system, if the process is transparent, and if relevant training is available, then the chances of success are greater than in cases where these processes do not take place.

In Part 4 there is an examination of employee development. In Chapter Eight theories and models of individual learning are examined, drawing upon the work of major psychologists. The behaviourist, cognitive and humanist schools of thought are discussed and then related to theories of individual learning. Learning is not confined to formal contexts and occurs continuously throughout all aspects of experience. Both internal cognitive processes and the application of external reinforcers influence the learning process. The goal-seeking behaviour of individuals can influence the outcomes of learning. It is also established that many aspects of HR other than employee development strategy and practice are influenced by theories of individual learning.

In Chapter 9 key distinctions are made between education, training and development and these must be taken into account for the practice of employee development. In particular, organisations professing a HRM approach must pay serious attention to the integration of training and development strategies. On the other hand organisations taking a short-term view tend to see training and development as a cost rather than an investment.

The role of the government in encouraging companies to participate in training and development is examined and the British voluntarist approach is contrasted with more interventionist approaches. Next, the extent of company training provision in the UK is discussed which leads on to a discussion of a range of factors that influence the role of employee development in organisations. Here the roles undertaken by employee development specialists are important and a typology to analyse these is discussed. Similarly, two typologies to understand organisational approaches – the Ashridge and the Meggision models – are examined. Lastly, a number of different methods available to identify training and development needs are examined, as are a range of training solutions before the chapter concludes with a discussion of the issues surrounding the evaluation of training.

Finally, in Part 5 there is an examination of employee relations issues. After considering how actors in employee relations may seek to understand their world through a frame of reference, the essence of the unitarist, pluralist and Marxist frames of reference are outlined. This then leads on to a consideration of possible management styles based on the interplay of collectivism and individualism. Before considering how these factors may impact on management's strategic choices for managing the employment relationship, there is a discussion of the factors employees might consider in deciding whether or not to join a trade union. The decline of trade union membership in Britain since 1979 is analysed, as is the current legislation on union recognition. The interplay of all these factors creates three strategic choices for management-union recognition, union substitution or union avoidance and each of these is considered. Finally, there is a discussion of partnership as an alternative model.

Chapter 11 concerns managing employee participation and involvement where the focus is more on the individual employee. A clear distinction between employee participation and employee involvement is made, especially in terms of participation being union led and involvement being management led. A model of a participation continuum is presented to assist our understanding of which participants are seeking what type of scheme and why. Evidence is presented to show a shift in focus away from participation in favour of involvement and that management has led this change in order to gain employee commitment to organisational goals.

Three examples of indirect employee participation – joint consultative committees, joint health and safety committees, and European Works Councils – are examined in detail. Consideration is then given to the four main approaches to employee involvement: downward communication, upward problem-solving, task participation and financial involvement. Finally, the Marchington *et al.* (1993) model of the dynamics of schemes over time is used to assist our understanding of the processes involved. Particular consideration is given to the notion of the horizontal fit between different forms of employee participation and involvement and the relationship of these to overall human resourcing strategy.

This is followed by a chapter on regulating the employment relationship where the focus is mainly collective relationships. Unilateral, joint and third-party ways of creating procedural and substantive rules are examined. Collective bargaining is then defined and the pros and cons of this form of joint decision-making are discussed. The decline of collective bargaining is explained, as is the decentralisation of the bargaining that remains. Consideration is then given to handling grievance, discipline and dismissal cases, taking account of legal obligations and good practice and the roles of line managers and human resource specialists. Finally, aspects of state regulation of employment are explored. After summarising the thrust of the previous Conservative governments' policies is this area, consideration is given to two aspects of the employment relationship – low pay and long hours – where the Labour government has introduced statutory protections.

Case Study 1.1

Strategic choices on greenfield sites

In the UK in the 1980s, as 'human resource management' as a distinct, individualist approach to the management of the employment relationship developed, it was argued that managers on greenfield, as opposed to brownfield, sites would be better able to introduce such practices. The greenfield situation supposedly gives managers advantages from starting with a congruent total system. However, research has found that not all organisations chose to take advantage of the greenfield site situation to introduce new policies. In some situations managers by choice have continued with a traditional personnel management approach (Leopold and Hallier, 1997). We look at two examples of the employment relationship policies that managers chose to introduce in greenfield sites in the start-up situation. The cases are drawn from a Scottish study of start-up and ageing in greenfield sites and concern the Bank of Scotland Card Services centre in Dunfermline and the OKI electronics plant in Cumbernauld. Both were created on greenfield sites but adopted rather different approaches to managing the employment relationship.

At the Bank of Scotland personnel policies and procedures were laid down in a manual from head office. This manual is very detailed and covers issues such as the clerical grading scheme, the job evaluation scheme, set procedures for working, and appraisal. Pay was determined through negotiations between the Banking, Insurance and Finance Union (BIFU) and the bank for both clerical and managerial staff. It was expected that card services managers would implement these procedures which were standard throughout the bank. One rationale for this was that staff could be transferred to and from the branch banking system and the centre. It was reported that employees who possessed work experience outside the bank, except in local government, found the detailed procedures difficult to accept, but school leavers were socialised into the system more easily as this was their first job. The emphasis on recruitment was not on attitudes towards the new management philosophy but on job-related aptitudes and skills. A predominately female workforce was recruited which was mainly composed of women returners who had updated their keyboard skills in local Further Education colleges.

At OKI, on the other hand, there is evidence of senior managers making a clear break with their managerial past. The plant general manager and HR director both had experience in the electronics industry in Scotland and had previously worked together. Their view of the future was shaped by their experience of job demarcation, union control, lack of flexibility, low productivity and functional specialisation. Not only did they desire to avoid these features but very soon after appointment, along with a new Japanese managing director, they set out to fashion a clear philosophy of the HR features they wished to adopt at OKI. Significantly this was not meant to be a slavish reproduction of the Japanese parent company practices but rather a combination of the best of Japanese and British approaches. Key terms and phrases in this philosophy included 'professional', 'successful', 'in Scotland to stay', 'Japanese

Case Study continued

but understand the local culture', 'works with customers and suppliers', 'tough but fair', 'respect for people' and 'a name for quality'. In HR terms, policies to be adopted included many of the features recognisable as HRM-style: involvement, communication, rewarding good performance, internal promotion and single status.

In order to emphasise the break with the past, there was a focus on recruiting people aged under 24. Management believed that younger people would be untainted by the old values of unionisation and hence they avoided employing former Burrough's workers, despite their experience in the industry. Aptitude tests were used to help identify flexibility and dexterity, although it was later recognised that these were quite crude instruments. More emphasis was given to interviews which were used to ascertain whether candidates were likely to work as members of a team and would be committed to work hard for long hours in the start-up period.

On greenfield sites there is a start-up phase, lasting two to three years, where there is a buzz of excitement, a common sense of euphoria and a willingness to work beyond the call of contract and duty. At OKI the start-up phase was somewhat frenetic and after two years or so management realised that a consolidation period was required, as this pace could not be maintained. The pressure to achieve output and quality meant that managers perhaps behaved in a more autocratic way than was expected of them. Confirmation of this came from appraisal interviews where employees expressed some of their discontent. Indeed, by this time labour turnover had reached 27 per cent and was seen as being too high. The transition from start-up to consolidation also caused tensions within the engineering staff, as the emphasis shifted from the initial setting-up of production and getting all systems working to achieving production targets at quality standards and within budget.

Changes in senior management can also influence the management philosophy and practices of the greenfield site. At OKI, for example, a new general manager was appointed who had the priority of making the site more efficient. This sharpening of the business focus was introduced because of new competitive pressures in the printer market. The new manager's priority was the measurement and control of factors such as productivity, quality and costs. Thus there was some tension between this approach and a previous initiative based on a visioning exercise. This earlier initiative had been introduced as part of the consolidation process and sought to develop an agreed vision for the company. With the assistance of external management consultants, senior and functional managers and, later, a cross-section of the whole workforce developed this vision. It emphasised partnerships with customers and suppliers and the continuous development of people and systems to become a world-class manufacturer of high-quality goods. Despite the efficiency drive, the exercise was not abandoned, as many of the messages about values and culture were incorporated into a new staff handbook and many managers tried to adopt the values in their style. But for the general manager progress and reward of managers was judged mainly in terms of their effectiveness and efficiency in meeting the cleanly stated business objectives. The HR contribution also became more focused on the business, perhaps approximating more closely to the 'hard' resourcing version of HRM. For example, training became focused on company-driven training needs, rather than individual employee needs, and measures of training effectiveness were adopted to evaluate its contributions to meeting business objectives.

While the OKI case illustrates changing market situations and the need to respond flexibly and quickly to these changes, the Bank of Scotland case is rather different. The nature of work in a card-processing centre has been likened to a computer-based assembly line and in such a case a personnel management system that stressed order, routine, stability and control was appropriate.

Activity 1.2

1 What features of an HRM-style approach are apparent in the approach adopted by managers at OKI?

2 What differences can you find with the approach adopted by Bank of Scotland Card Services?

3 What can you detect or infer about the relationship between line managers and HR specialists in these two cases?

4 To what extent were the approaches adopted by the respective managements appropriate for their business strategy?

5 What changes in circumstances led to changes in the employment management practices of the companies?

6 Were these changes appropriate?

SUMMARY

In this chapter the following key points have been made:

- Personnel management has gone through a number of stages of development from its origins as welfare work at the end of the nineteenth century.

- These changes are reflected in the name and size of the professional organisation for personnel and human resource managers, now the Chartered Institute of Personnel and Development.

- At various points in time personnel specialists have emphasised different aspects of their work: these include welfare, establishment control, professional distance and business orientation.

- There is a distinction between the personnel function (the tasks that have to be fulfilled in managing the employment relationship) and personnel management (the group of managers who specialise in this area of work).

- This distinction means that many aspects of the personnel function are carried out by line managers, although often with the support of personnel or human resource specialists.

- The different emphasis and orientation of personnel specialists has given rise to problems of ambiguity, marginality and trashcan.

- There is a need to establish an appropriate working relationship between personnel specialists and line managers.

- HRM-style policies can be seen as an attempt to overcome these problems and to emphasise a business orientation focus.

- The term 'human resource management' can be interpreted in four different ways.

- The Guest model of HRM emphasises strategic integration, commitment, flexibility and quality.
- We can distinguish between a 'hard' HRM-style approach, which emphasises *resource* and a 'soft' model, which emphasises *human*.
- A number of problems with the HRM-style approach have been identified, including both its imprecision and its prescriptiveness.

DISCUSSION QUESTIONS

1 What do the changing names of the body that is now the Chartered Institute of Personnel and Development tell us about the composition of its membership and the focus of their jobs?

2 What differences can you detect between a traditional personnel management approach and an HRM-style approach to the management of the employment relationship?

3 Why do you think there are tensions and ambiguities in the relationship between line managers and HR specialists? How might they be overcome?

FURTHER READING

There are a number of other undergraduate texts available that are aimed at human resource management specialists and therefore explore the issues introduced here in more detail. These include Beardwell and Holden (2001), Bolton (1997), Bratton and Gold (1999), Foot and Hook (1999) and Stredwick (2000). Students wishing a more advanced discussion of the issues raised should consult Legge (1995), Leopold, Harris and Watson (1999), and Storey (1995).

If you would like to explore the World Wide Web as a way of accessing information of the issues raised and discussed in this book, a convenient starting point is the *Human Resource Management Resources on the Internet* web page run by the Department of Human Resource Management at Nottingham Business School. From here links can be made to employers' bodies, professional associations and trade unions, and the material can be searched by topic as well as by organisation.

The address is
http://www.nbs.ntu.ac.uk/DEPTS/HRM/
Then click on HRM External Links and away you go!

Part 2 Employee resourcing

Chapter 2

Strategic planning for human resources

Hazel Williams

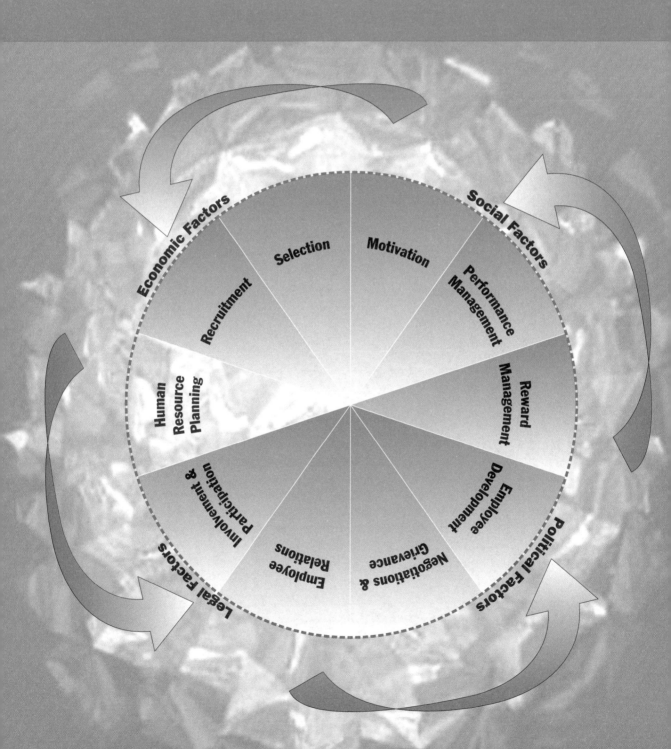

Having completed this chapter and its associated activities, readers should be able to:

- understand the impact of strategic human resourcing on the planning process
- appreciate the differences between manpower planning and human resource planning
- explain how the external and internal environment impacts on the process of human resource planning with particular reference to issues of flexibility
- undertake straightforward quantitative and qualitative calculations
- examine the implications of information systems on human resource planning
- apply the learning to a case study or organisation familiar to the reader

How can we ensure a good 'fit' between HR practices and the wider business goals?

The need to consider strategic planning for human resources has been recognised in the HR literature (for example Guest, 1987) over the last couple of decades and more recently by chief executives and senior HR specialists. Various external factors – such as a move towards globalisation, changing economic trends, changes in the demographic make-up of the labour force and a shortage of key skills, knowledge and experience – have contributed to the urgency with which the subject is now debated. Also there is a realisation within organisations of the changing and more 'flexible' nature of the workforce and their need to combine diverse careers with their personal lives.

In order to be effective a strategic human resource plan must recognise the constraints of the external and internal environment and provide a useful and managed link between strategic corporate plans and strategic human resourcing (see Figure 2.1). The outcome of this process is a number of HR policies and pro-

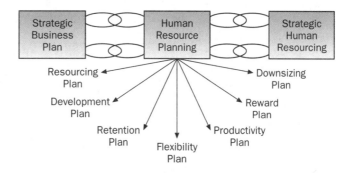

Figure 2.1 HR providing the link between business planning and human resource management

cedures – referred to as HR-style practices in this text – that offer a vertically and horizontally integrated HRP strategy (after Marchington and Wilkinson, 1996) specific to a particular organisation, which aim to gain employee commitment. A number of writers (including Pfeffer, 1994: 64) offer a prescriptive set of practices (for example Table 2.1) that are meant to lead an organisation towards its planned goals. These practices correspond with our understanding of HRM discussed in Table 1.1 in the previous chapter and empathise with the model of HRM proposed by Guest (1987) discussed in Chapter 1.

Table 2.1 Pfeffer's seven people management policies for success

An HR strategy comprises a set of (approximately) seven people management policies that 'seem to characterise most, if not all, of the systems producing profits through people'. These include:

- An emphasis on providing employment security
- Putting in a lot of resources to recruit the right people in the first place
- An extensive use of self-managed teams and decentralisation
- Wage levels that are high and are strongly linked to organisational performance
- A high expenditure on training
- Attention being paid to reducing status differentials
- A willingness to share information

Source: Pfeffer (1994: 64)

Although the policy names may be little different between organisations, it is their specific content and emphasis that ensures the right 'fit' to a particular organisation – referred to as 'bundles' of HR practices by others (Huselid, 1995). An appropriate analogy here is the human body. Each of us has the same basic skeleton with the same number of bones in approximately the same place; however the exact shape of our bone structure and muscles means that each of us is a recognisable individual. Thus, although the overall shape may be similar, the detail of an HRP for two organisations in the same type of business will not be exactly the same; for example, in terms of the content, the methods used and the outcomes expected.

It is interesting (and somewhat intriguing) to note that the ability to use quantitative and qualitative people planning methods is the one with which the majority of HR specialists and line managers are most uncomfortable. Traditionally, people management subjects are not associated with statistical modelling techniques or financial planning, but the ability to take a 'hard' view of people management in planning terms strongly suggests that this is an essential skill. Indeed many organisations are now recruiting numerate line managers and HR specialists who are equally comfortable with 'soft' management skills and techniques – the right and left hand of people management.

For the purposes of this discussion, line functions are defined as those 'which have direct responsibility for achieving the objectives of the company' (Stewart 1963: 32–3, cited in Storey 1992: 190). For line managers, the dilemma would appear to be three-fold. First, an acceptance of active people management responsibilities within the line management role. Secondly, an understanding of

Table 2.2 'Hard' and 'soft' human resource planning

'Hard' HR planning	'Soft' HR planning
• 'top down' activity	• 'networked' activity
• direct control	• indirect control
• unitarist view	• pluralist view
• assumes planned strategy	• responsive to emergent strategy
• rational, scientific approach	• employees seen as assets
• employees seen as costs	• processual perspective – plans 'emerge'
• systems perspective, static	

the underpinning concepts and processes of HRM, particularly with regard to the distinction between 'hard' and 'soft' HRM first proposed by Storey (1992) and summarised in the previous chapter. Table 2.2 considers the notion of 'hard' and soft' human resource management from a planning perspective – this will be considered further in the final case study at the end of this chapter. Finally, the use of techniques from disciplines such as statistics and finance within the context of people management.

The continuing introduction and sophistication of human resource information systems (HRIS) offers the chance to automate some of the calculations implicit within HRP. However, the more highly developed HRIS also presents the opportunity to go further and suggest possible decision choices to both the line management and the HR specialist. A cautionary note, however, is that many managers are not yet competent in this area (Parker and Caine, 1996: 30). There is a growing conviction at a senior level, for example the CEO of BOC, that the integration of information management and HR is vitally necessary and empirical evidence to support this comes from organisations such as the NHS where this partnership is changing the relationship between HR and the rest of the organisation (Williams, 2000).

> I can't help feeling that there is going to be an enormous convergence – and it's happening already – of the two disciplines of HR and information management. The application of IT and management systems will be crucial to the way that organisations work. So an HR professional's capacity to understand how these can be structured and developed is going to be very important.
>
> Don Beattie, Chief Executive for Personnel, BOC
> *People Management* (October, 1998: 35)

This chapter aims to examine the relationship between planning of human resources and strategic human resourcing. It will also draw out the differences between the traditional and limited scope of manpower planning and human resource planning in such a way as to demonstrate how elements of the external and internal environment can be presented in quantitative and qualitative terms to support the human resourcing strategy for an organisation. Finally, the role of HRIS will be considered in terms of how this 'tool' can assist strategic human resource planning. This discussion will be considered within the human resource planning framework offered by Bramham (1994).

1 As a line manager with a staff of five employees, who range in age and personal circumstances, what issues would you need to plan for over a 12-month period?

2 Your organisation's product range and your function are expanding over the next five years. You are expected to present your projected people plans to senior management in one week. What kind of information would be helpful to know about:

a) your current workforce?
b) the impact on your department of the expansion plan?

Manpower planning or human resource planning – vive la difference?

The confusion between personnel management and human resource management summarised in Table 1.2 is perpetuated throughout any discussion of HR processes and practices. A simplistic answer to the question posed above is that manpower planning *belongs* to personnel management and human resource planning *belongs* to human resource management. On the surface this statement is true and this would certainly fit with the renaming offered in Table 1.2.

Although the term 'manpower' is not really acceptable now in a politically correct environment, it is retained here because it denotes a more global generic term for labour. In essence, manpower planning has been associated with a more tactical approach of getting the right people, with the right skills, in the right place, at the right time. The definition of 'right' is not made in the literature, but should be taken to mean 'what is right for a particular organisation'. Part of the difficulty with this rationale is its static nature, where people are seen as a cost to the organisation (Bramham, 1994) instead of an investment.

Manpower planning has been associated in much of the literature, perhaps erroneously, as a linear process (Hercus, 1992), others see it as a continuous process (Hendry, 1995). The focus of manpower planning is on management and control. It usually includes various statistical calculations that are not always evident in practice: both short-term quantitative techniques (for example, labour turnover analysis) and more long-term qualitative techniques (for example, succession charts, attitudinal surveys).

The recession of the early 1990s provided a ready supply of labour in terms of numbers, which meant that in practice the emphasis on people planning *per se* was much reduced – an ideal opportunity for a rethink of the process was presented. Other texts (for example Bramham, 1994; Bratton and Gold, 1999) provide a more detailed review of the fundamental differences between manpower planning and human resource planning. This text will focus on strategic human resource planning, which is arguably more relevant for the line manager in the twenty-first century along with practical activities that will help to achieve a strategic approach.

Many writers have attempted to define human resource planning depending on their own discipline, organisational context, HR philosophy, and in many cases their personal practical experience. The view proposed in this text is that human resource planning is a strategic activity. This statement could be seen as contradictory, in that the notion of strategy comes before any subsequent activity. Indeed, consideration of the various definitions of strategic HRP demonstrates both the clarity and confusion of the statement as it is helpful to consider it in both ways.

A dynamic process, strategic human resource planning in this text will include reference to the four elements of Guest's (1987) four policy goals:

a) Vertical and horizontal strategic integration.
b) Be able to elicit employee commitment behaviours.
c) Provide a flexible workforce for a changing external and internal context
d) Be able to drive through quality people management and development that will impact on the products or services provided.

Thus the combination of these four elements will promote an environment able to achieve competitive advantage.

> A strategy for the acquisition, utilisation, improvement, and retention of an enterprise's human resources.   Department of Employment (1974)

This early definition offered by the Department of Employment (DOE) is useful in that it gives a clear focus for the planner. However, it was immediately noted that this definition is quite limited in that it does not include reference to corporate objectives (Stainer, 1971). In this way the strategy referred to may imply horizontal integration but not vertical integration. Clearly there is some synergy with the notion of manpower planning – implicit in getting the right people, with the right skills, in the right place, at the right time.

> The creation of explicit proposals by HR specialists, corporate and line managers (and sometimes other employees) to enable the supply or dispensation of the human resources necessary for the acceptable performance and long-term survival of an organisation.
> Tansley (1999)

The more recent definition proposed by Tansley (1999) reflects the dynamic nature of HRP and includes reference to the role of line management and possibly other employees. This definition is in line with the notion of HRM proposed by Guest (1987) as it suggests that line management and HR professionals (among others) are encouraged to take part in the creation process – thus gaining commitment to implementation. However, the definition stops short of implementation: in practice many strategic plans are created, but not implemented.

Another way of considering human resource planning is as a process (IPD, 1995; Reilly, 1996; Walker, 1980). There is an emphasis on the continuing need to change, modify and update HR-style policies and practices, clearly articulated in the definitions offered below. These definitions can be seen as a framework for managing information related to human resourcing issues. Current, accurate and complete information is essential to effective human resource planning

– human resource information systems can assist this management process and the more sophisticated information systems can offer alternative scenarios for decision-making.

> The systematic and continuous process of analysing an organisation's human resource needs, under changing conditions and integrating this analysis with development of personnel policies appropriate to meet those needs. It goes beyond the development of policies on an individual basis by embracing as many aspects of managing people as possible with a key emphasis on planning to meet the skill and development needs of the future.
>
> IPD (1995)

> Human resource planning can be defined as 'a process in which an organisation attempts to estimate the demand for labour and evaluate the size, nature and sources of the supply which will be required to meet that demand'.
>
> Reilly (1996)

What is distinctive from all of these definitions, and recognised in the literature, is the attempt to directly link the process of human resource planning to the overall planning of the organisation and thus weave together vertical and horizontal integration (Walker, 1980; Ulrich, 1987; Buller, 1988). Using Guest's model (1987) it can be seen that vertical integration indicates reciprocal relations between strategic planning and the process of human resource planning. Equally, horizontal integration suggests that the outcome of the process is a co-ordinated set of policies and practices in terms of the acquisition, utilisation, development and retention management of people as discussed in later chapters of this book.

As summarised in Table 2.3, manpower planning has made the transition to strategic human resource planning over a period of time and is characterised by a number of key points.

For the future, strategic human resource planning can be defined as a management process that provides a definitive connection between the strategic goals of the organisation and the qualitative and quantitative analysis, implementation and review of HR-style practices in both the short and long term, thus providing an HR strategy that fits holistically. The main purpose of strategic human resource planning is to support management decision-making: tactically for line management and strategically at corporate level.

Table 2.3 Manpower planning to strategic human resource planning – a continuum of development

Manpower planning		Human resource planning
Phase I	Phase II	Phase III
• Focus is short-term • Attempts to regulate and control employees	• Focus is short- to medium-term • Attempts to manage and control to meet with organisational objectives • Beginning to focus on employee behaviour, but tends to be disjointed	• Focus is long-term • Attempts to achieve competitive advantage through strategic orientation • Managing employee behaviour through involvement

A framework for strategic human resource planning

Although there are a number of models that are helpful to understanding human resource planning, Bramham (1994) provides a simple, but not simplistic, four-part framework: (see Figure 2.2). This model will provide a format for the discussion of strategic planning for human resources and identify its relevance for line management activities.

There are four phases to the framework. The first phase is the analysis and investigation, which considers the influence of the internal and external environment, a review of key elements of the organisation, and their impact on corporate strategy. Phase II examines techniques to assist the forecasting of the demand for labour and the internal and external supply of labour, thus identifying a human resourcing imbalance. Phase III establishes the key policy areas and offers a range of generic HR plans as to how this imbalance can be addressed. The final phase ascertains the ways in which the various plans can be implemented and controlled, with particular discussion of the role of human resource information systems.

Phase I – Analysis and investigation

This first phase of the human resource planning framework, containing four elements, is concerned with identifying and analysing the environment within

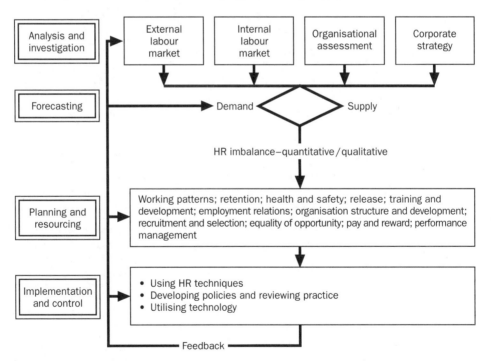

Figure 2.2 Model of human resource planning

Source: This material is adapted from *Human Resource Planning*, J. Braham 1994, with the permission of the publisher, the Chartered Institute of Personnel and Development, CIPD House, Camp Road, London SW19 4UX.

which strategic human resourcing takes place. An understanding of the external environment is fundamental to an appreciation of strategic planning for human resources and this will be dealt with in some depth in this text. The internal labour market refers to the flows of 'stocks' of employees at different levels both in and out of the organisation. The third section focuses on assessing different HR-style policies and practices and in addition the organisational culture is reviewed. The final element relates to the future corporate strategy and how this impacts on the human resourcing strategy.

The external labour market

The external labour market has changed markedly in the last two decades. The technological and communications revolution has changed the relationship between the supply of labour and the geographical base of that labour. Any review of the external labour market should take a global perspective. It is likely that organisations that do not take the global labour market into consideration will lose competitive advantage in the longer term. Therefore an appraisal of the external labour market should consider local, regional, national and international perspectives. A number of organisations undertake regular surveys to ascertain, among other things, the current state of the external labour market. For example a recent survey by PricewaterhouseCoopers (2000) notes that in the East Midlands there has been a general increase in recruitment overall and that almost half (48 per cent) of the companies surveyed thought that it was becoming increasing difficult to recruit workers, particularly skilled workers (50 per cent).

One approach to scanning the external labour market is by using the mnemonic PESTLIED, which represents various environmental factors. This is summarised in Table 2.4.

Table 2.4 PESTLIED – scanning the external macro-environment

P	**Political** factors with reference to European and national parliament and local government policy	L	**Legislative** factors – seeing an increasing amount of legislation emanating from Europe
E	**Economic** factors – fiscal policies notably changes in the interest rates, the potential impact of the euro	I	**International** factors particularly with regard to commercial regulation and population movements, mainly impact of Europe and USA
S	**Social** factors – the increasing impact of local community issues and the resurgence of concerns with regard to all forms of discrimination	E	**Environmental** factors – the impact of 'green issues' on corporate strategy making
T	**Technological** factors – increasing personal use of technology as well as in the workplace	D	**Demographic** factors with regard to the age and ability of the workforce and the socio-economic groups of the general population

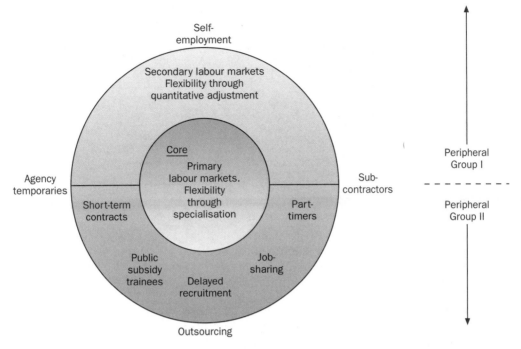

Figure 2.3 Core and peripheral workers

Source: Adapted from Atkinson and Meager (1986)

Perhaps the most influential work with regard to the current state of the external labour market is the much quoted model of the 'Flexible Firm' proposed by Atkinson and Meager (1986) – see Figure 2.3 – that conceptualises the different elements of the core and peripheral workforce. The inner circle represents the workers considered by the organisation to be vital to its success. They are likely to be full-time, highly skilled with good career prospects and remuneration packages. The first peripheral group is characterised by roles that are specific to that organisation – women have traditionally done many of these jobs particularly in retail, hospitality, education and health-related industries (Cully *et al.*, 1998). The second peripheral group is often integrated with the first peripheral group and mainly reflects the type of employment contract. Outside of these are other external groups, typically specific consultancy or subcontract-type jobs with around 90 per cent of workplaces contracting out basic services such as cleaning, training and security (Cully *et al.*, 1998).

The core and peripheral model has synergy with different types of flexibility (see Figure 2.4). *Numerical flexibility* is visible within the first and second periphery groups, with some support for *functional flexibility* (mainly at the core) at the edges. Implicit within is *temporal flexibility* in that some of the contracts may be for specific periods of time, possibly reflecting the seasonal nature of some organisations. *Geographical flexibility*, the ability to work away from an organisation (for example home-working), is not really demonstrated within the Atkinson and Meager's (1986) model of the flexible firm. There is a significant minority of workers (25.2

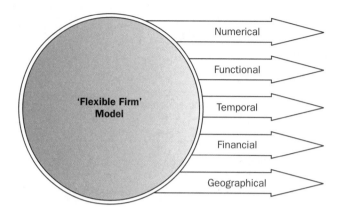

Figure 2.4 Types of flexibility within a flexible firm

per cent) who do all or some work from home, with the largest element being those in professional occupations (54.9 per cent) (Unknown, 2000). These forms of flexibility are apparent within the core and peripheral model discussed above.

- **Numerical flexibility** The ability of management to adjust the number of employees according to need, particularly useful for seasonal businesses.
- **Functional flexibility** The ability of employees to undertake different tasks due to their level of training and development, trained and qualified. Examples include multi-skilling and multi-responsibilities, high-tech and low-tech home-working.
- **Temporal flexibility** The ability of management to adjust the hours worked according to business needs through a range of contracts such as annualised hours, part-time work, job sharing, zero-hours and portfolio working, flexi-working.
- **Financial flexibility** The way in which employees are rewarded, with particular emphasis on enabling the employer to control expenditure. Examples include competence-based pay, performance-related pay, various flexible benefits schemes, team performance-related schemes.
- **Geographical flexibility** The management of the place of work that is often enabled by a high degree of investment in technology: for example, email, video- and tele-conferencing, tele-working (e.g. call centres).

Although there are a number of criticisms of this model it is helpful to understand the make-up of the labour market at any given moment of time, but it does not offer an organisation a prescription for re-organising its structure. There are several criticisms that are worth reviewing here.

- **The methodology utilised** Penn (1992) suggests that too small a sample was used on which to base firm conclusions.
- **Core-peripheral description** Some observers believe that this is far too simplistic a description as it would appear to suggest a standardisation of work practices.
- **Little evidence in practice** Larger longitudinal studies, such as the *Workplace Industrial Relations Survey*, did not find any substantial evidence of flexibility at work and where it is found it is not a widespread pattern of practice (Brown, 1990).

- *Numerical flexibility* Claims of numerical flexibility are overstated (Marginson, 1989).
- *Functional flexibility* There is little evidence for functional flexibility during the 1980s and it was possible to meet any demand through the use of computer-based technologies (Piore and Sable, 1984).
- *Peripheral workers* Some writers have commented that the number of peripheral workers is contingent on a variety of factors (Pollert, 1988b; Penn, 1992).
- *Other factors are involved* Various writers have suggested other factors influence an organisation's work philosophy: for example, high unemployment (MacInnes, 1988; Penn, 1992), competition (Walsh, 1991), demographics (Pollert, 1988a, 1991).
- *Lack of strategic intent* A key reason for concern relates to the lack of an appropriate written strategy concerning a comprehensive and systematic approach to the core-peripheral model based on a conscious and deliberate focus on developing flexible working practices (McGregor and Sproull, 1991; Proctor *et al.*, 1994). There is some evidence for different forms of flexibility in practice, but not in terms of a coherent and strategic approach.

So is there really any evidence that the flexible model has validity in the labour market?

- *Employers using flexible working practices* The initial findings from the longitudinal study, the 1998 Workplace Employee Relations Survey (WERS, 1998) (Cully *et al.*, 1998), suggest that there is evidence that organisations are taking a more flexible approach to employment, although this tends to be focused on numerical flexibility rather than functional flexibility: perhaps this is due to the continuing skills shortages experienced by some organisations (PricewaterhouseCoopers, 2000).
- *Peripheral workers* There is a greater use of freelance, agency and contract workers. There are some 1.7 million temporary workers in the UK who make up about 7 per cent of the workforce (IDS, 2000). Additionally there has been a growth in part-time work both in the UK and in most of Europe over the last few years (see the comparative note below), although this did slow down during the recession of the early 1990s (Brewster *et al.*, 1994; Mayne *et al.*, 1996). Women continue to view flexible working hours as critical to enhancing the role of women in management (PricewaterhouseCoopers, 2000).
- *Industry specific* Recent evidence suggests that some industries, such as the financial sector, are less likely to allow staff to transfer from full-time to part-time work (Rowe, 2000).
- *Employee options* Some even argue that part-time work should not be included as there may be little option for flexibility for employees, especially where many part-timers are employed (Walsh, 1999). This may cause some legislative concern – for example the recent part-time workers legislation.
- *A question of definition* Hunter *et al.* (1993) note that part-time work can be a euphemism for a few hours a week to 30 hours a week. They go on to observe that the distinction between temporary and permanent work can be quite blurred and that self-employment is another difficult area.

Comparative note

'Part-time work is on the increase and is playing an important role in Europe. Across Europe, a significant percentage of employers have increased their use of part-timers (38 per cent of respondents to the 1995 Cranet-E project reported an increase since 1992), with the northern countries of the EU (for example, the Netherlands, France, Switzerland, Germany and the UK) showing greater increases than their southern counterparts such as Spain and Turkey (Meulders *et al.*, 1996; De Grip *et al.*, 1997). Based on surveys of HR practices in some 14 European countries, Brewster *et al.* (1997: 119) suggest that almost "one in every seven people in the European Union is working part-time and part-time employment has been the major area of growth during the last decade".'

Extract from (Clifford *et al.*, 1997: 556)

The internal labour market

It is important to analyse the internal labour market to establish the current situation. This consists of an inventory exercise at different levels. This is a review of the make-up of employees: the actual number overall and in different areas of the business; age profile; the skills of employees; the demographic profile of employees; labour turnover and absence analysis for all types and levels of employee; performance/productivity levels; personal, management and technical competences. The outcome of this analysis is a snapshot of the human assets at a given moment in time. The advantage of this snapshot is that it provides a base line from which planning for human resourcing can begin.

Organisational assessment

An area often overlooked in the analysis is the wider organisational issues that impact on planning. This involves an examination of a number of key areas: the main philosophy of the organisation; the cultural aspects including employee attitudes; the organisational structure; the way in which employees are viewed – as a cost to the organisation or an investment; the people-related costs including remuneration, development and termination; the effectiveness of HR-style practices; and various trends such as absenteeism, labour turnover, etc. There has been a move towards flatter organisational structures in the last decade, initiated as a result of the recession at the beginning of the 1990s. Also the 1980s have been described as a period where the focus was on changing the organisational culture.

The main difficulty with this type of analysis is the lack of specific techniques readily available to help. They have tended to be organisation specific and the line manager may often use their own subjective judgement rather than a valid analytical process.

Corporate strategy

Perhaps the fundamental difference between manpower planning and strategic human resource planning is the attempt to actively match the organisational strategy. Some writers see the human resourcing strategy as a second or third order strategy (Purcell, 1989) – i.e. a functional strategy that is derived from the corporate strategy. Others, such as Torrington and Hall (1998), believe it is possible for corporate strategy and HR strategy to be mutually dependent or even to be HR led. For most organisations it is the first case that will most often be true. Purcell (1989) provides a concise appreciation of how the two integrate and the main areas of consideration, indicating discussion of the market place and financial targets.

Impact of the analysis for line managers

Undoubtedly this high level of analysis is likely to be undertaken centrally. Therefore line managers might question their ability to be involved in this process. However, there are clear opportunities for input. It is highly likely that the line manager will have a comprehensive knowledge of the issues that affect the external labour market in their particular area of expertise. Professional journals have regular articles on issues pertaining to a specific occupation. A cursory glance at the job advertisements section will reveal the value placed on certain jobs and it is relatively easy to see where the remuneration is being driven by a scarcity or dearth of skills in the marketplace. Line managers are able to analyse the make-up of their own department/function, although they may need help from HR with regard to the organisational assessment. It is likely that in many organisations where employee involvement practices are pursued that line management are aware of the corporate strategy – these are often synthesised in, for example, mission statements and road shows. What is clear from this discussion is that line management have a role to play in partnership with the HR specialist so that a comprehensive analysis of the external environment takes place.

Activity 2.2

Consider the course you are studying.

1 Are you being taught by a mixture of full-time and part-time lecturers?

2 Why do you think that universities and colleges are using elements of the flexible firm to provide teaching?

3 How does this mixture of teaching staff benefit the:

a) students
b) faculty/department
c) university as a whole?

Forecasting supply and demand

Traditionally, this would have been thought of as the 'hard' element of planning. A number of researchers have attempted to quantify people related data in order to derive a formula for calculating the demand for human resources in the future and the potential internal and external supply of human resources available for dispersal in the organisation. The outcome of the forecasting phase is to devise a human resourcing plan that will identify key areas for implementation. This may sound fairly straightforward, but basically it is a calculated guess – and as with all such guesses the more data that is available, coupled with previously known outcomes, permits the planner to become more accurate over time. But in the final analysis it is still only a (good) guess!

Perhaps the best illustration of this difficulty of crystal ball gazing is from the late 1980s. Well-respected opinion, both academic and organisational, pronounced that the 'demographic time bomb' – the result of a reduced number of births in the 1970s – would have a serious impact on industries' ability to recruit, retain and remunerate young people. Although true, this 'fact' was seriously overshadowed by the recession of the early 1990s, which resulted in a high number of redundancies including professional as well as manual labour. This example demonstrates the importance of weighting the relevant factors in terms of their influence on the planning process and outcome.

Phase II – Forecasting demand for labour

Fundamental to the success of demand forecasting is an accurate picture of the external, macro environment in which an organisation is operating. The CIPD suggest a course of action (see Table 2.5) that is derived from the environmental analysis (Table 2.4). A picture will emerge that indicates the new jobs or tasks that need to be recruited or the retraining required for current employees to produce the planned product or service. This leads to the development of skill and competencies sets to do these jobs/tasks. Additionally if the organisation needs to change its philosophy, structure or cultural style, the impact on the type of people employed will need to be determined.

Table 2.5 Extract from the IPD statement on human resource planning – forecasting demand

- Assessing the impact of business plans and objectives on the methods of working for: numbers and skills of employees; the structure and culture of the organisation; employee relations and employee development
- Analysing unit labour costs and productivity ratios in the light of business plans and objectives and the context of competition
- Forecasting future staffing requirements qualitatively and quantitatively

There are a number of quantitative and qualitative approaches summarised in Table 2.6 that can help this process.

- *Ratio-trend analysis* attempts to provide ratios for specific types of jobs or skills. For example, how many customer enquiries can be effectively taken by one call-centre operator within a set period of time.
- *Eco-centric modelling* allows data to be analysed to establish relationships between different types of variables, for example, the relationship of sales to

Table 2.6 Techniques for forecasting the demand for labour

Quantitative analysis	Qualitative analysis
• Ratio-trend analysis	• Managerial judgement
• Eco-centric modelling	• Delphi technique
• Work study	• Nominal group technique

the number of employees. Once developed these models can be extended to cover other key variables.

● *Work-study*, an outcome of scientific management techniques, is a system of assessing work by observation. Historically this technique has been used in manufacturing, however, it is possible to see it being used in the fast-food industry today.

● Perhaps a more subjective approach is *Managerial Judgement*. This method considers the 'best guess' of knowledgeable senior and line mangers and technical staff. Over time this method can become very refined, but with erratic external environment changes it is less reliable.

● The *Delphi Technique* is a more refined approach based on the systematic collection and analysis of anonymous managerial opinion. The main disadvantage to this process is that it can take some considerable time in a large organisation, during which the contextual issues may have changed.

● A quicker approach is an adaptation of the Delphi Technique. The *Nominal Group Technique* is a face-to-face meeting of relevant experts, who write down their ideas and then discuss and rank them. There is little empirical evidence to support these last two techniques, however, these are often discussed in texts on planning.

Forecasting supply for labour

Perhaps easier for the line manager and HR specialist is forecasting the supply of labour. This focuses on what is happening within the organisation and is in line with the IPD recommended course of action (see Table 2.7).

The *internal supply of labour* is characterised by the analysis of labour turnover in different ways. Generally speaking most organisations undertake this type of analysis to some degree, but not usually to the depth needed to elicit useful and meaningful information. Often employee turnover figures are discussed for the organisation as a whole, which does not expose particular problem areas with

Table 2.7 Extract from the IPD statement on human resource planning – forecasting supply

● Analysing existing human resources, e.g. age, length of service, skills and knowledge, future capability, flexibility, etc
● Estimating the impact of early and normal retirements, resignations and labour turnover
● Forecasting the future availability of people qualitatively and quantitatively
● Monitoring and analysing trends from opinion surveys, exit interview and subsequent follow-up

Table 2.8 Techniques for forecasting the supply of labour

Quantitative analysis	Qualitative analysis
• Stocks and flows analysis	• Succession planning
• Staff profiles	• Career planning
• Labour turnover analysis	
• Stability index	
• Half-life analysis	
• Cohort analysis	
• Retention profile	
• Census technique	

regard to recruitment or retention of specific skills or jobs. In recent years there has also been a focus on employee development. Another key area is the increasing focus on the age of the workforce, a growing area for computer modelling (Mohapatra *et al.*, 1990).

There are a number of quantitative analyses often associated with forecasting the internal supply of labour, summarised in Table 2.8.

- *Stocks and flows analysis* identifies the key entry and exit points, key promotion and transfer information. This analysis exposes any blockages to progression and can indicate potential problem areas in the future.
- *Staff profiles* provide indicators in terms of age, gender and ethnic distribution, and skills profiling.
- *Labour turnover analysis* expresses the number of leavers in a certain period as a percentage of the number of employees in that period.
- *Stability index* assesses the number of employees with (one) year's service as a percentage of the number employed one year ago.
- *Half-life analysis* assesses how long it takes a certain group of employees, e.g. graduates, apprentices, to reach half their original number. This is useful to track retention patterns throughout an organisation.
- *Cohort analysis* monitors a specific group of employees, e.g. production engineers, over a period of time to determine what happens to them over time.
- *Retention profile* expresses the survivors of a specific group as a percentage of the number of joiners usually in a particular year and is often displayed graphically as a histogram.
- *Census technique* expresses the number of leavers over a specified period (e.g. one year) as a percentage against their length of service and is often displayed graphically as a histogram. This is useful to track loyalty patterns throughout an organisation.
- *Succession planning* attempts to identify potential gaps in the organisation's capabilities in terms of specific employees. The aim is to put a specific name in a box. This is generally done at a senior level in the organisation or for specific knowledge-sensitive positions.
- *Career planning* may be used to support succession planning activities.

Table 2.9 External supply of labour factors

Economic factors	• Rate of unemployment in the immediate area • Impact of mortgage interest rates • Communications infrastructure, road networks and public transport • Size of local labour market and make-up of their skill base • Number of organisations in the immediate area with similar skill requirements
Demographic factors	• Density of local population, their type and age breakdown • Geographical movement of population in and out of the area • Composition of the local labour skills
Organisational factors	• Perception of the organisation's public reputation as a 'good' employer • Ability of organisation to adapt to local work culture
General factors	• Make-up of industry in the area • Availability of external funding for training and development • Links with local training and educational institutions

It is also necessary to review the *external supply of labour*. Key areas for consideration are noted in Table 2.9. Generally speaking this area is not examined in depth unless an organisation is considering relocation to a new area or diversification into a new range of products or services.

Using the information from the forecasting phase

The outcome of the supply and demand forecasting phase presents information in both quantitative and qualitative formats. Once the facts are established and the information analysed, it is possible to examine appropriate options to redress the HR imbalance (see Figure 2.2).

Impact of supply and demand forecasting for line managers

Drucker (1974) considers that the line management's job consists of five basic operations: setting objectives; organising; motivating and communicating; measurement; and people development – planning for people is not really implied as a key activity here. Indeed there is very little evidence in the literature that line managers undertake supply and demand forecasting as a regular and routine part of their activities. However, this does not mean that they should not do so. It would seem that if line managers understand the process and the benefits of HRP they would be better able to contribute to forward planning exercises taking place in their organisations and better able to 'see the wood for the trees' with regard to the human resource requirements for their own department.

The advent of information systems such as spreadsheets has provided the tools necessary to conduct the various calculations suggested above. Should the line manager prefer the HR specialist to undertake these task, it is likely to be completely fairly swiftly if the line manager is able to provide accurate, up-to-date and complete data, thus promoting a philosophy of partnership suggested by much of the literature in this area. The role of human resource information systems in the planning of human resources will be discussed later in this chapter.

Case Study 2.1

Retail is You

Retail is You is a general retail company with four store units based in four locations: Edinburgh, Birmingham, Manchester and Plymouth. The company currently employs 991 people with between 224 and 265 employed in each store and 40 based at the Nottingham warehouse.

In the last five years there has been a focus on recruiting graduate trainees (see Item 1) although some appear to be leaving within a short period of time (see Item 2).

Item 1 Number of graduate trainees recruited over a 5-year period

	Birmingham	Edinburgh	Manchester	Nottingham	Plymouth	Grand Total
1995	8	5	6	1	8	28
1996	9	6	8	0	9	32
1997	10	8	8	1	10	37
1998	10	9	9	0	11	39
1999	10	10	10	1	11	42

Item 2 Number of graduate trainees who left over a 5-year period with at least 1 year's service

	Birmingham	Edinburgh	Manchester	Nottingham	Plymouth	Grand Total
1995	4	2	5	0	3	14
1996	4	3	1	1	3	12
1997	3	3	2	1	3	12
1998	4	3	3	0	4	14
1999	5	3	3	0	4	15

Activity 2.3

Calculate the labour turnover and stability index at each location and for *Retail is You* overall.

Phase III – Planning and resourcing

The third phase of Bramham's model discusses the outcomes of human resource planning: i.e. the different resourcing, retention, development and termination policies that are developed as a result of the information collected and analysed in the previous phases. These policies or strategies are developed to address the issues raised during the forecasting phase. Ideally they should demonstrate horizontal integration such that they 'fit' with each other and do not conflict in any way. Typical policy areas, further developed in later chapters of this book, will include:

- *Resourcing plan* – what type of people are required, where are they likely to be now, what is the best mechanism to use to attract them to apply for vacancies, how will the effect of this approach be evaluated (see Chapters 3 and 4).
- *Development plan* – what skills are needed in the future, what mechanisms will be used to develop these skills, how will the skills base be increased and maintained, how will career planning and succession planning take place, how will the effect of this approach be evaluated (see Chapters 8 and 9).
- *Retention plan* – once recruited, what mechanisms will be put in place in order to retain employees who contribute to organisational performance, need to consider both 'carrot' and 'stick' options, key areas include remuneration, performance management, training, development and promotion opportunities, encouragement of commitment to the organisation (see Chapters 5 to 7).
- *Flexibility plan* – what types of flexible working patterns analogous to the notion of the 'Flexible Firm' will enhance individual and organisational performance (see Chapter 5).
- *Remuneration plan* – how will employees be rewarded, what benefits will be offered, how will the reward strategy remain competitive (see Chapter 7).
- *Productivity plan* – mechanisms that enable aspects of business process re-engineering, links with incentive measures (see Chapter 7).
- *Downsizing plan* – what are the triggers that indicate fewer employees are needed, what mechanisms will be employed to ensure that the process of downsizing is completed in a legal and ethical manner (see Chapter 6).
- *Control and management of HR plans* – what mechanisms will be used to manage the integration of the policies and plans discussed above to ensure they compliment each other, how will the success of these plans be evaluated (see Chapter 1).

Impact of planning and resourcing for line managers

It is clear that the responsibility for the development of the above plans is that of the HR specialist. However, it is argued here that line managers can make a vital contribution to ensure that the plans are workable and 'fit' the front-line needs and requirements. Consultation should take place such that appropriate timescales are established; procedures should be documented with clear responsibility lines identified.

Consider the resourcing plan. From the list below determine whether the task should be the responsibility of:

a) line managers
b) human resource specialists
c) both together:

    i)   designing the job
    ii)   deciding what qualities are needed in a prospective candidate
    iii) placing the advertisement
    iv) sending out application packs
    v)   shortlisting applicants
    vi) contacting applicants for interviews
    vii) conducting interviews
    viii) corresponding with applicants with the outcome of the interview
    ix) writing offer and rejection letters
    x)   greeting new employees on their first day
    xi) conducting organisation induction training
    xii) conducting initial job training etc.

Phase IV – Implementation and control

Bramham (1994) suggests that implementation and control of human resource planning is achieved by a) using HR techniques, b) developing policies and reviewing practice, and c) utilising technology. HR techniques appropriate for line managers will be discussed in further chapters of this text. The development of appropriate policies has been discussed in the previous section and will be further developed in this book. The latter two elements, reviewing practice and utilising technology, will be focused on in this section.

Once developed, a policy needs to remain current and appropriate to the internal and external environment in which the organisation is operating. Unless formal mechanisms are in place, a regular review of policies and practices is less likely to happen. Part of the reason is because of the general day-to-day work of line management and HR specialists in 'managing the moment'. Another cause may be that both are more tactically focused. Strategic human resource planning is tactical at the implementation stage, but in order to remain effective in the long term there must be some opportunities built into management activity to step back and review practice. This could be undertaken annually, bi-annually or quarterly. One effective method is to have a rolling management agenda that reviews different elements of HRM. This ensures that all aspects of functional impact are considered on a regular basis.

Utilising technology – Human Resource Information Systems

A recent review of the software offered by the on-line *People Management* site revealed that there are now over 100 computerised human resource information

Table 2.10 The use of personal data in employer/employee relationships

Data Protection Draft Code of Practice
• Take seriously and be seen to take seriously the protection of employee data
• Establish who is responsible for ensuring the firm's employment practices comply with the Data Protection Act 1998
• Explain to people who reply to job ads who they are giving information to and how it will be used
• Do not take information from a recruitment agency without the individual knowing
• Use an automated system in shortlists only if it can be shown to produce results that are consistent and fair to applicants
• Carry out pre-employment vetting only when a decision has been taken that the applicant should be appointed
• Don't keep recruitment records for longer than four months for shortlisted applicants
• Don't seek personal information from new employees that is irrelevant or excessive to the employment relationship
• Hold sickness records of staff only if you have the explicit consent of each employee

Source: *Personnel Today* (17 October 2000, p. 3)

systems (HRIS) available. Two important issues *vis-à-vis* the use of electronic data collection and analysis software are privacy and security issues. The recent updating of the data protection laws enshrined in the Data Protection Act 1998 and the introduction of the Human Rights Act 1999 has raised a number of concerns for employers and employees resulting in the drafting of a code of practice that will affect the way in which information systems are used to manage employee data – see Table 2.10.

There is evidence to suggest that many organisations are not using their HRIS as effectively as possible and that where they did its use was somewhat limited (Hall and Torrington, 1989; Broderick and Boudreau, 1992). Often the HR function has been the last to benefit from the introduction of a dedicated information system. Part of the reason here is the lack of emphasis placed on information systems by the HR specialist (Kinnie and Arthurs, 1993, 1996; Parker and Caine, 1996). Recent evidence from a joint survey by the Institute of Employment Studies (IES) and CIPD confirms that the main use of HRIS is as an 'electronic filing cabinet' to hold employee records and produce various types of reports (see Figure 2.5). Although this is the basic purpose of any HRIS they are capable of much more if those who use the system have the vision, skills and resources to do so.

Often there is confusion over the terminology: computerised personnel information systems verses human resource information systems. For the purposes of this text they will be assumed to be similar, but further clarification of these terms can be sought elsewhere (Williams, 2000). Table 2.11 below suggests the key differences between CPIS and HRIS.

A human resource information system is defined by Tansley *et al.* (2001) as 'a system which operates beyond the *usual* functional HR department's boundaries, enabling *significant* innovation of HR business processes and enabling the business drivers for change to HR processes in the network organisation' (emphasis added). This presupposes that HRIS can be useful to line managers in that it can provide information about people processes within their own sphere of influence,

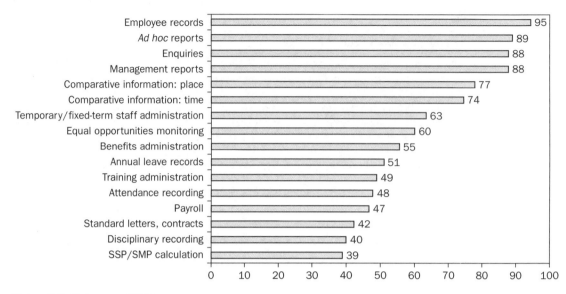

Figure 2.5 Main uses of HRIS

Source: IES/CIPD (2000: 1280)

Table 2.11 The difference between CPIS and HRIS

Computerised Personnel Information System	Human Resource Information System
• Owned by the HR department • Maintained by HR • Limited or no access outside of HR • Fed by paper or via a limited network • Limited assistance to HR processes • Limited by boundaries of location and geography	• Managed by the HR function, but owned by the organisation • Maintained by HR and line management • Access by line management and (possibly) individuals • Fed by intranet, email and workflow • Integral to HR processes • Boundaries no object

Source: Robinson (1997: 1)

taking into consideration the wider requirements of the organisation as a whole. In reality it would appear that most systems are more limited. However, they do provide line management with valuable employee information, such as that described in Table 2.12.

Much of the basic statistical analysis of the data collected in Phase II (Forecasting) has tended to focus on the analysis of employee supply-demand. The data can be processed speedily, efficiently and more accurately by a HRIS: indeed for many organisations this is the sole purpose of their system. Additionally HRIS are usually accompanied by a graphics package that allows the analysed data to be interpreted and presented graphically in different ways. Thus presentation to more senior colleagues is visual and backed by the actual data should individuals wish to have access to the background material. Among the very few models that have attempted to integrate the emerging (and increasing) role of

Table 2.12 Types of employee data

Individual HR data . . .	Collective HR data includes . . .
Application form, interview and test records, job history (transfers, promotions, etc.), current and historical pay details, inventory of skills and competencies, education and training records, performance assessment details, absence, lateness, accident, medical and disciplinary records, warning and suspensions, holiday entitlements, pensions data, termination record/exit interview/re-engage	Numbers, grades and occupations of employees; skills audit data – analysis of the skills available; absenteeism, labour turnover and lateness statistics; accident rates; age and length of service distributions; wage rates and salary levels; employee costs; overtime statistics; records of grievances and disputes and training records

part-time and flexible employment is that of Bechtold (1988), who developed a model for scheduling days off for part-time and full-time staff. In general, a computerised HRP model places the HR specialist in complete control of the analytical process.

More recent HRIS require data to be provided in a number of areas: corporate strategy; gender information; legal constraints; labour-market forces; demographics; financial constraints; alternative employment policies; various costs including outplacement and downsizing; employee morale and attitude; employee turnover trends; potential applicants. Many also have the capacity to integrate with other databases and business systems.

HRP and the intranet

The use of an HR intranet has grown significantly in recent years (IES/CIPD, 2000) although maximising their potential use is a strategic issue, particularly as the relationship with line management needs to be redefined – to pursue a partnership *vis-à-vis* a human resourcing strategy – so that using an intranet becomes a part of day-to-day work. However, an intranet is only as good as its content (Mansell-Lewis, 1997) and may require its sponsors to demonstrate its business benefits (such as the reduction in duplication of information, reduction of all forms of copying, more direct access to information, etc.), before the more reticent allow paper-based and legacy systems to be discarded.

Intranets are private computing networks, internal to an organisation, allowing access only to authorised users. They may include an internal 'web' along similar lines to the World Wide Web with multiple websites and web pages, electronic mail, newsgroups, online meeting facilities and any number of applications. Web browsers are used to navigate across information on the network and, whilst authorised users can cross into the Internet, those outside the organisation cannot cross into the Intranet.

(Curry and Stancich 2000: 250)

The content of an HR intranet will vary from organisation to organisation, but some generic elements are recommended in the list below. Information can be passed to and from employees and line managers in a more efficient and timely manner; for example, the results of employee surveys, notification of vacancies, notice of promotions and appointments, changes to policies, information from the external environment regarding the current state of the labour market, etc.

- HR policies
- Contact information
- Benefits information
- Employee surveys
- Appraisal forms and processing
- Internal/external recruiting
- Organisational charts
- Newsletters
- Absence monitoring
- Company calendar
- Training and development calendar
- Employee classifieds
- Guidelines for implementation of policies
- Contents of staff handbook

There are a number of business benefits to using an intranet to integrate human resourcing into the day-to-day working of the organisations. These include automated business processes, dissemination of information, facilitation of a collaborative culture, increased employee satisfaction and a mechanism to receive feedback.

HRP and the internet

The recent IES/CIPD (2000) survey found that well over half of the 552 respondents were using the internet as well as an intranet, but only 21 per cent were using them in conjunction with HR software. Where the HR software is being used with the internet and intranet it is mainly for employee resourcing (particularly for advertising, acknowledgement of applications and occasionally for psychometric testing) and information gathering. There are some definite advantages to be gained from using the internet for resourcing, for example:

- Employers can develop a database of CVs, completed application forms and other personal details about an applicant.
- Pre-selection criteria can be applied for a specific job and suitable candidates can be identified.
- Candidates can be emailed with notification of the vacancy, asked if they still have an interest and proceed with an application.
- If the database of pre-registered applicants is of sufficient size, the candidates identified in this way are likely to be both of interest to the employer and interested in the position.

One concern about this use is the recent draft code of practice regarding the use of personal details from the Data Protection Registrar. At the time of writing it is still unclear as to how much information can be kept, for how long and for what reasons.

Impact of implementation and control for line managers

It is clear that HRIS can facilitate information provision for line management. A constant danger is the likelihood of being overwhelmed by information in a forward thinking, proactive and appropriately resourced organisation. Dissemination of information can take place through traditional monthly/quarterly management meetings that may have standing agenda items to discuss people management issues as well as those needed to 'manage the moment'.

HRIS can greatly assist the line manager undertake their people responsibilities, particularly HRP, in an efficient, timely and cost-effective manner. The appraisal system, absence monitoring systems and resourcing are excellent examples.

- *Performance appraisal* There is often a general resentment of the amount of form filling required by HR at line level. Using the HR intranet the line manager should be able to complete the minimum of forms on-line, with clear benefits for completion outlined to line management. This information can be integrated into the career management, succession planning and training and development elements of HRIS with the minimum of effort and the outcome displayed in, for example, the training and development calendar. Individuals can be personally notified of the next programme date.
- *Absence Management* Timely reports can provide comparative data against other functions/departments, identify emerging trends of absence and patterns of behaviour, be graphical wherever possible, with appropriate detail available and various options for action should line management need to take necessary remedial action.
- *Resourcing* Information regarding the current state of the external and internal labour market can be assessed by line management prior to the decision to recruit. Line management can notify HR of their intention to recruit, complete/update job descriptions and person specifications on-line, allowing HR to devise appropriate advertising and establish the recruitment media with the minimum of paperwork. Design and copywriters can produce draft adverts which can be placed on the organisation's website, forwarded to a recruitment agency web site, or placed in appropriate journals and other media with the minimum of delay. Skill profiling software can facilitate a match between the applicants' data and the competences required by an organisation both visually in the form of spider diagrams or graphs and numerically by percentage 'fit' so that the line manager and HR specialist can make informed judgements on who to interview.

Activity 2.5

1 What type of information about students would be helpful for administrators and lecturers for planning for the next year's intake, programmes, courses and modules?

2 What type of information about students would be helpful to describe the current state of the student population?

SUMMARY

In this chapter the following key points have been made:

- Strategic human resource planning makes the link between corporate strategy and human resourcing strategy. It recognises the need to allow for changes in, and the impact of the external environment. This information is used during the forecasting of the supply and demand for labour to develop an appropriate range of HR-style policies and practices. These can be implemented, managed and controlled using various tools, including, for example, human resource information systems.

- Human resource planning can be defined both strategically and as a process. Generally HRP occurs once the corporate strategy is established. It is difficult to establish a point at which manpower planning developed into human resource planning – it happened over a period of time and is characterised by a number of key points.

- The key difference between traditional manpower planning and strategic human resource planning is the involvement of the line management and potentially other employees (to encourage commitment) in the latter process – this is a key theme in much of the literature. Some organisations, such as Marks & Spencer, have always attempted to have few functional distinctions between line and personnel managers because 'good human relations is something that cannot be left to the personnel department' (Tyson and Fell, 1992). Indeed there is some recognition in the literature that line managers are involved in some HR planning activities, however, their level of influence is questionable, although evidence suggests that these activities are defined differently by line managers and HR specialists (McConville and Holden, 1999).

- Fundamentally the difference between manpower planning and HRP is one of scope. Manpower planning has traditionally been associated with the 'hard' numerical elements of forecasting supply and matching it with the demand for staff. However, there is considerable confusion even in current literature.

- It has been suggested elsewhere that the HR specialist has four planning concerns (Richards-Carpenter, 1989). First, HRP is an activity that should be taken seriously by all involved. Therefore training is needed and should be offered as a standard activity so that the process is well understood, data can be interpreted and the subsequent findings can be translated into effective policies. Secondly, HRP takes time, effort, commitment and resources, thus all involved, particular line management, should see it as a worthwhile management activity. Thirdly, all involved need to understand what HRP is and how it can make a difference to achieving corporate and departmental objectives. Lastly, the HR specialist must establish how HRP links into the corporate culture of the organisation.

- Bramham's (1994) framework of human resource planning is a useful visual representation to help make sense of the HRP process. The four key elements (analysis and investigation, forecasting, planning and resourcing, implementation and control) provide a phased approach to HRP that facilitates a process whereby a detailed snapshot of the organisations can be established and suitable responses can be developed.

- The model of the *Flexible Firm* offered by Atkinson (1984, 1985) provides a conceptual framework for reviewing the external labour market. Some evidence is offered suggesting that a more flexible approach to employee resourcing is helpful when planning for human resources.

- Information is only useful if it is used; otherwise it is just an expensive way of producing data. The real question is how can information systems support the work of line management and produce meaningful data in useful formats that help make sense of the data held by the organisation. Human resource information systems are becoming more sophisticated, not just 'electronic filing cabinets', but also tools that enhance decision-making. More recent HRIS are able to make use of up-to-date technology including the intranet and internet.

? DISCUSSION QUESTIONS

1   What are the differences between manpower planning and human resource planning?

2   How useful is the flexible firm model for undertaking current employment strategies?

3   What are the pros and cons of using quantitative and qualitative techniques for forecasting labour supply and demand?

4   How may information systems facilitate human resource planning for line managers?

R FURTHER READING

Students interested in further information on this topic should consult Bramham (1994) or Torrington and Hall (1998).

Chapter ③ Recruitment

Sue Simpson

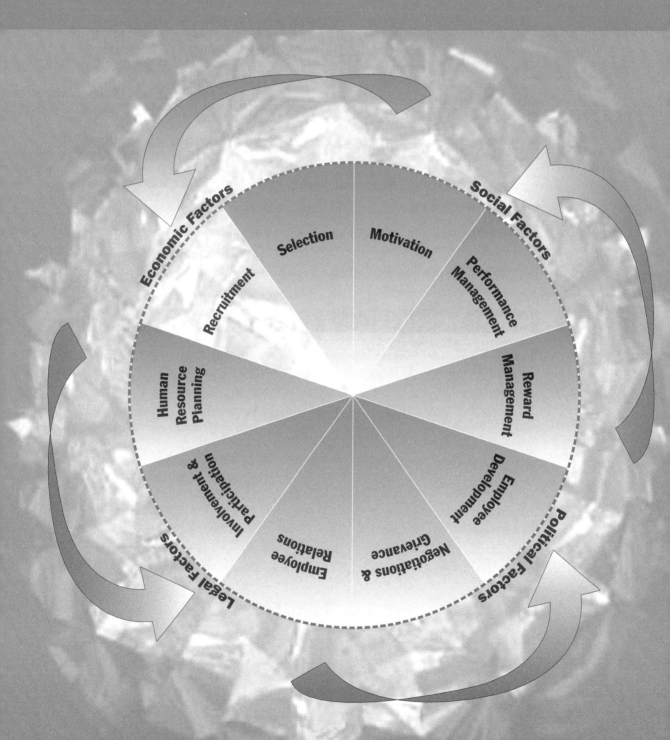

Having completed this chapter and its associated activities, readers should be able to:

- appreciate how recruitment strategy and practices 'fit' with the human resource and organisational strategies and the variation in different occupational contexts
- understand that an organisation's management may adopt a variety of strategies and methods for recruitment, using these singly or together as appropriate to the current and future vacancies
- distinguish between recruitment and selection but appreciate the links between the two
- consider the rationale for equal opportunity and diversity strategies, and some of their impacts
- appreciate the implications of the 'mix' of internal promotions and external recruits and the choices available as alternatives to filling vacancies
- distinguish between job descriptions and person specifications and use of these to create an appropriate advert for the vacancy
- consider the role line managers play in the recruitment process and the way this interacts with human resource specialists
- appreciate that recruitment is a two-way process, dependent on attracting a 'pool' of applicants

INTRODUCTION

Recruitment is one of the most visible roles undertaken by the personnel or human resources department of an organisation, indicated by the very word. Recruitment tasks need to be carried out even if there is no dedicated 'named' department or functional area in the organisational structure specified for it. Indeed some organisations view the human resource function as an unnecessary and wasteful 'cost' to the business and operate successfully on this principle, only providing the minimum, legal, requirements. This seems to bear out Armstrong's view (1995: 158) that 'accountancy controls and logic . . . undermines the case for a distinctive "personnel" approach'. Where there is no human resource function, recruitment may be the responsibility of a variable mix of line managers from the appropriate area or department, together with outside agencies advising or providing personnel to carry out the recruitment tasks. Irrespective of the actual format chosen, however, some overseeing by senior management from the host organisation will always be required. Similarly, the development and use of recruitment policies also varies; some organisations have codes of conduct and defined standards to be achieved; or perhaps more accurately, codes they aim to achieve. Other organisations may have no written policy but operate by custom and practice and pragmatism, doing what is required as circumstances dictate.

Recruitment can be considered as part of a trio, 'recruit, reward and retain', which includes performance management and can be described by the broader term 'resourcing'. While in the 'personnel' model, recruitment may have been viewed as delivering the short-term goal of producing the product or service, the various HRM models outlined in Chapter 1 indicate a more vital role for recruitment in ensuring the organisation has the right mix of skills and expertise to deliver the organisational strategy. For instance, Guest's 1987 model requires recruitment to help deliver three of his four 'goals of HRM', the three being employee commitment, flexibility/adaptability and finally, quality, where appropriately skilled and motivated staff are essential (Guest, 1987). Recruitment together with training, development and appraisal facilitates enhanced performance within the organisation, including outsourcing for certain roles and products as appropriate. The approach taken to recruitment can be seen to embody the organisation's values, whether positive or negative. These will impact on its culture, perpetuating or changing it – whether unplanned, by accident, or planned, by design. This reflects tangible and intangible factors such as the relationship of existing and new organisational members.

Recruitment may be thought of as a positive process of generating a 'pool' of candidates by reaching the 'right' audience, suitable to fill the vacancy while selection can be seen as a more negative process of choosing or 'picking' from among that 'pool' the most suitable candidate(s), both able and willing to fill the vacancy. The two processes are closely linked and interdependent, indeed their division is rather arbitrary and variable. Imagine the recruitment process as a net, attracting and catching candidates, with funnels and filters to select them by whatever criteria. Taylor (1998: 105) describes 'wide trawls . . . [which] bring in lots of different fish, while wide nets only catch the biggest'. They are each useful but in different situations. The wide trawl has to grab your attention, while the wide net can be restrained to reach a narrow audience who self-select from the detailed description of the job and person required. Developing this further, the wide trawl may catch a lot but then discard many, both before and after employment commences; while the wide net may catch fewer and use more sophisticated methods of selection prior to engagement. This analogy suggests that the two processes of recruitment and selection, run somewhat in tandem, rather than entirely sequentially.

Start-up companies will have the task of staffing the organisation from scratch, a 'green field' relatively free of pre-established attitudes. This offers an almost unique opportunity to create an organisation with the personnel it recruits, usually reflecting the owner's or senior managements' values. The example of BellSouth, a cellular telephone company, shows over half the workforce were recruited in one year at start-up, '60 per cent of those recruited were aged under 30 and for many of them BellSouth was their first employer. The average length of service for the whole workforce is less than two years' (Leopold, 1997: 38). In contrast, established companies need to look at vacancies arising from expansion, internal promotion or leavers. Each situation presents a slightly different environment for recruitment. By considering the broader contextual factors surrounding a particular post, such as the tasks to be included and the levels of reporting within the organisation, appropriate levels of status and remuneration can also be identified.

This takes into account both internal relativities, based on any job evaluation systems in use in the organisation, and external comparability, based on labour markets for occupations and jobs (see Chapter 7).

In this chapter, we will outline and explain the origins and development of recruitment strategies and the processes and techniques associated with them, establishing the significance of the recruitment tasks involved.

Activity 3.1

Think about organisations you have worked in or read about.

1 How did they approach the recruitment of staff?

2 Was recruitment done by word of mouth, or in the local job centre?

3 Were the same methods used for all occupational groups or jobs?

4 What might be the advantages and drawbacks of the methods used?

Another way to help you understand recruitment issues is to recall how you approached applying to university. How did you find out about the courses available and the different universities? Did you look on the web, read prospectuses or use other means – whether advice from school, parents, friends or people who already attended particular institutions? You may have used a combination of these. How did they attract your attention? What criteria did you use to select your choices: reputation for teaching or research, position in various 'league tables', location (city centre or campus site), ease of entry, distance from home or likelihood of employment after graduation? Any other factors? Almost without realising it, you have already experienced many aspects of the recruitment process.

Overview of recruitment

Development of approaches to recruitment

The evolution of the Chartered Institute of Personnel and Development, outlined in Chapter 1, can be mirrored in parallel developments in recruitment and selection. Traditionally, recruitment would be based around relatively simple methods, locally based. *Ad hoc* arrangements, which may depend on word of mouth, seeing an advert in a corner shop or in the local press, have advantages. They may be appropriate for jobs where there are many potential applicants, available locally.

Such basic recruitment methods can only ever reach a relatively narrow group of potential employees and are therefore less likely to attract either the right skills for the organisation's needs or to offer equality of opportunity to the individual, compared with more broadly based methods. If, for instance, there is a strong tradition of recruiting family and friends of existing employees to a particular organisation, those groups not already represented tend to be permanently excluded, with implications under equal opportunities legislation.

Comparative note

It is easy to underestimate the influence of different cultural traditions, where guiding principles like 'the right way of behaving' may be surprisingly different from those assumed 'correct' in the West. In the Islamic world, there is traditionally a dependence on personal relationships, trust and loyalty. This may be expressed as a strong tradition of recruiting family and friends of existing employees to a particular organisation, seen not as 'nepotism' but as the right approach to recruitment (Hickson and Pugh, 1995).

The practices occur in both indigenous societies and in the diaspora, even though the latter will be mediated by the host culture(s). For instance, Hickson and Pugh (1995: 171) describe the characteristics of a typical Chinese small business as 'paternalistic and personalistic', based on traditional Confucian principles of benevolent authority and responsibility for the welfare of other family members. These morally binding relationships are based on trust and loyalty. The owner manages by direct personal involvement; family members are brought in, chosen for their abilities and supported during their education and training, including perhaps, postgraduate degrees. The paternalism does not have the stigma of over-dependence associated with it in more individualistic cultures such as the UK or US.

The economic environment and availability of sophisticated management systems are important factors affecting recruitment to management positions in developing countries. Negandhi states '. . . the personal nature of such recruitment in India, where it is largely confined to relatives and friends, and the performance of these recruits is not seriously evaluated. Why recruit strangers when their credentials cannot be checked?' Negandhi sees this not as backward but showing high adaptation to circumstances. (Adapted from Hickson and Pugh, 1995: 228)

Skill shortages and a desire to provide 'equal opportunities for men and women, . . . realizing a proportional representation of women' in the Dutch Air Force, are discussed by Schruijer (in Vickerstaff, 1992: 95). One of the main barriers to recruitment and integration was the technical nature of many jobs and a positive action plan to overcome these involved thinking creatively about increasing the 'pool' of applicants. Innovative new recruitment material included cassette tapes of interviews with women working for the Air Force, raising the sort of issues and questions potential recruits ask and their responses. In addition, brochures were written specifically for women, using text and photographs from the interviews, and the career opportunities described include detail on flight training.

Increasingly therefore, the limitations of these methods are seen and criticised in individualistic Western contexts where the aim of achieving equal opportunity, increasing diversity (and plurality), is generally sought through scientific, rational solutions including systematic selection procedures and psychometric testing with statistical justification. One reason for the growth in personnel management as a function was the potential this offered to develop a more professional and systematic process of recruitment (see Chapter 1). The development of systematic, rational policies and procedures, which reflected changing legal requirements, meant it was possible for all candidates to go through essentially the same process, thus ensuring fairness as far as possible, as well as reaching sufficient numbers of suitable candidates to ensure successful recruitment.

Systematic procedures tend to be associated with large bureaucratic organisations, having well-developed human resource functions and specialist recruitment staff. Indeed in the larger and more sophisticated organisations, the recruitment department would itself have a large and varied staff, each specialised in different aspects of recruitment and selection for different occupational groups. Such organisations are adapted to the time lag associated with following all the detail of systematic procedures. These procedures, while helping ensure equality of opportunity, almost inevitably slow down the recruitment procedure; it is very difficult for such organisations to fill vacancies quickly.

Recent factors influencing approaches to recruitment

The recent widespread increase in competitive pressures, discussed in Chapter 2, make cumbersome systems less appropriate, especially in more volatile sectors of the economy, such as IT or e-commerce. Recently, under pressure of competition with reductions in personnel and influenced by internal politics, it is reported that recruitment responsibilities are increasingly devolved to non-specialists (IPD, 2000b). Another response is to streamline recruitment processes, targeting the potential labour market more specifically even at the cost of a loss of some coverage of that market. Speeding up the whole recruitment process, so a 'just in time' approach can deliver staff where and when they are required, is often desired. The 'flexible firm' described in Chapter 2 has implications for recruitment as well as training and rewards. Employees may be recruited using the criteria of dual or multi skilling (achieved or potential) or a willingness to work on a casual contract or variable hours. The most extreme example is the 'zero hours' contract, where employees remain at home, unpaid, until they are called into work. Acceptance of such contracts is most likely to reflect a lack of alternative opportunities. This contrasts with 'golden hellos', of several thousand pounds, used to attract the brightest graduates into high-profile occupations or companies, or, alternatively, those where competitive pressures mean insufficient applicants are generated. Both illustrate the dynamic nature of recruitment, inevitably governed by economic factors.

Writers such as Guest (1987), Legge (1995), Iles and Salamon (1995: 206) identify the movement towards human resource strategies in the 1980s as many North American and European organisations 'began thinking of their recruitment and selection processes as major levers to support strategic and cultural change', recognising the role human resources play in providing competitive advantage. Iles and Salamon also identify a concern with efficiency in two approaches to selection, namely the psychometric 'scientific selection' model and the social process model, the latter 'constructing' the individual by identifying qualities, beyond those purely job related, which are required for success in the organisation. One way in which such changes are manifested is in the 'competency' movement. This focuses on outputs, typically performance criteria including consideration of skills and examples of how they have been demonstrated, rather than the traditional focus on inputs, typically education and experience, as a basis for success in the organisation.

Another recent driver affecting recruitment has been that of equality of opportunity, particularly concerning gender, race, disability, marital status and certain criminal convictions. Leighton (2000: 43) predicts wider anti-discrimination measures based on a draft EU directive on equal treatment in employment covering 'age and sexual orientation . . . religion and belief'. Direct discrimination occurs when one individual is treated less favourably than another on one of the above grounds. Here the action is explicit. Indirect discrimination occurs when although the requirement applies to all, some groups are disadvantaged as they are unlikely to meet the criteria. It must be shown that the requirement is a genuine and substantial reason, for instance it must be necessary in order to do the job successfully. Recruitment and selection are themselves essentially based on discrimination – to find suitable employees; the critical concern is what is deemed acceptable discrimination and what is unacceptable or even illegal. The equality of opportunity which enables individuals to take part in working life (and hence social and economic integration), also helps to achieve a diverse labour force for the employer, which a recent IPD Report (1999a) identifies as leading to improved business performance.

The comparative note earlier gives examples of how societies differ in what they term 'acceptable' in this area. Even in the same society differences occur over time; in the UK married women were prevented from working, unless in unpleasant 'working-class' jobs until the Second World War. Women's employment outside the home was alternately approved (and required in wartime due to labour shortages) and disapproved (when jobs were required for male 'breadwinners' not for women's 'pin money'). Perceptions of neglect of their prime role of childcare and domesticity remained until the 1970s, and resurface periodically. Today debate focuses on issues such as the relaxation of restrictions on women's roles, including military service on the front line in the case of Western powers.

Corbridge and Pilbeam (1998) use Straw's three-level model to consider equal opportunities. These are 'EO as equal chance' 'EO as equal access' and 'EO as equal share'. They represent a hierarchy and are progressive, with the ideal being all groups represented at all organisational levels. Legal strengthening of equal opportunities is represented by recently implemented legislation on data protection and on human rights which is expected to have a profound effect on recruitment and selection. Under Article 8 of the Human Rights Act respect for privacy, family life, home and correspondence are protected. Leighton (2000) lists the areas affected including advertising, psychometric testing, references and health checks. The questions asked on application forms will be under scrutiny, so they should be concerned solely with job-related qualifications, experience and skills. The precise effects of the legislation are untested but unjustifiably intrusive questions are clearly to be avoided.

Organisational and occupational contexts for recruitment

Organisational contexts for recruitment will vary and the organisational contingencies, the choices made between effort and reward, reflect this. Put simply, the relative importance of the vacancy and the difficulty of filling it will determine how it is handled in terms of resources required and made available.

One general way in which organisations have responded to competitive pressures is to move away from many specialised job descriptions to fewer, much broader, generic ones. Fincham and Rhodes (1999) comment on the link identified by Burns and Stalker in 1961 between organic structures and changing product or market environments. In addition, 'delayered' organisations undergo a planned reduction of the number of their hierarchies, the organic structure focusing on the dispersion of expertise throughout the organisation rather than concentrated at its apex. In the early 1970s Ford (UK) had a mechanistic, bureaucratic organisational structure which reputedly had 40,000 detailed job descriptions, presenting a virtually impossible task of continual updating. A more organic structure replaced this and Storey (1992: 55) reports of one particular agreement with the trade unions that '500 different job titles were reduced to just 50', allowing management more flexibility in the utilisation of labour.

Another example illustrating this change is, for instance, the traditional 'secretarial' job. These are no longer specific to individual managers' roles in the organisation or specified departments, but are typically represented by a few generic types. These can be classified by, and reflect, skill levels but also allow flexibility so the job-holders can be deployed across the organisation where appropriate. The skills and abilities required for a secretary or personal assistant at directorate level are very similar irrespective of the functional area in which they are located: confidentiality, discretion and organising skills. In contrast, word-processing skills as well as functional skills – for instance, accuracy and a liking for dealing with numbers in the finance function – are likely to dominate the requirements for secretaries at a middle managerial level. At a more junior, entry level, basic word-processing will be required as well as the temperament to take on routine clerical work, such as filing, efficiently. The 'flattening' of the hierarchy focuses attention on both the transferable skills common to all these jobs and the skills differentiating the various levels. In one respect, all secretaries have some duties in common so in any given week they may expect to do a range of duties from filing to dealing with unexpected situations or difficult people. The clerical assistant will spend the majority of time on the former, while the personal assistant will focus their time on the latter duties. This also provides a reminder that obtaining the 'right' candidate rather than necessarily the 'best qualified' one should be the aim. Today, IT skills are so ubiquitous that it is even questionable whether secretarial roles still exist in the high-tech world.

What might be termed the 'positional contingencies' of the labour force, such as occupational characteristics, are also significant in terms of recruitment procedures. For instance, some occupations have a tradition of changing jobs frequently and with minimal delay. An example is hair stylists: it is quite usual to find hairdressers have changed employer or 'gone mobile' – travelling to customers' own homes to style their hair – in a short space of time. Imagine establishing a new salon and recruiting stylists. The decision-making process, including shortlisting, may take three weeks, meaning the typical quick turnover presents problems. Quite simply potential recruits are likely to have accepted other offers rather than wait for a lengthy recruitment process to conclude. If the occupational norm is frequent and fast job changes, requiring only one week's notice, a three-week recruitment procedure is unrealistic. There is considerable variation between occupational sectors; factors such as the level of skill or professional background, organisational type, employer and location are all influential, as is the availability of alternative opportunities. It is important to be careful when making assumptions about any of these aspects; such assumptions can easily be misleading and lead the unwary into poor decision-making.

It can be seen therefore that a balance may have to be struck between speed in filling vacancies and the complexity and length of the procedures followed. This is not a simple relationship, as shown above. The approach taken to recruitment in the organisation is partly a strategic choice, decided by management. It may be that sophisticated, lengthy procedures are adopted where it is vital to secure scarce personnel with knowledge and skills critical to the core business and able to offer inspirational leadership to develop its future potential in an unpredictable market. However, it should be remembered that 'cheap and easy' options remain preferable on a cost-effective basis for the majority of vacancies. Reliable, up-to-date knowledge of the labour market, both internal and external to the organisation, is essential to a recruitment strategy if it is to be successful.

Systematic recruitment process

While a systematic recruitment process is usually adapted in some way to suit the organisational contingencies and circumstances of the labour market, the generalised process provides a useful structure to consider all the alternatives available in recruitment. We can get a snapshot overview of the recruitment and selection process by looking at Table 3.1.

Is there a vacancy?

The first step in the recruitment process is to ask if there is a vacancy. This is fundamental if a strategic decision is to be made rather than merely replicating what has gone before. Organisations and tasks change and alternative solutions may emerge once this question is answered. Factors such as the length of time the extra skills that are required and their availability inside or outside the organisation are significant. Reorganising the work by mechanisation, using overtime or staggering the hours, making the job part-time, subcontracting the work or using agency labour may all be alternative solutions, preferable to a permanent full-time replacement. Skill shortages in both the short and long term need to be assessed. These might be on a macro-level, such as the issue of a UK shortage of IT specialists reported by Lamb (2000) prompting targeted recruitment from India or a transfer of the contracts to India. Where it can be demonstrated that a specific candidate can contribute to the future needs of the organisation and strengthen the range of abilities and experience available, there is a strong case for permanent recruitment. Where the contribution required or contributed is less and the timescale short, casual recruitment is likely. The 1984 flexible firm model of Atkinson may provide a rationale for these decisions (see Chapter 2). Planning is relevant as a process to help decision-making, rather than necessarily providing a concrete solution here.

Table 3.1 Recruitment flowchart

Stage	Question	Action
1	Examination of strategic implications of vacancy in light of organisational philosophy and circumstances (buy in/grow own) and capability. Will recruitment be targeted and how?	Review in line with organisational and functional strategy, senior management, recruitment strategy, business cycle. Exit interview?
2	Replacement or new position? Authorisation? Yes	No? Obtain authority
3	Existing job description and person specification? Up to date? Yes	No? Job analysis exercise for JD, then do PS No? Review and amend
4	Terms and conditions agreed? (relate to Stage 1) Yes	No? Negotiate and agree within organisation
5	In-house or external trawl? Advertise? Advertise in-house	External – to Stage 6 Not necessary; offer promotion/ redeployment To Stage 10
6	Decide target group	Problems if this is too broad, too narrow, failing to create a diverse workforce, not reflecting community in which located, or its customer base.
7	Decide appropriate recruitment methods	Seek specialist advice or refer to past practices, revised as necessary with regard to cost-effectiveness.
8	Decide communication methods and action	Use information and experience from HR department or outside specialists
9	Decide organisation's response to initial enquiry Information pack? Yes No? Pre-screen? Yes No Send application form or request CV/letter Shortlist and send rejection letters Invite to organisation for interview	Design and send information pack Arrange pre-screening Arrange shortlisting meeting, reasons for rejection or selection (Equal Ops) and administrative follow up
10	Selection If no suitable candidate, revise and repeat recruitment exercise	Feedback from interviewers and candidates for evaluation
11	Evaluate effectiveness of recruitment/ selection, (short and long term) and implement improvements	Feedback above and induction, immediate manager, appraisals, exit interviews, labour turnover

Source: adapted from Beardwell and Holden, 1994: 193–4 and Bolton, 1997: 34

Specifying characteristics of the job and the person

Job analysis

Job analysis, the process of collecting and analysing information about the tasks, responsibilities and the content of the job, is the next stage of recruitment. It is useful as a 'tool' to examine whether existing job descriptions are appropriate for future needs and looks at the job, rather than the job-holder, though in practice these are difficult to separate. Schmitt and Chan (1998) recognise the importance of job analysis, however informal, as central to the need to ascertain the nature of the vacancy by specifying work behaviours involved. Analysing the job and the organisational context in which it takes place generates a set of required 'Knowledge, Abilities, Skills, and Other characteristics' (KASO). These can be 'firmed up' into statements which then constitute the job requirements, formalised into a job description. If a more sophisticated approach is required, measures of KASO can be developed and the scores become specific selection criteria.

Four questions need to be asked to determine the dimensions of the vacancy:

- What does the job consist of?
- In what ways is it to be different from the job done by the previous incumbent?
- What are the aspects of the job that specify the type of candidate?
- What are the key aspects of the job that the candidates want to know before applying?

Methods of analysis vary in terms of sophistication, cost, convenience and acceptability. Four types of method are used: observation, diaries, interviews and questionnaires. Observation, the first method, is the most straightforward, least costly and easily available. Observers see the job at first hand and can question the job-holder directly for clarification. Disadvantages include difficulties in the interpretation of what the job includes, the impact of observation itself on job behaviour and the differing interpretations of different observers. Overall reliability needs to be questioned and, finally, some tasks occur only infrequently and cannot be observed.

The latter problem also affects the second, work-diary method where job-holders record their work over a period of time. A high degree of commitment and co-operation, including even insignificant information, is required. A third method, interviews, may be structured and inadvertently exclude areas the questioner is unaware of. If unstructured the information may be unsystematic and hard to analyse without further clarification. Combining both in a semi-structured format allows systematic coverage but the interviewee can stress significant details, otherwise missed. The major advantages of the interview method are cost, convenience and the interaction it allows between colleagues. Disadvantages include the likelihood of bias and lack of reliability as well as the dependence on the skill of the interviewer for its success. Finally, questionnaires are the fourth and most sophisticated and complex of all methods, usually involving the use of computer packages. These methods require specialist training and expertise, providing statistically reliable and valid measures, with corresponding increases in costs.

The main contribution of job analysis is probably identifying critical incidents relating to the performance of the job, irrespective of the methods used. These may be directly used to specify excellent, average and unsatisfactory performance. It is easy to see how they can be linked to prediction of success in the job and provide criteria for selection, since they focus on key aspects of job performance. In the longer term, they can be used in the appraisal of performance. Finally, cost is significant in the choice of method and should be assessed in terms of the reliability of the results obtained.

Schmitt and Chan (1998) point out that often job analysis is only piecemeal, which helps to explain why little research has been carried out to find the links between job analysis and successful selection decisions and thereby justify more sophisticated methods.

Job description

Job descriptions can be written from information obtained whichever method of job analysis is used. Organisations use job descriptions for a variety of purposes, including rewards as well as recruitment, so the information included may well vary. There is also a legal requirement that employees receive a copy of their job description. At present this is within the first eight weeks of starting the job but, of course, legal requirements may change. However, it should also be remembered that this includes a tacit, informal contract (including discussions at the interview for instance) as well as the written details. The job description usually includes:

- Job title
- Location/department
- Who the job-holder is responsible to; and who they are responsible for
- Main purpose of the job/overall objectives
- Relationships both internal and external to the organisation
- Specific responsibilities/duties
- Working conditions including physical or economic conditions
- Any other duties

Statements of specific responsibilities and duties comprise the largest section of the job description. Recently, the traditional job description comprising a list of tasks has been increasingly replaced by specification of required behaviours, relationships and accountabilities, reflecting increased flexibility in the workplace and a focus on performance. The 'competency' approach has been adopted by leading companies, complementing their procedures for training and development and performance appraisal.

Person specification

Person specifications relate to the person doing the job. Two well-established systems of person specification discussed by Marchington and Wilkinson (1996: 113 and 114) are Roger's seven-point plan and Munro Fraser's similar five-point plan, both dating from the early 1970s. They vary slightly in the mix of attributes included (see Tables 3.2 and 3.3):

Table 3.2 Roger's seven-point plan

Physical make-up	Health, strength, personal appearance, energy
Attainments	Educational qualifications, vocational training and experience
General intelligence	Thinking and mental skills, specific intellectual skills
Special Aptitudes	Particular skills needed for this job
Interests	The personal interests that could be relevant to the performance of the job
Disposition	The personality type that is most suitable for the position
Circumstances	Special circumstances that might be required of candidates

Table 3.3 Munro Fraser's five-point plan

Impact on others	Physical make-up, appearance, speech and manner
Acquired qualifications	Education, vocational training, work experience
Innate abilities	Natural quickness of comprehension and aptitude for learning
Motivation	Kinds of goals set by the individual, consistency, determination in following them up, and success in achieving them
Adjustment	Emotional stability, ability to stand up to stress and to get on with people

These provide a structure which enables the recruiter to focus on the knowledge, skills and personal attributes needed for the job, considered as an 'ideal', away from the arena of 'real' candidates. Personal attributes are identified from an updated job description, reflecting the real needs of the post using aspects of the above lists. The value of the person specification is its use in allowing comparison of 'real' candidates against this 'ideal', giving selection some objectivity.

Person specifications should distinguish essential attributes from desirable ones. This can be difficult but the rigour required in distinguishing between these provides a useful tool for later selection decisions. The absence of an aspect deemed 'essential' removes that candidate from consideration, since they would not be able to fulfil the required duties. In contrast, 'desirable' aspects, the optional extras, provide criteria from which the 'best' of remaining candidates can be chosen via the selection process.

In the 1990s, aspects of the above person specifications such as 'circumstances' or 'disposition' were seen as inappropriate. As Marchington and Wilkinson (2000: 113) point out, 'Although the broad framework may still be valid, it is now unethical, inappropriate and potentially discriminatory to probe too deeply into some of these areas of the person specification.' Now it is often preferred to use a profile of the competencies required to perform well on the job, or identifying the potential to achieve these competencies with training. These competencies are expressed in terms of statements, prefaced by verbs, of behaviours needed with standards required stated in terms of required outcomes. However, Whiddett and Kandola (2000:30) identify drawbacks with this approach in the context of graduate recruitment. Specifying the large number of competency behaviours can limit diversity and there is no certainty the behaviours demonstrated in selection will be transferred to the actual work. They comment that 'indeed little attention is paid to whether they actually complete the task successfully', suggesting that the organisation focusing exclusively on competencies may, as a result, then recruit inefficient workers.

Recruiters need to be aware that making essential characteristics too demanding presents a barrier, deterring or debarring applicants who are, in reality, suitable. These are counter-productive, prevent the vacancy being filled and provide grounds for potential cases of discrimination to an industrial tribunal. For instance, an organisation which 'over-recruits', requiring say, bilingual secretaries whose skills are rarely used, but reflect their bosses' ego, causes frustration and boredom for the individual. Demotivation impacts on other staff too and labour turnover is likely to increase as those affected seek more suitable work elsewhere. The end result is negative for both individual and company (see Chapter 5) and 'realistic recruitment' can be seen as a constructive development.

The opposite, setting requirements too broadly, potentially hinders recruitment by generating too many applicants, slowing down the shortlisting process unless computer-screening of applicants can be implemented. Some recruitment is targeted at individuals with relevant experience in the type of work, perhaps in a similar organisation, on the likelihood that, having job-specific skills, they will soon be fully effective in the new post. A counter-trend in graduate and management recruitment is to look for those with limited experience but with the potential to 'grow' or develop and fill senior roles in the future. Indeed, while some recruitment is targeted at specific tasks and jobs, other recruitment may be much more general for a variety of roles. Some organisations prefer candidates without previous experience, presenting a 'clean slate' to be moulded to the organisation's own values. Personal traits and transferable skills such as communications, teamwork and ability to handle change are likely to determine suitability. This is a more strategic and longer-term view of recruitment. Advertisements wll have a correspondingly different focus depending on these contrasting approaches.

One of the key findings of the IPD Survey Report (2000b: 1) is that '60 per cent of organisations experienced difficulties in filling one or more of their vacancies over the last year'. The main reasons given are lack of required experience in applicants, lack of technical skills and 'wanting more pay than we can offer'.

There is an inevitable trade-off between detailed, slower administrative procedures and 'broad brush' approaches relying on speed and pragmatism. The former allow full consideration of aspects such as equal opportunities but at the cost of longer time taken and loss of applicants to alternative employers. The latter, more opportunistic methods, 'seizing the moment', also have drawbacks: insufficient attention to avoiding bias and a tendency to rationalise decisions later. However, a speedy response to the market may be an advantage. Recruitment is a fine balancing act and perhaps it is best to assume that solutions are difficult to find in reality and do not provide a perfect 'fit'; in any case contingencies are always changing. Imagine a 3-D jigsaw where having completed the uppermost side, the jigsaw is reversed to reveal a secondary pattern. This degree of complexity means it is extremely unlikely all will match. In reality, some sort of solution will be chosen or 'emerge', probably a 'least worst' one based on pragmatism, using methods appropriate to the organisation and occupational type with fair but workable procedures. It may fall short on some, ideal, criteria but overall business priorities are likely to provide the most persuasive and viable options.

Activity 3.2

1 Why might traditional forms of person specification be inappropriate?

2 What information do non-traditional job descriptions contain and how do they benefit the organisation?

3 Are there any drawbacks to using competency-based tools such as these in recruitment?

Recruitment methods

The various methods all have benefits and drawbacks and choice depends on the particular vacancy and the type of labour market in which the job falls, bearing in mind the previous discussion. There are two categories:

Internal recruitment

Internal recruitment may offer development to staff from within the organisation either broadening their range of operation into a new area or promoting those within the area but at a more junior level. This can also be useful where variation in the demand for products or services, in turn leading to contraction of some areas with the potential for redundancy, can be alleviated or minimised. Internal records can be searched to supplement those applying voluntarily and suitable staff redeployed to the vacancies.

The advantages are that internal recruitment is a cheap and relatively easy first option. It may be seen as an opportunity for career progression so energising employees. Retention of existing employees, particularly high-performing ones, is seen as very desirable, particularly as the alternative may be they join a competitor. It is mutually beneficial and does not require sophisticated techniques, though in future it is likely to be monitored to ensure equal opportunities. Such problems arise where the vacancy is advertised but the successful candidate is already a foregone conclusion. Monitoring is likely to increase in the future in respect of internal appointments which were previously unchallenged. There is a need for organisational cultures that support diversity at application stage as well as at interview. Perversely, however, this can be counter-productive, causing employers to stick rigidly to the laid-down procedures so that candidates' real track records are ignored.

Finally, it should be remembered that internal recruitment does not avoid the necessity for external recruitment; this is still required but in a different part of the organisation, in order to fill the vacancy left by the internal candidate.

External recruitment

This splits into direct and indirect methods. Direct methods mean the vacancy is handled by the organisation itself, usually the HR department, placing an advert in the media or with a job centre. In contrast, indirect methods occur where the HR department decides it is preferable to have part or the whole of this process handled externally. This may be done for a variety of reasons: lack of expertise or of time may make using an external source with known expertise and a defined budget an effective alternative compared with resourcing within the organisation for relatively few occasions each year. Setting up a new business venture or recruiting 'new blood' into an existing organisation may require the guarantee of confidentiality of using a third party, if the business strategy is not to be compromised or the existing employees alienated.

Indirect methods devolve recruitment to a third party, such as external selection consultants, allowing the entire process to be completed outside the host organisation if desired. Job centre recruitment services have the advantage of direct contact with those seeking work, facilitating selection from nationwide sources with computer-based data. It is socially responsible and secure, and allows a quick response for applicants. Disadvantages of job centre recruitment are that registers are mainly of the unemployed as opposed to those seeking a change of employment; this may reflect inappropriate skills and inconvenient locations.

The use of external consultants depends on the level and nature of the recruit being sought. 'Head-hunters' or executive search consultants may know individuals who can be approached directly, useful if the employer has no previous experience in a specialist field, for instance, recruiting for an overseas location. Drawbacks of this method include the cost involved (10 per cent or more of the starting salary, proportionately repayable if the employee leaves within specified periods), the fact that good candidates outside the head-hunter's network are excluded and the possibility that the recruit may remain on the list and be head-hunted again.

External recruitment can also be carried out by commercial employment agencies and recruitment consultants. These are well established for certain categories of staff such as administrators or accountants and require little in the way of administration for employers. The drawback is that these can hide high costs if the staff only stay a short while. They may also provide a poor 'fit' with existing staff. The status and pay of existing staff needs consideration, so internal relativities and differentials within departments are recognised and consideration given to how these help deliver the organisation strategy. Management selection consultants provide an opportunity to seek applicants anonymously – though in a neat reversal of roles, the companies' own staff can use the same agents to find alternative work – and use the expertise of the specialist consultant. Again, cost is a factor and the fact that internal candidates may well feel excluded from the opportunity of promotion. The advantages are quick and acknowledged access to the specific labour market of candidates potentially willing to change employer.

In the public sector of the economy, there is normally a degree of openness with regard to employee mobility, indicated by permitted time off to attend interviews.

In contrast, the private sector is often marked by secrecy, such that if the present employer were to be aware an employee is even looking at other employment 'their card is marked' adversely, creating even more secrecy. Time off for interviews in competitor organisations is out of the question so interviews may be held out of office hours or sickness or holiday entitlement used. This shows the extreme sensitivity of the issue. Indeed given that companies also recruit clandestinely using box numbers, the employee could, unknowingly, even apply to their existing employer. Discretion by the agency together with knowledge of those companies to whom the applicant does not wish to apply should enable both recruiter and candidate to continue their respective relationships with the agency.

Finally, Taylor (1998) cites an opinion poll suggesting almost a half of employees are recruited into their present jobs by a direct approach or word of mouth. Elsewhere it has been suggested that 30 per cent of vacancies are never advertised, despite pressure to do so in the interests of efficiency and equal opportunity. Marston (1997) describes British Airways scheme to 'recruit a friend' by offering £2000 to employees when the 'friend' has been in the post a month. BA report that this has increased the number of applicants especially for specialist areas like computing, improved the recruitment success rate and removed the need to pay agency fees. Such payments are a variation of the 'golden hellos' paid to new employees in some sectors.

Activity 3.3

1 What issues need to be considered if 'recruitment bonuses' are paid?

2 How would you deal with the problems arising from internal methods of recruitment?

3 If you wanted to obtain a more diverse workforce, what methods would you use and what information might help you?

4 What might be the rationale for a sophisticated company to prefer recruiting by word of mouth, assuming this is not based on nepotism?

Recruitment advertising and media

Recruitment advertisements are created to attract attention to the vacancy and the organisation using a mixture of graphics and key words about the job or qualities of the person required. Normally elements from the job description and person specification are included, giving essential and desirable attributes for successful performance in the job. Designing appropriate advertisements depends on factors such as the perceived difficulty of filling the vacancy, whether it is a specific job or general occupational group and if a particular age group is required. Potential applicants can then ask themselves 'Is this the type of work/employer I want? Have I got the right abilities for the job?' Details of how to obtain further information, make an application and any closing dates are given. Careful wording is required to interest the casual reader but Taylor (1998: 105) warns that for popular jobs it may be advisable to include 'realistic' as opposed to entirely 'positive' information. The logic is that people then self-select and those tempted to try for every job, irrespective of whether they satisfy the requirements, are dissuaded. In the long run, it is probably both good practice and pragmatic to be honest in recruitment literature.

Lewis (1985) identifies four rules for recruitment advertising:

- Target using appropriate media.
- An adequate number of replies should be generated to ensure selection can occur.
- The advertisement should minimise wasted replies, reducing the selectors' work and increasing the probability of identifying all suitable candidates.
- Opportunities to promote the organisation as a good employer with good public relations, including accurate job advertisements.

Audiences should be targeted by choosing the most appropriate media. Knowledge of the appropriate sector of the labour market and the media sources which serve them is necessary if the advertisement is to be effective both in terms of reaching the appropriate audience and also in value for money. The *IPD Survey Report* (2000b) compares a variety of recruitment methods from a survey of 262 telephone interviews, including changes since 1999. They also identify the characteristics of recruitment of three specific groups: managers, professionals and skilled manual workers. The findings are set out in Tables 3.4 and 3.5.

Table 3.4 Recruitment methods 1999–2000

Recruitment methods	2000 (%)	1999 (%)
Ads in specialist or trade press	86	86.9
Local newspaper ads	81	85.8
National newspaper ads	68	74.7
Job centre and employment services	68	62.6
Employment agencies	66	60.6
Speculative applications	56	64.6
Word of mouth	53	52.5
Internet	47	36.4
Links with schools and colleges	44	49.5
Head-hunters	29	33.3
Local radio ads	12	11.1

Source: IPD Survey Report (2000b)

Table 3.4 shows the relative importance of each recruitment method and the increase or decrease in its use over the previous year.

The most frequently used recruitment methods for these three groups can be seen in Table 3.5.

Finally the most effective methods, identified by those using each method, for the three groups is shown in Table 3.6.

Table 3.5 Most frequently used recruitment methods

Most frequently used recruitment methods	Managers 2000 (%)	Prof'n 2000 (%)	Skilled manual 2000 (%)
Ads in specialist or trade press	55	71	17
Local newspaper ads	55	64	72
National newspaper ads	57	50	
Job centre and employment services			58
Employment agencies	42	50	33
Speculative applications	40		38
Word of mouth		40	38
Internet	36 (1)	42 (2)	22 (3)
Links with schools and colleges	8	22	24
Head hunters	29	14	1
Local radio ads	3	5	

Note: (1) 22% in 1999, (2) 34% in 1999, (3) 12% in 1999
Source: *IPD Survey Report* (2000b)

Table 3.6 Most effective recruitment methods

Most effective recruitment methods for those using each method	Managers 2000 (%)	Prof'n 2000 (%)	Skilled manual 2000 (%)
Ads in specialist or trade press	49	54	4
Local newspaper ads		21	66
National newspaper ads	33	26	33 (1)
Job centre and employment services			17
Employment agencies	34	38	21
Speculative applications			2
Word of mouth		2	10
Internet	2	1	2
Links with schools and colleges			
Head-hunters	27	16	
Local radio ads		1	

Note: (1) only used by 13% of all organisations
Source: *IPD Survey Report* (2000b)

An adequate number of replies should be generated to ensure selection can occur. The UK has found difficulty in recruiting teachers in recent years; the slogan 'everyone remembers a good teacher' attempts to reach a new audience and promote feelings of appreciation. Similarly nurses may be recruited by stressing the satisfactions of the job and recently enhanced prospects. The recruitment of most of Britain's new doctors from abroad, with other European countries and Africa being particularly targeted, began in 1993, according to Hall (1998). Other sources, either attracting British graduates into medicine or those already qualified back to the UK, are estimated to require improved pay and conditions packages of the order of 50 per cent, together with more flexible hours and child care facilities. Though the NHS plan to train an extra 1000 medical students a year for the next seven years this can only be a long-term solution. It takes six years to train a doctor and 15 to 20 years to reach consultant status, so this aim will have no positive impact until 2010 at the earliest.

Efficiency criteria suggest the advertisement should minimise wasted replies, reducing the selectors' work and increasing the probability of identifying all suitable candidates. If the organisation is overwhelmed with applications which do not meet the essential characteristics, good applicants may be missed or only contacted after accepting jobs elsewhere. Extra staff may be needed to deal with the backlog of correspondence, so costs increase and candidates are more likely to experience negative impressions of the company and adverse public relations if unsuccessful candidates do not receive a reply. The organisation can be caught in a vicious circle, failing to recruit successfully, so problems generated by ill-advised wording or choice of media serve as a salutary lesson when the recruitment exercise is next undertaken.

Opportunities to promote the organisation as a good employer help to attract applicants, taking into account factors like the attractiveness of the post and labour market availability, so the advert should encourage 'realistic' recruitment. The recruitment process is also a valuable opportunity for public relations and as such the advert reaches a broad but significant audience. In an ideal world, even unsuccessful candidates will be so impressed with the organisation and how they have been treated that, despite their disappointment at not being appointed, they still recommend the company to others. Attitudes of recruiters often fail to recognise that the process is two way. Corbridge and Pilbeam (1998: 93) point out that 'applicants have considerable control because they can, at any stage, decide to exit from the process'. Unsolicited applications may also be retained for a few months to be considered with other applications, likewise a record is usually kept of former employees with recommendations as to whether re-employment is encouraged or not.

Activity 3.4

1 If you were responsible for recruiting, what methods would you use to fill these jobs: a design engineer in the car industry, a laboratory technician in a hospital, a manager for a retail shop, a labourer on a building site, a hotel cleaner, a qualified accountant?

2 If you were seeking an opening in, say, marketing or finance, where would you look assuming (a) you wished to work locally and (b) you were prepared to be mobile in your choice of location?

3 Which groups of potential employees would you aim to attract with the slogan 'everyone remembers a good teacher'?

4 Identify the issues which need to be addressed in regard to shortages of groups such as doctors.

5 To what extent can these shortages be considered 'recruitment' issues?

6 What issues arise when recruiting qualified and professional staff from overseas?

Recruitment media

These vary in appropriateness and cost. Knowing the target labour market is the first requirement for decision-making. The comparative availability and attractiveness of the vacancy in the context of the economic cycle, the location, alternative occupations and employers all need to be taken into account. Essentially, the more difficult the task of filling the vacancy the more necessary it is to reach a broader population. National media, high-profile methods and greater financial investment may be required.

Advice from specialist consultants and agencies, as well as expertise within the company, is valuable. Past experience of such recruitment will help in the choice of media and best options for success, including measures such as using head-hunters or targeting particular occupational groups or organisations. Knowledge of local, national and international labour markets and occupational traits is vital.

The Internet and other electronic media are used by half of the public sector according to the *IPD Survey Report* (2000b). Electronic methods are mainly for recruitment purposes: e-mail applications, posting vacancies on company Internet and internal intranet sites, but they are not yet seen as effective 'stand alone' methods of recruitment. Finn (2000) discusses the likely transformation of this fast-changing and competitive market, with the Internet potentially reaching a huge number of candidates at low cost.

Activity 3.5

1 What type of vacancies or careers are advertised on TV or at the cinema? Why might these media be chosen?

2 Look at a selection of adverts. What do they tell you about the organisation, the type of work, education, experience or the sort of person required?

3 Look at the information in Tables 3.4, 3.5 and 3.6. What conclusions would you draw about using the following media: word of mouth, adverts in specialist or trade press, employment agencies, national newspaper adverts, head-hunters, the Internet?

4 What disadvantages may arise in recruiting online?

Case Study 3.1

Strategic choices and practices in recruitment

The two cases here look at typical policies and practices in recruitment used in the UK in 2000. In Chapter 4 the case study uses the same examples to consider selection procedures and practices. The cases are written around real companies and illustrate the variation in recruitment methods occurring between industrial sectors, occupations and jobs within the same company.

Case Study continued

The first case, ServiceCo, is in the high-tech electronics industry with a turnover of £40m, part of a £2bn diverse international organisation. The company is highly regarded because of its financial management and stock market performance. During the previous decade it moved away from manufacturing to buying in the product, installation and maintenance.

This type of company is perhaps typical of some of the changes which have occurred with the emergence of human resource management, where a 'minimalist' approach is seen as appropriate. The personnel function exists solely at head office fulfilling legal duties relating to contracts, pensions and termination. Locally the individual businesses vary but the essentials of a 'personnel' function are entirely carried out by line managers, who have had no specific training, while the remainder of the role is, quite simply, absent. This is interesting simply because it uses little of the systematic recruitment and selection procedure deemed as essential good practice by many companies. There is no tradition of 'managing people' strategically, though operationally informal *ad hoc* methods based on pragmatism and reflecting day-to-day pressures are used. Direct overheads are kept low, an espoused and actual organisational priority of the parent company. There seems no real pressure or good reason to alter policy or practices, since the costs of the present policies are generally indirect and diffused around the company.

Recruitment policy is unwritten and has developed in an *ad hoc* manner. Most staff and management are long serving and there is a high degree of continuity. Senior management are well qualified in their specialist field. Management vacancies are usually advertised internally except where the post is identified as appropriate for internal promotion with a particular candidate in mind. Job-specific skills are sought, backed as appropriate by professional qualifications. There are no procedures to formalise internal promotions, for instance, an annual appraisal system. For key personnel with scarce skills, where there may be only a few suitable individuals available nationally with the range of abilities and experience required, external methods are used. These are outside executive search consultants, also known as 'head-hunters', or executive selection. Long service inevitably involves changes of roles among managers and roles are adapted, sometimes by default, to fit the new incumbent, suggesting that knowledge of the industry, the organisation and their own personal contacts are valued. There may also be an element of concern that internal applicants could move to a competitor, or, alternatively, set up their own business or consultancy, which in practice may have the greatest effect on recruitment decisions.

Technical staff are recruited mainly from within the business or other companies in the group. Other methods found effective include the grapevine and local or personal contacts, for instance, fellow students on professional or postgraduate courses, together with head-hunters. The method of recruiting clerical staff is mainly from a local employment agency, often via the temporary route.

Thomas, a recently qualified professional accountant with a degree in business studies, is recruited via just such an employment agency. When the job was placed with them, they contacted all those suitable on their books and any new registrations. They checked the candidates have the job-specific skills in accounting required by ServiceCo. After the agency discussed his suitability with ServiceCo, Thomas is called for interview with the Finance Director. This seems to go well and at the end he is told he will be notified the next week after other candidates are seen. The staff at ServiceCo think about their decision. They have been seeing candidates once a fortnight, on average, for the past eight weeks. Thomas seems to have the right experience to do the job but a decision seems difficult to take. Finally, they decide to invite him in again to see the Managing Director. On reflection they

Case Study continued

feel that they would like to see an earlier candidate again but he is already placed and the stream of candidates has dried up. They feel pressure to fill the vacancy, so as a result, they offer Thomas the job.

The second case is SuperCo, a large supermarket group. Recruitment is identified as a key lever to staff the organisation at the point of customer contact with employees who are customer-focused and enjoy selling food. Typically these jobs involve checkout and restocking duties. The requirements are for transferable skills, including reliability, organisation, motivation and teamwork. A simple direct link is drawn between successful recruitment (and training) using the established procedures, leading to better service, more customers, greater potential increases in sales and success in meeting financial targets. The advertising of vacancies is done internally on web- and paper-based staff news, as well as on store noticeboards.

It is company policy to fill vacancies by promotion and/or transfer within the company as far as possible. The appraisal system helps identify individuals who have the potential to fill promotional vacancies that may arise.

Company policy also requires any internal advertisement of vacancies to be accompanied by external advertising. It is also company policy to consider how members of staff who become disabled can be retained in employment. Every effort should be made to maintain a normal age mix in each store but stores may actively recruit the over-65s for any job, where failure to do so would lead to long-term vacancies.

The external sources used are direct applications to the store, job centre notification for all non-management and assistant manager vacancies and press advertisements, agreed with and placed by the authorising personnel office. Internal and 'held' applications are considered and advertisements only placed if these are not successful. Finally, recruitment boards in all stores display the vacancies to customers.

Assistant manager posts are seen as promotional opportunities and preference is always given to suitable current senior staff. External applicants may be considered if they fulfil several criteria, including, for instance, having a degree of responsibility and experience of supervising staff in a previous employment, being willing to accept shift patterns, and experience in stock control.

Bakery staff need either previous bakery experience or the appropriate City and Guilds qualification.

Graduate recruitment for all functions within the company is co-ordinated by a specialised unit at head office with some assessment and selection at regional level, and the focus here is on the need for transferable skills, backed by evidence of their application.

Fiona, a placement student at SuperCo on a business studies degree, is given a project by the HR Manager. While the company has an internal recruitment policy, popular with staff as it offers promotion, there are difficulties in arranging prompt release dates from departments. Some managers are so reluctant to lose good staff to other parts of the organisation that in a few cases the issue has dragged on so long that the employees have taken matters into their own hands and taken jobs in a rival organisation. Fiona is given the task of devising a procedure which satisfies all parties as far as possible. She knows that in order to achieve her deadline she needs the co-operation of line managers who, with the best of intentions, find that the pressure of their work often means HR activities get pushed onto the 'back burner' and forgotten until a crisis brings them into prime position again. She also knows that the HR Manager feels line managers fail to appreciate her contribution and that delivering timely constructive support is vital towards earning her bonus.

1 What are the strengths and weaknesses of the approach to recruitment adopted by ServiceCo?

2 How do the methods used at ServiceCo compare with the information in the *IPD Survey Report* (2000b)?

3 What issues arise from the method used by ServiceCo to recruit Thomas?

4 What features of a systematic recruitment process are apparent in the approach adopted by managers at SuperCo?

5 How would you summarise the approaches taken by the two organisations?

6 Give a rationale to justify these contrasting approaches and methods.

7 Draw up a report for Fiona with a workable procedure for the transfer of staff to present to the HR Manager.

8 What might be the views of line managers to any proposals?

9 Imagine you are a consultant brought in to advise the two companies on their recruitment policies and methods. Write a brief report for consideration by their respective senior management. You may make assumptions but state clearly what these are.

SUMMARY

In this chapter the following key points have been made:

- Recruitment strategies and practices are chosen to help deliver the human resourcing and organisational strategies, and they may vary even within the same organisation at the same time, with parts of the organisation expanding while other parts contract.

- Recruitment and selection are distinct but complementary processes, the former generating a 'pool' of applicants and the latter 'picking' the most appropriate from this pool.

- Vacancies may be 'filled' by a variety of alternative strategies such as overtime or outsourcing the work.

- Management have the choice of a variety of strategies and methods for recruitment, including use of recruitment agencies and executive consultants as appropriate.

- Up-to-date job descriptions and person specifications help set objective criteria against which to assess applicants and also help create advertisements based on the real needs of the vacancy.

- Advertising agencies and specialist publications ensure that advertisements reach the appropriate readership, while increasing the amount of information provided reduces the number of inappropriate applications.

- Internal promotions offer career progression to existing employees while external recruits bring in new faces and skills to the organisation.

- Line managers play an increasing role in the recruitment process, and ultimately it is they who have to rely on the success or otherwise of the choices made, so it is right they share authority for these.

- Recruitment is a two-way process, success being dependent on agreement by both sides and dependent on a degree of openness and trust.

- The need for efficiency and for equality of opportunity and diversity can appear conflicting but a case can be made for the contributions each make to the business.

- New ideas such a competency have been introduced in many organisations but they may have weaknesses in terms of promoting diversity and ensuring candidates are recruited who can deliver results.

? DISCUSSION QUESTIONS

1 What do the approaches taken to recruit graduates tell you about the significance of graduate placements to companies' overall recruitment strategies?

2 What approach would you suggest to ensure the recruitment of employees with scarce skills?

3 What methods could you adopt to encourage these candidates to apply to your company?

4 Which of these methods would you recommend, and why?

5 What significant differences might be apparent between line and HR specialists in their approach to recruitment?

6 What rationales could you offer for these differences?

7 Assess the constraints and solutions regarding shortages of doctors or IT specialists.

8 What are the advantages and possible drawbacks of presenting salary details in advertisements?

9 How would you assess the level of development of a company's equal opportunities policies and procedures using Straw's (1989) model?

10 What is the current assessment of areas of concern in respect of data protection and human rights legislation regarding recruitment?

R FURTHER READING

There are a number of other undergraduate texts available, some of which are aimed at human resource management specialists and therefore explore the issues introduced here in more detail. These include Beardwell and Holden (2001), Bolton (1997), Bratton and Gold (1999), Foot and Hook (1999) and Stredwick (2000). Students wishing a more advanced discussion of the issues raised should consult Leopold, Harris and Watson (1999), and Storey (1995). Texts concentrating specifically on resourcing issues include Corbridge and Pilbeam (1998) and Taylor (1998). Many relevant and accessible articles are available in *People Management* on recruitment topics (also available online).

Chapter 4 Selection

Sue Simpson

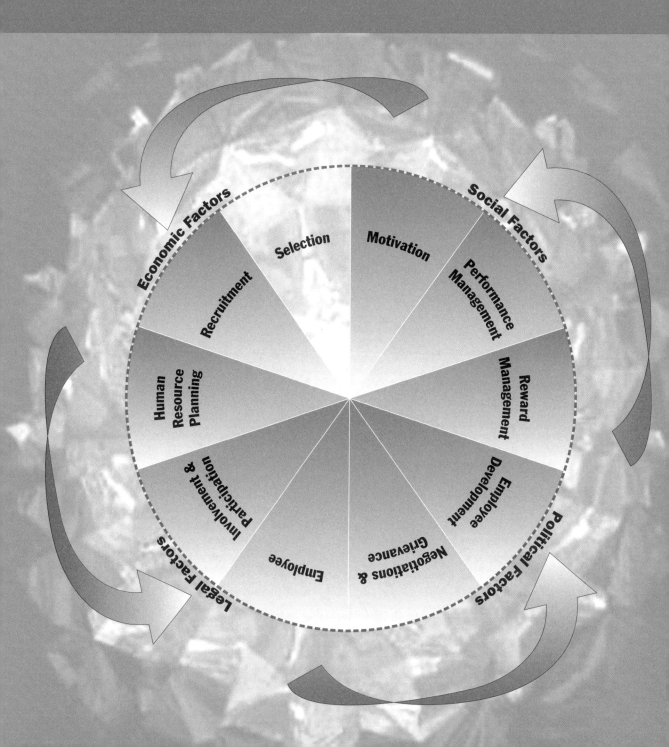

Having completed this chapter and its associated activities, readers should be able to:

- appreciate the limitations and subjectivity of selection methods: interviews, application forms and references

- distinguish the different organisational and occupational contexts and the influence these have on selection

- recognise the added value of valid and reliable methods of selecting employees

- see the different contributions of selection focused on skills, experience, attitude and/or future potential

- understand the contribution of involvement by the HR function, line management and outside agencies

- see the strengths and limitations of the different techniques, and how these can be improved

- appreciate the need to assess all the information on each candidate, to reach the best selection decision and understand the subsequent benefits for retention and good organisational performance

- consider that selection is a two-way process, crucial to identifying the human expertise and potential needed to generate the organisation's competitive advantage, effectiveness and long-term future

INTRODUCTION

The selection process is the key to ensure an appropriate quality of personnel, previously identified as required within the organisation. Selection has been defined in the previous chapter as the process of choosing the 'appropriate' candidate(s) both able and willing to fill the vacancy. Clearly then selection is constrained by the success or otherwise of recruitment summed up by Watson (1994: 203) that 'selection techniques cannot overcome failures in recruitment: they merely make them evident'. Various methods of selection are used to identify, then reduce, the pool and to find the candidate(s) most suited, not necessarily the 'best' candidate, for that particular vacancy. Other organisational aspects such as the rewards structure, styles of management and approaches to motivation, dealt with in other chapters, are influential in the recruitment and selection process and the retention (or otherwise) of these employees once they are appointed. Various methods of selection, alone or in combination, are usually used, involving techniques chosen to be:

- Based on relevant aspects of the job.
- Valid, in that they test what they are meant to test. In the case of psychometric tests in particular, the following attributes may be desired

- face validity: does the test 'feel right' to the applicant?
- predictive validity: can the test distinguish between good and bad performers and can this then transfer to job performance?
- content validity: can the required characteristics be defined and tested appropriately?
- reliability, giving the same results when repeated (Beardwell and Holden, 1994: 248).

A systematic, rational approach to selection is thorough and balanced in the interests both of the candidates and the organisation but as with recruitment, there are trade-offs between sophisticated, costly methods and simple, quick and cheap ones. Equally selection may be focused on an immediate, specific job or broad largely unknown future jobs.

Who should be involved?

Selection is usually carried out with a significant input from within the organisation, reflecting the importance attached to this activity. Even in organisations where the recruitment process, or a specialised part of this such as psychometric testing, has been outsourced to consultants or other agencies, the HR department and line management (from the functional area or department) will have some involvement in selection. Management has a direct interest in ensuring the new employees selected are the most appropriate available, due to managers' responsibility for, and reliance upon, the new employees' performance.

If the candidates available do not match expectations, a decision is needed to either modify requirements on that occasion and make a job offer, or to repeat the process and thereby hope to find more suitable candidates. Both of these alternatives (diluting the quality of recruits or increasing the time taken to complete the process) involve compromises which may be acceptable or not in the light of past experience and current or expected business pressures.

If the interests of line management in selection are self-evident, what role remains for HR to play? On the one hand, line management, although typically lacking professional HR expertise but confident to seize the initiative with a 'can do' mentality, may leave HR with only minor administrative duties. On the other hand, HR departments usually maintain an overview of the whole process to ensure organisation policies and practices are fulfilled, particularly in relation to equal opportunities and other legislative requirements where they can offer specialist advice to line management. They develop recruitment and selection strategies for the supply of suitably skilled personnel at the right time. Policies and procedures relevant to the sector and its labour markets can then be drafted to achieve the HR and organisational strategy. Where the relationship between line management and HR is close, focused on achievement of shared business objectives, it is likely that HR involvement in selection is greater, easing pressure on line management both in terms of expertise and time. However, line management may also have an interest in involving HR in other circumstances, providing a convenient target to blame if problems arise, or vice versa depending on the internal organisational politics.

HR departments in large organisations may be very specialised, not only in relation to the type of employees recruited (for instance, graduates, technical, international staff) but also in their professionally qualified staff, such as occupational psychologists where the demand for their services in terms of say, psychometric testing, can be justified.

In some organisations, due to the closely interdependent nature of the work and the group dynamics, arrangements will be made to involve members of the department where the vacancy occurs in the selection process. At higher organisational levels this is sometimes seen in the selection of senior staff and even Chief Executives. Taking into account the views of a wide section of the organisation's members provides a useful vehicle to get their commitment to the choice made, providing they are aware of all the job requirements. However, if this involvement is merely to rubber stamp others' decisions rather than requiring a genuine contribution, the overall effect may be negative and cynical.

We will outline and explain the origins and development of selection strategies, processes and techniques, to help understand their significance and applicability.

Activity 4.1

1 Think about organisations you have worked in or read about. How did they approach the selection of staff after recruitment was completed?

2 Was selection done by 'hunch' or gut feeling, or were more sophisticated methods used?

3 Were the same methods used for all occupational groups or jobs?

4 What might be the advantages or drawbacks of the methods used?

5 Why might tensions arise between line management and HR specialists involved in selection?

6 If line management want more involvement in selection, what would you advise in preparation for this?

Another way to help you understand selection issues is to recall the selection processes you went through in your applications for university. How many of your choices responded to you? Did they make offers straight away or was there a selection process? Were you called to an open day or for an interview? Were any samples of your work required such as writing an essay on the day or bringing one with you? Were any tests used? What might be the rationale for this? How did you approach the decision of which offers to hold? What happened when you received your results? Was there flexibility in the institution's attitude if your results were different from those originally required? Did you need to go into 'clearing' and with what outcomes? How did you make the final decision of the course and institution? How did your experience of the selection process differ from your friends at other universities? Are you aware of any differences relating to different subjects studied? Almost without realising it, you have already experienced many aspects of the selection process.

Overview of selection

Development of approaches to selection

The most basic and universal selection method is probably a simple interview, for instance, when recruiting staff to temporary posts in a pub or local shop. Both the organisation and its methods are fairly informal. The owner or manager typically has no training in selection, its rationale or up-to-date methods. The use of what Taylor calls 'cosy one-to-one interviews' (1998: 132) is likely to lead to selection of the 'blue-eyed boy' with whom the interviewer can identify in some way, blind to the possible weaknesses of such a candidate. Indeed, relatives or friends of existing employees may be deliberately sought rather than placing an advert. As with the recruitment process, selection based on such *ad hoc* arrangements has some limitations. Taylor (1998: 119) quotes Cook who used the term 'the classic trio' in respect of interviews, application forms and references; Cook goes on to add that these are all popular selection methods but equally all of limited usefulness. Application forms may be biased, perhaps unwittingly, in the questions asked and also the recruitment methods used may only reach a restricted audience. References tend to be subjective and lack openness. Perceptual errors such as relying on stereotypes or the 'halo' effect, seeing a positive attribute and assuming all the remaining attributes are positive (or vice versa) mean these basic selection methods are of doubtful value. They provide only limited evidence for decision-making, ignoring the qualities of other candidates and may contravene new legislation according to Leighton (2000). Overall, a failure to recognise the link between good selection methods, selection decisions and outcomes for their organisation is a significant drawback. Indeed, Taylor (1998: 138) again quotes Cook; the subjectivity of such commonly used, unsophisticated selection methods is such that 'as predictors of job performance [references have] low validity and [. . .] often contain more information about its author than about its subject'.

Comparative note

The influence of different cultural traditions has an impact on the methods of selection used.

In the Islamic world, there is traditionally a dependence on personal relationships, trust and loyalty within a framework of rules for living which are all valued more than the hard efficiency seen as typical of the West. A highly regarded individual will be found a job rather than the Western custom of finding the right person for the job (Hickson and Pugh, 1995).

A similar approach can be seen in the deeply rooted traditional Confucian philosophy of the Chinese; respecting ancestors, valuing stability in society and recognising responsibilities for the extended family. Typically work is 'usually of lifetime employment of long-term mutual obligation' (Hickson and Pugh, 1995: 181). This background means 'promotion is not seen as individual preferment but influenced by the collective views of workmates, including the candidate's moral and political attitudes, respect for the age and seniority of the candidate and of others who might be affected' (Hickson and Pugh, 1995: 167). In contrast to Western expectations, neither ability at the job nor experience seem to be criteria here. The development of a capitalist economy and privatisation have undoubtedly caused change in recent years but the values embodied in such deep-rooted approaches to organisational life may well prove surprisingly durable. While hard work is valued a significant cultural difference is personal modesty regarding achievements; drawing attention to these may destroy the harmony of the work-group and attract bad luck. This contrasts with the Western regard for individual success; it makes application form or interview questions requiring candidates to talk about their 'greatest achievement to date' inappropriate as a technique of selection.

A selection method widely used on the Continent is graphology, the analysis of handwriting. In continental Europe, 'graphology is used extensively in decisions about recruitment, promotion and team compatibility' (Vickerstaff, 1992: 103). In European companies, a survey by Vickerstaff showed 80 per cent used graphology, of these 40 per cent used it 'all the time' and only 20 per cent never used it. It is such a common practice that, in Switzerland 'candidates are often asked to supply their own graphological report', to the prospective employer, for which they also pay. On the Continent, its value lies in revealing the candidate's public personality and hidden areas of weakness and vulnerability embedded deep in the subconscious. Attitudes in Britain to this selection method contrast sharply. Vickerstaff reports a comparative survey by Industrial Relations Review and Report in 1991, comparing French and British methods of selection: the greatest contrast is in the British approach to graphology, seeing it as on a par with astrology as a predictive tool.

Selection methods used	France %	Britain %
Interviews	100	100
Graphology	77	1
References	11	97
Tests		48–58
Assessment centres		30

Taylor (1998: 123) sees the attraction of graphology as being its reliability. Individual handwriting remains very similar throughout adult life, with a high level of agreement among graphologists about a candidate's personality. However, it has poor predictability, indicated by its lack of validity and shown in its failure to identify personality traits or job performance, and he cites Watson (1994: 208), who cannot find insufficient evidence to support the use of graphology as part of a fair and objective selection procedure.

Clearly there are some significant differences in the choice of selection methods. It is easy to dismiss methods not favoured in a particular society as irrational or based on nepotism, for instance. Perhaps it is more helpful to see them as culturally defined, and perfectly rational in their specific context, each with their own, different strengths and weaknesses. Both the local pub and high-performance teams still put emphasis on selecting work colleagues who can be trusted. As 'known quantities' the risk of selecting the 'wrong' person may be reduced as much by recruiting a friend as relying on the 'rationality' of a systematic selection procedure.

Recent approaches to selection

There are two, complementary, reasons to move on from basic, *ad hoc* approaches to more transparent, systematic and structured methods in selection. First, at the organisational level it is likely to become obvious that performance is deficient, traced back in part to poorly performing employees, which in turn reflect weak selection processes. This is of increasing significance to the organisation in the truism 'people are our most valued asset', recognising employees as the variable differentiating organisational performance, judged by value added and profitability. Storey (1992: 35) identifies selection as one of the 'key levers' available to management to deliver this, contrasting the role of selection in the contrasting 'ideal types' of personnel and industrial relations as a separate, marginal task, while in the HRM type, it is an integrated, key task. Selection is clearly identified as a critical factor in achieving organisational objectives. Secondly, from the potential employees' point of view, the basic, *ad hoc* selection methods described are liable to fail some sections of the population, requiring more inclusive transparent methods to ensure diversity in the workforce.

Corbridge and Pilbream (1998: 134) point out that a business case will be a more persuasive argument for equal opportunities. Audit, monitoring and policy review are diagnostic tools to evaluate progress. The value of a diverse workforce, beyond the minimum required by law, includes:

- Increasing diversity, stimulating change and creativity in the organisation
- Enhancing the people dimension of quality initiatives
- Representing customer diversity in the workforce
- Recruitment and retention of employees from wide, unbiased talent bases, with a culture of fairness, equity and 'inclusion'
- Encouraging employees to give of their best, knowing they are not discriminated against
- Bottom-line considerations; low staff turnover reduces costs in resource terms, creating a positive and dynamic work environment

The process of making selection more systematic and accountable, so all candidates are considered using the same processes and against the same, possibly statistically significant, criteria gives credibility to the selection process. However, other approaches target groups normally neglected, using positive discrimination. Beardwell and Holden (1997) report research by Hogarth and Barth in 1991 that B&Q, the home improvement store, concentrated selection on the over-50s age group in one store. They report 'an overwhelming success. . . . In commercial terms the store has surpassed its trading targets' (1997: 294). They represent a more reliable workforce relating well to customers with the patience and experience to answer their queries'.

Desirable characteristics for selection

One aspect of the increased focus on selection is the widely held perception that the 'right' employees are required in terms of educational level, skill, experience and, particularly, 'attitude'. Legge (1995: 181) identifies 'replacement strategies of recruitment, selection, intensive socialisation; or [. . .] recruiting compatible beliefs' as some of the alternative methods for managers interested in changing or managing a culture, 'on the assumption that appropriate behaviour will follow'. Development of a 'strong or quality culture [. . .] points to standardisation of employees via highly selective recruitment practices and intensive socialisation in the preferred values' (Legge, 1995: 223). Compatible beliefs are usually taken to mean a compliant disposition, accepting management authority. The rationale for this, usually unsaid, is concern that dismissing 'unsuitable' employees is more difficult and costly once in employment than identifying such individuals and excluding them from selection before the offer of employment is made. 'Unsuitable' can, for some employers, be taken to include criteria such as a record as a trade union activist or even membership of a trade union, a record of ill health or reluctance to work flexible hours.

However, while these attributes of experience and attitude may be necessary in a successful candidate, they do not guarantee good performance in the job itself. This is one potential danger in selection; identifying successful candidates in terms of the selection procedures but finding that their performance as employees on the actual job falls short of that required is mentioned by Whiddett and Kandola (2000) even in the context of a competency framework discussed in Chapter 3. Such examples may represent shortcomings in the selection process or in the methods themselves. This shows both the weakness and the potential of selection for the organisation. The need for self-motivated employees with the 'right' attitude, individually ambitious and rewarded by performance-related pay, (rather than 'the rate for the job') became more apparent as companies responded to increased competition from the 1980s. In turn, this raises the profile of selection and the resources, both financial and time, assigned to it.

Organisational and occupational contexts for selection

Organisational contexts vary and the particular organisational contingencies are deciding factors in calculating the effort-reward equation for a given vacancy. These translate into the resources the organisation is prepared to commit to selection given the importance of the recruit, perhaps in terms of added value. It follows that sophisticated methods may be justified where selection is concerned with scarce high-value employees making valuable contributions to realise the organisation's future potential, but cheap, easy options for selection may be more appropriate in the opposite circumstances.

Examples of the former would be the selection of key players in a senior managerial team. This would require excellent performance and skill levels in a variety of areas, including the functional specialism, strategic vision, increasing market share and achieving financial targets. Finally, the personal skills both to work as a member of such a team and to lead, by recruiting, motivating and retaining staff to deliver this, are also required. The demanding requirements of such a role mean the recruitment and selection process is likely to be long, thorough and costly, justified by the relative scarcity of individuals who could excel in all the areas required, and the organisational cost of errors if bad selection choices are made. A firm of head-hunters may be engaged, expensive advertisements placed in the national press, exhaustive checking of biographical data and costly interviews arranged in presti-gious premises as part of this selection. The 'fit' in terms of the job require-ments and the existing management team is vitally important. Despite all the sophisticated techniques used giving vital supporting evidence, the critical factors in deciding who is appointed will probably be the dynamics of the relationship with a key decision-maker, probably the Managing Director or equivalent role, a combined process of elimination where deficiencies can be identified, and fol-lowing 'gut instinct'.

In contrast, where the vacancies to be filled are relatively straightforward and there is a readily available pool of suitable applicants, the selection process may simply consist of an application form, interview and checking of references; relatively quick, easy and cheap. In each case the methods chosen represent value for money.

How selection criteria vary in similar roles

Occupational characteristics and contingencies are significant in terms of different career paths, even within very similar jobs. In certain occupations and companies job changes are frequent; in others the norm is loyalty to one employer, with con-sequent implications for selection criteria. With the former, career progression will be achieved through the individual both seizing and creating opportunities, identifying strongly with their occupational identity. The latter, more stable environment, allows its employees to achieve a varied career through company-identified needs, so the individual may even change career path within the com-pany, reflecting strong identification within the one organisation.

A good example of this is in the HR function itself. The more frequent job change may be represented by a professionally qualified HR specialist who in the course of their career has practised in a variety of industrial sectors (pharmaceutical, bank-ing and insurance, for instance), and may reflect development of expertise in one particular aspect of selection. In addition, each job change will be reflected in a career move up the different organisational hierarchies, from HR assistant through to HR manager, their key expertise being the professional contacts across the func-tion, adaptability and familiarity with best practice. In contrast, an example of the infrequent job change would be an individual who may have begun their career in a different functional area (finance, operations or technical, for instance). Later they move into an HR role within the same company, probably a sideways move with responsibility for the same functional area or for a company-wide HR remit such as graduate recruitment. The company values their experience and the networks they have built up and developed over several years within the company; training to fill gaps in their HR knowledge can be accessed as required. Selection criteria would be quite differently focused for each. Management decisions in terms of selection as well as those of candidates are likely to be influenced by a wide variety of factors and will be partly governed by the strategic choices available at that time.

Systematic selection process

A systematic process of selection provides a useful basis to consider all candidates, equally, in contrast to *ad hoc* arrangements. The challenge of obtaining good results from selection while achieving acceptable cost levels and acceptable timescales is the main focus of attention in this area. Taking the recruitment and selection process of Table 3.1 in Chapter 3, the aspects of a generalised selection process are itemised in more detail in Table 4.1, allowing consideration of the issues and the alternatives available:

Table 4.1 Selection flowchart

Stage	Question	Outcomes
1	Application form/CV Compare with job description and person specification	Pass/fail/possible by filtering May be computer scoring
2	Telephone interview 'off-guard' and possibly with a senior manager	Pass/fail, cost-effective filtering Proceed to next stage
3	Compilation of shortlist, probable/possible Scores and reasons for inclusion/exclusion	Some candidates may decide not to proceed with application
4	Final tailoring of selection methods, clarification of roles (e.g. for interviews) and procedures	
5	Testing: Intelligence(s) Aptitude Personality	Suitably trained/appropriate (valid and reliable?) Arrangements for feedback
6	Interview: Panel Individual Sequential	Role and rationale, HR take overview?
7	Exercises at assessment centre or similar In-tray Group Presentation Leaderless discussion	Trained/qualified observers at each exercise to evaluate candidates against agreed criteria, may include potential
8	Debrief assessors and scoring	Discuss compromise between actual candidates and specification
9	Clarify decision and offer	May do verbally first, agree date then confirm by letter
10	Debrief candidates	Ethical and PR implications
11	Evaluate effectiveness of recruitment/ selection (short and long term) and implement improvements	Informal or formal

Pre-selection

Pre-selection involves filtering of application forms, CVs and covering letters, using agreed job description and person specification criteria. Attracting a broad, mixed group of applicants may be desired, 'including in' by glamorous or 'wacky' adverts. In contrast, if rather tightly focused selection is required, this can be anticipated to some extent in the wording and placement of the advertisement, encouraging candidates to self-select in terms of whether they fit the criteria and feel an application is worth while. However, the scarcity of jobs and a lack of realism in assessing their own skills and experience against the limited criteria given will encourage some candidates to 'try their luck' against the odds for that particular vacancy. If there is a poor response to the advertisement, due to problems in recruiting for that position, they may indeed be lucky and be considered further. Usually, however, those candidates not meeting the essential characteristics would be rejected at this stage, on the grounds that they would be unable to perform the job. Those meeting the criteria are considered probable or possible candidates for shortlisting.

One area seen as of increasing importance in recent years is rigorous pre-employment vetting of CVs and references. Midgley (1999: 58) finds 'more and more prospective recruits are being tempted to embellish – if not falsify – the contents of their CVs'. There are considerable pressures on companies to ensure selection is tightened but at the same time the impact of human rights legislation has important implications in protecting individuals, discussed in Chapter 3.

Another screening method which may also save valuable time and expense in the long run is telephone interviewing. This is typically unannounced, informal and may include a problem-solving exercise. Though the candidates are usually warned in advance, nevertheless they are caught off-guard, in their own surroundings but subject to all the ongoing, everyday pressures of their normal life. This one-to-one conversation, perhaps with a senior manager, may take the form of a hypothetical situation where they have to offer solutions to a developing scenario, showing their ability to think on their feet in a very practical way, demonstrating logic and creativity. Organisations using such methods, costly in terms of time, feel the results justify the investment in terms of identifying individuals they would want to assess more thoroughly in the next stages of the selection process. This is cost-effective of managers' time, allows some checking of application form details and allows two-way communication.

Activity 4.2

1 What are the advantages in adopting a systematic approach to selection?

2 Are there any disadvantages and, if so, what might these be?

3 What approach to selection would you suggest to maximise the outcomes for the organisation in cases of plentiful, good candidates?

4 What approach to selection would you suggest to maximise the outcomes for the organisation in cases of few candidates in a scarce but essential job?

5 How would you ensure candidates' qualifications and experience are 'bona fide'?

Shortlisting

Once pre-selection is completed, a shortlist can be compiled. This is likely to involve assessing the details on the individual application form against the requirements of the job. The CV alone is unlikely to provide sufficient detail in the specific categories required to facilitate this, which is why an application form and a covering letter may also be required. It is usual for large companies to have different application forms for different employee groups (manual, clerical, professional and management). These can then be tailored to the particular occupational group, with appropriate questions and depth of detail to help selection. They will be designed to be 'user friendly', encouraging completion.

Shortlisting strategies will obviously vary according to the number of candidates. Simply looking for a key 'essential' variable in the person specification can be used to filter 'out' unsuccessful applications. Responses may be 'marked' like an examination and applications not reaching a minimum mark are automatically excluded. A more detailed examination of remaining applications, to sift through all having 'desirable' attributes, can then be made. The HR department is likely to complete initial sifting but employees and managers from the functional area have a critical interest in the new appointment and are likely to be involved in final shortlisting. A shortage of candidates will see all probable and possible candidates included, while an abundance of candidates remaining at this stage suggests that the criteria could have been drawn more tightly. A workable shortlist for a single vacancy is usually in single figures. The HR department needs to follow up all the administrative requirements, including suitably worded letters of rejection to unsuccessful candidates thanking them for their interest once it is established that they are not successful. This includes an ongoing administrative task of keeping candidates appropriately informed of the next stages of the selection process.

Recently, online applications have been adopted by organisations involved in frequent recruitment generating a large volume of applications. 'Scoring' or marking such applications, using key word searches, is fast and the number of applications is not an issue. This method is cost-effective and avoids bias and error, due to selective perception and stereotyping, creeping in. However, careful design is required; few candidates are prepared to spend, say, 45 minutes completing a form online.

In parallel with the shortlisting process, the HR department needs to check and finalise selection methods, ensuring the line managers who are involved are fully trained and aware of the parameters within which they operate, including legislative ones.

Testing

Testing is a more frequently used method of selection in recent years (*IPD Survey Report*, 2000b). In some measure it is a check, on behalf of or by the employing organisation, to ascertain the actual skills or personality profile of the candidates. Typically these are in the form of questionnaires, offering several choices to assess the individual's ability or personality (indicated by attitudes or values etc.) and are known as 'psychometric tests'. In cases where qualifications have been obtained some years ago or the employer wants to be more certain that the candidate can make practical use of skills indicated by examination passes, these tests can provide additional evidence for selection decisions.

Ability or aptitude tests may test general skills (numeric, verbal, analytical or problem-solving) or specific job-related ones. Tests in basic skills may be useful to screen out the weakest candidates. Performance at ability tests may indicate performance in the job, for instance, a chef preparing a meal. Others may test their skill at learning, appropriate if they are applying for jobs with complex, new skills. Selecting between high-performing candidates can be made by identifying performance falling outside a specified range, say, the upper quartile, indicating failure in that aspect, and 'norms' for success in particular jobs will enable direct comparison. This may be an eliminator or be considered alongside other measures of selection and an overall decision reached. The positive aspects in terms of equality of opportunity are the equal treatment of candidates without formal qualifications; the drawbacks are that meeting the test criteria may provide a barrier to certain groups, making selection more difficult for them. Indeed, if the tests are not appropriate to the tasks in the job itself, not valid in terms of what they test or reliable in giving the same results when repeated, they may be unfairly discriminatory, as discussed in terms of equal opportunity in Chapter 3. Not only will the organisation be liable to lose any legal challenges but also the tests will not serve the selection process well in terms of being a good method of finding future employees.

The main advantage of ability tests are the relatively high validity they offer, compared to other methods (see Figure 4.1).

Personality tests can be divided into two broad groups, normative tests looking at traits and ipsative or ideographic tests which, typically, look at behaviours, ranking the strength of reaction to the different aspects. Criticisms are especially directed at personality tests where even if candidates' traits are correctly identified, there is a huge assumption as to whether this indicates they would be successful or not in performing the job. The various tasks of a job often require a mix of skills rather than particular personality traits, since jobs can usually be successfully performed by a variety of individuals each doing the particular job in a slightly different way. Also personality is not 'cast in stone'; people learn and develop as they respond to the changing circumstances in which they are required to work including changing management styles and changing colleagues.

However, as stated earlier, much importance is now placed on employees having the 'right' attitude. This is much harder to achieve than changing surface behaviour and is ethically questionable. The area of personality testing is one of the most sensitive areas in selection and is now under increased scrutiny and legal challenges, as discussed in Chapter 3.

Perhaps more than any other method, the use of tests needs to be considered carefully concerning appropriateness, is the information sought relevant to the job? This is more open to interpretation in the case of selection for broad-based, developmental roles. Also the availability of sufficient resources, confidentiality, laws regarding copyright, storage of results and feedback need to be considered. The CIPD and others warn that it is unethical merely to use tests to try to justify 'scientifically' selection decisions made by other, possibly discriminatory, methods. Cobridge and Pilbeam (1998: 111) quote the criticisms of Blinkhorn and Johnson who suggested in 1991 that personality tests are 'stage-managed bits of flummery intended to lend an air of scientific rigour to personnel practice'. Also, suppliers of tests should provide evidence that their tests do not unfairly disadvantage certain groups. Recent legislation means the burden of proof is now on the employer to prove they did not discriminate, rather than the earlier, less rigorous need for the candidate to prove discrimination.

One important consideration in the use of tests is the cost involved. Specialised companies organise training and accreditation for staff and supply recognised tests. Recognised qualifications in psychology may be required to administer tests and interpret the results. Professional codes of practice, including those of the CIPD, require individual feedback to be offered to candidates taking such tests, together with counselling if required. This represents a considerable investment of time and money, only justified by the benefits it offers in improving the quality of selection decisions, borne out by later performance 'in the job'. It follows that such methods are more likely to be focused on key roles or senior positions within the organisation, shown in the *IPD Survey* (2000b) information later in this chapter. Doubts have increased with the availability of web-based testing, reducing costs but moving away from the high-quality, personal feedback felt to be best practice in this area.

One area where testing is being increasingly used is that of call centres (Whitehead, 1999). He reports that call centre work is the fastest growing job category but there are recruitment and turnover problems with some experiencing turnover as high as 80 per cent, attributed to the intensity of the environment. At an estimated direct cost of £2000 per head, this is a significant problem affecting their profitability. One solution is to improve selection using personality testing, since the 'ideal' call centre worker is an introvert, diligent person, with good attention to detail. Traditionally, call centres recruited extroverts, who are easily bored, while personality tests show the preferred personality to work as a team member (people oriented) is different from the personality of a team leader (task oriented). This seems a clear case for using personality tests but other specialists say personality tests are a waste of time, since as long as they can perform the duties efficiently, handling repetitive work and learning quickly, searching for an 'ideal' personality is pointless. Alternatives such as work sample tests or simulations, or structured learning exercises to test underlying abilities, are preferred. In the future, genetic testing for employment may become a serious issue with implications for unfair discrimination.

Activity 4.3

1 Which people do you think should be involved (or represented) when shortlisting candidates for a vacancy?

2 Why should they be involved?

3 Could online facilities help in this process and, if so, how?

4 Are there any drawbacks to using the web for shortlisting which need to be addressed?

5 Why are psychometric tests increasingly used?

6 What are the major criticisms about them?

7 When would you recommend personality tests be used?

Interviewing and its improvement as a selection tool

The interview is the most frequent method of selection and most applicants as well as organisations would feel the process of recruitment somehow incomplete without a face-to-face meeting. It is widely held that the crucial selection decision is taken in the first three minutes of an interview, based on first impressions, making this a poor tool on which to base the entire selection decision. Much of the training now seen as a requirement for all involved in interviewing is concerned with redressing such shortcomings to improve the success and impartiality of decisions. Ensuring the interview is conducted professionally, usually involving more than one person to provide a balanced assessment and counter criticisms of bias, involving line management and exploring techniques of questioning are all methods of improvement.

Another method of avoiding interview bias is to use a fairly structured format so each candidate is asked the same questions, allowing direct comparison of the manner and content of the answers. A simple structure using the acronym 'WASP' (Argyle, 1972) described in Table 4.2, with a beginning, middle and end, is effective in ensuring all the major areas are covered. Argyle also suggests a fifth phase of negotiation about the job offer requiring further social skills. Thinking carefully not only about what questions to ask but also how they are asked, for instance avoiding multiple or leading questions and probing answers both from the application form and responses in the interview, is important.

Behavioural interviewing techniques include questions about past performance, hypothetical questions ('What if . . .') and contra-evidence. While some hold that hypothetical questions are unfair since the candidate may well not have had a particular experience, others see these as evidence of empathy and lateral thinking, which may be very desirable qualities, and could be taken as evidence of a degree of maturity. Usually a mixture of direct 'closed' questions, focusing on confirming or clarifying factual information, and indirect 'open' questions requiring elaboration or opinions to be given in lengthier answers, are used.

Open questions can be challenging in terms of the quality of responses given by the candidate, drawing on their own skills and experience; what is not said may be more significant than what is said. Follow-up questions may highlight areas which are left vague, perhaps deliberately so as to deflect exploration of weaknesses. Similarly, clarifying dates to show gaps or the actual length of time of involvement in a particular role can be very revealing as to the actual significance of the work undertaken. Some statements may need to be followed up; the candidate may be vague about details of the actual work undertaken or levels of responsibility. For instance, membership of a project team may be actually setting up and leading the team or merely acting as a 'gofer'.

Interviewing skills can also be improved by training including analysing a video recording of practice interviews. Techniques of questioning such as summarising and reflecting upon the responses given, referring back to the interviewee may be useful for clarification ('So what you're saying is . . .'). The skill of the interviewer in putting the candidates at ease and allowing their strengths to shine while following up any areas of weakness is of great value. Body language,

Table 4.2 Selection interviews: problems and possible solutions

	Interview problem	Possible solution
1	Perceptual bias; dominance of first impressions	Training in interview technique, gathering comprehensive information; giving value to later as well as early information
2	Difficult to ensure all areas where information needs to be gathered (or given) are covered for each candidate, due to *ad hoc* approach	Structuring interview (WASP = Welcome; Acquire information from candidate; Supply more details of job; Parting and what happens next). Gather information systematically on all aspects and all candidates for comparison
3	Failing to satisfy requirements of line management or future colleagues	Involve line management and future colleagues in whole interview process, including training and briefing in preparation for this
4	Candidates evade questions; reflection after the interview indicates questioning ineffective, perhaps borne out later by behaviour in the job	Effective questioning technique to avoid leading, multiple or rhetorical questions; follow up 'gaps' in application form; follow up applicant's statements to clarify by obtaining detailed evidence of specific experience using open and closed questions
5	Fail to identify good candidates because their abilities and experience do not 'fit' the exact form required by the established procedures	Selection procedures need to be sufficiently flexible to allow for unconventional candidates, reflected also in questioning technique. A 'focused' approach may help, allowing some flexibility to the interviewer to follow 'leads' in the conversation, avoiding the rather narrow mechanistic structured approach. Systematic coverage but the format allows discretion
6	Problem of applicants successful at the interview and selection stage who then do not make the transition to settled employee	May be some value in using personal recommendation and contacts, where the informal relationship allows a freer discussion of critical or negative aspects of the job prior to selection, resulting in more awareness and a realistic appraisal of the actual work before starting

facial expression, posture, personal distance, voice tone and speech patterns are observed for both passive and aggressive behaviours. Questions are likely to range from the relatively superficial level of clarifying facts to deeply held attitudes and values at the other extreme, dependent on the nature of the job.

There are a wide variety of interview formats available; with one or two interviewers, together or sequential, or in some organisations more interviewers are involved as a panel. There may be a mixture of formality and informality, junior and senior staff as well as a variety of functional areas involved, HR, line management, other staff with a direct interest in and need to work with the individual recruited. In combination, these allow a composite, multi-dimensional picture to emerge, seeing the candidates 'in the round' and assisting comparison. Indeed, a lengthy process of selection allows more evidence to be gathered and the pressure of this process could be taken as an indication of how the individual responds at the end of a tiring day to the pressures of the 'real' job. This is a 'real' rather than a rehearsed portrait. A similar justification can be made for 'stress' questions and techniques. Panel interviews in particular need to be carefully structured, often with each individual member having a distinct area and question to raise, otherwise a 'free for all' may leave certain areas blank. Structuring also allows each candidate to be questioned similarly in the interests of fairness. The validity of the interview can be significantly increased in a variety of ways, indeed it is suggested that the main problems lie not with the interview as such, but with the interviewer, where awareness and training can overcome many of the problems.

Activity 4.4

Think about selection in organisations you have worked in or read about.

1 What interview styles have your friends and colleagues experienced?

2 What were their reactions to these?

3 Why are interviews criticised as a method of selection?

4 What steps can be taken to remedy these criticisms?

Assessment centres

Many of the above points are addressed with an even greater level of confidence using the selection technique known as an 'assessment centre'. This involves a battery of complementary selection methods to allow candidates to be considered by several qualified and experienced assessors, including senior managers, in various contexts over a period of one to five days. The methods chosen should clearly discriminate between candidates in order to help selection, but should meet validity, reliability and fairness criteria. Typically they include psychometric tests, personality tests and several interviews (for instance, technical and personal) described above, and also:

- *In-tray exercises* where a typical day's work, perhaps tasks for the particular job, are given to candidates and they indicate priorities and how they would deal with each task in a time-constrained exercise, perhaps providing a sample of the work achieved.
- *Presentations*, perhaps with a topic of their own choice, selected and prepared prior to the assessment centre, and likely to be a component of the actual job.
- *Problem-solving* where a specific operational issue for the business is examined in a limited time of, say, 40 minutes, producing a rationale with both a strategic and a tactical plan drawn up and presented.

- *Discussion* with the other candidates, on a given issue, perhaps on an item of current affairs impacting on the business. This would involve putting forward one's own views, listening to others' views and responding to them, handling conflicts of fact or opinion, demonstrating awareness and skill in handling group dynamics and achieving an outcome if that is required, usually in a fixed time. The discussion may be led or leaderless, the latter revealing natural tendencies of candidates either to take control or to avoid confrontation, to emerge during the exercise.
- *Group activity*, perhaps a physical problem-solving exercise, getting a team and equipment across an imaginary barrier with limited equipment and time, or leading blindfolded members round an obstacle course. This exercise has potential for role reversal, the need to rely on others if the task is to be successfully completed and the likelihood of having to display vulnerability.

These last two exercises are often extremely revealing of the candidates' real personalities and previously hidden strengths and weaknesses. There may be no right or wrong answers but the aim is to reveal the 'real' personality. These include reactions to stress or criticism, relationships with one's peers and ability to 'think on their feet'. In normal circumstances the candidate would probably prefer to keep some of these hidden or under control. The high cost of assessment centre selection makes it appropriate for selecting between many good candidates when the consequences of inappropriate recruitment is expensive to the business.

At the end of the assessment centre, assessors compare notes on each candidate in each situation in which they were observed together with test results and discuss whether on balance they merit consideration for an offer or not, on this occasion. Assessors are debriefed and follow-up administration completed. Candidates should also be offered debriefing since the whole exercise, especially if it results in rejection, may be a traumatic experience. Schmitt and Chan (1998) discuss different types of assessment centre design together with criticisms of the method, including the increasingly relevant need to assess candidates as potential members of teams.

Biodata

This selection tool typically involves the collection of biographical data by means of a battery of multiple-choice questions about work and personal details, generated from existing employees. These are identified as falling in categories of 'successful' and 'not successful' in their jobs. The candidate's data can be compared to the biodata for successful employees by computer, indicating predicted success and hence selection. Biodata shows good validity but its wide use is impractical since each vacancy requires the whole process of generating appropriate questions to be repeated. Also it is often perceived as arbitrary and unfair since there may be no obvious link with the job but a statistical link to successful performance, according to Arnold, Cooper and Robertson (1995). Its main use is for screening purposes by large organisations where high development costs can be justified by the number of candidates and the importance of the right selection decision, for instance for graduate recruitment.

References

References are the third traditional method of selection (with interviews and application forms), though Taylor (1998: 138) comments that researchers find them to be of 'very limited value'. Perhaps this is because even the most unlikely candidate can find someone, somewhere, to write positively on his or her behalf. The limitations given by Taylor are subjectivity, giving the same rather than varying ratings for all aspects in respect of an individual, a bias towards good ratings and avoidance of extreme ratings. Their main use seems to allow the double-checking of factual information, such as dates of employment, and confirming general impressions made at interview. However, employers are increasingly cautions to commit their knowledge or opinions on previous employees to paper, so avoiding any adverse legal implications. For certain jobs such as working with children and for internal promotions within organisations they remain influential, since they provide a check on false claims of qualifications or expertise.

Clarifying the selection decision

The focus on the personal attributes needed for the job, considered as an 'ideal' away from the arena of 'real' candidates, is now reversed. In the selection process, there is an attempt to gather evidence impartially based upon the needs of the job and job-holder. The task at the end of the selection process is to collect and review all this evidence on the actual candidates, ideally with the staff involved in the exercises. This has the advantage of making a conscious effort to include all evidence, positive and negative, early or late, into the decision-making process, giving added value to selection by avoiding or compensating for known weaknesses in the selection process. It also draws into the process any dissenting voices having been involved in the selection and able to express their opinions before the decision is made. It may be that the person specification drawn up near the start of the recruitment process is closely matched; if not, a compromise is required. Either the attributes of the actual candidates seen have to be accommodated or else a decision not to appoint but to repeat the whole process, perhaps targeting a broader population, must be made. Recruitment provides the candidates for the selectors to judge, which returns to Watson's (1994: 203) statement in the introduction to this chapter that 'selection techniques cannot overcome failures in recruitment'. The problems generated by poor wording or selection of media, attracting too many or a poor selection of candidates, serve as a salutary lesson when the recruitment exercise is next undertaken. Problems may serve to reinforce existing cultures, limiting diversity and continue existing employment imbalances in gender, race and disability.

Evaluation of various selection methods

Taylor (1998: 120) reports that a recent compilation of hundreds of studies from many countries assessed in meta-analyses by computer, 'show that traditional methods of selection . . . are markedly poorer at accurately predicting job performance than more sophisticated techniques such as personality tests and assessment centres', as shown in Figure 4.1. Indeed, Taylor (1998: 121) goes on to

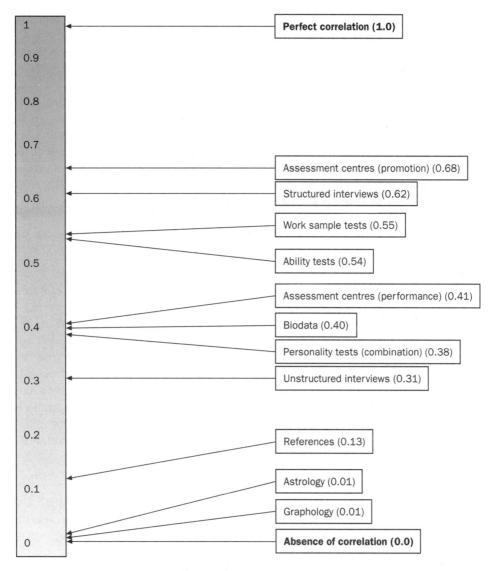

Figure 4.1 Validity of some methods of selection in predicting job performance

Source: Adapted from Corbridge and Pilbeam (1998)

reiterate the observation by Robertson and Makin in 1986 that in the UK 'the frequency of a method's use is inversely related to its known validity'.

The figures shown represent correlation coefficients calculated from many studies, the correlation coefficients are measured on a scale 0 to 1, where 0 represents an absence of correlation and 1 represents perfect correlation. A good correlation suggests a reliable indicator.

In terms of the validity of methods of selection, this figure shows that

- Astrology and graphology appear to be extremely poor predictors.
- References appear to be only slightly more accurate.

- Unstructured traditional interviews suggest more significance to 0.31.
- Personality tests (which may be used in combination) with a correlation coefficient of 0.38, bio-data at 0.40 and assessment centres designed to focus on performance in the job at 0.41, still only suggest relatively low levels of significance.
- Finally, ability tests at correlation coefficient (0.54) work sample tests (0.55) and structured or focused interviews (0.62) appear to have greater significance, rising to 0.68 for assessment centres designed for promotion or development purposes. The difference between the two types of assessment centres is probably explained by the fact that the latter, designed to assess suitability for promotion or development, by definition assesses individuals already belonging to the organisation and socialised to its norms. Prediction of success is more accurate here than for assessment centres focused on predicting job performance, since these draw candidates from outside the organisation, not socialised to its norms. Even the 'best' selection methods still fall short of perfect prediction.

The various methods all have benefits and drawbacks. The choice of method has to be made in relation to the particular vacancy and the type of labour market in which the job falls. Adverts need to be carefully worded, as discussed in Chapter 3, to avoid a vicious circle, unable to identify and select good applicants due to the huge number responding. Job requirements need to be realistic and not too demanding or too broad if selection is to be both possible and efficient. The organisation can also be promoted as a good employer to attract applicants and enhance its overall public profile. In an ideal world, even unsuccessful candidates will be so impressed with the organisation and their experience of the recruitment process that, despite their disappointment, they still recommend it to others.

Evidence of selection in practice

The *IPD Survey Report* (2000b) findings are summarised in Table 4.3.

The IPD report that there is more similarity of selection methods used across groups of workers as compared with the recruitment methods used to generate the

Table 4.3 Most frequently used selection methods

Most frequently used selection methods	Managers (%)	Prof'n (%)	Skilled manual (%)
Interview	98	99	81
Application forms	70	70	68
CVs	70	71	45
Candidates' covering letters	61	61	41
Ability or aptitude testing	36	37	24
Personality questionnaires	35	26	7
Assessment centres	22	15	2
Telephone-based screening	11		6
Biodata	5	5	2
Graphology	1	1	0.004

Source: *IPD Survey Report* (2000b)

original field of candidates. In general the more sophisticated and costly tools are used for managerial and professional groups rather than skilled manual workers, where the interview remains popular. Overall, a general increase in the use of psychometric tests and assessment centres, structured interviewing (for consistency) and variation in questions to avoid the 'practice effect' of questions being repeated were noted. Another recent development is the use of electronic media, by 40 per cent of organisations in the survey, especially in the public sector. The main methods of selection were posting vacancies on internal 'intranets', using a dedicated Internet recruitment site. Only 3 per cent administering selection tests via the Internet.

Table 4.4 gives an indication of the effectiveness of these selection methods. The figures identify the single most effective method for those using each of the methods. Almost inevitably, therefore, the interview leads the field: it can be assumed to be ubiquitous, despite its weaknesses. Assessment centres follow in second place, reflecting not so much their lack of accuracy as the cost in terms of time, money and other resources, and the seniority of the appointment. A number of organisations identify ability or aptitude testing, alone, as their most effective selection method, particularly for manual workers.

Table 4.4 Single most effective selection method

Selection methods	Managers (%)	Prof'n (%)	Skilled manual (%)
Interview	57	61	69[1]
Application forms	6	9	12
CVs	11	10	8
Candidates' covering letters			
Ability or aptitude testing	8	6	16
Personality questionnaires		4	
Assessment centres	40	31	20[2]
Telephone-based screening			
Biodata		8[2]	
Graphology			

Source: *IPD Survey Report* (2000b)
(1) confidence in interviews still high for skilled manual workers compared to a fall-off in interview confidence for managers (75% in 1999) and for professionals (76% in 1999)
(2) very few users

Activity 4.5

1 Using what you now know about selection methods, which ones would you use for the following jobs?

 a) a design engineer in the car industry
 b) a laboratory technician in a hospital
 c) a manager for a retail shop
 d) a labourer on a building site
 e) a hotel cleaner

Activity continued

Induction

In some sense, the departure from the organisation of recent joiners (termed 'early turnover' or 'early leavers') can be considered an extension of the selection process. Employees may find difficulty adjusting to the reality of the organisation, the job itself or their colleagues, perhaps causing them to think more deeply about their career aspirations. Induction, the intensive socialisation by the employer to help the transition into the workplace, can also be seen as part of the selection process. It can easily be ascribed to the 'training' function, orientating the new employee to the systems, processes and personnel of the organisation as they start the job. There are elements concerned with the immediate job, the department or functional area and finally the organisation as a whole. Normally such a period of intensive training would take place as the employee begins the job or within a few weeks of this, though aspects could be staggered and some elements may be centrally organised, running, say, twice a year.

Fowler (1996) comments that 'early leavers' reflect the increased likelihood of resignation during their first few months of employment. He points out that a low level of turnover represents stability, seen as an important characteristic of an effective, well-motivated labour force (see Chapter 5). It appears that workers who undergo an initial intensive induction training course are less likely to leave in the early stages of employment. As well as the disruption to that job and closely associated job-holders, the notice period is normally insufficient to recruit a replacement, thus incurring additional costs of temporary staff, if available. There may also be staff dismissed at an early stage of their employment. Whichever side instigates a withdrawal from the process, it can be viewed as a final stage in the selection process, which is always a voluntary one and can be broken at any stage, by either party.

One of the problems leading to early departure is the creation of false expectations during recruitment, including too optimistic predictions of interesting and varied work, promotion and training opportunities or levels of overtime and extra pay. Once reality sets in, based on comments by other employees with a discrepancy between this and the picture given at interview, they may soon leave. Likewise, the reality of the organisational experience, where they find the culture difficult to adjust to, too bureaucratic or unfriendly, or they have personality clashes with their immediate manager or workgroup, may make them feel they won't 'fit in'. The latter is a good example of the benefits of wider involvement of line management and the peers of the new employee in selection. Exit interviews may indicate the reason for leaving and the role played by the organisation as well as the individual in this. However, the tendency is usually to give an uncontroversial reason, such as 'leaving for more money' to avoid any confrontation, when in fact they tell their workmates quite a different reason. Rather than seeing all turnover, particularly of new employees, as negative and a 'problem', it is perhaps more constructive to see some turnover as inevitable and even a healthy process, since it helps ensure a degree of 'fit' between the organisation and its employees. However realistic, the selection process cannot be fully completed until the individual experiences the 'real' job and organisation, albeit at some cost in resources of time, money and frustration.

Evidence of evaluation of recruitment and selection

The *IPD Survey Report* (2000b) states that evaluation is now acknowledged to play a central part in good practice, but is hindered by lack of resources, lack of scope to implement findings and internal difficulties. The most popular method is informal feedback from recruits to their managers, analysing labour turnover, appraisal and assessment ratings, though one organisation evaluated the survival rates of recruits chosen by an assessment centre. However, the *IPD Survey Report* (2000b: 17) goes on to say 'a formal validation of the recruitment and selection process by an occupational psychologist or consultant is used by only 3 per cent of organisations'.

Case Study 4.1

Selection methods in practice

These examples look at several of the methods of selection in the UK in 2000. Chapter 3 uses the same examples in a case study to consider recruitment procedures and practices. The cases are written around real companies and have been chosen to illustrate the variation in selection methods occurring between industrial sectors, occupations and different jobs within the same company.

The first case is ServiceCo in the high-tech electronics industry with a turnover of £40m, part of a £2bn diverse international organisation. The parent company is highly regarded because of its financial management and stock market performance. In terms of the HR function, 'ServiceCo' is best described as 'minimalist', with legal requirements fulfilled at head office and line managers carrying out the essentials for managing personnel.

Selection policy is unwritten and has developed in an *ad hoc* manner. Most staff and management are long serving and there is a high degree of continuity. Deeply held values are articulated in terms of technical expertise and financial success. Requirements are for expertise in the job and willingness to work the long hours. Previous career history is taken as an indication of this. Technical skill may supercede even the usual need to 'get on' with the boss and ability to work as part of a team is of secondary importance.

Normally external recruitment is used for senior management vacancies: executive search consultants identify likely candidates and, on behalf of the company, advertise and shortlist. Previous experience of the industry and acceptability to the board are the prime criteria.

Case Study continued

Recruiting for, say, a Chief Executive by placing an advert of one-eighth page size, with a repeat the following week, could cost £20K in a national broadsheet newspaper. Using a third party, an executive search company, requires a fee of about 15 per cent of a starting salary of, say, £100K, proportionately reduced if the employee leaves early. Total recruitment cost would be in the order of £40K. Management roles are adapted to fit the new incumbent, suggesting that individuals are valued due to their knowledge of the industry, the organisation and their own personal contacts. In practice, where evidence emerges that the individual recruited at this level cannot achieve the financial targets or lacks sufficient technical expertise, they quite simply leave.

Similar methods are used for selecting technical staff. Initial interviews are completed by a specialist agency. Second interviews are then held in the organisation, on an *ad hoc* basis after normal working hours, with the immediate manager and a team member. Promotion to management level may be internal, the candidate having demonstrated ability and motivation. Where a vacancy can be predicted by planned changes in the company, there may be the opportunity to provide fast-track grooming for the post several months ahead of requirement. This pre-empts ambitious individuals leaving for competitors. Where they fail to meet the requirements of the job, termination of employment is usual. The method of selecting clerical staff is either from a local agency or more usually via the temporary employment route. Selection is by considering the potential employee 'in situ', having worked for the company for some weeks or months.

Staff turnover is rarely a concern at this company, and despite the keen financial regime, evaluation is not an issue. There is no department or specialised staff to do this and is infrequent recruitment. References are considered important, they are not evaluative but confirm factual details of previous employment, this reflects the legal implications surrounding references. Since all the company now report through devolved business units, issues concerning equal opportunities or diversity in the workforce are not felt to be significant.

Thomas, the recently recruited accountant introduced in Case Study 3.1, has been in the job four months when a clerical vacancy occurs and he suddenly finds himself doing the selection for the replacement. He is always eager to take on new tasks and sees the interview as 'a bit of a chat'. He knows that in a small department such as at ServiceCo, there is a lot of pressure to ensure all staff are contributing fully One of the areas he questions the two candidates, female, married and in their late twenties, is their intentions to have a family. It is only later, over a drink in the pub with a friend, that he realises this might not have been a good idea.

The second example is typical of large supermarket groups, SuperCo. It embodies the systematic, bench-marked 'good practice', even at the base of the organisation. Recruitment and selection are identified as a key lever to staff the organisation at the point of customer contact with employees who are customer focused and enjoy selling food.

The selection of candidates for hourly paid posts, in particular cashier and shelf-stocking duties, involves a two-stage selection process. Each stage identifies behaviours and 'competencies' using a 'person specification by picturing the type of person needed', focusing in turn on different job skills in order of priority. These must be demonstrated before the candidate can move on to the next stage:

Stage 1: Application form and assessment
Required behaviours are interests in selling and helping, tested by short questions on motivation. A further assessment exercise then identifies other required behaviour, such as

Case Study continued

attention to detail in noticing people's behaviour and using common sense. Testing methods include an exercise where candidates watch a video of people in the store and record what they notice.

Stage 2: Interview

Candidates need to demonstrate an interest in helping customers, ability to follow instructions, cope with routine, enjoy the 'hands-on' environment, show an interest in selling and in food, which all demonstrate competency in the required behaviours for the job. The process is designed to advance the company equal opportunities policies.

Each stage is scored by the assessor using a matrix of questions. For instance, the Stage 2 rating sheet lists six questions on each of the specified behaviours under three categories (unsuitable, meets specification, good candidate), requiring a yes or no answer. Any negative answer in the first column rules the candidate out, and further columns are then scored and totalled but progress to the final 'good candidate' column only occurs if all the previous results are successful.

Detailed training for everyone conducting selection is carried out, and no one is allowed to interview unless this training has been successfully completed. This involves welcoming, structuring the interview, planning the questioning strategy and probing by follow-up. Behavioural interviewing techniques include past performance, hypothetical questions and contra-evidence. Interviewing skills include summarising and reflecting, as well as open and confident body language. Ideally the candidate speaks for most time during the interview, which is conducted by personnel. Normally the line manager of the recruiting department will also see the candidate before a job offer is made to check suitability, availability and liaise with personnel to arrange induction, health and safety, and cashier training.

Graduate recruitment for all functions within the company is co-ordinated by a specialised unit at head office with some assessment and selection at regional level. Management are normally recruited internally by progression within the stores, though a proportion of 'new blood' from outside the company are also recruited, often from the hospitality industry. Senior management selection is split equally between the internal route and 'new blood'.

Fiona, the placement student introduced in Case Study 3.1, has been asked to take on another project. Given the high cost of recruiting graduates, the central HR department is alarmed at the relatively high turnover among this group who, typically, complain that they have spent time a lot of time 'stacking bananas' in their first six months with the organisation. It is requested that Fiona examines current selection methods, making recommendations to address the problem of the early graduate leavers.

Activity 4.6

1 What features of a systematic selection process are apparent in the approach adopted by managers at SuperCo?

2 What differences can you find with the approach adopted by ServiceCo?

3 To what extent are these differing selection processes successful? What additional information would help you to assess this?

Activity continued

4 What advantages and disadvantages are there for involving the following in selection:

(a) outside agencies?

(b) line management?

5 What are the pressures and/or vulnerabilities in their selection practices, actual or potential, in each of the companies?

6 What changes would you recommend to avoid these?

7 What do the approaches taken by the ServiceCo and SuperCo companies tell you about the significance of selection techniques to these companies' overall resourcing strategies and tactics?

8 Is Thomas right to feel some unease at his questioning tactics in the interview?

9 What alternative approach to the selection of a new clerk could Thomas have taken?

10 What are the issues Fiona needs to address regarding graduate leavers?

11 What recommendations would you make to the central HR departments in both companies?

SUMMARY

In this chapter the following key points have been made:

- Selection has gone through a number of stages of development from its rather subjective origins of interviewing, application forms and referencing.

- These changes are reflected in the search for valid and reliable methods of selecting employees, each method having strengths and limitations but there are recognised ways of minimising the weaknesses.

- Selection can focus on skills, experience, attitude or potential, or a combination of these.

- Selection involves contributions from the HR function, line management and outside agencies.

- Different organisational and occupational contexts influence the choice of selection approaches and methods.

- All the information on each candidate needs to be reviewed and evaluated to reach the best selection decision.

- Consider that selection is a two-way process, crucial to identifying the human expertise and potential needed to ensure retention, generate the organisation's competitive advantage, organisational performance and effectiveness in the long term.

 DISCUSSION QUESTIONS

1 What approach would you take for the selection of employees with readily available skills?

2   Which methods would you adopt to ensure the most appropriate candidates are selected in this scenario?

3   What steps can be taken to make selection interviews a more reliable tool of selection?

4   What issues arise in using selection tests?

5   Why and how would you select employees on the basis of 'potential'?

6   Are there any drawbacks to selecting on the basis of competencies?

7   What arguments would you use to convince senior management investment in more sophisticated methods of selection is worthwhile?

8   How can the selection process assist in addressing high turnover?

9   When applying principles of equality and teamwork to selection, what issues might you expect to arise?

10 Does the recent emphasis on style and presentation in recruits have any implications for equality of treatment?

11 How might the issues identified in the previous two questions be resolved?

12 In what circumstances might a 'focused' approach to selection be preferable to a strictly systematic one?

(R)   FURTHER READING

There are a number of other undergraduate texts available, which are aimed at human resource management specialists and therefore explore the issues introduced here in more detail. These include Beardwell and Holden (2001), Bolton (1997), Bratton and Gold (1999) and Foot and Hook (1999). Students wishing a more advanced discussion of the issues raised should consult the chapter by Iles and Salamon in Storey (1995) and Leopold, Harris and Watson (1999). Texts largely concentrating on recruitment and selection are those by Taylor (1998) and Corbridge and Pilbeam (1998). Fuller discussion of validity and utility in selection is also available in Arnold, Cooper and Robertson (1995). Many relevant and accessible articles are available in *People Management* on selection topics (also available online).

Part 3 Employee reward

Chapter 5 Motivation to work

Yvonne Leverment

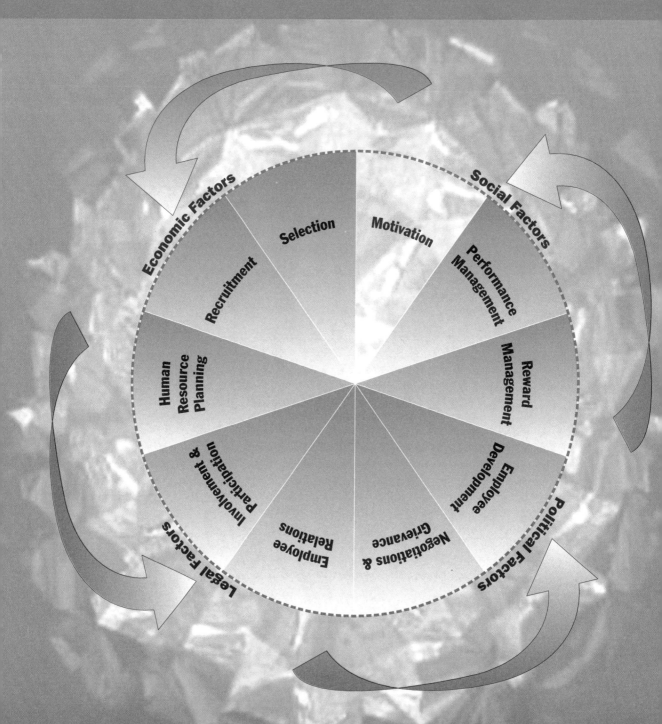

Having completed this chapter and its associated activities, readers should be able to:

- explain the main theories and concepts that underpin motivation to work
- identify the factors that contribute to the needs and expectations of people at work
- discuss and be able to evaluate their relevance in the work situation
- outline the key factors that contribute to a person's sense of job enrichment

INTRODUCTION

This chapter considers the concepts of motivation and job satisfaction and examines the issues that are important in the creation of a stable and well-motivated workforce. What motivates people to work is a key issue for any organisation to address. This is because the relationship between the organisation and its workforce is governed by what motivates people to be fulfilled in the work that they do. The implication of this for the manager is the need to recognise how to elicit effective performance from their team of workers, in order to achieve the goals and objectives of the organisation. Although there is no single, universally accepted definition of motivation, what is clear is that people are usually motivated to do something. What should be remembered here is that this may not always be positive! A person may be motivated *not* to do something – a piece of work, communicate with colleagues – which may prove to be detrimental to the outcome. Also, factors that motivate one individual to perform well may not be the same factors that motivate another. Finally, it is important to accept that motivation is not the only important determinant of work performance and that factors such as ability, resources and interaction with others all play a part.

Activity 5.1

Think of your university work or current part-time job:

1 What motivates you as an individual?

2 What motivates you to carry out your work well?

3 How do you influence people in the work/university situation?

Early ideas on work motivation began with the scientific management approach taken by F.W. Taylor. In the late nineteenth century Taylor developed a science of work which involved the detailed assessment of work processes in order to improve efficiency and productivity (Taylor, 1947). In recommending the detailed division of skills into small fragmented tasks Taylor degraded the labour force by reducing its skilled component. The purpose of this was to simplify tasks in order to increase the flexibility of the labour force. This, in turn, allowed for greater efficiency and increases in productivity. At this time it was considered that workers were motivated by pay and working conditions above all else. Thus, research of the day concentrated on ways in which workers' productivity could be increased.

In the 1920s a group of experiments known as the Hawthorne studies challenged the notion that first, individuals acted only in isolation, and, second, that individuals were only responsive to rational economic and physical stimulation. The Hawthorne studies marked the beginning of the human relations approach to work which stresses the importance of social factors in the world of work. The role of management was to harness worker co-operation through team-building, improved communication and worker participation in the decision-making process.

From this time the development of many competing theories on the nature of work motivation began to emerge. Two contrasting approaches were adopted. The following part of this chapter outlines these two approaches.

Theories of motivation

Motivational theories can be divided into two categories – *content* and *process*. Content theories or *need* theories are based on the assumption that all individuals possess the same set of needs and, as individuals, we behave in ways which satisfy these needs. In other words, this set of theories places importance on *what motivates* people to perform well at work. These theories consider human behaviour to be 'reflexive' and instinctive in nature, driven by unconscious drives. Process theories, on the other hand, acknowledge the differences in people's needs, focusing on the *processes* that create these differences. They assume that people are aware of their goals and behaviour and assume that people are purposive and rational. Also known as cognitive, the process theories identify how behaviour is initiated, directed and sustained. Each set of theories will be considered separately.

The content theories

The major content theories of motivation are:

- Maslow's hierarchy of needs
- Alderfer's modified need hierarchy model
- Herzberg's two-factor theory

Maslow's hierarchy of need theory

Published in 1943, Maslow's theory was based on the basic assumption that people are always wanting, that is, they want more and what they want is dependent on what they already have. This basic assumption gives rise to what is known as Maslow's hierarchy of needs – a series of levels based on a hierarchy of importance.

The hierarchy comprises five levels beginning with physiological needs, which then ascend through safety needs, love needs, esteem needs and, at the highest level, the need for self-actualisation. Maslow argues that self-actualisation is the ultimate human goal, acknowledging the challenge for society is to enable individuals to develop their capabilities to the optimum. He believed that few people ever reached this level, thereby postulating that self-actualisation is a need that we, as individuals, strive for all our lives.

- *Physiological needs* – these include needs for food, warmth, clothing and shelter. Also, sleep, maternal behaviour and sensory pleasure.
- *Safety needs* – these include the need for safety and security, freedom from pain, protection from danger and deprivation and the need for predictability and order.
- *Social needs* – these include affection, a sense of belonging, social activity, friendships and relationships.
- *Esteem needs* – these include the need for recognition and belief in oneself. This may include self-respect and the esteem of others, together with the desire for confidence, strength, independence and achievement.
- *Self-actualisation needs* – this involves the need to develop one's full potential.

Maslow argues that once a lower need on the pyramid is reached or satisfied, it no longer acts as a motivator. Instead, the needs in the next level in the hierarchy demand satisfaction and become the motivating influence. Therefore, only unsatisfied needs motivate an individual. However, he also makes it clear that the hierarchy should not necessarily be a fixed order. Indeed, there may well be a reversal of the hierarchy. Some examples of this include:

- For some, the drive for self-actualisation may surface despite lack of satisfaction of more basic needs.
- For the unemployed, particularly those who can be classed as long-term unemployed, higher levels may be lost as the individual strives only to be satisfied at lower levels.
- Self-esteem may seem to be more important than social needs to some individuals.

Turning to the work situation, there are a number of problems relating to Maslow's theory:

1 Individuals do not necessarily satisfy their needs through the work situation alone. Therefore the manager needs to have some understanding of a person's private and social life as it may affect their behaviour in the work situation.
2 Individual differences and preferences means that people place different values on the same need.
3 Rewards or outcomes at work, such as higher salary or promotion, may satisfy more than one need.
4 Motivating factors between individuals may not be the same, as individuals seek satisfaction in different ways.
5 In Maslow's theory satisfaction is seen as the key motivational outcome. However, job satisfaction does not necessarily lead to improved performance.

Although Maslow's work was not originally intended as an explanation of motivation in the workplace, it has nevertheless been popular as a theory of motivation. It draws attention to a number of different motivators and provides a framework for viewing the different needs and expectations that individuals have. However, the theory holds little empirical support (Hall and Nougaim, 1968; Lawler and Suttle, 1972) and Maslow himself recognises the limitations of his theory as it provides no operational definitions of the needs he describes.

Alderfer's modified need hierarchy

Alderfer's model (1972) suggests that individual needs can be divided into three groups, based on the core needs of existence, relatedness and growth (ERG):

- *Existence needs* – these include nutritional and material needs concerned with sustaining human existence and survival. In the work situation, working conditions and pay would fall into this group
- *Relatedness needs* – these include relationships which can be met through family and friends socially and through peers, colleagues and supervisors at work
- *Growth needs* – these include needs which are concerned with the desire for personal development

Whereas Maslow proposed a progression up a hierarchy, Alderfer suggests that these needs should be viewed as a continuum. More than one need can be activated at the same time and the individual can progress *down* as well as *up* the hierarchy. In what Alderfer refers to as the *frustration-regression* process he suggests that if an individual is frustrated at attempting to satisfy one set of needs, he can reassume a lower set of needs as important. In this way, unsatisfied needs become less rather than more important. Additionally, research carried out by Wanous and Zwany (1977) found that relatedness and growth needs become more important once satisfied. This suggests that employers can more easily satisfy the needs of their employees.

Work carried out by Mumford in 1976 used the broad categories of Maslow and Alderfer to identify more specific categories for workers' needs. The assumption underpinning these categories was that employees had needs which directly related to their work:

- *Knowledge needs* – work that utilises their knowledge and skills
- *Control needs* – these are satisfied by the provision of information, good working conditions and high-quality supervision
- *Psychological needs* – these include the need for recognition, responsibility, status and advancement
- *Task needs* – the need for meaningful work and some degree of autonomy
- *Moral needs* – the need to be treated in the way that employers would themselves be treated

Herzberg's two-factor theory

Research carried out by Herzberg *et al.* (1959) involving interviews with 200 accountants and engineers, identified two sets of factors that affected motivation

Hygiene factors

Relationship with colleagues
Job security
Working environment
Salary
Company policies
Level and quality of supervision

Dissatisfiers

Motivation and job satisfaction

Satisfiers

Responsibility
Recognition
Personal advancement
Achievement
Nature of role

Motivators

Figure 5.1 Hertzberg's two-factor theory of motivation
Source: Adapted from Mullins (1999: 495)

and work. One group of factors, which if found to be absent, caused dissatis-faction. This included working conditions, salary, job security, company policy, interpersonal working relationships. This grouping of factors was termed *hygiene* factors as they served to prevent dissatisfaction. The second group of factors, termed *motivators*, represented sources of satisfaction. This group included responsibility, recognition, promotion, achievement (see Figure 5.1).

Using this theory, it would appear that job satisfaction and dissatisfaction are caused by two different sets of factors. Motivational factors affect feelings of satisfaction or no satisfaction. Their absence did not cause dissatisfaction. Hygiene factors afford the workers an acceptable working environment. They do not lead to increased satisfaction or job involvement yet their absence leads to dissatisfaction, for example, low pay.

Herzberg's two-factor theory is more directly applicable to the work situation and this application can be used to incorporate more motivators when areas of work are redesigned (see Figure 5.1). The theory indicates that it is more likely that good performance leads to job satisfaction rather than the reverse. Although through his interviews Herzberg attempted to take an empirical approach to the study of work motivation, support for the theory is mixed. Two common criticisms centre on the validity of the methodology adopted in the research. First, the independent effects of hygienes and motivators is open to question. In addition, the interview approach may not have been the most appropriate way to determine people's reflection on their performance. Secondly, a study on accountants and engineers with interesting and lucrative jobs may not be applicable to people with largely unskilled work, which is uninteresting, repetitive and of limited scope. Later in this chapter we shall return to Herzberg's work when the motivational effects of job redesign are discussed in the section on job enrichment.

The content theories dominated work motivation for a number of years. Yet, evaluations of them reveal a number of significant flaws which Arnold *et al.* (1998: 248) summarise as follows:

- Needs did not group together in the ways predicted
- The theories were unable to predict when a particular need would become important
- There was no clear relationship between needs and behaviour
- Needs were generally described without sufficient precision
- The notion of need as a biological phenomenon is problematic as it ignores the capacity of people to construct their own perceptions of needs and how they can be met

Activity 5.2

1 Consider your own needs: do you recognise them in your own behaviour?

2 Do your needs always drive your behaviour at work/and or at university?

The process theories of motivation

In attempting to identify the relationships among the variables that make up motivation, the process theories provide a further contribution to understanding the nature of work motivation. The key process theories include:

- Expectancy-based models, such as Vroom, Porter and Lawler
- Equity theory
- Goal-setting theory

The expectancy-based models

The basis of expectancy theory is that people are influenced by the expected results of their actions. Therefore, motivation is a result of the relationship between:

- the effort used and perceived level of performance, and
- the expectation that the desired outcome or reward will be related to the performance

For this to happen there must also be the expectation that a reward or desired outcome is available.

The most popular expectancy-based theory is that of Vroom. The publication of Vroom's study *Work and Motivation* in 1964 aimed to explain the links between people's perceptions of their role at work, with the amount of effort needed and the degree to which they felt rewarded for this effort. Also referred to as the *valence, instrumentality and expectancy (VIE) theory*, Vroom argues that people prefer certain outcomes from their behaviour over others. Satisfaction is felt when the preferred outcome is achieved. Definitions of these three variables are as follows:

1 *Expectancy* – If I try, am I able to carry out the action I am considering?
2 *Instrumentality* – If I carry out the action, will it lead to an identifiable outcome or reward?
3 *Valence* – How much do I value those outcomes and rewards?

According to Vroom, a person's motivation for a certain form of behaviour is determined by the combination of valence and expectancy. This is termed the *motivational force*. The strength of the force of the individual's motivation to behave in a particular way is evaluated in an equation as:

$$F = E \times V$$

Where F = motivation to behave
E = the expectation that a behaviour will result in a particular outcome
V = the valence of the outcome

The motivational force of an action is unaffected by outcomes which either have no valence or are thought of as being unlikely to result from a certain course of action.

An example of this:
Imagine you are a professional tennis player, about to take part in a match. The first question you might ask is, 'How capable am I of winning?' (*expectancy*). The considerations you might make would be the amount of training you have done, your level of fitness, your level of experience in competition and the level and skill of your opponent. The next question you might ask would be, 'How likely is it that I will win?' (*instrumentality*). The considerations here might include your opponent's ability, the playing conditions, your present standard. Finally, you might ask, 'How much do I value winning?' (*valence*). The considerations you might make would be the amount of recognition you would receive, the progression and advancement of your career and the monetary rewards gained.

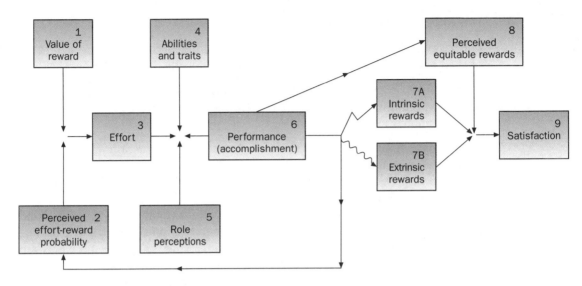

Figure 5.2 Model from Porter and Lawler (1968)

Vroom's theory has been further developed by Porter and Lawler (1968) who go beyond motivational force and consider performance as a whole. From the work perspective the motivational force of a job is compromised by factors such as the individual's abilities, traits, perceptions of role and opportunities. They suggest *rewards* to be an intervening variable. In addition they suggest that motivation, satisfaction and performance are separate variables with a somewhat complex relationship (see Figure 5.2).

- *Value of reward* – similar to the valence in Vroom's model in that people wish for outcomes/rewards which they hope to achieve from their work. The value placed on this is dependent upon the depth and strength of people's feelings towards it.
- *Perceived effort-reward probability* – similar to expectancy in that it refers to a person's expectation that outcomes/rewards are dependent on the amount of effort given.
- *Effort* – is how hard the person tries. The amount of effort is dependent on the interaction of the variables such as the value of the reward and the perception of the effort-reward relationship.
- *Abilities and traits* – in suggesting that effort does not lead directly to performance, Porter and Lawler suggest that factors such as intelligence, skills, knowledge and personality contribute to a person's ability to perform an activity.
- *Role perceptions* – is the way in which a person views their work and the type of role that they should adopt. This not only influences the effort used but also the direction and level of action deemed necessary for effective performance.
- *Performance* – is dependent not only on the amount of effort used but also on the person's own abilities and traits and their perception of role. Therefore, if the person lacks either the ability or personality or does not have an accurate

perception of what is required, a large amount of effort may still result in poor performance.

- *Rewards* – these are the desired outcome of the task. They are both intrinsic, for example, sense of achievement, feelings of recognition and responsibility, and extrinsic, such as salary and working conditions. Porter and Lawler suggest that although both are important, intrinsic rewards are more likely to produce job satisfaction related to performance (rewards are discussed further in Chapter 7).
- *Perceived equitable rewards* – is the level of reward people feel they should fairly receive for a performance.
- *Satisfaction* – is seen as an attitude that is determined by the actual reward and the perceived level of award for a given task or performance.

What does all this mean to the manager in terms of how to motivate people in the work setting? While expectancy theory is helpful in identifying key factors that motivate workers, it pays little attention to the explanation of *why* an individual values or does not value particular outcomes/rewards. However, it does help to explain the nature of behaviour and motivation at work and thus can help to identify problems in performance. In order to achieve this, managers need to consider four key aspects of work:

1 The need to focus on the use of appropriate rewards for which to provide incentive for improved performance. It could be that in some instances workers may value recognition and praise rather than monetary reward.
2 The need to establish clear relationship between effort–performance and reward as perceived by the individual worker. This may mean improved training, guidance and support.
3 The need to take into account variables such as abilities and traits, perceptions of role, and organisational procedures, which may affect performance.
4 The need to minimise undesirable outcomes which may be perceived to be a result of high performance, such as short-term contract working, redundancy, and industrial accidents.

Equity theory or organisational justice theory

The central theme in this theory is the notion that people's feelings of how fairly they are treated are assessed through comparison to others. This can be likened to a form of exchange process where a person expects certain outcomes in exchange for certain contributions or inputs. Equity theory is most associated with the work of Adams (1965). The assumption that underpins this theory is that social comparison in our relationships is governed by our concern as individuals for fairness or equity. In doing so, an individual perceives effort and reward in relative, rather than absolute terms. If the perception is one of inequity, the more distressed the individual feels, and the more tension this distress causes, and the more motivated they become to restore equity through changes in either perceptions, behaviour or both. A simple diagram to explain Adams's equity theory is shown in Figure 5.3.

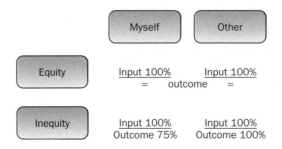

Figure 5.3 Description of equity and inequity
Source: Adams (1965)

More recently, organisational issues such as downsizing, delayering and change in management programmes have impacted on how people view the organisations in which they work, and how committed and motivated they are within their work situation. In these incidences people may well express a sense of injustice in the work process and be less motivated and committed to the organisation. If a strong sense of injustice exists, people are likely to reduce their contribution to the organisation as a whole. A distinction can be made between *distributive justice* (whether people believe they have received or will receive fair rewards) and *procedural justice* (whether people believe that the organisational procedures that deal with rewards are fair). A good example of this is any form of assessment that you undertake as part of your undergraduate studies. Consider the work and effort that you would put in to preparing for an assessed seminar. You know that you have to prepare well in order to gain a good mark. You expect that the organisational procedures and systems are in place that will secure you a mark that is fair. Indeed, you are unlikely to prepare well for the assessment if you do not believe that you will receive a fair mark for your attempts. However, the resulting mark may not be what you had hoped for when you consider first, the amount of effort that you have made in your preparation, and secondly, if you begin to compare your mark with that of others. You may well begin to question the organisational procedures that are in place. These may include the provision of adequate and reliable assessment criteria prior to the assessment, the skill and depth of knowledge of the subject matter of the assessor, together with their level of experience of carrying out the assessment and subjective bias of the assessor.

Goal-setting theory

Viewed as much as a motivational technique as a theory, work carried out by Locke (1976) is based on the notion that a person's goals or intentions determine their behaviour. The combination of goal difficulty, and the extent to which a person is committed to achieving a desired goal, determines the level of effort used in realising the goal. Thus, goals guide people's responses and actions, ultimately directing work behaviour and performance. To be effective goals need to be:

1 *Specific* – specific goals tend to lead to higher performance as they create a basis for a precise intention or form of behaviour. Here, the implication for the manager/employer is that specific goals should be identified by the manager in order to direct behaviour and maintain and enhance motivation.

2 *Realistic* – while difficult goals lead to higher performance than easy goals as they produce more effective behaviour, goals should be set at a challenging but realistic level.

3 *Achievable* – goals at the limits of a person's ability will not result in higher levels of performance. If goals are unachievable it will produce demotivational behaviour and reduce level of performance.

There is strong evidence to support goal-setting theory (Mento *et al.*, 1987; Locke and Latham, 1990) and Arnold *et al.* (1998: 258) points out that it is 'probably the most consistently supported theory in work and organisational psychology'. Feedback on behaviour and performance (also referred to as knowledge of results) is an important feature in goal-setting theory. Although it is well recognised that feedback on performance *is* motivational, it still remains that many organisations give little or no information regarding performance. More often, feedback and knowledge of results is only given when performance falls short of what is required. This gives rise to the fourth practical implication for the manager:

4 *Feedback* – feedback and knowledge of how an individual is performing is associated with high performance. Accurate and timely feedback acts as a progress check and can form the basis for revision of goals. In addition, feedback should be positive and any negative feedback should be dealt with in a sensitive manner.

A further issue in goal-setting theory concerns level of participation and its effect on performance. It is thought that goals set by others are more likely to be accepted if there is participation in determining the goals. It is assumed to be effective because it increases an individual's understanding of what is fair in the process. It also gives the individual a degree of control over the situation, thus enhancing their commitment to achieving the goal.

Activity 5.3

1 How far can you say that human beings are as rational as expectancy theory suggests?

2 What are your own goals at work or university? How do they motivate you to improve your performance?

Job enrichment

The concept of job enrichment involves changing the design and experience of work in order to enhance satisfaction for the employee in the workplace. It anticipated that by doing this job satisfaction will lead to improved motivation and a good performance output. Various aspects of a job may influence an individual's level of satisfaction with it. Extrinsically this may include factors such as pay, working conditions, peers and superiors. These factors are valued outcomes that are controlled by others. Intrinsic factors may include recognition, responsibility, advancement and achievement. The relationship between intrinsic rewards and performance are more immediate and more in control of the individual. It is argued by Lawler (1973) that it is these intrinsic rewards that are the most important influences on motivation to work.

An individual's role and job design can have a marked effect on how they experience work and achieve satisfaction in what they do. In their model Hackman and Oldham (1975) suggest that it is the *characteristics of the job* that lead to job satisfaction. Huczynski and Buchanan (1991) state that this model is the basis of Herzberg's expectancy theory of job enrichment strategy. In this model five core dimensions are used in which to analyse the job and role of an individual. These core dimensions are as follows:

- *Skill Variety* (SV): the extent to which a job makes use of different skills and abilities
- *Task Identity* (TI): the extent to which a job involves a whole and meaningful piece of work
- *Task Significance* (TS): the extent to which a job affects the work of other organisation members or others in society
- *Autonomy*: the extent to which a job gives the individual freedom, independence and discretion in carrying it out
- *Feedback*: the extent to which information is given about level of performance and which is related back to the individual

If the content of the job is assessed on these five dimensions a *motivational potential score* (MPS) can be calculated using the following equation:

$$MPS = \frac{SV + TI + TS}{3} \times (autonomy) \times (feedback)$$

The motivating potential is low if one of the three main components is low. In addition, autonomy and feedback are considered to be more important in their influence over motivation. Thus a zero or near zero rating on either of these would result in a significantly greater lower score.

If jobs are redesigned in such a way that the presence of these five dimensions is increased, three critical psychological states can occur in workers:

- *Experienced meaningfulness of work*: determined by the level of skill variety, task identity and task significance and the extent to which work is meaningful, valuable and worthwhile
- *Experienced responsibility for work outcome*: determined by the amount of autonomy afforded and the extent to which an individual is accountable for the output of that work
- *Knowledge of results of work activity*: determined by the amount of feedback given and the extent to which an individual knows and understands how well they are performing

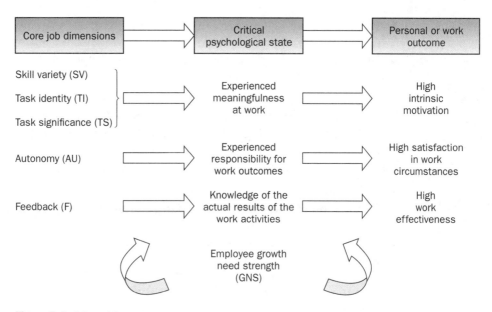

Figure 5.4 Job enrichment

Source: Adapted from Hackman, Oldham, Jansen and Purdy (1975)

Work motivation and job satisfaction will be high when these three critical psychological states are experienced. In addition, behavioural outcomes such as work attendance and the quality of work produced may be improved. One further dimension to the model was a personal attribute termed the *growth need strength* (GNS). Hackman and Oldham (1975) believed that this moderated the extent to which the three critical psychological states could be experienced. If an individual has drive and potential their GNS will be high and they will experience the three critical psychological states strongly (see Figure 5.4).

It can be seen how Hackman and Oldham's model encompasses job characteristics, job satisfaction, principles of work design, psychological state and motivation. Although the model has been universally accepted over the years Roberts and Glick (1981) point to two major criticisms in its usage. First, that the model says little about how to change a job in order to increase the amount of core characteristics it offers and, secondly, the model says little about how to redesign jobs for people low in growth need strength. Huczynski and Buchanan (1991) illustrate how the model shows that the motivating potential of jobs *can* be improved by applying five implementing concepts. These, then, do have implications for managers in the workplace:

- *Combining tasks* – increasing the variety of the work carried out by an individual will increase the contribution that the individual makes
- *Forming natural work units* – increasing the contribution that the individual makes to the work will increase the significance of the job
- *Establishing relationships* – giving employees responsibility for establishing contacts both within and outside of the organisation increases variety and affords the individual more freedom. Furthermore, it increases the potential and opportunity for direct feedback

- *Vertical loading* – giving responsibility normally allocated to superiors increases individual autonomy
- *Opening feedback and communication* – allows improvement for the feedback of performance

These five concepts have a considerable impact on the nature of the relationship between employee and employer and reflect on what Schein referred to in 1988 as the psychological contract. This implicit contract is based upon a series of assumptions on this important employee–employer relationship. These assumptions are outlined as follows:

- That employees will be treated fairly and honestly. That they will be afforded information about changes in working conditions and practice and that they will be treated justly and with equity.
- That employees should be able to expect a degree of security in return for loyalty to the organisation.
- That employees should expect employers to recognise their work, value the contribution that they make and satisfy their needs of fulfilment and job satisfaction.

From these basic assumptions it can be seen that the contract is largely a tacit agreement between employee and employer – nothing is formally written down and agreed upon between the two. Even though the contract is at the core of the employee–employer relationship, it is neither fixed nor ever stable. In addition, it is an agreement between unequal parties. The input of the employee will be dependent on their skills and knowledge and what motivates and interests them as individuals. These will be influenced by factors such as class, education, family circumstances, gender and race. The priorities of the employee are to receive what *they* perceive to be appropriate rewards and recognition for their work effort. For the employer, economic forces and capital resources will be crucial factors in how they allocate reward and recognition.

The trend towards increased efficiency – the 'notion of more for less' – and the increased expectancy of 'what is reasonable' by the employee, threatens the stability of the psychological contract between employee and employer. Watson (1995) suggests that different types of contract are made between an individual and their employer, depending on their position within the organisation and the type of work carried out. Two broad categories are used by Watson to explain this:

- Managerial/professional positions. Individuals in these positions tend to use discretion in their work and so have a high trust relationship with their superiors. In return for a high level of reward (salary, opportunity, status, satisfaction) these individuals use their own initiative and comply with the requirements of the organisation.
- Less skilled manual work, routine clerical and service work. The generally lower level of monetary reward (often on an hourly or weekly basis) for these groups is characterised by a low trust relationship with superiors. Work tasks are monitored under a basic contractual commitment and there is less in the way of potential for career advancement.

Clearly, if either party fails to meet the basic assumptions and expectations of the psychological contract, serious consequences may develop. For the employee, these may include lack of morale, demotivation and lack of advancement. For the employer, it may include absenteeism, lack of employee effort and high employee turnover. In addition, it is reasonable to suggest that the psychological contract does not hold as true in the new millennium as it did in years gone by. In Chapter 2 we have seen how the concept of the 'flexible firm' has challenged the notion that the relationship between employee and employer, as described above, remains strong. Individuals now work longer hours, are more accountable, more flexible and more disposable than ever before and the psychological contract can no longer be taken for granted.

Due to the uncertain economic climate where competition is strong and change inevitable, the response from within organisations has been to focus on adaptability and responsiveness to change rather than continuity and stability. This has been reflected not only in the psychological contract as described above but also in the nature of the more formal employment contract. Today there are a variety of employment contracts other than full-time and part-time permanent positions (see Chapter 2). The use of part-time and short-term contracts limits the commitment of the employer to the employee and can be justifiably (by the employee) seen as a form of control. This control often precipitates the need for the employee to work harder and for longer hours, often working beyond contract in an attempt to gain a degree of security.

Activity 5.4

In considering Hackman and Oldham's model, look for areas where your own work could be redesigned in order to increase your own motivation and work performance.

Motivation, performance and commitment

If we refer back to the Guest model of HRM (1989) in Chapter 1, in discussing policy goals related to human resource management, he argues that the policy goal for commitment is to ensure that employees feel bound to their organisation and are committed to high performance via their behaviour. One of the more popular ways of dividing organisational commitment into various components is described by Allen and Meyer (1990):

- *Affective commitment* – concerns the individual's emotional attachment to the organisation
- *Continuance commitment* – the individual's perception of what it would cost and the personal risk involved in leaving the organisation
- *Normative commitment* – the individual's own feelings of obligation to the organisation as their employer

It is true to say that people can feel multiple commitments in the workplace. These may not only be to their particular organisation, but also to their department, locality, trade union or professional association (Aranya and Ferris, 1984; Barling *et al.*, 1990). It is believed that an individual's commitment to their work can be enhanced through affording them the opportunity to encounter positive experiences in the workplace. Aspects intrinsic to the job are more important than extrinsic factors such as pay and working conditions. For example, Matthieu and Zajac (1990) found autonomy to be positively associated with organisational commitment, which Iverson (1996) suggests has a positive impact on attitudes in the workplace. This would seem particularly pertinent for the affective component of commitment where commitment is based on emotional attachment.

The link between commitment and performance is a lot less clear. Iverson, Deery and Erwin (1994) suggest that role ambiguity, or lack of role clarity, role conflict or inconsistent demands of the role and role overload will have a negative impact on organisational commitment. While Meyer *et al.* (1993) found that workers with high affective commitment tended to be better performers, a person is unlikely to perform well if they are unable to achieve, either through lack of ability or any of the above. If this is so, it can be expected that there will be a stronger link between commitment and performance for aspects of performance that depend more on motivation than ability. Finally, intention to leave the organisation is the most cited reason for low organisational commitment. Additionally, as Matthieu and Zajak (1990) point out, a person who does not feel committed to his organisation is more likely to want to leave it, than a person who does feel committed.

Case Study 5.1

Working for patients but demotivating the professionals?

Roymary NHS Trust is a large district general hospital undergoing a radical whole hospital change programme. The hospital's musculoskeletal process deals with any type of orthopaedic condition. The range of patient age and type of condition on these wards is enormous – from elderly fractures of the hip to young football players breaking legs, from traffic accidents to the less severe, but equally debilitating slipping and falling over, breaking arms, legs and backs. In the organisational change process four previously mixed acute/rehabilitation trauma wards have been restructured in order to accommodate two wholly acute and two wholly rehabilitation wards.

Previously on admission, patients had been admitted to one ward for the duration of their stay. Following the restructuring this no longer happened. The acute wards now accepted the patients on admission. It was from these wards the patients went to theatre and subsequently spent the initial few days of their post-operative recovery. The rehabilitation wards, as their name suggests, serve to accept the patients in preparation for discharge back into the community. Nursing staff worked in teams – two teams per ward – but all other health professionals, for example members of the therapy professions, treated patients on any of the four wards.

One of the jobs to be *formally* redesigned was that of the traditional ward sister. As a direct result of the organisational change programme this role no longer existed, having been replaced by Team Leaders. These newly created roles incorporated new job descriptions, which

Case Study continued

saw an extension in the roles and responsibilities beyond nursing itself and into the realms of middle management. In addition, a new role of Support Worker was added to the team, which nursing and therapy assistants had been encouraged to apply for. Underpinning this new Support Worker role was the introduction of a hospital-led training programme. This programme had a number of objectives. It was anticipated that by improving the support worker knowledge base the continuity of care, and handling and rehabilitation of the patient would be enhanced. In addition, the blurring of professional boundaries through the newly trained support workers role enhanced skill mix on the unit through providing some therapy intervention at weekends and promoting rehabilitation outside of formal treatment sessions. To further the concept of a skill-enhanced support worker, an in-house competency-based training package was developed, based on the National Vocational Qualification system. This centred on basic nursing, physiotherapy and occupational therapy skills which included dressing practice, wound care and simple exercise regimes. This specifically designed package allowed the support worker to concentrate on skills related to rehabilitation and allowed them to obtain a recognised in-house award – the one incentive they had received for taking on the new role.

Other than this the traditional team-based nursing existed. That is, nurses, including the support workers, were organised into teams comprising a mix of seniority and skill. Each team had responsibility for the welfare of a fixed number of patients. As far as possible the workload was organised such that patient allocation was based in bays. Each team took on the workload of two bays and a set number of side rooms.

Although attached to the ward through secondment, the physiotherapists and occupational therapists were actually based in their own departments in another part of the hospital. Located within their own small teams, both professions worked on the wards and in the gymnasium adjacent to the wards on a daily basis and for much of the day. The nature of the musculoskeletal work was such that the therapy professions were heavily involved in the treatment and recovery of the patients. To this end, a new initiative introduced by management had been the introduction of newly designated therapy treatment rooms within the confines of the musculoskeletal unit. This provided them with their own base close to the ward setting from where they could treat patients without taking them to their main department elsewhere in the hospital.

A further new initiative had involved the use of multiskilling. Professionals had been encouraged to identify tasks that could be 'shared' in order to enhance the treatment of the patient and speed up recovery. An example of this was the introduction of nurses being allowed to supervise exercise regimes on the wards – a role which had previously been performed by the physiotherapists. Another example was the ability of the nurses to assess patients attempting the stairs post-operatively – a pre-requisite for being discharged. Again, this had previously been under the umbrella of the physiotherapists.

The organisational change programme had brought about significant improvement in patient care in terms of level of care, patient recovery, theatre waiting times and increases in bed occupancy. The health professionals themselves, however, portrayed a mixed response to what was happening around them. For the most senior nurses, acceptance of change was more evident in those who experienced a sense of enrichment in their roles which tended to be confined to those whose jobs had been formally redesigned. For the nurse, the higher up the hierarchical ladder, the more upbeat and positive the attitude to change. For the more junior nurses, there was evidence of increases in workload among those whose jobs had not changed following the restructuring, but who were experiencing changes in role as a result of changes in the nursing hierarchy. In addition, increases in tasks and task variety were seen as intensification

Case Study continued

of work rather than increases in job satisfaction. Lack of recognition of this work intensification was often cited as a major concern. The new support worker role had provided variation and increases in scope of practice for nursing and physiotherapy assistants, but other than an in-house qualification had failed to provide little incentive for the role to succeed.

In spite of concerns over the intensification of work the nurses viewed the issue of multi-skilling more positively than the therapy professions. Much was made of the benefits to patients through providing a more comprehensive level of care and enhancing their own skill base. The therapy professions, although pleased with the management initiative of providing on-site treatment facilities, demonstrated a real of fear of losing their skills to other professions and viewed the whole process of multiskilling as 'deskilling'.

Activity 5.5

1 Discuss how expectancy theory and equity theory contribute to the understanding of the situation described above for the:

   a) team leader
   b) nurses
   c) support worker
   d) therapy professions

2 What are the implications for management in dealing with the situation?

3 How can management enhance the commitment of the professionals to the change process?

SUMMARY

In this chapter the following key points have been made:

- There are two contrasting approaches to the theory of work motivation
- Content or need theories are based on the assumption that psychological needs lie behind human behaviour
- Process theories concentrate on the cognitive process of determining levels of motivation
- Fairness and justice are becoming more prominent in organisational life
- The setting of goals that are specific, achievable yet sufficiently difficult can often improve a person's work performance
- An individual's role and job can affect how they experience work and achieve satisfaction
- The psychological contract is based on a series of assumptions and is an important element in the employer–employee relationship
- Individuals can have multiple commitments in the workplace
- Organisational commitment is encouraged by positive experiences at work

DISCUSSION QUESTIONS

1 What are the differences between content and process theories of motivation? Outline and discuss the main motivational theories.

2 How far can management 'assume' a well-motivated, fully committed workforce?

3 Discuss the various considerations that a human resources manager would have to make when redesigning work and introducing new roles into the organisation.

FURTHER READING

Students seeking further detail on the issues raised in this chapter should consult Arnold *et al*. (1998), Fincham and Rhodes (1999) or McClelland (1999).

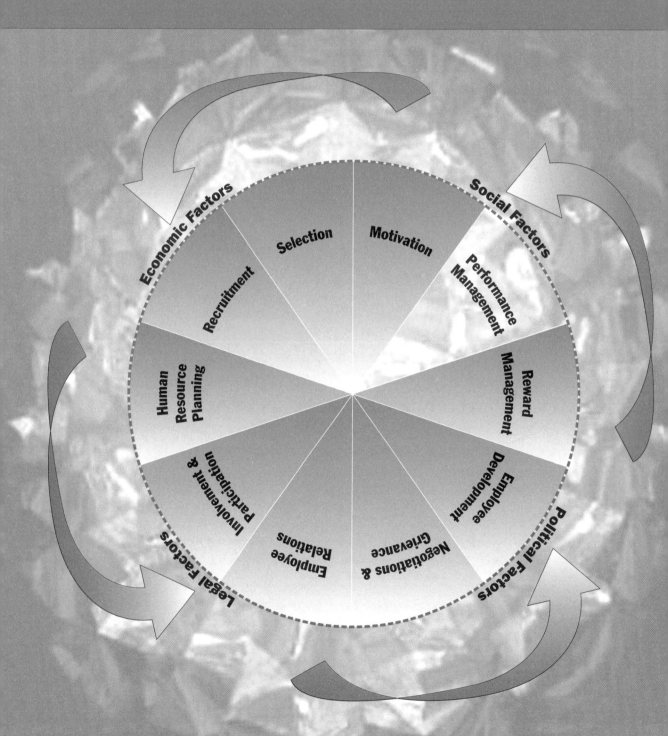

Having completed this chapter and its associated activities, readers should be able to:

- understand the purpose and process of performance management
- describe the 'paradox' inherent in the performance management process
- understand the role of performance appraisal within the process of performance management
- understand the formal and informal components of performance management
- describe various approaches to performance management, and the advantages and disadvantages of each
- understand the reasons for resistance to performance management methods
- appreciate the complexities in dealing with the outcomes of the performance management process
- understand the need for an ethical approach to performance management

INTRODUCTION

External forces such as competition, regulation and other environmental factors all impact on organisational performance. It is generally agreed, however, that the behaviour and quality of employees within the organisation have a fundamentally important effect on organisational performance. Much of the managerial discourse asserts that organisational goals are largely achieved through the effort of employees, and if employee performance is improved, the organisation will in turn be more productive. Performance management can thus be defined as the policies, procedures and practices that focus on employee performance as a means of fulfilling organisational goals and objectives.

Despite the perception that performance management is a necessary managerial function, it is often a problematic process. Managers are typically loath to pass judgement on employees, employees often report that the process of having their performance appraised is a futile exercise, and HRM practitioners are sometimes inclined to see the process as a laborious administrative chore. Why then is performance management so widely practised? Some theorists (for example, Barlow, 1989; Fisher, 1999) have presented the view that the process of performance management is merely a means of achieving an illusion of control. They argue that the processes of measuring, monitoring and evaluating performance gives the *appearance* of management control. The extent to which the control aspect of the performance management process is 'illusional' is debatable. Figure 6.1 clearly shows how performance management can be a powerful form of controlling employee behaviours to bring them in line with organisational goal attainment.

Hendry, Woodward, Bradley and Perkins (2000) assert that control-based performance management systems serve to undermine rather than contribute to

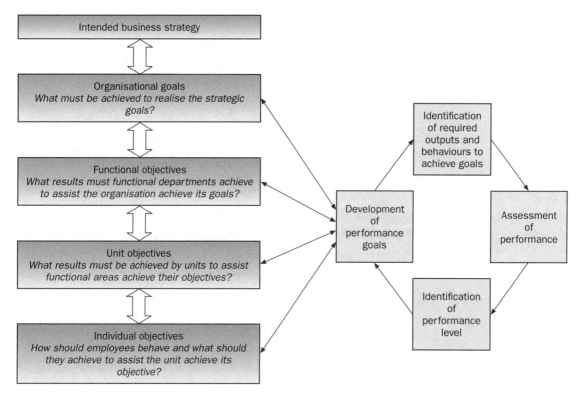

Figure 6.1 A model of performance management

performance, and they go on to present a cogent plea for a strong developmental approach to the performance management process. It can be argued that in recent times there has been an attempt to lessen the 'control' aspect of performance management, and to emphasise the developmental aspect of the performance management process. We have witnessed a move away from simplistic 'trait' methods of performance appraisal and a movement towards methods that provide more elaborate and detailed feedback, and that emphasise future tasks and goal achievement (these different systems are described in sections of this chapter).

Despite the move towards developmental performance management, the tension between performance management as a controlling/judgemental process and as a supportive/developmental process is still a contentious issue and is likely to stay topical for some time.

Leaving such debates aside, there are a number of specific uses and applications related to performance management:

- *Strategic link* – facilitates the setting of individual objectives which support achieving the business strategy
- *Performance measurement* – it establishes the relative value of an employee's contribution to the organisation
- *Training and development* – it identifies performance deficiencies and thus highlights training needs

- *Rewards and benefits* – it helps determine appropriate pay for performance and equitable salary and bonus incentives based on merit or results
- *Human resource planning* – it provides information which assists in succession and career planning
- *Communications* – may facilitate a dialogue between employees and management

In addition to the functional uses of performance management outlined above, the process of performance management can be a powerful motivating tool for employees. For example, performance management involves significant feedback on performance. Positive feedback typically has a motivating effect, yet even negative feedback, *as long as it is constructive,* can serve to provide employees with clear directions for improved performance that in turn may also positively affect motivation. Linked into the provision of feedback are the notions of recognition and reinforcement, both of which have strong motivational value. Performance management also provides the opportunity for growth and development, through the drawing up of personal development plans. Given the motivational value of feedback provision, reinforcement and growth opportunities, theorists argue (see, for example, Rudman, 1995; Armstrong, 1996) that performance management should be a continuous process, rather than an annual event. Employees should receive ongoing feedback and reinforcement, as well as ongoing opportunities for development.

The chapter opens with a discussion of some of the complexities associated with the performance management process. This is followed by an examination of formal and informal methods of performance management and their appropriate applications. Different types of performance appraisal methods are then outlined, and the advantages and disadvantages of each method are discussed. This is followed by a discussion of the management of ineffective performance, and finally, ethical issues associated with performance management are discussed.

Performance management: system or process?

A common criticism of performance management is that it is characterised by rigid, bureaucratic 'top-down' *systems,* imposed by management who are seeking simple solutions to complex problems. As Armstrong (2000) correctly asserts, a better way of conceptualising performance management is as a *process.* Conceptualised in this way, performance management can become a flexible, continuous and evolutionary process, more suited to contemporary organisational structures. Viewing performance management as a process involves a move away from the traditional 'top-down' approach, and paves the way for a more 'upwardly-managed' approach.

Conflicts associated with performance management

As with most practices associated with managing the employment relationship, the process of performance management is complex, largely due to the different interests and concerns of the parties involved.

One conflict arises from the fact that organisations and employees have different goals: employees are seeking reassurance, reinforcement, as well as additional rewards, while the organisation wants to monitor output, and wants employees to accept constructive criticism in order to improve performance. Winstanley (2000: 189) sums up the situation neatly:

> At the nub of the performance management paradox is the pursuance of a dual and contradictory approach to performance management. Employees are treated as intrinsically valuable, self-actualising individuals and the organisation provides an arena in which their developmental potential can be realised. At the same time the organisation pursues conditions of worth approaches, which require constant evaluation, grading, classification and measurement and individuals are subjected to systems which constantly remind them of their contingent relationship with the organisation.

Another conflict arises in the fact that performance management requires a dual role from managers since they are required to be both *judge* and *helper*. It is difficult for managers to perform these roles simultaneously. When the aim of the process is appraisal, the system provides a means for managers to make long-term decisions (for example, regarding promotion) and short-term decisions (related to pay, for example) associated with an employee. This is a potentially adversarial role, which may impact negatively on the developmental objectives of the performance management system. The manager's role as coach and helper involves different communication processes and skills to that of communicating a set of appraisal decisions.

The conflicting roles of management as both judge and helper has led some theorists to argue that performance management systems should be restricted to performance matters, and not extended to training, career decisions, remuneration decisions and other areas of human resource management. Some organisations address this issue by designing separate systems for *appraisal* and *development,* or alternatively, by conducting separate appraisal and developmental reviews at different times.

Formal and informal performance management processes

From the discussion so far, we can ascertain a number of clear functions of the performance management process. First, it can provide a means of 'measuring' the employee's effectiveness on the job. Second, it can identify areas where the employee is in need of training. Third, it can maintain and improve motivation through feedback and the setting of specific goals on the basis of this feedback.

Large or complex organisations will almost certainly require a formal performance management process to provide adequate 'data' for workplace planning and to assist employee development. As Armstrong (2000) notes, formal performance reviews provide a strong focus on motivational, performance and developmental issues. Key questions that can be answered from the formal review process are 'Where have we got to?' and 'Where are we going?' (Armstrong, 2000: 70).

Formal performance management processes tend to involve a series of steps as outlined below:

1 A performance 'agreement' is established with the employee. This agreement is linked to the business plan.
2 Performance data is gathered and measured via a specific appraisal methodology (for example, either a results-oriented approach or a competency-based approach, both of which are discussed later in this chapter).
3 Performance is reviewed via a formal appraisal interview, where performance 'data' is analysed and discussed.
4 Feedback is provided to the employee.
5 Depending on the outcomes of the performance management process, pay or development needs (or both) are addressed.

There are numerous advantages in having a formal performance management process. First, they are less subject to personal bias if properly developed and implemented. A related feature is that they can provide more comprehensive and accurate information regarding employee performance and potential. This is especially useful as a means of providing an information base for workforce, career and succession planning decisions. Another advantage is that formal performance management methods can assist less skilful or inexperienced managers, since the process is structured for them. One often cited although contentious advantage is that formal performance management systems give the *appearance* of being fair and objective. Arguably, they should not just *appear* to be fair, they should in fact be designed with fairness and equity as major concerns. Finally, formal processes provide a neat way of assembling large amounts of performance-related information in large and complex organisations.

There are, however, some disadvantages associated with formal systems. They can become cumbersome, complex and time-consuming to administer, and, similarly, they may become overly formal and bureaucratic. There may be time delays in 'follow-up' that can serve to undermine the process. Formal systems may also be misused; for example, they may be viewed entirely as an administrative 'chore' or record-keeping function. Finally, it is sometimes difficult to adapt and change one formal performance management system for another one. This is an important issue given the pace of change in organisations and the need for considerable flexibility in organisational direction and resultant policies.

Performance management need not be confined to a formal interview whereby a manager discusses the extent to which specific and agreed performance standards are being met. Rather, performance management may also be an *informal process*.

Informal performance management methods are more usually found in small organisations, partly because day-to-day communications with employees is easier than in large organisations. However, size of the organisation is not the only factor to consider when choosing between informal or formal performance management methods. On important consideration is the desired output of the process. For example, if there are few opportunities for promotion of career development, or if the organisation operates in a highly erratic and unpredictable industry, then an informal system may be more appropriate. The context just described is not really suitable for a formal system since it may provide information that cannot be utilised and creates unrealistic expectations in the minds of employees.

As with formal processes, there are certain advantages and disadvantages to informal performance management methods. One advantage is that informal appraisal promotes more personal contact and opens communication channels between managers and employees. Also, there is a sense of immediacy with informal appraisal since appraisal and feedback occur almost simultaneously. Another advantage of informal performance management is that it is more flexible since it is not constrained by guidelines and procedures. A related feature is that it is cheaper and more easily carried out. Finally, informal performance management methods are highly suited for small organisations where it is possible to maintain sufficient contact with all employees.

The disadvantage of informal performance management systems include the possibility that informal methods may be too subjective and biased, and too dependant on the individual appraiser. Similarly, there are fewer checks in informal systems, to ensure objectivity and honesty. Informal methods may not be comprehensive enough, and the appraiser may forget certain items without a record of what to do. Finally, it is much more difficult to check if it is being properly carried out.

It could be argued that organisations should have both formal and informal systems of performance management running concurrently. In essence, the performance management process should be a continuous process, and the use of informal assessment alongside more formal methods help to maintain the momentum of ongoing performance management.

Case Study 6.1

Appraisal and performance

'Hello Clare,' greeted team leader Gerard Greene. 'Could you possibly meet me in my office in ten minutes before you go home? Your annual performance appraisal has to be done today. Shouldn't take long.'

Clare had not been previously informed that the performance appraisal was due. Nevertheless, she was now keen to have the meeting with her team leader, as she had lately been thinking that she would like to revise some of her performance goals. Additionally, Clare, who was by nature a 'perfectionist', had been a little concerned of late that her performance was not up to her usual standard, and she was a little anxious to get some feedback and clarify her situation.

Clare arrived punctually at the team leader's office at the requested time. She arrived to find Gerard madly rushing to finish last-minute tasks. 'Oh Clare, I've completed your appraisal, have a look at it and sign it. I've actually given you excellent ratings on all the factors, but everyone received top ratings this year. I was really pleased with the way that the team worked together in order to get the Sheffield order out this month. That order was incredibly important to us. I have nothing more to add other than keep up the good work.'

Clare could tell that Gerard was really busy and flustered. She looked over the appraisal and signed it, and then left so as not to interfere with Gerard's last-minute activities. As she left her team leader's office, Clare felt disappointed with the interview.

Performance management and appraisal

A central component of an organisation's performance management system is the process of performance appraisal. This tends to be a formal procedure that consists of systematic and scheduled performance reviews accompanied by appraisal interviews. There are numerous performance appraisal methods, and a number of these are discussed below. However, before going on to explore the different appraisal methods, we will consider how the choice of appraiser may impact on the appraisal process.

Different people at various 'levels' of the organisation may carry out performance appraisal:

- an employee's manager
- self-appraisal
- peers
- subordinates
- person(s) outside the employee's immediate work environment
- a combination of the above, termed 360-degree appraisal or multi-source feedback, both of which are discussed later in this chapter

Manager

Manager-conducted appraisal can potentially strengthen the work relationship between manager and employee but not all managers have the necessary interpersonal skills. However, an unfavourable appraisal may prejudice future work relations. Another disadvantage is that the manager may be too removed from employees' environment to be able accurately to gauge actual work performance.

Self

Self-assessment is suitable for employees in jobs with a high level of autonomy, or who work in isolated areas, or for employees with rarely held skills. It usually needs to be combined with another form of assessment. Another advantage is that it obviously involves employees directly in the appraisal process. However, self-assessment may be difficult to control and co-ordinate and may be abused if strongly linked to rewards and promotion. Another problem is that studies suggest low correlation with assessment by supervisors, and research findings indicate that there is significant gender effect in self-assessment whereby women tend to rate themselves lower than do men.

Peers

Work colleagues and group members are well acquainted with the employees' work behaviours and outputs, and thus can provide a valuable source of assessment. In this way, multiple assessments are obtained which may increase objectivity and fairness.

Peer assessment is suitable for jobs where managers cannot readily determine work outputs or observe on-job behaviour. However, this method is not suited to highly competitive work situations. Other problems include the fact that it is time-consuming, and employees may see it as a means of dividing them.

Subordinates

Subordinate assessment may assist in manager and supervisor self-development. Managers and supervisors are provided with direct feedback and the averaging of several judgements is more impartial. However, employees may feel threatened by having to assess their boss, and managers may feel they are being undermined. Additionally, employees may assess only according to how their manager meets their own needs. Finally, like other multi-source feedback methods, this form of 'upward' appraisal can be time-consuming.

Outside assessors

The use of outside assessors (through the use of consultants or assessment centres) provides a measure of impartiality. An advantage of this is that there is less chance of future work relationships being affected. It is suited to the selection of staff for future development. However, it should be borne in mind that external assessors are likely to have insufficient knowledge of or contact with the employee, and that such methods are costly. In addition the use of outside assessors may encourage managers to ignore an important part of their job, namely provision of communication, feedback and motivation.

Types of performance management methods

Over the years numerous types of appraisal methods have been established, ranging from trait methods and simple ranking systems through to more complex and sophisticated techniques. In this chapter we will outline and critique the following appraisal methods:

- trait methods
- objective-based methods
- competency-based methods
- 360-degree appraisal.

Trait methods

Trait appraisals were an early form of appraisal method, popular in the 1970s. This method (sometimes called conventional rating) involves the listing of traits or 'attributes' that are rated on a continuum according to the extent to which the trait or attribute is present. An example of a trait-oriented system is provided in Figure 6.2.

Employee Name:			
Department:	Section:		Position:
Reporting Period:			
Rating Key: a = superior	b = above average		c = average
d = below average	e = unsatisfactory		

1. Ability to adapt a b c d e	2. Diligence and application a b c d e
3. Co-operation with others a b c d e	4. Quality of work a b c d e
5. Communication skills a b c d e	6. Leadership a b c d e
7. Planning a b c d e	8. Manner and appearance a b c d e
9. Loyalty a b c d e	10. Initiative a b c d e

Figure 6.2 Example of a trait-oriented performance appraisal rating

While trait appraisal systems are easy to develop, they are problematic and have greatly declined in use as a result. In fact, this system is being highlighted in this chapter as the sort of system that you would *not* want to design or implement. A major problem with such systems is that traits are often aspects of personality which have little bearing on the nature of the job being performed. Traits such as 'ability to adapt' and 'initiative' can be ambiguous terms with highly subjective interpretations. Trait-oriented systems have tended to be used across jobs and departments, yet for appraisal to be meaningful and to impact on performance, feedback should be related to specific aspects of an employee's job. Another problem is that trait rating systems are subject to error, notably error associated with leniency, strictness, central tendency and the halo effect. Leniency occurs when appraisers tend to give all employees favourable ratings, while strictness is just the opposite. Central tendency represents a tendency to evaluate all employees as average, while halo error occurs when a high rating on one factor considered important by the appraiser 'contaminates' the other factor ratings for that employee.

Trait systems are also criticised because they cannot be used for developmental purposes. While they may indicate 'trait deficiencies', they do not indicate to employees how improvement may occur, and are thus of little use for development purposes.

It can be demonstrated then, that trait systems are seriously flawed. Over the years commentators have argued cogently against such systems (see, for example, Latham and Wexley, 1981). The following quote from Drucker (1974: 25) neatly sums up the flawed nature of trait systems:

> An employer has no business with an employee's personality. Employment is a specific contract calling for specific performance, and for nothing else. Any attempt of an employer to go beyond this is usurpation . . . it is abuse of power. An employee owes no 'loyalty', no 'love' and no 'attitudes' – an employee owes performance and nothing else . . . Management should concern themselves with changes in behaviour likely to make an employee more effective.

Objective-based methods

As a reaction against the limitations and flawed nature of trait systems, and in a bid to more closely link employee behaviour with organisational goals, performance appraisal has become more concerned with behaviours, outputs and goal attainment. An early form of this approach was 'Management by Objectives' (MBO). Under this approach, organisational targets were translated into 'sub-targets' throughout the organisational structure, so that managers and employees had a specific set of goals to achieve. The process of MBO involved managers and employees discussing the goals of the business unit as well as how the employee's job contributed to achievement of those goals. A time period would be set, and the manager and employee would (ideally) negotiate the goals to be achieved during the assessment period. At the end of the time period (and ideally at various stages throughout the assessment period), goal attainment would be reviewed, and new goals would be set for the next assessment period.

While the objective-based system is a vast improvement on earlier performance appraisal techniques such as trait systems, it does have its problems:

- The goals set may be short-term goals, and other long-term goals may be neglected.
- Goals may be set 'too low' so that success is ensured.
- Not all jobs have easily measureable objectives.
- Goal attainment may be affected by factors outside the locus of control of the employee. This could lead to low appraisal ratings when in fact the employee was performing effectively.
- It is difficult to make comparisons between different employees for the purpose of assessing grounds for promotion or pay increases.
- It may work against a team-based approach if individual goal attainment takes precedence over team goals.
- Desirable behaviour (for example, innovation) which does not impact on goal attainment may be discouraged.
- There is too much emphasis on outcome (results) rather than on process (*how* the job is carried out).

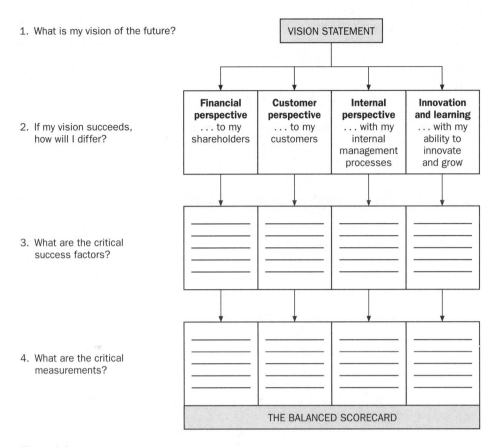

1. What is my vision of the future?

VISION STATEMENT

2. If my vision succeeds, how will I differ?

| **Financial perspective** ... to my shareholders | **Customer perspective** ... to my customers | **Internal perspective** ... with my internal management processes | **Innovation and learning** ... with my ability to innovate and grow |

3. What are the critical success factors?

4. What are the critical measurements?

THE BALANCED SCORECARD

Figure 6.3 The balanced scorecard

Source: Adapted from Kaplan and Norton (1993: 139)

A more recent objective-based approach is the 'Balanced Scorecard' method first proposed by Kaplan and Norton (1992). This method is essentially a management system that utilises a 'stakeholder' approach to performance management. Four different perspectives are incorporated into the balanced scorecard approach: financial, customer, internal business and innovation and learning. The system thus extends beyond the traditional financial, short-term approach to performance management. The balanced scorecard approach is illustrated in Figure 6.3.

From Figure 6.3 there are four main steps in the balanced scorecard approach. First, the 'vision of the future' must be decided. This is followed by interpreting the vision and resultant competitive advantage from four different perspectives: shareholders, customers, internal management processes and ability to learn and develop. The third step involves the critical success factors that stem from these different perspectives. The fourth step involves the identification of critical measurements for determining how far the organisation is along the path to success.

While this system appears to be an *organisational* performance management system, it is increasingly being used as a means of assessing individual performance. Winstanley (2000) cites evidence from a UK bank, where the balanced scorecard has 'cascaded' into individual scorecards that are linked to group and organisational scorecards, representing a type of 'golden thread' linking organisational and individual performance.

Competency-based methods

In recent years there has been has a move away from performance management systems which rely exclusively on the achievement of quantifiable and measurable objectives and targets. The competency-based approach to performance management stresses the role of process: *how* a job is performed is seen as just as important as what outputs are achieved. The issue of how a job is performed is of particular importance in performance management within the service sector, where the process of quality service provision (which is difficult to measure in quantifiable terms) is paramount.

One method that lies within the competency approach is Behaviourally Anchored Rating Scales (BARS). There are various ways to devise these scales. However, the development of BARS usually includes the following steps:

- Instances of behaviours reflecting effective and ineffective performance are compiled by job experts.
- These examples are assembled into performance dimensions.

BEHAVIOURALLY ANCHORED RATING SCALE	
Job Title: Project Manager Job Dimension: Organising and conducting meetings	
EXCELLENT	1. Displays exceptional ability to assess the progress of a meeting and alter its sequence, pace or format quickly 2. Ensures there is mutual agreement among participants as to work to be done as a result of each meeting before it closes 3. Anticipates questions which will be asked during meetings. Provides clear, concise and accurate answers 4. Makes use of visual aids which are creative, interesting and enhance understanding of subject matter 5. Receives positive feedback during and after meetings
AVERAGE	1. Capable of conducting entire meeting. Makes adequate prior preparation 2. Shows some awareness of level of understanding by audience. Usually alters presentation if necessary to make allowance for this 3. Presents information clearly, concisely and unambiguously. Usually answers questions directly 4. Occasionally uses visual aids 5. Uses written agenda
UNSATISFACTORY	1. Finds it very hard to respond to level of understanding of audience. Sticks rigidly to same presentation and style 2. Fails to prepare for meetings 3. Unable to display link between actions and objectives 4. Finds it very hard to respond even to simple questions on status of work 5. Creates hostile environment by criticising members of audience openly 6. No use of written agenda or other documentation

Figure 6.4 A sample behaviourally anchored rating scale

- This process is repeated by a second group in order to check the validity of the process.
- The examples within each dimension are rated on a numerical scale.

With the BARs method, the rater must have substantial job knowledge. The system has potential for objectivity, and by providing specific examples of behaviour for each level of job performance, it is possible to be exacting about what constitutes effective job performance. Perhaps the main disadvantage of the system is its complexity, and the fact that it is a fairly costly and time-consuming method. An example of BARS is provided in Figure 6.4.

Activity 6.2

Design a BARS performance appraisal instrument that assesses and rates the performance of lecturers at your university.

360-degree methods

So far we have reviewed forms of performance management that all involve a 'top-down' approach. An obvious problem with such approaches is that they rely solely on the evaluation of one person, moreover, that person has considerably more power than does the employee being appraised. By using a variety of sources to evaluate performance, the process of performance management becomes more informed, valid and convincing. Turnow (1993) states that 360-degree appraisal rests on two main assumptions. First, our self-awareness is increased by the knowledge of discrepancies between how we see ourselves and how others view us. Second, enhanced self-awareness is necessary for improved performance and becomes a necessary foundation block for leadership and management development programmes.

360-degree appraisal methods basically involve an employee being rated by subordinates, peers, superiors and sometimes customers, as well as self-assessment.

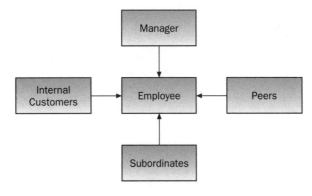

Figure 6.5 360-degree appraisal

Questionnaires are used to gather the data, interviews are rarely used in 360-degree appraisal. Assessments from the various sources are collected and then consolidated by a relevant third party (such as the HR manager or a consultant), and a profile of performance as seen by the different perspectives is prepared. This profile is relayed back to the target manager, and an appropriate action plan is designed which serves to deal with identified developmental needs. An example of some of the areas covered by a 360-degree appraisal questionnaire is provided in Table 6.1.

Multi-source feedback methods have represented a challenge to traditional hierarchical concepts of management, and more specifically a challenge to management's use of performance appraisal as a means of control. Perhaps for this reason, multi-source feedback methods have traditionally been less popular than other performance management methods. Nevertheless, Fletcher (2000) suggests that since the 1990s, 360-degree appraisal has increased in popularity in the UK, largely attributable to the decline in traditional notions of hierarchical management.

Obvious advantages of 360-degree schemes include the provision of high-quality feedback since the feedback stems from a variety of different sources. There is evidence to suggest that employees perceive greater fairness in 360-degree appraisal than in single rater systems. Greenberg and Lind (2000) report on findings whereby employees who were evaluated by multiple sources responded more positively than those who were evaluated only by their superiors. Specifically, employees evaluated by multiple sources expressed greater job satisfaction and commitment, and they felt that their appraisal was fairer than the employees expressed under a single source system. A related advantage is that employees are more likely to alter their work behaviour as a result of multi-source feedback. Finally, 360-degree appraisal indicates to employees that performance management is taken seriously by the organisation, and may contribute to a strong culture of development.

Disadvantages associated with 360-degree appraisal are related to the fact that it is fairly resource intensive, time-consuming and costly. Also, there is some debate as to whether such schemes should be related to pay (see, for example, Redman and Snape, 1992; Harris, 1999). On an individual level, employees may be hurt by significant negative feedback, and such instances must be handled sensitively.

Table 6.1 Sample headings used in 360-degree appraisal questionnaires

Leadership	Defined as: shares a clear vision and a focus on achieving it. Demonstrates commitment to the firm's mission. Provides direction and purpose, and inspires staff.
Team player/manage people	Defined as . . .
Self-management	Defined as . . .
Vision	Defined as . . .
Decision-making	Defined as . . .
Communication	Defined as . . .

Source: Adapted from Armstrong, M. (2000)

The management of ineffective performance

The issue of how to manage ineffective performance may seem somewhat negative and distasteful to some readers. Nevertheless, it is important to realise that the process of performance management will reveal some employees whose performance is adequate, some whose performance is outstanding and some whose performance may be ineffective. This section will focus mainly on the management of ineffective performance, since it is this issue that can be the most problematic.

The performance management process is incomplete if it identifies performance problems without attempting to fix them. Where performance has been identified as ineffective, a serious and thorough investigation is warranted. In overview, the main categories of ineffective performance include the following:

- unsatisfactory work (in terms of quality or quantity)
- personal problems affecting work behaviour and output
- violation of work-related rules

Before even contemplating 'punishment' of the employee or disciplinary action, the organisation must consider its role in such ineffective performance. For example, the organisation is responsible for selecting the employee for the job and for the design of training to equip the employee with the necessary skills. The following areas highlight the potential role of organisations in instances of ineffective performance.

Recruitment and selection

Problems in performance may arise if the needs of the job are not understood (such as in the case where a job is 'over-sold' at interview), or if the employee is over- or under-qualified. The selection procedure must be examined to ensure that job descriptions and selection criteria are accurate, and that the experience and skills of recruitment staff is appropriate (refer back to Chapters 3 and 4).

Promotion

Ineffective performance may occur where an employee has been over-promoted or promoted too quickly, or where an employee has been promoted into an unsuitable or 'disliked' position. Training and career development programmes should be examined, as should the supervision of the employee.

Conditions

A lack of equipment or resources, and unpleasant or unsafe conditions may also lead to ineffective performance. Inadequate or uncompetitive pay rates may also lead to sub-standard performance (see Chapter 7). Feedback should be sought from employees with regard to equipment and conditions, and the work environment should be monitored in terms of safety conditions. A review of the pay structure (for example, through marketplace surveys) will reveal any discrepancies in pay rates.

Communication and role negotiation

Problems in performance may arise if there is work role ambiguity and confusion. Job descriptions should be checked and communicated, and jobs should be clearly discussed with employees to alleviate any ambiguity (see Chapter 3).

Staffing levels

Work overload can also lead to ineffective performance. This is an important consideration after any down-sizing strategy.

Stress

Stress (either personal or work-related) can have a marked effect on performance. Where an employee is showing certain behavioural signs of stress, counselling may be necessary and any organisationally induced causes must be identified.

Work organisation

Poor supervision and problems of work flow may also lead to ineffective performance. Supervisors should be consulted and monitored, and in the case of workflow problems, jobs and work processes may need to be redesigned (see Chapter 5).

Case Study 6.2

Managing ineffective performance

David was a relatively new employee with an East Midlands textile firm. He showed promise right from the start, and after six months as an administrative assistant he was promoted to the position of Human Resources Manager. David's manager thought that he was an extremely capable 'star' employee, who could train himself on the job to do no matter what the position required. It came as a shock to David's manager when an HR audit conducted by a consulting firm revealed serious flaws in the way that David was implementing the firm's policies and procedures. The revelation occurred only three days before David's probationary performance appraisal interview. Discussion of David's 'performance problem' constituted the entire interview, and resulted in David's demotion with an extended probationary period. David left the interview devastated, and he contemplated resignation.

 Activity 6.3

How could David's ineffective performance be addressed more successfully?

Ethics and performance management

While performance management is typically viewed as a strategic management process aimed at increasing organisational effectiveness, it should not be forgotten that performance management involves the evaluation and assessment of *people*. The argument can be made that employees should be viewed as *resourceful humans* rather than 'human resources' (Hendry *et al.*, 2000: 47). Performance management should thus be a humanising process, not a process steeped in mechanical identification of 'predictors' or the measurement of quantifiable outputs. Winstanley and Stuart-Smith (1996) correctly argue that performance management should be carried out with certain ethical principles in mind. First, at all times of the process there should be respect for the individual. Employees should be treated as people who are 'ends in themselves' and not as 'means to an end'. Similarly, all parties involved in the performance management process should respect each other's needs, and mutual respect should underpin the process. Procedural fairness is another important aspect of an ethical approach to performance management. The procedures involved in the performance management system should be carried out fairly and in a just manner. Finally, there should be a level of transparency in the performance management process. Employees should be given the opportunity to scrutinise and appeal any performance-based decisions that are made.

SUMMARY

In this chapter the following key points have been made:

- Rather than just be an evaluation mechanism, performance management can be a powerful motivational and development tool.
- Performance management should be a continuous *process*, rather than a rigid and bureaucratic *system*.
- Formal and informal performance management processes are appropriate at different times and in different organisations. They can ideally be used in tandem in larger organisations.
- The choice of appraiser impacts on the performance management process. Different appraisers are appropriate according to the situation.
- Trait systems of appraisal are highly problematic due to their subjective and overly evaluative nature. Objective-based, competency-based, and multi-source feedback approaches are more recent innovations. While they do have certain disadvantages, they are preferred over the earlier 'attribute-focused' performance management systems.
- The management of ineffective performance deserves careful handling. Before any sort of disciplinary action is undertaken, management must conduct a thorough investigation of relevant factors, such as the organisational and work context, surrounding the identified under-performance.

- Employees should be viewed as 'resourceful humans' rather than 'human resources'. The process of performance management should thus demonstrate respect for the individual, and be carried out in a transparent and fair manner.

DISCUSSION QUESTIONS

1 Should small businesses have formal performance management systems?

2 Should appraisal be conducted for evaluation or development?

3 How do the questionnaire headings used in 360-degree appraisal differ from the attributes used in early trait systems?

4 Why do you think some managers resist the use of 360-degree appraisal?

5 Why are ethical issues associated with performance management important?

FURTHER READING

Students wishing to explore further some of the more specialist areas associated with performance management should consult Armstrong (2000) or Walters (1995). On the issue of ethics and performance management, students are directed to Winstanley (2000). Hendry *et al.* (2000) provides a comprehensive summary of the problems associated with performance management, and for an interesting and at times amusing critique of performance management systems, consult Fisher (1999).

Chapter 7 Reward management

Diannah Lowry

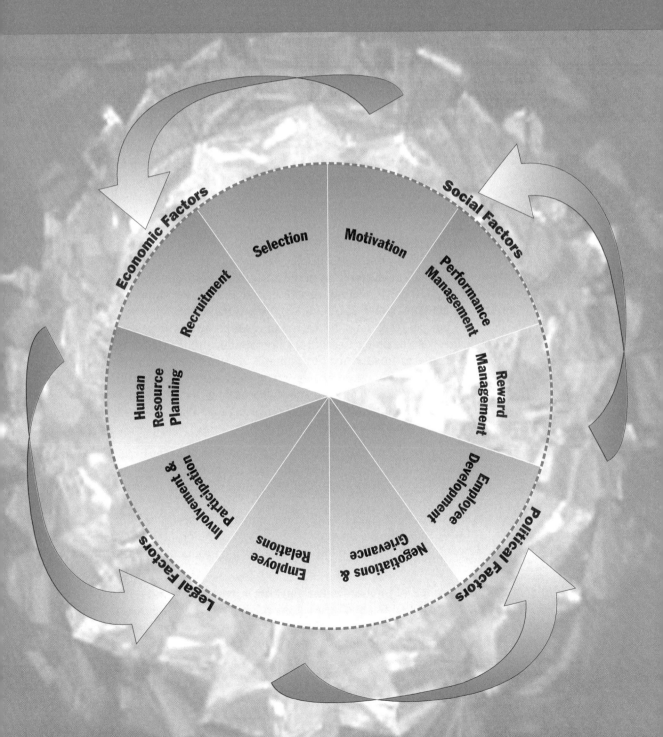

Having completed this chapter and its associated activities, readers should be able to:

- understand the purpose and components of a reward system
- appreciate the evolving nature of reward systems and the external factors which impact on organisational rewards
- outline some of the main theoretical perspectives and motivational theories underpinning notions of reward
- understand the broad dynamics that underlie the design of pay structures
- describe various forms of payment systems
- describe various forms of employee benefits
- appreciate the importance of communication, participation and employee involvement in the design of reward systems
- outline the broad activities and process of managing consultants who are employed by an organisation to design a reward system

INTRODUCTION

Work is a significant component of most people's lives. While some of us may be lucky enough to derive feelings of satisfaction and self-worth from the nature of our work activities (refer to Chapter 5), we are hardly likely to be fully satisfied if we are not paid well enough for the jobs we perform. All things being equal, people are likely to prefer to work for organisations that provide better rewards than others. As was mentioned in Chapter 3, reward is part of the trio of 'recruit, reward, retain'. On the surface, the design of adequate organisational reward seems simple enough. Yet, the creation of adequate reward systems that suit all employees is often a difficult and elusive task. The reasons for this are two-fold, involving both social and economic factors:

- Employees have certain expectations associated with both intrinsic and extrinsic rewards. For employees, rewards constitute a significant source of income and purchasing power, as well as social well-being. Employees thus usually seek to maximise rewards.
- Organisations have considerable concerns about the cost of reward systems and the impact of such systems on cost-effectiveness and profitability. Managers are thus consistently aiming to improve quality and productivity while controlling wage costs.

These two sets of interests must somehow be reconciled, and it is in this merging process that the design of reward systems becomes a complex activity.

The reward system is important in attracting and retaining employees who will assist the organisation achieve its goals. The reward system can have a significant

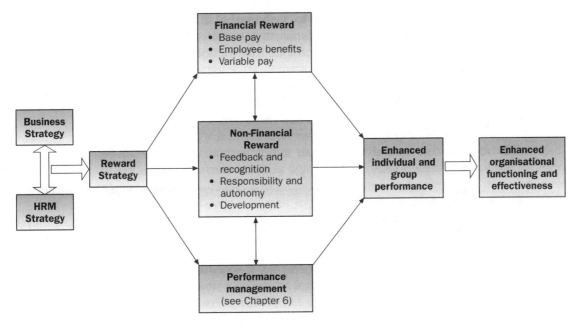

Figure 7.1 Reward system model

impact on the success of organisational change programmes and on the push to improve organisational performance.

Reward systems are composed of both financial rewards (often referred to as 'direct' or 'extrinsic' rewards) and non-financial rewards (often called 'indirect' or 'intrinsic' rewards). These are outlined in Figure 7.1 and are discussed in greater detail in a section below.

As with other HRM activities, the design of reward systems is affected by external considerations. Globalisation, increased competition and environmental uncertainty have resulted in significant organisational restructuring. Increasingly, reward systems are being designed to reflect such business and structural changes. Reward systems have thus changed dramatically over the last twenty years, and we are now witnessing what some theorists refer to as the 'new pay' (Lawler, 1995). The essential feature of 'new pay' is the linking of pay and business performance. According to Heery (1996), the 'new pay' is broadly characterised by the following:

- a heightened awareness of the need to link pay with business strategy
- the use of reward systems to reinforce flexible forms of organisation
- an emphasis on 'variable pay', in other words, pay that is contingent on performance or the acquisition of skills and competences. Variable pay is seen to realign employee interests with the interests of the organisation by providing workers with a financial stake in business success.

This chapter opens with a discussion of the elements of reward systems, then moves on to explore some of the relevant motivational theories that underpin the concept of reward. We then turn our attention to issues more closely aligned with financial or direct reward. The notion of pay structures is discussed, and different forms of pay structures are presented. This is followed by an examination of various pay systems. The chapter then turns to the issue of non-cash reward or 'employee benefits' as a component of reward systems. Issues related to communication and employee involvement in the design of reward systems are discussed, followed by a brief discussion on the use of consultants in the design of reward systems. Finally, the concept of integrated reward systems is examined.

Elements of reward systems

As indicated on Figure 7.1 above, reward systems are comprised of both financial and non-financial rewards. While financial rewards are of significant importance to most employees, the importance of non-financial rewards differ according to the orientation of the employee. For example, some employees regard the level of responsibility and autonomy of a job as intrinsically rewarding, while other employees would find very little attraction towards such job attributes. Likewise, some employees may find that job security is a form of intrinsic reward, while other employees feel comfortable with their 'mobility'. An important aspect in the design of reward systems is to achieve a certain balance between financial and non-financial rewards.

Financial rewards

These are sometimes referred to as 'direct' or 'extrinsic' rewards. There are various types of financial rewards that can make up a reward system:

- *Base pay* is the 'guaranteed' payment associated with a job, usually determined on a time basis (hourly, weekly, monthly or yearly).
- *Variable pay* is contingent on individual, group or organisational performance. It is defined strictly as pay that does not become a permanent part of base pay. In recent times there has been a growing emphasis on this variable pay system as a means of aligning employee interests with organisational strategy.
- *Employee benefits* consist of 'perks' such as company cars, pension schemes, child-minding facilities, private health insurance, holidays and stock options. Depending on the nature of the organisation, there is a vast array of benefits available.

Non-financial rewards

- Job satisfaction (satisfaction with the actual process and outcome of job-related activities) is perhaps one of the most important forms of intrinsic reward (refer to Chapter 5).
- *Feedback and recognition* are much under-emphasised in organisations, yet they are an important aspect of any reward package. Employees need to know that good work is viewed positively (refer to Chapter 6).
- For some employees, the presence of *responsibility* and *autonomy* in their jobs is a form of intrinsic reward.

- Security of employment can be a form of intrinsic reward, despite its obvious link to financial rewards.
- Development, both personal development and career development, are also important forms of intrinsic reward for many employees.

Motivation and reward

There are numerous theories that inform the design of reward management systems. Given the trend of organisations towards flatter structures and increased use of teamwork, reward should be considered at the group at organisational levels, rather than just at the individual level (Bartol and Durham, 2000). With this in mind, this chapter examines individual theories of motivation and reward as well as relevant organisational theories. The first three motivational theories discussed in this chapter have already been discussed in Chapter 5, while the remaining organisational level theories are covered in this chapter for the first time. It is suggested that you re-read the relevant sections in Chapter 5 if necessary.

Individual theories

Equity theory

According to equity theory (Adams, 1965), employees compare how much work they put into their job and the resultant outcomes (rewards) with the work effort and outcomes of other employees. Employees will then form judgements about the fairness of their own rewards. If employees perceive that their work effort and resultant rewards are basically equal, then the situation is perceived to be equitable. Perceived inequity will lead to tension, and employees are likely to try to reduce this tension. This is typically achieved by negative means such as reducing participation and involvement in the employment relationship. The dissatisfaction resulting from perceived inequity may even lead to absenteeism, sabotage, expressing hostility, and turnover.

A major implication of this theory is that organisations should seek positively to influence equity perceptions by exercising great care in the allocation of rewards. One way of achieving this is by giving employees some voice in the design of their reward management system. Additionally, it supports the idea that the reward system should be linked to the performance management system to ensure equitable reward allocation.

Expectancy theory

Expectancy theory (Vroom, 1964) suggests that workers will work better when they believe that they are capable of achieving the task at hand and when they are confident that valued rewards will result from their work effort.

The implication for reward systems is that the most motivating reward systems will be those that make clear linkages between performance and the rewards that employees really want.

Goal-setting theory

Goal-setting theory (Locke and Latham, 1990) states that specific difficult goals, together with feedback on performance, will lead to higher performance levels by focusing employees' attention, effort and persistence towards task achievement.

The implication for reward systems lies mainly in the design of the 'goal', and is particularly relevant in the case of some performance-related pay systems (covered in a section later in this chapter). While goals should be difficult, they should not be 'unattainable' or any effort to achieve them will appear futile to employees.

Organisational theories

Agency theory

You will recall from the introductory discussion that the issue of reward is a complex issue because of the divergent interests between employees and managers. Agency theory (Eisenhardt, 1989) focuses on the different interests between a principal (one who delegates work, a manager for example) and the agent (one who performs the work, or in other words, an employee), and seeks to 'align' such interests. A key question is seen to be 'How can agency costs be minimised?' Agency theory is thus concerned with determining the most efficient contract between a principal and agent. The theory states that the principal should choose a contracting scheme that serves to align the interests of the agent with the interests of the principal, in other words, one that reduces agency costs. Contracts can be classified as behaviour-orientated (for example, merit pay systems, dealt with in a section below) or alternatively, outcome-orientated (for example, gain-sharing and profit-sharing schemes, discussed later in this chapter).

Prospect theory

Prospect theory (Kahneman and Tversky, 1979) is a theory of decision-making under conditions of risk. Since few employees determine their own reward systems, the theory addresses how an employee evaluates and makes choices about plans that are either in place or are being modified in some way (such as when an employee is considering a new job, or is involved in organisational change programmes). The theory has been mainly applied to employee evaluations of 'at-risk' pay plans, where employee's base pay is reduced and supplemented by performance-based incentives. Essentially, the theory suggests that the likelihood of taking a risk depends on whether or not the alternative is viewed as a loss or gain. For example, when facing a pay system change, rather than consider 'What will my financial position be under this new system?', employees will ask 'How much more or less will I make than I do now?' The theory states that employees are likely to take a greater risk in preventing any loss of payment, and are likely to avoid risks that are associated with possible gain. Essentially, the theory states that loss aversion is greater than gain attraction. Furthermore, the theory suggests that over time employees adjust and become satisfied with existing pay arrangements, and thus become averse to losing any part of their reward package. Additionally, employees value what they possess more than an equally attractive alternative, so that equal trade is essentially unattractive. For any alternative to be acceptable, it must be perceived as superior to the existing situation (Bartol and Durham, 2000).

Institutional theory

This theory attempts to determine why organisations take the forms that they do. The theory posits that organisational design is not rational but emergent. Organisations respond to internal and external pressures in such a way that, over time, they will start to resemble each other. Four main reasons have been offered for this process. First, environmental forces such as government legislation and cultural expectations define responsible management and lead to accepted standards of management practice. Second, organisations tend to become similar through imitation and processes such as 'bench-marking', as well as through receiving similar advice from consultants. Third, the workforce is increasingly similar (especially in managerial ranks) due to participation in professional organisations and participation in similar professional training. Finally, once an organisational procedure (say as pay systems) is established, it seems to be somehow viewed as the only legitimate and acceptable way of getting things done. Institutional theory thus predicts that organisations in a given field are likely to employ similar pay practices in order to appear credible. The theory states that pay traditions have the potential significantly to inhibit economically rational thinking about what practices will lead to the best outcomes. Flying the 'new pay' banner, Bartol and Durham (2000: 13) thus conclude that the main principle to be drawn from this theory is:

> to the extent possible, organisations should avoid the trap of institutionalisation . . . this is not to suggest that organisations cannot learn from others' experiences and practices or that they should ignore employees' legitimate concerns, but rather that they should make well-considered choices that fit their individual strategies and cultures.

Case Study 7.1

Richard's dilemma: move or stay?

Richard is a 27-year-old Marketing Supervisor with Freightship, an established container shipping firm with headquarters in Suffolk and regional bases in Europe, the Middle East, Asia and Australia. Richard has worked with Freightship for the last five years, progressing quickly from a graduate 'entry-level' position to his present supervisory role. Over the last eighteen months, Richard has made intense efforts to develop his career further, mainly by participating in training, applying for promotion and by instigating numerous career development discussions with his manager. Senior management had always been very impressed with Richard's performance over the years, and regarded him as a 'star' performer. Despite Richard's reputation as an exceptional employee who was keen to take on further responsibilities, and despite his own efforts to move his career along, Richard seemed to hit a brick wall every time a potential career opportunity came along. He was consistently passed over for promotion and international transfers, and his requests for increased responsibilities were

Case Study continued

ignored. Management didn't seem to understand that Richard required further challenges and responsibilities as he developed within the organisation.

Richard gradually grew frustrated with the fact that no matter how well he performed, his efforts went apparently unnoticed. He started applying for jobs that offered greater development opportunities and rewards in other organisations around the country. An obvious 'star' performer, Richard's job-hunting efforts were successful and he was very soon offered a job as Marketing Director with a 'start-up' company in London that specialised in freight and storage. The job as Marketing Director involved a three-year contract, with contract renewal likely although contingent on performance.

The London job involved a much more creative and strategic role than Richard's job in Freightship, which was largely operational. As part of his new reward package, Richard was offered a base pay level 2 per cent less than his pay at Freightship, but with an additional variable component (based on performance) of up to 15 per cent. Performance rating would be determined and reviewed by senior management every six months. A company car was part of the package. Richard noted that the new company was a small company, and opportunities for further advancement were likely to be limited. Nevertheless, after careful consideration and negotiation on some minor points, Richard was satisfied with the reward package and he indicated that he would formally accept the position.

Unexpectedly, when Richard announced his intention of resignation to his manager at Freightship, a counter-offer was made within four hours. Freightship now offered Richard a promotion to Marketing Manager, with an increase in tasks and delegation responsibilities. A 5 per cent increase in base salary accompanied the promotion. At this point Richard had to think long and hard about which position to accept. The London job appeared exciting – a fresh start in a strategic and important role, a promotion in job title, not to mention the possibility of a significantly increased salary through the performance-based supplement. However, the Freightship counter-offer was also attractive. The increase in challenges and responsibility guaranteed further career progression and secure employment in an expanding company that Richard knew and understood. The base salary increase meant that Richard was assured of a pay increase. Additionally, the new role involved significant international travel, an aspect of the job that Richard greatly enjoyed. Importantly to Richard, the Freightship offer meant that he could stay in Suffolk and enjoy his house, friends, sport and lifestyle. The move to London would involve some element of upheaval, and the increased property prices and general cost of living in the London area would absorb any potential increase in salary.

After carefully weighing up the costs and benefits of each job, Richard decided to accept the Freightship counter-offer.

Activity 7.1

1 In the case study above, what role does reward play in employee attraction and retention?

2 Identify the extrinsic and intrinsic rewards in the case study.

3 Which of the individual and organisational motivational theories discussed in this chapter seem most applicable to the case study scenario outlined above?

4 Which job offer would you have accepted and why? What does this reveal to you about your own 'motivators'?

Financial reward: structures and systems

There are two main components in the design of financial reward. The pay structure relates to the pattern or structure of pay relationships. Pay systems, on the other hand, are the procedures involved in remunerating employees *within* the structure. Essentially, the pay system is a set of rules that link reward, effort and status.

Pay structures

Internal and external pay relationships are the two main considerations in designing pay structures. Both are concerned with the concept of fairness, identified earlier in the chapter as being closely related to motivational issues.

External pay relationships

Prior to examining internal pay relationships, the organisation will need to know its place in the marketplace with regard to appropriate pay levels. A number of factors impact on external pay relationships, these are broadly determined through market tracking and pay surveys:

- Government legislation impacts on levels of pay through the National Minimum Wage (NMW), the Equal Pay Act 1970 (as well as the Equal Value Regulations 1983). The NMW sets a minimum wage for different employee groups: adult workers, workers under the age of 21, and workers 'in training' over the age of 21 years (refer to Chapter 12). The Equal Pay Act and Equal Value Regulations prescribe that men and women should be paid the same rate of pay if they are doing broadly the same work.
- Macro-economic issues impact on pay through issues related to the supply and demand for labour (refer to Chapter 2). The state of the economy, unemployment levels, and the Retail Prices Index are all particularly relevant here. This is a complex area and a detailed discussion is beyond the scope of this book. Suffice to say that high unemployment usually means new staff can be recruited at lower rates, and is also likely to mean lower pay increases.
- The availability of skills can also affect pay. For example, skills shortages usually result in increased pay rates. We are currently witnessing this phenomenon in the information technology industry. In recent times employees in the IT industry have enjoyed rapid pay increases as the increased usage of technology and the rate of innovation has led to a high demand for appropriately skilled workers.
- Unions and their bargaining power also impact on pay levels (refer to Chapter 12). Some researchers have suggested that a strong union presence within an organisation leads to better pay outcomes for workers.
- Last but certainly not least, the ability of the organisation to pay is viewed by some as a fundamental issue in the design of pay structures. For example, a common managerial stance during union negotiations is to argue that the

organisation does not have the capacity for an increase in pay. It should be noted that this stance is fairly unconvincing if senior management are awarding themselves hefty pay increases. Nevertheless, some organisations (especially in the public sector) may experience genuine problems related to capacity to pay, especially when faced with limited external funding.

Activity 7.2

As mentioned above, government legislation impacts on levels of pay through the National Minimum Wage (NMW) which sets a minimum wage for different employee groups: adult workers, workers under the age of 21 and workers 'in training' over the age of 21 years.

Is it fair that workers under the age of 21 years are paid less? Give reasons for your response.

Internal pay relationships

Internal pay relationships are usually determined through a process of *job evaluation*, a procedure that attempts to make objective and systematic comparisons between jobs. Through the process of job evaluation, a hierarchy of jobs is formed. Job evaluation can be carried out using a number of different techniques, some more objective than others:

- *Job classification* – every job is classified into a grade using a specially prepared set of grading classifications. The grades are described in terms of such factors as experience required, supervisory issues and whether or not routine tasks constitute the job.
- *Job ranking* – jobs are basically ranked in order according to responsibility or skill level and level of responsibility
- *Factor-point systems* – each job is evaluated against a grid of factors and points. Factors include job-related descriptors such as 'problem-solving', 'complexity' and 'accountability'. This type of method aims for greater objectivity than the job ranking or job classification methods. Consultancies have developed fairly sophisticated factor-point systems, an example of one widely used factor-point system is the Hay Guide Chart-Profile.

After creating an internal job hierarchy through job evaluation, and after determining the external factors related to market position, a pay structure can be formulated. There are a number of different types of pay structures, each having specific characteristics that are rewarded in preference to others. *Graded pay structures* emphasise length of employment and hierarchical progression (see Figure 7.2). This type of structure is composed of a series of job grades, whereby jobs of equivalent value are fitted into the relevant grade.

As organisations pursue the 'Holy Grail' of flexibility, graded pay structures are increasingly being seen as rigid and overly hierarchical. A more flexible structure is found in *broad-banded pay structures*, where the number of grades is reduced

Figure 7.2 Traditional graded pay structure

and the pay range (band) is broadened. This type of structure facilitates overlap between different occupations and levels of responsibility, thus increasing job flexibility and providing employees with more opportunity for pay 'movement' or progression, as well as career development (see Figure 7.3). A recent study by the IPD (IPD, 2000a) indicates that broad-banding is widely practised and is increasing in popularity.

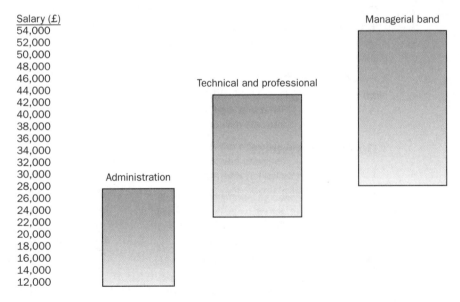

Figure 7.3 A broad-banded pay structure

Pay curves are another form of pay structure. Pay curves consist of different pay movement tracks depending on competence, skill, responsibility and performance. 'Exceptional' performing employees would be located on a higher pay curve than 'effective' employees (see Figure 7.4 overleaf)

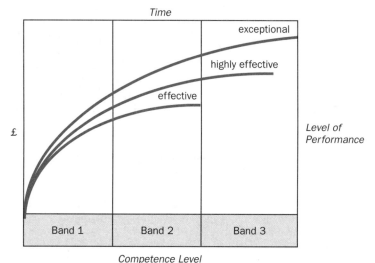

Figure 7.4 A pay curve

Pay systems

Pay systems are the processes involved in remunerating employees *within* the pay structure. Traditionally pay systems were more collectivist in nature, and involved 'natural' incremental progression along the pay structure. Employees were basically treated the same in terms of such pay progression. More recently, there has been a strong move to replace this collectivist approach with a more individualised focus. In essence we have witnessed a shift from job-based pay systems to performance-based pay systems. The main types of pay systems are outlined below. Each payment system can be used on its own or in conjunction with another.

Time-based systems

This is the traditional system of payment. The employee is paid by time, tradition-ally for hours of attendance, although it could be for attendance on a daily, weekly, monthly or yearly basis. Notions of management discipline and control and 'moral obligation' are relevant concepts here that assist to ensure that the employee puts in a fair day's work (Sisson and Storey, 2000). Advantages of time-based systems include their low administration costs, their ability to assist managers forecast labour costs, and the fact that such systems are easily understood by employees. A criticism of time-based systems, however, is that they provide little incentive for employees to improve productivity.

Competency and skill-based pay

Technically these are two different pay systems, but for the purposes of this chapter they are treated the same. Under these types of systems, the employee is paid for clearly identified skills (inputs) and competences (behaviours). Skill-based pay is often associated with an occupational standard, and can be linked to National Vocational Qualifications. Competency-based pay is a more recent system, and involves the formulation of specific competences related to employee behaviour and performance. There is a broad range of skills and competences that can be rewarded, ranging from 'soft' interpersonal skills and competences, to more technical skills and competences. A fundamental rationale underlying such systems is that employees are required continuously to develop and improve their work practices. In this way, skill-based and competence-based systems are thought to impact significantly on organisational competitiveness. There is some evidence to suggest that this type of pay system is increasing in popularity in the UK (Armstrong and Brown, 1998).

Individual (or group) performance-related pay

Performance-related pay systems (PRP) have proved increasingly popular over the last decade. Indeed, Harris (1999) has argued that the growth in PRP in recent years is perhaps the most significant development in the practice of HRM. According to a recent IPD survey, the growth of PRP is more marked in the private sector (*IPD Survey Report*, 1999b). In this chapter we will examine this reward strategy in some detail, given its popularity and increasing usage.

Performance-related pay strategies lie at the heart of the 'new pay' discussed in the introduction to this chapter. Increasingly competitive open markets have forced the adoption of human resource management strategies that clearly contribute to the enhancement of business performance. The fundamental assumption underlying PRP is that motivation and performance is increased by the contingent distribution of monetary incentives. Additionally, it has been argued that there is an element of fairness in such systems, on the grounds that employees who make the greatest contribution should be paid more. This last point is somewhat problematic and is discussed in more detail in a critique of PRP at the end of this section.

Under a PRP system, the employee is paid for either individual and/or group performance. Pay can be related to productivity as indicated by direct indices of performance associated with standards of productivity (for example, payment by financial results achieved through sales). This type of system is usually termed an 'incentive pay plan' and tends to be more objective in nature. Alternatively, PRP may involve a more subjective managerial assessment of the contribution made by an individual or group of employees. Merit pay plans and discretionary bonuses are examples of these forms of PRP. The rationale underlying PRP is simply that employees are likely to perform better if rewards are clearly attached to their performance. In overview, PRP systems aim to achieve a number of objectives:

● to motivate employees
● to direct attention toward organisational goals
● to change the culture of the organisation
● to deliver equitable rewards
● to emphasise individual work or teamwork as appropriate

Despite these ambitious objectives, PRP systems have proved over time to be somewhat problematic. Kohn (1993) argues that PRP fails to achieve its objectives since the psychological assumptions underlying such plans are inadequate. He argues that any benefit from PRP is essentially short-term compliance rather than commitment to organisational success, since extrinsic motivators such as pay fail to alter fundamental attitudes that underline behaviour. He also proposes that incentive systems treat symptoms rather than causes, in other words, PRP systems can become a substitute for effective management and leadership. Furthermore, Kohn argues that PRP systems act to reduce risk-taking, and since some PRP systems emphasise minimum standards of performance, they reinforce a rigid focus on behaviour. In this way, desired outcomes such as quality, creativity and individually motivated improvements are jeopardised.

In addition to the problems identified by Kohn above, there are also problems related to the use of PRP as both 'carrot and stick' (Harris, 1999; Hendry *et al.*, 2000). As discussed above, PRP rests on a number of assumptions related to its motivational value. One issue is that PRP is perceived to be fair since high performers should receive the highest reward. However, PRP seeks to motivate all workers, and raise performance *where performance needs to be raised*. A recent *IPD Survey Report* (1999b), however, shows that this is not entirely the case. Table 7.1 reveals that poor performers show the least change in their behaviour under a PRP scheme, followed closely by average performers.

Table 7.1 The effect of PRP on employee behaviour

	A large improvement %	A small improvement %	No real change %	A small deterioration %	A large deterioration %
High performers	27	44	28	0	0
Average performers	6	56	35	3	0
Poor performers	4	38	46	10	2

Note: Data shown is for private sector only.
Source: This material is taken from the Institute of Personnel and Development Survey Report 'Performance Pay Trends in the UK' (1999b) with permission of the publisher, the Chartered Institute of Personnel and Development, CIPD House, Camp Road, London SW19 4UX.

In addition to these findings, the 1999 IPD survey also revealed that the benefits in terms of improved performance were only slight (see Table 7.2). From the table it can be seen that PRP had very little impact on an employee's choice to remain within an organisation, and had little perceivable effect on facilitating organisational change. In addition, PRP had little effect on stimulating creativity and innovation (in keeping with Kohn's criticism), and slight effect on team-working (although it should be noted here that the data refers to individual performance-related pay, which is acknowledged to work at odds with team-based structures).

Table 7.2 The impact of individual performance-related pay

	A large improvement %	A small improvement %	No real change %	A small deterioration %	A large deterioration %
Employee performance	19	61	20	0	0
Employee willingness to stay with the organisation	7	34	54	5	0
Facilitating change within the organisation	15	31	50	3	1
Encouraging employees to suggest improvements and innovations	6	27	64	3	1
Effective team working	4	27	58	10	1

Note: Data shown is for private sector only.
Source: This material is taken from the Institute of Personnel and Development Survey Report 'Performance Pay Trends in the UK' (1999b) with permission of the publisher, the Chartered Institute of Personnel and Development, CIPD House, Camp Road, London SW19 4UX.

Thus, despite the immense popularity of PRP systems, it is worth noting that there is a lack of empirical support for PRP. Critical research has demonstrated that PRP may make a minority of employees work more intensively, but that morale and work relationships may suffer.

Organisational performance pay

Employees can also be rewarded for organisational performance. The goal of such pay systems is to merge the interests of employees with the performance of the organisation by sharing in some portion of the profits made, or, alternatively, in the reduction of costs. Profit-sharing schemes and gain-sharing are two main types of organisational performance pay. Recent governments have sought to encourage adoption of profit-sharing schemes through making them tax efficient for both the employee and the organisation. Under profit-sharing systems, a proportion of the organisation's pre-tax profits is paid to employees. Gain-sharing involves the payment of bonuses (usually on a quarterly basis) depending on the financial gains achieved by the organisation's improved performance. Unlike profit-sharing which uses the organisational-level performance measure of profits, gain-sharing programmes measure group or plant performance, which are likely to be seen as more controllable by employees. An advantage of gain-sharing is improved communication and problem-solving, since employees need to be kept constantly informed on relevant performance and goal achievement.

One of the disadvantages of organisational performance pay schemes, particularly with profit-sharing, is that they can be complex and difficult for employees to understand. Additionally, some factors are thought to moderate the effect of reward under such schemes. For example, the extent to which employees desire participation and the position of employees in the hierarchy of the organisation will impact on the motivational value of reward under organisational performance pay systems.

Employee benefits

Employee benefits are the components of a reward package provided in addition to cash pay. Benefits can impact on employee attraction, retention and motivation. While benefits used to be associated more closely with salaried (non-manual) workers, recent moves towards 'single status reward schemes' (created in order to merge the employment conditions of manual and white-collar employees) have meant that employee benefits are an increasingly common component of a total reward management system. Armstrong (1996) notes that employee benefits can be deferred or contingent, or immediate. Deferred or contingent benefits include pension schemes, sick pay and medical insurance. Immediate benefits include a company car or a loan.

There are three main categories of benefits for employees:

- *'Welfare' benefits* consist of health insurance, prolonged disability schemes, life assurance, pensions and sick pay.
- *Family-friendly benefits* are becoming increasingly common as awareness is raised on the importance of maintaining a healthy balance between family and work demands. Family-leave policies and child-care traditionally constitute such benefits packages. For example, compassionate leave, maternity and paternity leave, as well as the provision of child-care vouchers and creches are specific components of family-friendly benefits.
- *Job-related benefits* may include such things as a company car, relocation allowances and protective clothing allowances, as well as company discounts. There are a vast variety of possible benefits in this category, depending on the nature of the job and organisation.

In recent times there has been a shift to 'flexible benefits'. With flexible benefits, employees choose their benefits while the fixed total cost of remuneration is maintained. Employees can have either a choice within benefits or between benefits, and can thus choose benefits that suit their personal needs and other obligations. One of the main advantages of flexible benefits is that the requirements of different sections of the workforce can be catered for, for example, older and married employees will have different benefit preferences from young single employees. Also, motivational theory instructs us that it makes sense to provide benefits that employees consider to be valuable. A disadvantage of flexible benefits is the complexity and administrative load that accompanies them.

According to Armstrong (1996), it is essential to use professional advice in the setting up of a flexible benefit scheme, given the technical nature of flexible remuneration and the possible tax implications. The use of management consultants is dealt with shortly in a section below.

Communication, employee involvement and participation in reward systems

Armstrong (1996) correctly asserts that reward systems convey two messages to employees: how an employee's contribution is valued; what an employee is being paid for. Reward systems must be felt to be fair by employees, or they will have a de-motivating rather than a motivating effect. It is thus important to communicate to employees about the organisation's reward policies and practices, and how those policies affect them. Employees should clearly understand the pay structure and the benefits structure, and how pay progresses within the structure. They should have a good understanding as well of the methods of grading and regrading jobs, for example, employees should have some knowledge of the job evaluation scheme in operation. Employees should also clearly understand how any performance-based pay systems or competency-based system works.

Importantly, however, the communication process should not just be 'top-down'. Employees should be actively involved in the decision-making processes associated with the development of reward systems and policies. This can be achieved through the use of project teams and working parties. Trade unions and their representatives should play a role in the consultation process (refer to Chapter 12). Their views should be sought well in advance of any reward system implementation, and they should be involved throughout all stages of the development of the reward programme.

The use of management consultants in the design of reward systems

As the design and development of appropriate reward structures and systems becomes an increasingly specialised task, management consultants are frequently utilised. They can provide specialist expertise and additional resources in the introduction of new pay structures, pay systems and benefit schemes, and can provide an 'independent' means of conducting diagnostic reviews and evaluations of existing reward systems.

Armstrong (1996: 396) proposes that it is necessary to perform the following activities related to the use of management consultants:

- The consultants should be carefully selected, and should fit the culture and management style of the organisation.
- The objectives and expected 'deliverables' of the project should be clearly stated to the consultants.
- Explicit terms of reference should be agreed, and a project plan that covers outcomes, a timetable, resources required and costs should be developed and agreed.
- Management should carefully scrutinise any proposals made by the consultants, ensuring that proposals are relevant to the objectives of the project, within the cost budget and realistic.

- After the project has started, regular progress reports should be submitted by the consultant. These should be checked against the project plan.
- If the project starts to slips behind schedule or if expected deliverables look like not being produced on time, corrective action should be taken quickly.

Integrated reward systems

This chapter has explored a variety of reward management approaches and options available to organisations. It is important to note that there is no universally acclaimed 'one best way' of designing reward systems for organisations. Instead, it is argued that organisations should adopt a 'holistic', integrated and contingent approach towards the concept of reward (Hackett and McDermott, 1999; IPD, 2000a). For example, if organisations have adopted a team-based work structure, then reward should also be team-based (group-based) rather than individually allocated. Additionally, pay structures such as broad-banding and competency-based or skill-based reward systems need to be supported by adequate training provision. Importantly, it is argued that the reward system must be closely tied in with the business strategy of the organisation, so that the behaviours and outcomes that lead to organisational goal attainment are rewarded appropriately and fairly. A recent report by the IPD (IPD, 2000a: 4) argues that if there is a 'best practice' approach to reward management, it is a contingent approach that involves the 'generic' activities of employee involvement, communication and training.

SUMMARY

In this chapter the following key points have been made:

- Reward systems are an important means of attracting, retaining and motivating employees.
- The design of reward systems is a complex area since management and employees have different concerns and interests.
- In recent times there has been a move to the 'new pay', which involves a focus on linking pay with business strategy and the use of variable pay.
- Employee involvement and participation in the design of reward systems should not be neglected if the reward system is to be considered fair and serve a motivational purpose.
- For some employees, intrinsic rewards are as important as extrinsic rewards.
- Pay structures relate to the patterns of pay relationships, with a focus on external and internal relationships.
- Pay systems are the procedures involved in remunerating employees within the pay structure.

- Despite the emphasis on variable pay as part of the 'new pay' agenda, pay systems such as performance-related pay do not appear significantly to enhance individual or organisational performance.

- Employee benefits can be used as part of a reward package. Flexible benefit schemes should be designed with the help of specialist advice.

- The design and implementation of reward systems is generally becoming an increasingly complex area, and in some cases it may be necessary to use management consultants. Consultants used in the design and implementation of a reward system should be carefully selected and projects carefully monitored, in order to ensure the ongoing success of the reward system.

- There is no 'one best method' of reward system. It depends on the nature of the organisation and the employees involved. There is, however, 'one best way' of designing and implementing reward systems and that is to involve employees in the process, ensure the process is transparent and communicated at all levels of the organisation, and ensure that relevant training is available.

DISCUSSION QUESTIONS

1 In what way do reward systems impact on:

a) employees?
b) organisations?

2 In your view, what is the relative importance of extrinsic and intrinsic rewards?

3 To what extent should pay be contingent on level of performance?

4 Why do you think that PRP has been adopted so widely by organisations?

5 What are the advantages and disadvantages in using management consultants in the design of reward systems?

FURTHER READING

Students wishing to explore further some of the more specialist areas associated with reward should consult Armstrong (1996). On the issue of 'new pay', students are directed to Lawler (1995) for the philosophy and rationale behind the concept, and to Heery (1996) for an interesting critique. Further information on the use of consultants in the design of reward systems can be found in Armstrong (1994).

Part **4** **Employee development**

Chapter 8 Individual learning

Jim Stewart

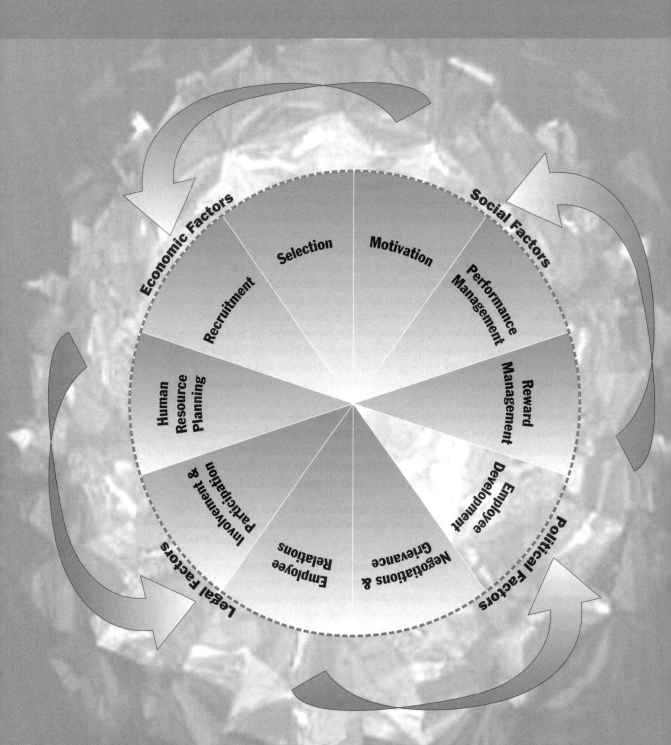

Having completed this chapter and its associated activities, readers should be able to:

- explain various theories of individual learning

- describe the various traditions of psychological thought from which these theories arise

- articulate and compare the complementary and contradictory features of the various theories of individual learning

- outline the relevance and application of individual learning to HR practice and, in particular, training and development practice

INTRODUCTION

Understanding individual learning processes and associated attempts to control and predict the outcomes of individual learning are a central feature of the study of organisation behaviour (Buchanan and Huczynski, 1997; McKenna, 2000). Such understanding also has obvious relevance to HR strategy in informing policy and practice in relation to training and development. It does though inform other aspects of human resource strategies such as selection and rewards management. For example, the old adage that 'you cannot teach an old dog new tricks' might be one explanation for the practice of ageism which leads organisations to discriminate against people over a certain age in their recruitment and selection. The belief is that older people cannot 'unlearn' established behaviours and so cannot be trained to adopt new behaviours and, therefore, should not be selected. Another adage of HR and management practice is 'what gets rewarded gets done' (see Chapter 7). In other words, employees will engage in behaviours and activities, and will pursue objectives and outcomes, that result in them achieving some valued reward such as more pay or promotion. This adage is a direct articulation and application of behaviourist learning theory, which will be discussed later in this chapter. The point here is that learning theory has wide application in human resourcing strategies.

Activity 8.1

1 Think about organisations you are familiar with. Is the adage of 'you cannot teach an old dog new tricks' applied there?

2 Based on your experience of 'older people' (defined as you think appropriate!), do you think the adage has any validity?

3 Taking organisations you are familiar with again, produce a list of examples which support the adage that 'what gets rewarded gets done'.

4 Now do the opposite. Produce a list of examples which would contradict the adage.

Attempts to understand and explain individual learning are primarily produced within the discipline of psychology (Myers, 1995; McKenna, 2000). Work done in the disciplines of social psychology and sociology are also of relevance (Rollinson et al., 1998; McKenna, 2000). These latter disciplines are perhaps of more interest when attempting to explain and understand the notion of organisational learning (Stewart, 1999). Before examining specific theories of learning, therefore, it will be useful first briefly to review the discipline of psychology in order to identify the main schools of thought which have influenced the development of theories of learning.

Perspectives in psychology

Human resourcing strategies might be characterised as the practical application of the social sciences to the management of people in work organisations. This follows from the fact that the social sciences are concerned with understanding and explaining human experience and behaviour. Thus, the essential theories of HR practice are drawn from those produced in the social sciences. Psychology is one of the social sciences. A significant factor which is used to distinguish one social science from another is the level of analysis adopted as the focus for the science. Sociology, for example, adopts a macro-focus and therefore 'society' as a macro-level of analysis. Social psychology adopts an intermediate focus and therefore focuses on interactions between two or more individuals as the level of analysis (Myers, 1995). Psychology adopts a micro-focus and therefore the individual as the micro-level of analysis.

These distinctions are not 'hard and fast' and there can be exceptions as well as degrees of overlap. They do though serve a purpose and it is useful to bear them in mind. Psychology is primarily concerned with understanding and explaining the experience and behaviour of *the individual human being*. Two definitions illustrate this point:

- The science of behaviour and mental processes (Myers, 1995)
- The science of mental life (Miller, 1966)

Obviously, any unit of analysis above an individual cannot be said to have or to experience mental 'life' or 'processes' and so the definitions illustrate the individual focus of psychology. Two other significant points emerge from the definitions. First, both emphasise that psychology is a 'science'. This is significant since, as will be discussed later, different traditions in psychology have attached different interpretations and emphases to the meaning and importance of the notion of 'science'. Second, while both use the word 'mental' only the first definition uses the word 'behaviour'. The distinction between these two concepts and phenomena is significant for two reasons. First, it is associated with the differences of view on the meaning and status of 'science' just mentioned. Second, the distinction can lie at the heart of debates within HR practice. For example, within the area of equal opportunities practice and managing diversity there is great interest in understanding and perhaps eradicating the causes and effects of sexism and racism. A big question here is whether practice should be concerned with sexist or racist beliefs and attitudes both examples of 'mental life' or 'mental processes'; or whether the focus should be exclusively on 'behaviour'. A bigger question is whether this question is the right one or even a valid one! (See Stewart, 1996)

> **Activity 8.2**
>
> 1 Produce a list of advantages and disadvantages of focusing on the individual as the unit of analysis.
>
> 2 Think about the implications of focusing on 'mental processes' to the exclusion of behaviour.
>
> 3 Think about and identify other examples of where the distinction between 'mental processes' and 'behaviour' might be significant for HR practice.

Different writers propose different categorisations of perspectives, or 'schools of thought' in psychology. Ribeaux and Poppleton (1978) suggest two broad perspectives, Arnold *et al.* (1998) suggest five while McKenna (2000) identifies four. There is therefore no single or definitive or correct categorisation of perspectives. There are, though, three perspectives which are generally identified in the literature and which are of particular relevance to this chapter (see also Stewart, 1998, 1999). The first of these is the behaviourist perspective.

Behaviourist psychology

Behaviourist psychology is a perspective associated with the pioneering work of J.B. Watson and B.F. Skinner (Buchanan and Huczynski, 1997). Development of the perspective was in some ways a reaction to earlier approaches and priorities attached to what was then an emerging discipline or science (Rollinson *et al.*, 1998; McKenna, 2000). Related to this, behaviourism can be said to have two defining characteristics. First, there is a general rejection of the internal workings of the mind as an area of study and investigation. Thus, behaviourist psychology attaches greater weight to the first definition given above because of its inclusion of and focus on behaviour. Second, and relatedly, adoption of an overriding principle that human behaviour is the product of experience of and within physical and social environments. Thus, ideas about innate or biological causes of individual behaviour are rejected.

The two defining characteristics detailed above are perhaps presented in extreme form. They were though highly influential in the behaviourists' attempts to establish the credibility and status of psychology as a 'science'. To achieve this, behaviourists such as Skinner believed that psychology should adopt the same research paradigm and methods as the established natural sciences such as physics and chemistry. In turn, this meant focusing on only that which is observable, measurable and capable of manipulation under laboratory conditions as the basis of research and study. The answer to this of course is 'behaviour' which meets all of those conditions, and thus the term 'behaviourist psychology'. This is not to say that behaviourist psychologists either did or do reject the existence or influence of 'mental processes' or innate, biological causes of behaviour. Their argument was and is simply that such phenomenon are not amenable to scientific investigation, and that theories developed by studying behaviour provide all the explanation necessary.

Contemporary psychology and psychologists tend to temper the strict and inflexible application of the behaviourist tradition. However, its principles inform the development of theories of learning to be examined later in the chapter and so it is important that they are understood.

Cognitive psychology

In contrast to behaviourism, cognitive psychology focuses on and emphasises the significance of mental processes. These form the major area of study for cognitive psychology and so this perspective can be said to reflect both of the definitions given earlier. In common with behaviourism, however, this perspective also adopts the view that the experience of individuals in their physical and social environments is a, if not the most, significant factor in understanding and explaining individual behaviour. Study of the interactions between individual mental processes and the physical and social environments as the source of explanations of human behaviour could be said to be the defining characteristic of cognitive psychology. Recent research also suggests that this perspective is now the most dominant within the discipline of psychology, at the expense of the behaviourist tradition (Robins *et al.*, 1999; see McKenna, 2000).

In common with behaviourism, cognitive psychology broadly accepts the paradigm and methods of research applied in the natural sciences. The key difference is that this perspective claims to be able to apply that paradigm and those methods to the study of mental processes. This leads to a conceptualisation of individual human beings as 'information processors' (Ribeaux and Poppleton, 1978; McKenna, 2000) interacting with environments. Thus, mental processes such as forming and changing attitudes and beliefs are seen as the result of processing information resulting from the individual's experience of interactions with their environment.

There are two other concepts in addition to that of 'information processor' within this perspective which are important to the purpose of this chapter. The first is that of 'maturation' developed by Piaget in his work on child development (Myers, 1995). The second is that of 'personal constructs' developed by Kelly (1955). Both of these have applications in cognitive learning theories.

Humanist psychology

The third perspective of relevance here is the school of thought generally known as humanist psychology. This perspective includes a significant departure from the two previously discussed. The scientific method broadly accepted and applied by both behaviourist and cognitive psychology assumes that the world has objective existence which is independent of the observer, and is therefore amenable to objective investigation and explanation. Humanist psychology, broadly defined, rejects this assumption. This does not mean that this perspective is 'unscientific'. For humanist psychologists, being scientific means being systematic and rigorous. It does not though mean detaching the observer from that which is studied. So, within humanist psychology, the broad tradition of phenomenology is adopted (Arnold *et al.*, 1995; Buchanan and Huczynski, 1997).

Phenomenology is a tradition within philosophy as well as within the social sciences. The perspective argues that any 'objective' definition or understanding of reality is merely a widely agreed interpretation rather than a specification of objective fact. These interpretations are not and cannot be universal over time and space since all human experience is 'subjective' and therefore subject to unique and individualistic interpretation. The idea of individual and unique 'world views' (Buchanan and Huczynski, 1997) is an effective means of capturing this argument.

One further principle of this perspective is important to emphasise here. This is that individual human behaviour is purposeful and goal directed (McKenna, 2000). One significant goal is to fulfil our potential, or to 'self-actualise' (Maslow, 1959; see also Chapter 5). In summary, therefore, the two defining characteristics of this perspective are a phenomenological view of the nature of reality and a belief in self-actualisation as an overriding determinant of behaviour. These characteristics are again significant influences on learning theories associated with this perspective.

Activity 8.3

1 Think about and identify the most significant similarities and differences across the three perspectives on psychology described here.

2 How will these similarities and differences influence the approach to studying and explaining human behaviour?

3 How will they affect and influence the development of learning theories within each perspective?

Individual learning

The basic question addressed by theories of learning is 'How do individuals learn?' To some extent, the question of *why* individuals learn is also a matter of concern. Specific theories of learning vary in the extent to which they seek to answer both or only one of these questions. They also vary in their ambition. Some are limited to merely describing the process of individual learning; others seek to explain the process by identifying and specifying causal relationships; the most ambitious claim to provide prescriptive models based on predictive theory. In addition, specific theories are also influenced by the central tenets of the perspective or schools of thought in which they were produced.

What will become clear is that specific theories have features or elements which support, contradict or complement other specific theories. The fact that this is the case suggests that no one theory is comprehensive or definitive, and that therefore there is as yet no single or universal answer to the questions posed at the beginning of this section. It also suggests though that principles which find support in more than one theory might be considered to have greater validity than would otherwise be the case. It will be useful and instructive therefore to look for similarities and differences as the examination of specific learning theories unfolds.

Definitions of learning

It is always useful to begin with definitions. Though it is not easy to define learning as the word can be used as a noun and as a verb. This is apparent in the following definitions.

> Learning is the process of acquiring knowledge through experience which leads to an enduring change in behaviour.
>
> (Buchanan and Huczynski, 1997: 107)

> . . . an experiential process which results in an individual displaying relatively permanent changes in underlying values of behaviour so that the individual is able to adapt to a changing environment.
>
> (Rollinson *et al.*, 1998: 212)

Both of these definitions include references to a process, thus using the word 'learning' as a verb, and to the outcomes of this process, thus using 'learning' as a noun. The latter usage is emphasised in the definition offered by Myers (1995) which focuses on behaviour as an outcome of learning, and similar definitions are applied in most texts concerned with HR strategy and practice through employee training and development (Harrison, 1997; Reid and Barrington, 1997). But answers to the questions which started this section can only come about by examining the process; in other words by using the word learning as a verb. This is in fact the primary focus of the theories explored in the following pages. The two definitions given above provide strong clues as to the specific focus adopted by the various theories, and that is, of course, individual experience. The theories vary in their interpretations of that experience.

Behaviourist learning theory

The first specific theory to be examined is behaviourist learning theory. There are in fact a number of related theories which can be grouped under this heading, and each will be examined in turn. One significant point which is important to state at the outset is that in one sense there is no theory of learning in behaviourist psychology. This rather strange claim arises because this tradition arose out of a concern to understand and explain the causes of human *behaviour*. Thus, behaviourist psychology did not produce a theory of one aspect of human behaviour which is called learning. What was produced was an explanation of the totality of human behaviour, and this rested on the proposition that *all human behaviour is learned*. So, for behaviourists, learning is the explanation of human behaviour. This point is best illustrated by the work of Skinner, an early and influential behaviourist psychologist, who labelled his theory of human behaviour 'learning theory' (Myers, 1995). Attempts to understand this process in more detail are what are now generally referred to as behaviourist learning theories.

The basic building block of behaviourist learning theory is the idea of *association*, or associative learning (Myers, 1995; McKenna, 2000). This idea suggests that some organisms, humans included, can learn to link in some relationship two or more otherwise independent events. An example might be the amount of effort put into a task and the quality of the output; a student's essay for, instance, or an employee's attempt to write a report. Or, perhaps, an academic's attempt to write a book chapter! Taking this building block further led to the idea of *conditioning*. Here, an explanation is provided about why some events are associated rather than others. In other words, why an organism associates event A with event B rather than with event C or D. To continue one of the examples, the student associates effort (event A) with the quality of the outcome (event B) rather than with the results of student elections (event C) because of the consequences in the form of a mark arising from event B.

There are two significant modes of conditioning. The first is known as 'classical conditioning' and is associated with the work of Pavlov (McKenna, 2000). Pavlov's work with salivating dogs is widely known and referred to in many texts. Probably his most important contribution is the distinction between *conditioned* and *unconditioned* stimuli and responses. Basically, this distinction holds that unconditioned stimuli or responses are the result of automatic, physiological or biological processes and are therefore *not learned*. The example from his experiments with dogs is that food in the mouth is an unconditioned stimuli, and salivating when food is present in the mouth is an unconditioned response. Introducing an initially neutral stimulus demonstrates the existence and nature of associative learning, and the meaning of conditioned stimuli and responses. In Pavlov's experiments, this neutral stimulus was a particular sound. This sound was played as the dogs were provided with food. The dogs eventually came to associate the sound with being given food and so would salivate on hearing the sound irrespective of whether food was provided. Thus, the sound became a conditioned stimulus and the salivating a conditioned response. The latter was no longer an automatic, physiological response since food was not present in the mouth. The dogs had learned, through conditioning, to associate the sound with food.

The second mode of conditioning is that developed by Skinner and is known as 'operant conditioning' (McKenna, 2000). A significant distinction between the two modes of conditioning is that the first, proposed by Pavlov, focuses on stimuli and responses which the organism does not control. Operant conditioning focuses on the spontaneous and controllable behaviour of the organism. Such behaviour is referred to as *operant behaviour*. Building on what the early psychologist Thorndike called the 'law of effect' (Myers, 1995), Skinner proposed an association between operant behaviour and its *results* or *outcomes*. Operant behaviour has consequences and effects on and for both the organism and its environment. Thus, in operant conditioning, the key association is between behaviour and its consequences.

A second key element in Skinner's learning theory is the role of *reinforcement* in operant conditioning. If operant behaviour results in some valued outcome – what might be termed 'reward' from the perspective of the organism – then the behaviour becomes associated with the outcome. The behaviour then becomes more likely to recur. Operant behaviour which results in negative or adverse consequences or outcomes conversely becomes less likely to recur. Thus, through the influence of reinforcement working within a process of operant conditioning, organisms learn to behave in some ways rather than others.

Skinner introduced the term 'reinforcer' to refer to rewards, and defined the term to mean any event that increases the frequency of a preceding response (Myers, 1995: 270). Note the value free nature of this definition. A reinforcer is simply any event which has the effect of increasing, or making more likely, a specific behaviour. Skinner also distinguished between two different types of reinforcer. The first are referred to as positive reinforcers and constitute positive stimuli such as food, money, attention or approval. The second are negative reinforcers which strengthen a response, or behaviour, by removing adverse stimuli such as pain, disapproval or isolation. Note that negative reinforcement therefore does not apply to administering punishment. Skinner was consistent in arguing that his two types of reinforcer were much more effective in shaping behaviour than punishments.

Applications of Skinner's learning theory range from social policy to therapeutic interventions, from child-rearing practices to HR strategies in work organisations. The purpose in all of these applications is to 'shape' behaviour by reinforcing operant behaviour as and when it constitutes, or moves in the direction of, desired behaviour. According to Skinnerian principles, all other behaviour should be ignored and it will then cease. The value and frequency of reinforcers can be varied depending upon how closely operant behaviour meets the desired behaviour, culminating in maximum reinforcement of the actual desired behaviour.

The most obvious application of Skinner's learning theory in HR strategy is in the design and implementation of employee training and development programmes. These can merely reflect the general principles in a generalised way, or can apply what is known as *behaviour modification* interventions (Buchanan and Huczynski, 1997). These rely totally on Skinner's learning theory in their design and execution and utilise principles and practices first developed in the treatment of psychological disorders. However, employee development programmes based on behaviour modification designs can be utilised for any category or group of employees, and any category or type of knowledge, skills or behaviour; e.g. sales training, health and safety training, VDU operations, call centre operators or professional and managerial groups. Wider applications are also possible. The work of Hamner (1977) and Luthans and Krietner (1975) (see McKenna, 2000) apply behaviour modification designs to organisation-wide interventions. It can be argued that their works are early examples of attempts to design and implement what are now referred to as performance management systems. As mentioned previously, Skinnerian principles also inform and influence the design and operation of reward management systems in work organisations (see also Chapter 7). All of these applications are attempts to 'shape' the behaviour of employees to conform to that specified as desired or correct by the organisation.

Activity 8.4

Think about a recent or current education or training course you have attended and answer the following questions.

1 What principles of operant conditioning are applied in the design and implementation of the course?

2 What examples of positive and negative reinforcers can you identify in the operation of the course?

3 Does the course constitute an attempt at 'behaviour modification'?

4 What are your reasons for your answer to Question 3?

Social learning theory

Social learning theory is a development and refinement of Skinnerian behaviourism. It is arguable whether this theory is categorised as a behaviourist or cognitive theory of learning. This is because its originator, Bandura (see Myers, 1995; McKenna, 2000), was concerned with the role and impact of internal mental processes in human learning. However, he also accepted the basic principles of Watson and Skinner and incorporated operant conditioning into his own theory. It is therefore reasonable to claim that his theory is a refinement of behaviourism.

Bandura's theory is also referred to as 'observational learning'. This is because he believed that learning would be both laborious and hazardous if individuals had to rely exclusively on their own actions. Consequently, Bandura investigated the role of observation in individual learning, and developed and introduced the concepts of 'imitation' and 'modelling' into the learning process. Put simply, these concepts explain how individuals learn from and through others. So, behaviour is learned by observing and imitating the behaviours of other people. A number of factors have been found or suggested to be influential in determining which behaviours of which people will be imitated, and which will not. First, Bandura identified that operant conditioning will be influential. So, behaviours which, when imitated, receive positive or negative reinforcement will be adopted. Second, the perceived status of the person being imitated, or not, is significant. This factor relates to the idea of 'modelling' and gives rise to the idea of *role models*. The argument is that individuals will seek to 'model' themselves on those who they perceive to have high status, and will therefore 'imitate' their behaviours. The third influencing factor is consistency of the behaviour being imitated. The more consistent, the more likely the behaviour will be imitated.

Bandura's work and theory has had a wide impact. It is central to the idea of 'socialisation' which seeks to explain how children learn to behave in conformance with the norms of the societies into which they are born. It is also at the heart of debates on the role and impact of films and television in creating and perpetuating violent behaviour in society. The popular notion of pop stars, actors and high-profile sports stars acting as 'role models' is also a direct result of the application of social learning theory. It has also had significant impact on the design of HR strategies. The notion of 'socialisation' is directly applied in organisation induction programmes. It is also now more widely applied in programmes aimed at changing and/or maintaining organisation culture through HR strategies (McKenna, 2000). More specifically, Bandura's work provides the theoretical foundations for *mentoring* as an employee development method, as well as its variant of *buddy systems* as part of induction programmes. The theory has also been incorporated into some forms of behaviour modification designs in employee training and development programmes (Stewart, 1996).

Cognitive learning theory

It was explained earlier that a key distinction between behaviourist and cognitive psychology is the attention given to internal mental processes. Cognitive learning theories seek to explain individual learning by focusing on those processes. Recall also that a basic tenet of cognitive psychology is to conceptualise human beings as information processors. This also provides a basic model for the learning process within this perspective. The theory of learning developed by Gagne (1974), summarised as a series of stages in Table 8.1, is a useful illustration of this approach.

Gagne's theory reflects the focus and interests of cognitive psychology by incorporating factors such as memory, emotions and perceptions. These lead to the argument that while the *process* of learning is the same for everyone, the *outcomes* will vary because of individual differences in, for example, motives and emotions which will influence what information is selected, and how it is coded and interpreted. The overall theory though is straightforward; individuals learn by accessing, processing and transforming information from and about their physical and social environments.

Cognitive learning theory as expounded by Gagne does not necessarily refute behaviourist learning theory. It might be argued that it provides a fuller understanding by seeking to explain the role of cognitive processes. Investigation of these processes also led to the development of ideas on 'sign' and 'latent' learning (Hilgard *et al.*, 1971). These concepts inform an argument that individuals

Table 8.1 Gagne's cognitive learning theory

- *Motivation* to act exists
- Information is searched for and *apprehended*
- Information is *acquired* by coding and storing in the short-term memory
- *Retention* occurs by transferring information to the long-term memory
- Information is retrieved from the long-term memory through *recall*
- Recalled information is *generalised* to new situations
- Information is applied through *performance*. Changes or differences in performance confirm that learning has taken place
- *Feedback* is gained and monitored to assess whether the original motivation to act has been satisfied

formulate *cognitive maps*. The concept of cognitive maps suggests that each person produces a personal representation of their understanding of their environments, and their experiences within those environments. These maps are applied to inform behaviour but, and this is the significant point, independently of the immediate context of the behaviour. Cognitive maps are learned. They then inform future behaviour. Therefore, learning and behaviour can be separated in time and space.

A related but broader concept to cognitive maps is that of *schema*. This concept was originally devised by Bartlett (1932). It suggests that human beings organise information, received through the senses, into meaningful relationships and patterns. Individuals then use those patterns to make sense of and respond to their experiences in and of the world. A particular form of schema is the theory of 'personal constructs' devised by Kelly. Personal construct theory supports the argument that individual human beings produce unique responses to the same stimuli. That being the case, cognitive theories such as that produced by Gagne may explain the process of learning, but no theory is capable of predicting or controlling the outcomes of learning. So, while a number of individuals may engage with the same learning experiences, and while the process of learning may be the same for each of them, the outcomes from the experience will vary from individual to individual. This is a significant departure from behaviourist learning theory and a major challenge to the claims made by theorists such as Skinner (see Buchanan and Huczynski, 1997).

It is possible to argue that cognitive learning theories have wide implications for HR strategy. Ideas on mission statements and statements of organisation values are one example. Such statements are arguably examples of 'schema' which organisations wish their employees to adopt to inform their behaviour. Much writing on culture change emphasises the 'management of meaning' (see McKenna, 2000; Buchanan and Huczynski, 1997; Anthony, 1994). Cognitive learning theories, and cognitive psychology more widely, in part provide the theoretical foundations for culture change programmes premised on the importance of meaning. In terms of employee training and development, principles applied in the design and implementation of such programmes are directly derived from theories such as that devised by Gagne (see, for example, Harrison, 1997; Reid and Barrington, 1997; Stewart, 1999).

Activity 8.5

1 Identify some key principles which you have experienced in an education or training course which are associated with Gagne's theory.

2 How do these principles contradict or challenge those of behaviourist learning theory?

3 How do they complement those of behaviourist learning theory?

4 Which of the two sets of principles do you think are the most effective or appropriate to apply in education or training courses?

Experiential learning

An alternative cognitive learning theory to that of Gagne is experiential learning theory. This theory is both more widely known and more widely applied. It was originally developed by Kolb and his colleagues (Kolb *et al.*, 1984), and is commonly referred to as the experiential learning cycle. This name reflects the principle that learning is cyclical, a feature which is also implicit in the theory developed by Gagne. As well as being cyclical, experiential learning theory also suggests that learning is continuous. This means that learning does not occur only in formal situations such as education or training courses; it occurs in all settings and contexts including at work, at home and in social activities. This feature of learning is supported by all of the theories included in this chapter. It is therefore surprising that many or most people associate learning almost exclusively with formal learning settings such as schools, universities or training centres.

According to this theory, learning occurs through a process of four stages. These stages form the experiential learning cycle detailed in Figure 8.1. Each stage in the cycle needs to take place for effective learning to take place, although the cycle can be entered at any of the four stages. The theory also suggests that learning is goal directed. This means that different individuals will be pursuing different goals in their learning. Because of this, they are likely to pay particular attention to different stages of the cycle. For example, scientists are concerned with developing theories and will therefore be more interested in generalising concepts than non-scientists. Managers though are more concerned with identifying and applying practical solutions to organisational problems. They will therefore be more concerned with experimentation, to discover what works, than non-managers. This argument leads to the idea of learning styles. Variation in learning styles reflects the variation in types of goals being pursued (Stewart, 1996).

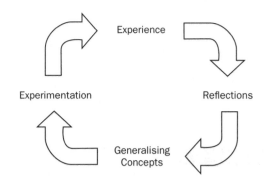

Figure 8.1 The experiential learning cycle

Kolb and his colleagues identified four broad styles. Each style reflects a preference for a combination of two of the stages in the cycle. The styles are detailed in Table 8.2.

A number of self-analysis instruments have been produced to enable individuals to identify their learning style. One of these is the Learning Styles Questionnaire

Table 8.2 Kolb's learning styles

The diverger	A combination of concrete experience and reflective observation produces this style. It reflects a preference for engaging in tasks and then thinking about the process and results.
The assimilator	Combining reflective observation and generalising concepts produces this style. Preferences for analysing data to formulate generalisations are reflected in this style.
The converger	A style which combines generalising concepts and active experimentation. Preferences are for formulating general principles and testing them out in practice.
The accommodator	A combination of active experimentation and experiencing produces this style. It reflects a preference for action over cognitive processes and for pragmatic results.

(LSQ) devised by Honey and Mumford (1986) which reflects their refinement of Kolb's original theory. This refinement includes two key distinctions. First, the work of Honey and Mumford suggests that learning styles are the result of preferences for only one stage in the cycle, rather than a combination of two stages which is the case with Kolb. Second, the LSQ focuses on behavioural preferences, rather than the cognitive preferences which is the basis of the instrument devised by Kolb. These distinctions led Honey and Mumford to propose a different set of learning styles. These are set out in Table 8.3.

Table 8.3 Honey and Mumford learning styles

Activist	Emphasises the experiencing stage of the cycle Enjoys the 'here and now' Corresponds with *Diverger*
Reflector	Emphasises the reflective stage Stands back and analyses Corresponds with *Assimilator*
Theorist	Related to generalising concepts Produces logical synthesis for wide application Corresponds with *Converger*
Pragmatist	Focuses on experimentation stage Tries out ideas in practice Corresponds with *Accommodator*

Humanist learning theory

There are some theories of learning which overlap the cognitive and humanist perspectives. One of these is the idea of learning through *insight* (Hilgard *et al.*, 1971).

This theory was developed in part because of dissatisfaction with behaviourist theories. A major tenet of the theory is an individual human being's free capacity to make their own sense of problems and to reach their own solutions. This is also a central feature of humanist psychology. Insight itself though is conceptualised as a cognitive process, hence the overlap.

Insight occurs when new or different relationships are formulated between given or existing elements in a situation. Common examples of insight are whenever someone utters 'Aha' or something similar. The saying 'the penny finally dropped' is also a colloquial illustration of insight occurring. The theory has little detail to explain the process, but the following features have been demonstrated (Hilgard *et al.*, 1971).

- *Insight depends on the arrangement of the problem situation* The original research involved studying the attempts of chimpanzees to secure food under experimental conditions. The animals had to move sticks of varying length to new positions in order to be able to move their food so they could secure it. This 'rearrangement' of the elements can, for humans at least, also be applied to abstract as well as concrete problems in order to gain 'insight'.
- *Once a solution occurs with insight, it can be repeated* This feature is self-explanatory. Similar problems will be approached with the insight gained.
- *Learning gained through insight can be applied in new or novel situations* This feature is again fairly self-explanatory. Relationships between elements, or variables, can be generalisable, especially if those relationships are causal.

Hilgard *et al.* (1971: 218) summarise the lessons of the theory of insight in the following statement: 'An effective learner is a resourceful, adaptable person able to use what he [sic] knows in new situations and to discover solutions to problems that he [sic] has never faced before.'

This quote reflects the essential nature of humanist psychology and especially the views and arguments of Rogers (1965, 1969), one of the leading theorists and writers in that school of thought. Rogers advocated a position which puts the individual, or the learner, in exclusive control of the learning process as well as learning outcomes. So, for Rogers, individuals are not the passive responders to external stimuli conceptualised in behaviourist learning theory and, to an extent, in cognitive psychology. They are rather active agents determining their own choices and decisions. This view is also reflected in the distinction Rogers draws between teaching and learning. He argued the dictum that one person cannot teach another person anything. All that can be done – according to Rogers – is to provide an environment, and perhaps an experience, in which another person is free to learn. Rogers's analysis and arguments therefore change the focus for the work of professional teachers, trainers and developers. Their role is one of 'facilitator', which is to create an appropriate and supportive social and emotional climate in which learning is possible and likely. That this view has been influential in the practice of employee training and development as part of HR strategy is evident from the emphasis given to facilitating, rather than training, in recent books on the subject (see Walton, 1999; Wilson, 1999).

Discussion

As has been made clear throughout the chapter, the study of individual learning, and the theories that have been developed as a result of that study, has significant implications for the design and execution of HR strategy. Examples have been given which illustrate that many HR strategies and practices found in work organisations at the present time rely, in part at least, on theories of learning for their theoretical foundations. Those who advocate such strategies and practices in academic or populist books on organisation and management do not always make these foundations explicit. Nor is it likely that practitioners in organisations do so. They may be unaware of the foundations when they advocate adoption of particular approaches to and strategies for the management and development of employees. It is the case that the more informed decisions on strategy and practice are, the more likely they are to be appropriate and relevant decisions. Understanding individual learning is therefore an important factor in devising HR strategy.

The clearest, but not the only, example of where this is the case is in employee training and development. An illustration of this is the work of Fitts, as long ago as 1962 (see McKenna, 2000). Fitts refers to three phases of skills development. The first is called *cognitive*, where the learner seeks understanding of the task and associated principles. The second is referred to as the *associative* phase. Here, the application of knowledge is emphasised, and practice with feedback is utilised to improve performance. The final stage is referred to as the *autonomous* stage. Performance of the task becomes increasingly automatic and there is less need for either reference to the memory for knowledge or for feedback on performance.

It should be clear that this model of skill acquisition draws on cognitive learning theories in the first stage and on behaviourist learning theory in the second stage. It also broadly reflects strategies adopted in work organisations for the training of new employees, or for training existing employees in new tasks. With or without the application of ideas around facilitation, employee training and development programmes commonly begin with 'teaching' knowledge before moving on to application and practice until the learner is proficient to carry out the task, having developed the necessary skills (see Buckley and Caple, 2000).

Activity 8.6

Think about a current or recent learning experience and answer the following questions:

1 What prompted you to learn?

2 What do you do to prepare to learn?

3 What happens to you as you learn?

4 How do you know you have been successful?

Use your answers to these questions to assess the validity of the theories described in this chapter and decide which theory most accurately answers the question 'How do *you* learn?'

Hislop Brewery

Janet Tanner works as HRD manager for Hislop Brewery. Janet began her working life with Hislop ten years ago as a commercial trainee manager, following graduation with a BA (Hons) in Business Studies. Her liking and aptitude for personnel matters and development has led to her present position, which she has had for two years. During her time with Hislop, Janet has seen and been part of many changes. Over the past two years she has initiated and managed a major change programme (of which more later) to support the company's intended business strategy.

Hislop is what is referred to as a 'regional brewery'. This means that the company limits its operations to particular geographic regions in the UK. While it is a publicly quoted company, Hislop is still managed by members of the founding family and the original owners. This, in Janet's view, has both positive and negative consequences. The positive outcomes are associated with the strong backing for HRD which Janet receives from both the chairman and the managing director. Negative outcomes arise from a long-serving and loyal workforce who still see Hislop as a family business and who therefore can be resistant to change.

The major objective for the company is to avoid takeover by one of the large, national/international brewery companies. Achieving this objective depends on the company continuing to satisfy existing shareholders which, in turn, depends on maintaining impressive business results. The company's declared and intended strategy to achieve this is to deliver first-class service and products to its customers. Standards to operationalise the strategy have been formulated in a number of 'hallmarks of service' statements for each area of the business. These statements specify and define what customers can expect to receive in terms of service from the company. Similar statements have been agreed for support functions in relation to their 'internal' customers.

Hislop employs just over 1500 staff. The vast majority of these – more than 85 per cent – work in retail operations managing and delivering services to the 'eating and drinking public'. The remainder are concerned with 'free trade' sales and support services such as distribution, property management, finance and HR. Janet reports through a group head of HR to the managing director and has responsibilities which cross the head office/retail divide. However, retail operations have their own training and development function which reports to the group sales director. The company has received Investors in People (IIP) recognition and has received many awards, both national and industry specific, for its employee development activities. Comprehensive training plans and programmes exist for all categories of staff and these are fully utilised. Support is provided for professional qualifications. Every member of staff receives an annual development-based appraisal with quarterly reviews and works to an agreed individual development plan. The HRD function is well resourced with a refurbished training centre, which includes a 'training pub' complete with kitchen and cellar, and a complement of twelve staff across group and retail departments. In a recent paper for the MD, Janet estimated that the company spends a total of £3 million on employee development (taking account of both direct and indirect expenditure) which represents more than 7 per cent of a total payroll of £40 million.

A major part of Janet's work over the past two years has been the Hallmark Initiative. This initiative has involved all employees in Hislop Brewery attending a two-day workshop on the concept of customer service. The workshops have enabled all employees to contribute

Case Study continued

to formulation of the Hallmark statements. Follow-up activities in departments and sections have led to production of mini-statements for those departments and sections and, in some cases, for particular jobs. The Hallmark Initiative is central to the organisation's business strategy of delivering first-class customer service, and the relevant statements have been issued to existing customers, are displayed in all Hislop's managed and tenanted sites and are used by sales staff in negotiating new customers/business. Other development initiatives to support the business strategy have included team development events for all established teams in Hislop, a newly designed management development programme and a series of 'challenge' events designed to encourage innovation and improvements in the company's operations. The 'challenge' events involve diagonal cross-sections of staff working in teams to develop their problem-solving and creative-thinking abilities which are then applied to specific areas of the company's operations.

As Janet reflects on the current position of the company and the role of HRD she identifies two reasons for satisfaction. First, all employees are supported in learning their jobs through well-designed training programmes. This helps to maintain the organisation's ability to continue to do its traditional business well. Second, the Hallmark Initiative and related activities help to support beneficial changes in what the company currently does. However, these initiatives and activities are beginning to bear fruit, and Janet wonders about the future direction and contribution of HRD to individual and organisational learning.

Activity 8.7

1 What theory or theories of learning do you think are being applied in developing the employees of Hislop Brewery?

2 What evidence supports your answers to Question 1?

3 How can learning theories help Janet make decisions for the future of HRD in Hislop Brewery?

4 Given your response to Question 3, how can learning theories help Janet tackle the particular problem of traditional employees who are resistant to change? And what should be the role of line managers in applying solutions?

SUMMARY

In this chapter the following key points have been made:

- Theories of individual learning are primarily developed in the science of psychology.

- There are a number of perspectives, or schools of thought, within psychology.

- Each of these perspectives adopt their own principles in relation to the nature of human experience.

- Learning is not confined to formal contexts and it occurs continuously throughout all aspects of experience.

- The learning process is influenced by both internal cognitive processes and the application of external reinforcers.
- The outcomes of learning are influenced by the goal-seeking behaviour of individuals.
- Many aspects of HR strategy and practice, including rewards, performance management and employee training and development are influenced by theories of individual learning.
- While learning theories can and do hold contradictions for each other, each can and does provide significant and useful principles to inform decisions on HR strategy and practice.

DISCUSSION QUESTIONS

1   What applications in HR strategies can you identify for theories of learning?

2   Which theories have particular reference for different HR activities; e.g. selection, training, reward?

3   Do theories of learning have implications for achieving equal opportunities in work organisations? If no, why not? If yes, what are these implications?

4   What implications arise from learning theories for the role of HR practitioners *vis-à-vis* that of line managers?

FURTHER READING

In order to explore further the links between learning and training and development practice, readers should consult Arnold *et al.* (1998), McKenna (2000) and Stewart (1999).

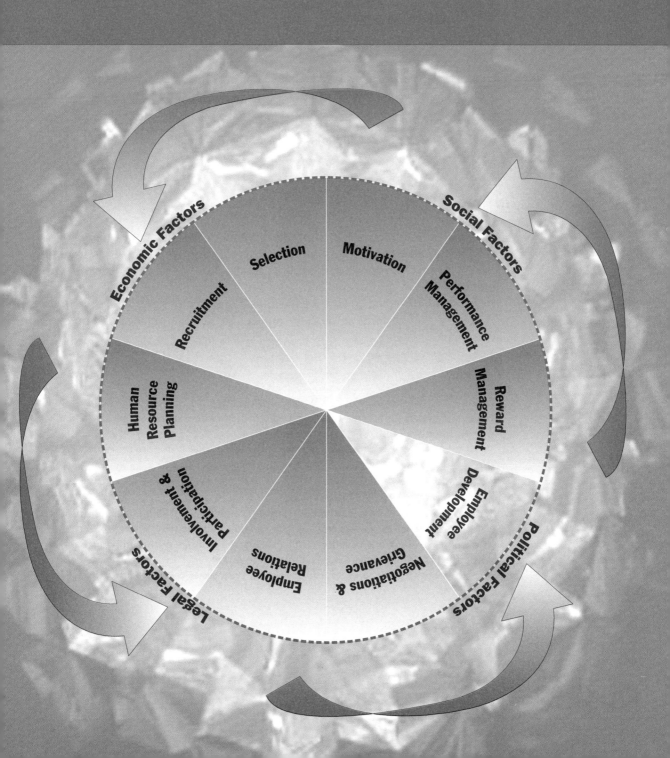

Having completed this chapter and its associated activities, readers should be able to:

● explain key concepts in relation to the field of employee development

● articulate the benefits of training and understand the challenges facing the training and development profession

● understand the relevance of the role of the government to the practice of training and development in the United Kingdom

● outline the types and levels of training provision in the United Kingdom

● compare the roles undertaken by employee development specialists

● outline and compare different organisational approaches to employee development

● understand and articulate the systematic approach to employee development

INTRODUCTION

An understanding of the key concepts in relation to the field of employee development and the role of the employee development practitioner are central to any discussion surrounding the role of training and development within the HR function.

Key definitions which focus on education, training and development help us to develop an understanding of their implications for the practice of employee development.

Education

Education is defined as activities which aim to develop the knowledge, skills, moral values and understanding required in all aspects of life rather than a knowledge and skill relating to only a limited field of activity.

(Manpower Services Commission, 1981, quoted in Reid and Barrington, 1997: 7)

Training

Training is a planned process to modify attitude, knowledge or skill behaviour through learning experience to achieve effective performance in an activity or range of activities. Its purpose, in the work situation, is to develop the abilities of the individual and to satisfy the current and future needs of the organisation.

(Manpower Services Commission, 1981, quoted in Reid and Barrington, 1997: 7)

Development

Developing people as part of an overall human resource strategy means the skilful provision and organisation of learning experiences, primarily but not exclusively in the workplace, in order that business goals and organisational growth can be achieved.

Such development must be aligned with the organisation's vision and longer term goals in order that, through enhancing the skills, knowledge, learning and innovative capability of people at every level, the organisation as well as the individual can prosper.

(Harrison, 1997: 7)

Activity 9.1

1 Focusing on the three definitions above, locate any recent learning events you have experienced; these can include events experienced at university/college or in an organisation.

2 Using your answers to Question 1 as a starting point, produce a list of similarities and differences between education, training and development.

By focusing on the definitions, a pattern of similarities begins to emerge. All three terms relate to issues of knowledge, skills and understanding. However, education refers to these issues in relation to 'all aspects of life', whereas the definitions of training and development have specified focuses in terms of the needs of organisations and of work.

These differences would suggest that in a text with a focus on the role of the practitioners in organisations, this chapter is more likely to be concerned with activities which focus on training and development as it is these two activities which would appear to relate more clearly to the organisation's needs. However, we must be cautious of assuming such clear differentiation.

Stewart (1999) identifies the current emphasis on ensuring compulsory *education* to the needs of employers and that higher *education* emphasises preparation for the 'world of work'. This brings to our attention the increase in formal qualification-based programmes for management development and the rise of partnerships between organisations and higher education providers.

The three definitions help develop an understanding of the vast range of activities and methods available to the employee development practitioner and the crucial role associated with identifying training needs and matching an appropriate method to develop the required knowledge/skill and understanding. This part of the role often referred to as 'identifying training needs' will be referred to later in the chapter.

Activity 9.2

Consider the discussion around the definitions of education, training and development. Can you give examples of learning events that might fit into each definition?

What are the benefits of training?

Linking the benefits of employee training and development to the concept of human resourcing strategies

> Well-trained labour forces are productive . . . cohesive, motivated and . . . capable of accommodating change and introducing new technologies.
>
> (Graham and Bennet, 1995: 254)

This quotation succinctly relates to a number of key benefits which can be attributed in part to effective training strategies and demonstrates the link between the practice of employee development and the policy goals of HRM (Guest, 1987), namely concepts of strategic integration, commitment, quality and flexibility (see Chapter 1, pp. 9–10). The quote refers to the terms 'cohesive' and 'motivated', which we can link to the view that organisations can build commitment by giving employees the opportunity to develop. This in turn highlights to the employees their individual importance in the overall organisational strategy and can help to increase motivation.

The statement *capable of accommodating change* implies that training labour forces can enhance flexibility and therefore the ability of an individual to cope with and be adaptive to change. This is particularly important to organisations in this period of rapid change and reflects the growth during the 1990s of the concept of 'managing change' or 'change management', which regularly appears in business journals, business texts and provides the focus for many training courses. The growing demand for flexibility in the workplace can also be attributed to growth of atypical employment contracts and changes in work practices (see Chapter 2). Chapter 2 introduces the concept of the flexible firm and it is apparent that for individuals to be able to cope with the growing demand for flexibility in terms of their skills (functional flexibility) their training and development needs are paramount. The Labour Market and Skills Trend Report 2000 cited that research had demonstrated that 'changes in work practices or multiskilling' are the second cited reason by employers for increasing skill needs preceded only by technological advance.

Apart from the benefits referred to in the quote, we can also look at the link between employee training and development and the concept of quality referred to in the Guest (1987) model of HRM policy goals. We can refer to Leopold's (Chapter 1, pp. 9–10) definition of this dimension:

> Here there is meant to be an interrelationship between high-quality employees in whom employers are prepared to invest and develop in the belief that such employees will in turn deliver high-quality goods and services which will help distinguish an organisation from its competitors.

The notion of investing and developing demonstrates the obvious link between employee development and the practice of human resource management. It is to this 'link' that we now turn our attention. An examination of Guest's model of HRM policy goals (1987) highlights the concept of 'strategic integration'. If we refer to Leopold's discussion of this concept (Chapter 1, p. 9) it is clear that the integration of the practice of employee development is vital to achieve both internal coherence and to promote the interrelationship between human resourcing strategy and business strategy. Keep emphasises the vital role of training and development in human resource management:

> the case that the adoption of a strategic approach towards the training and development of their workforce represents a vital component of any worthwhile or meaningful form of HRM (or HRD) is easily made.
>
> (Keep, 1992: 321)

From this short discussion of some of the key reasons for and benefits of training and development in organisations, it is clear that an organisation which professes to be practising 'human resource management', must pay serious attention to the integration of training and development strategies. So why do numerous reports, articles and texts refer to the relatively poor state of the United Kingdom' training provision? This brings us to the next section which primarily looks at the key debate in the field of employee training and development.

The challenges facing the role of employee training and development

> Companies that, for whatever reasons, are inclined to treat their employee simply as a cost or commodity, and who hence fail to invest in training and development activity cannot meaningfully be said to be practising human resource management.
>
> (Keep, 1992: 321)

This quote highlights a key problem with raising the importance of training and development in organisations. The key view which prevails in some organisations being that training is a cost not an investment. To explore this view in more detail consider the following:

Example 1
If a manufacturing organisation were proposing to spend £10,000 on a new piece of machinery for the factory, they would more than likely be able to justify the investment by producing statistics/data which demonstrates an increase in productivity. Therefore there is a clear link between the cost and benefit of this investment.

Example 2
If a manufacturing organisation were proposing to spend £10,000 on a new personal development programme for supervisors in the factory, it would be very difficult for the employee development function to produce statistics/data which would demonstrate the cost/benefit of the training for the organisation.

These two examples help to demonstrate the difficulty associated with demonstrating the immediate pay-back to organisations of training and development expenditure. Therefore an organisation which has a short-termist perspective might, as Keep (1992) states, see training as a cost not an investment. It can be seen from these examples the complexity of evaluating training provision particularly from a financial point of view and this aspect of the role is discussed in more detail later in this chapter.

Where organisations do view training and development activities as a cost and not an investment, their recruitment and selection practices will probably reflect this belief. An organisation unwilling to invest in training and developing employees will be likely to 'poach' employees and their associated skills from other organisations. This can create a vicious circle . . . if employees feel that by investing in training and developing, their employees will be more attractive to competitors and more susceptible to 'poaching' they might be wary of investing money in training and development due to the fear of losing the employees they have invested in.

The concept of HRM and strategic integration, however, suggests that if a company invests in training and development the internal coherence of their human resourcing strategy is vital. Human resourcing practices need to reflect this investment and employees need to be managed in order to retain these skills, which in turn increases the long-term benefits from the investment.

The notion of flexibility and flexible working practices has been introduced in Chapter 2, and the associated links and effects on the organisation's training and development policies require perusal.

The flexible firm model developed by Atkinson in the early 1980s (1984), introduces the concept of core and periphery workers, and has been explored in Chapter 2. It has been suggested that among the non-core workers, the 'emphasis on labour as a cost to be minimised is greatest' (Ashton and Felstead, 1995: 244). This would in turn suggest to us that if periphery labour is seen as a cost and not an investment, the associated investment in training and development of this group of workers would be minimal. Ashton and Felstead argue that 'HRM may fail to touch this growing army of peripheral workers – if HRM is to be found anywhere, it will be among a narrow band of core workers' (1995: 245).

However, we could consider the effects of an increase in functional flexibility (encourage multiskilling) and this could be suggested to lead to a need for training. While this training may not be formal/qualification-based training, it could nevertheless extend an individual's skills base.

Ashton and Felstead suggest that

> we can take the level of commitment a company shows towards investing in the skills of its workforce as a litmus test of whether or not British employers are changing the way they manage labour.
>
> (1995: 235)

If the organisation views its labour as a cost, it is less likely to invest in training and development and therefore will be reliant on the external labour market providing the required skills and knowledge it requires. If, however, the organisation manages labour as a resource and invests in the quality of its internal labour, it is more likely to demonstrate an investment in the importance of training and development.

The government's role in vocational training

It is important to consider the role of politics in the training and development provision in Britain.

> While the majority of EU states have some form of regulation in their training systems and also incorporate trade union interests in the policy making process for training, the UK is an exception.
>
> (Hendry, 1995: 410)

This quote provides us with a further avenue of exploration in terms of vocational training and development provision in the UK. While in Europe there is some degree of regulation in terms of the training provision by employers, 'in the UK vocational training is treated as the responsibility of the individual employer' (Hendry 1995: 410). To illustrate this difference we can look at examples from other European states.

Comparative note

In France a training tax (which in 1998 was a statutory minimum of 1.5 per cent of the annual wage bill) is primarily responsible for financing vocational education. This is termed a state-interventionist approach. Germany, Switzerland, Austria and Denmark operate a 'Dual System' where the provision of vocational education and training is a shared responsibility between the state and employers. This has been termed a 'corporatist' approach (for further discussion, see Hamlin 1999).

The UK, however, operate a 'voluntarist' approach to vocational training, meaning that it views issues relating to managing the labour force as the responsibility of industry and the employer and therefore the British government's intervention and involvement is not explicit. While not regulating provision in any way the UK government is involved in designing and launching training initiatives, for example, career development loans and training credits which aim to extend provision to all individuals, and essentially 'picks up the pieces', filling the gaps where employers don't offer any kind of training and development opportunities.

Activity 9.3

Consider the relative advantages and disadvantages of state involvement with vocational education and training policies.

Discussions surrounding the issues of voluntarism, which effectively places employers in control of levels of training provision, highlight a certain level of discontentment. To explore this let us consider a few critics of this policy.

> For almost 100 years – from the late 1880s to the mid-1980s – the history of training in the UK has been one of chronic under-investment, persistent failure and recurrent periods of acute skills shortages . . . the conclusion has been that countries such as Germany and France have had better national vocational training systems, more capable of quickly

responding to technological change and economic growth. In contrast the UK training system failed to produce the quantity of skilled labour required to meet national needs.

(Hamlin, 1999: 38)

If we compare Britain with other countries such as Germany and Japan, where the skill level is acknowledged to be higher, it is evident that the heart of the British training problem is the failure of employers to demand higher level skills.

(Ashton and Felstead, 1995: 241)

In the UK, the cost of industrial training is born in the main by employers and this goes far to explain the consistently inadequate investment made in training.

(Harrison, 1993: 79)

Despite a range of government initiatives over the years, the voluntary system has consistently failed to deliver sufficient effective training activity to create, in the UK, the necessary skilled workforce to match those of our competitors.   (DfEE, 2000a: 61)

Despite consistent criticisms, and in spite of some of the members' views, a National Skills Task Force produced the following statement in support of their proposals in the *Third Report: Tackling the Adult Skills Gap* (2000a: 46).

The Task Force has debated whether the framework we recommend should include a statutory delegation on employers to meet some form of minimum training requirement. Some members remain committed to the view that, without such an obligation, we will not succeed in delivering the full increase in adult learning which is needed. Other members, however, were convinced that the new framework ... can deliver the necessary progress and that a further statutory requirement is not appropriate. A new statutory delegation on employers does not form part of our recommendations.

Activity 9.4

Through research, consider the following:

Should 'a statutory framework be created that, through a system of tax incentives and, where necessary, tax penalties, ensures that the training issue is placed on every company's agenda?'   (DfEE, 2000a: 62)

Training provision in the UK

The 1985 survey by Coopers & Lybrand suggested that: 'Few employers think training sufficiently central to their business for it to be a main component in their corporate strategy' (1985: 4). While the previous section suggests that the UK still has a long way to go in terms of their training provision in comparison to their European counterparts, what do surveys and statistics tell us about developments in training provisions since the Coopers & Lybrand report?

To explore this we can consider Labour Force Survey Results from the Skills and Enterprise network on behalf of the Department for Education and Employment (see Figure 9.1).

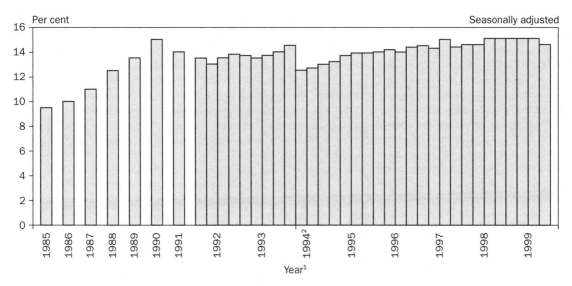

Figure 9.1 Trends in job-related training among employees[3] in the United Kingdom

Note:

1. 1984–1991 spring data only. 1992 onwards, spring, summer, autumn and winter of each year. Regrossed data from 1993–1999.
2. A discontinuity occurred in the data from summer 1994 onwards.
3. Employees of working age receiving job-related training (on or off-the-job) in the last four weeks (seasonally adjusted). Working age is defined as men aged 16–64 and women aged 16–59.
Source: Labour Force Survey, winter 1999/2000 in *DfEE Labour Market Quarterly Report* (2000c: 7)

The winter 1999/2000 Labour Force Survey results demonstrate a drop in the number of employees receiving job-related training. However, it can be seen from the statistics that the figures have risen by approximately 5 percentage points between 1985 and 2000, suggesting a gradual and relatively constant increase in the working population receiving training over this fifteen-year period.

The same survey shows that nearly two-thirds of all the job training is funded by the employer or potential employer (see Figure 9.2). The figures do show an imbalance in the number of males and females benefiting from this investment, with employers paying for 68.1 per cent of men's training as opposed to only 58.6 per cent for women. The figures suggest that more women are paying for their own training through various means, this could be suggested to be linked to women re-training after a career break.

It is evident from the 'Skill needs in Britain' survey (Figure 9.3) that we can establish a link between the types of training funded in Britain, and Ashton and Felstead (1995: 247) claim that 'the main determinant of company training appears to have been "push" factors such as BS5750, health and safety requirements and occupational regulations rather than the "pull" factors of HRM techniques'. A view repeated by the CIPD: 'training activities are still largely driven by the need to react to legislation' (CIPD 2000c: 12). However, these figures also demonstrate the pace of change in technology is having an effect on training provision. Foreign language training, despite globalisation, still appears to be a low priority on the training agenda of British organisations.

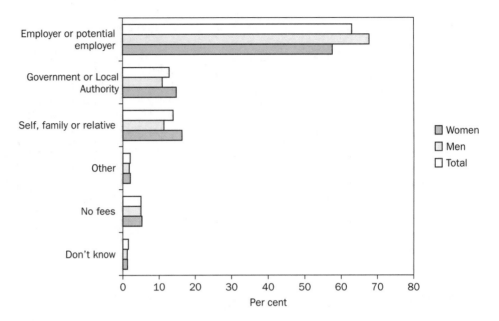

Figure 9.2 Who pays for training?[1]

Note:
1. Question is only asked of those doing some off-the-job training.
Source: Labour Force Survey, winter (1999/2000) in DfEE *Labour Market Quarterly Report* (2000c: 7)

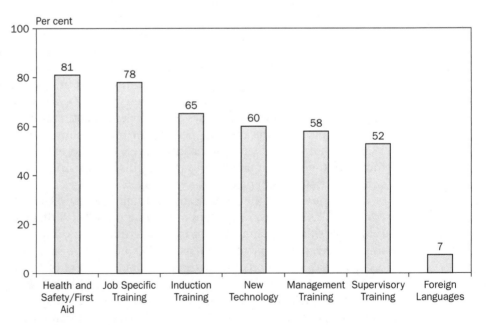

Figure 9.3 Type of off-the-job training funded or arranged by employers, 1998
Source: DfEE *Labour Market and Skills Trends* (2000d: 53)

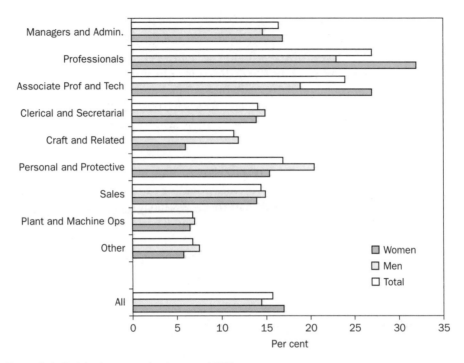

Figure 9.4 Training by occupation (autumn 1999)

Source: Labour Force Survey, autumn 1999 in DfEE *Labour Market Quarterly Report* (2000b: 7)

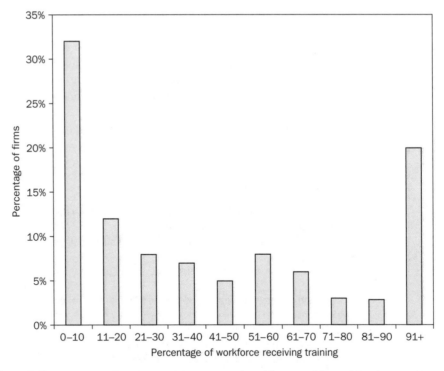

Figure 9.5 Distribution of training provision – proportion of firms providing training, by percentage of workforce covered   *Source*: DfEE *Towards a National Skills Agenda* (2000a: 25)

Studies have shown, e.g. (Prais, 1985), that a disproportionate amount of all training that does take place in the United Kingdom is aimed at the higher and more senior levels of the workforce. Figure 9.4 shows that, based on the labour force survey in autumn 1999, this does not appear to have changed 'people in the professional and associate professional and technical groups of occupations were nearly four times more likely to receive training than plant and machine operatives (26.8 per cent and 24.1 per cent as against 6.9 per cent)' (*Labour Market Quarterly Report*, 2000c: 7).

Figure 9.5 shows that a staggeringly high one-third of all employers provide training for only 0–10 per cent of their workforce. The same figure shows that one-fifth of all employers are providing training for over 90 per cent of their workforces. It is suggested that 'those less likely to receive training . . . include people working for smaller firms, with employers being less likely to provide training the smaller they are' (DfEE, 2000a: 22). This could be suggested to link to a number of reasons, probably most significant being lack of resources in relation to finance, specialist skills and knowledge activities.

Employee development roles

The role undertaken by the employee development specialist in an organisation will be influenced by a number of internal and external conditions. Stewart (1999) has produced a summary of key influences based on the work of Harrison (1997) and Reid and Barrington (1997). His list includes factors which are said to highlight the structural influences on the function in conjunction with the internal issues of interrelationships and interactions (see Table 9.1).

It has been suggested that 'Two of the key issues surrounding the status of training and development in many organisations are: who these organisational trainers are and what they do and how the effectiveness of their activities can be proved' (Stewart, Manhire and Hall, 1999: 222).

There have been several research studies undertaken that have produced typologies and models which aim to explore the different types of role taken by the

Table 9.1 Factors influencing the role of employee development

- Top management support for and interest in employee development
- Size of organisation in terms of numbers employed
- Nature of operations and 'business' of the organisation, e.g. degree of complexity, range of occupation groups
- Need demand for training and development, e.g. make-up of internal and external labour markets
- Location and hierarchical position of person with ultimate responsibility for employee development
- Culture of the organisation
- External factors, e.g. degree of legislative regulation
- Expertise, professionalism and credibility of development specialists

Source: Stewart (1999: 84)

trainer/employee development specialist in the organisation. The most often cited studies relate to the work of Pettigrew, Jones and Reason (1982) who produced a typology of trainer roles which we will explore later in the chapter.

The American Society for Training and Development (ASTD) commissioned research into roles adopted by HRD professionals published by Harris and De Simone (1994), and Bennett and Leduchowicz (1983) and considered the two key themes of why invest in training and how do we deliver it? These questions led to a model of four trainer roles derived from the answers to their research.

However, let us return to the work of Pettigrew, Jones and Reason (1982) whose research produced a typology of trainer roles (see Table 9.2).

Table 9.2 Pettigrew, Jones and Reason typology of trainer roles

The provider	A role emphasising the operational aspect of the trainer's role, and little integration with the organisational objectives and strategies. Activities focused on bringing about steady improvements. This role is often the 'traditional' view of employee development.
The passive provider	The role of the passive provider is reactive rather than proactive in approach. This reactivity and lack at 'promotion' if the role limits the activities to 'low level' involvement which have little influence on the organisation. Their role is often undertaken by an individual lacking in experience and expertise especially in relation to 'internal politics'.
The training manager	A managerial role with an emphasis on planning and resource allocation. The role will involve co-ordination of training activities and the responsibility for effective and efficient administrative systems.
The change agent	A role focused on the development and changing of the organisation rather than the maintenance. The role will closely link to activities associated with learning and development (organisational development) rather than prescriptive and traditional training courses. The role emphasises the need for the employee development specialist to act as consultant rather than provider.
Role in transition	A role which represents the movement of practioners from provider to 'change agent'.

The typology produced by Pettigrew, Jones and Reason (1982) illustrates the obvious links to factors which influence the role of employee development (Stewart, 1999). It is clear that the different roles presented in the typology will have an influence on the type of internal relationships the trainer has specifically with line and senior managers. The *provider* and *passive provider* will tend to be operating at a distance from management. The role of *training manager* as 'implied' in the job title will more likely have a close involvement with other managers in the organisation. The roles of *change agent* and *role in transition* have an emphasis on working with line management and therefore building good interrelationships and operating at a more strategic level will be an essential part of this role.

It could be suggested from this typology that the first two roles reflect conditions more in line with personnel management whereas the later roles due to increased involvement, influence and credibility reflect the 'strategic role' associated with the concept of 'HRM'. However, the question has been posed . . . 'Should not the practice of trainers, whether managers or not, be seen as influencing organisational performance?' (Stewart, Manhire and Hall, 1999: 222).

If we consider a more recent survey: IPD, (2000c) research was carried out to identify which skills training managers viewed as most important in their role. The most highly ranked skill was 'knowledge of people management', followed by 'knowledge of business objectives', 'training evaluation', 'knowledge of organisational development' and 'training needs analysis'.

It would appear from this ranking that trainers do see their role as having an influence on business performance. With the IPD research suggesting that the 'training function is becoming more closely aligned with business processes' (IPD, 2000c: 9).

Activity 9.5

1 Reflect on the typology by Pettigrew, Jones and Reason (1982). What are the potential advantages and disadvantages of each role from the perspective of:

   a) the trainer,
   b) the individual,
   c) the organisation.

2 Taking into account additional research by the IPD (2000c), which role do you feel most closely links with the current needs of the organisation and why?

Organisational approaches to employee development

A number of research studies have identified that organisations adopt different approaches to the practice of employee development. In this section we examine two often cited approaches, namely the *Ashridge research* (Barham *et al.*, 1987) and the *Megginson model* (Boydell, 1983).

The Ashridge research

This is the most recent of the research concentrating on approaches taken to the practice of employee development and was produced following a survey of a cross-section of organisations in the UK and a number of in-depth organisational case studies. This research highlighted that changes in the environmental context had an effect on the way that employee development was practised and managed in

Table 9.3 The Ashridge model

Approach	Typified by
The fragmented approach	• employee development is *ad hoc* and unplanned • employee development activities viewed as a cost not an investment • employee development activities do not link to the organisation's strategy and objectives • training and development activities are mainly concerned with knowledge organisation • training and development activities have an emphasis on prescriptive and directive courses
The formalised approach	• human resource development is clearly linked to both organisational objectives and individual goals • training and development activities often link with other HR functions (e.g. appraisal systems) • employee development activities link to organisational objectives but primarily are concerned with focusing on individual development • training and development activities have an emphasis on both knowledge and skill acquisition • increased involvement of line managers in employee development activities
The focused approach	• human resource development is clearly linked to both organisational objectives and individual goals • training and development activities encompass the practice of a wide range of activities to develop knowledge, skill, value and attitude • individuals are involved with identifying and managing their learning • line management have a greater responsibility for the development of their staff • emphasis on evaluating/measuring the effectiveness of human resource development

organisations. It was suggested that the current environmental context requires more flexible, customer-oriented and internationally focused organisations which require leadership rather than control and an emphasis on the development of employees to enhance potential.

The Ashridge group identified three phases in the changing approaches to employee development (see Table 9.3).

Stewart (1999: 130) suggests that the three approaches can be associated with different time periods which typify different environmental conditions. He suggests that the fragmented approach typifies the practice and context of the 1950s/1960s, the formalised approach is primarily linked to the prevailing conditions of the 1970s/1980s and the focused approach has relevance in the 1990s and beyond.

Activity 9.6

1 Review the three approaches outlined by the Ashridge model. Consider the advantages and disadvantages of each approach from the perspective of each of the following:

a) individual employees
b) employee development practitioners
c) senior managers

2 What links can you identify between the personnel vs. HRM debate and the three approaches outlined?

3 Consider the implication and consequence for the role of the professional development practitioners in relation to each of the three approaches. How do you feel the role will change and develop?

The Megginson model

While the Ashridge research which has been outlined reflects recent research into approaches of employee development, the Megginson typology is based on research carried out more than twenty years ago.

This research had a focus on approaches to training needs rather than employee development in general, and was carried out by researching the practice of training in a number of organisations. The research produced findings that influenced the following five-category typology (see Table 9.4).

Activity 9.7

Review the Megginson five-category typology.

1 Which of the approaches is most apparent in an organisation with which you are familiar?

2 What are the potential drawbacks of such a categorisation?

3 Which approach do you feel is most appropriate in the current environmental context and why?

To explore further a formal or planned approach to employee development in an organisation, we can explore the systems approach as outlined by Megginson. The systems approach is most often depicted as a cyclical model which encompasses four key stages (see Figure 9.6).

The model implies that links exist between each step and that the process is cyclical and therefore the learning process is continuous.

To generate a better understanding of the model, each stage will be discussed in more detail.

Table 9.4 The Megginson five-category typology

	Typified by	Advantages	Disadvantages
The welfare approach	• focused on the needs of individuals • training provided for the benefit of the individual • 'value' linked qualifications and certification which in turn are linked to career progression • training generally regarded as positive as long as it satisfies	• employee loyalty and commitment • strong organisational culture	• resource intensive • expensive • may not be linked to organisational strategy or employee development strategy
The administrative approach	• concerned with the design and delivery of efficient systems to monitor and record training and development activities • focused on organisation of information and data • activities which do not 'fit' the system may be overlooked • formulation of organisational-wide training and development plans which are rigidly followed • impartial and consistent application of the roles in approving expenditure and activities • maintenance of accurate and up-to-date records • suggested link to bureaucratic structures (Stewart 1999: 127)	• perceived fairness • training plans aligned with organisational objectives	• inflexible • system-based rather than a focus on organisational and individual needs, benefits and relevance
The political approach	• the profile of the employee development function in terms of power/status/influence • pursuit of credibility in the eyes of senior managers • training activities linked to what is valued with decision-makers • primarily concerned with satisfying senior management	• the function has a link to the organisational objectives and strategies through their liaison with senior managers	• individual needs ignored • difficult in times of senior management change
The organisation development approach	• link to the application of theory and research from social and behavioural science • approach linked to development of groups rather than individuals • emphasis on interpersonal relationships • emphasis on 'soft skills' rather than 'systems' • congruence and coherence between individual and organisational needs and aspirations (Stewart 1999: 128)	• emphasis on developing individual potential • improved flexibility and ability to respond to change	• could be viewed as unstructured with a lack of focus on organisational strategy • could ignore on-the-job skill and knowledge requirements
The systems approach	• link to 'scientific management' • referred to as 'formal' or 'planned' employee development • approach consists of following a 'cyclical process' • emphasises interrelationships of connected steps • related to 'continuous development'	• logical and rational process • provides predictability and control • ensures consistency in approach	• rigid • hard to apply to some occasions • developed in times of stability

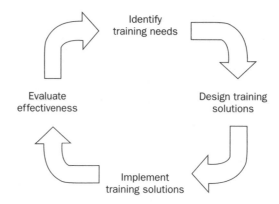

Figure 9.6 The systematic training cycle

The systems approach to employee development

Identifying training needs

> For training to be effective it is necessary to discern the training needs not only of the individual and the group but how their needs fit the overall organisational objectives.
>
> (Beardwell and Holden, 1994: 340)

This quote outlines key areas where training needs may exist and is well depicted by Boydell (1983) who suggests that training needs exist at three levels: the organisational level, the job/occupation level and the individual employee. Stewart (1999: 149) provides definition at these three levels as:

- *Organisational level* 'Knowledge, skills and attitudes which all members of the organisation, irrespective of their job or occupation, will be required to develop.'
- *Job/occupational level* 'What any individual needs to know and understand, and to be able to do in what kind of manner if successful performance in the job or occupation is to be possible.'
- *Individual employee* 'Individual training needs exist to the extent that there is a gap between the knowledge, skills and attitudes currently held by the individual and the knowledge, skills and attitudes specified at the job/occupation level.'

To identify further the methods which may be used at each level by the practitioner, it is possible to combine ideas relating to methods (Beardwell and Holden, 1994) with Boydell's (1983) three-level model (see Table 9.5).

The table does not intend to present an exhaustive list of methods available; this would be difficult as different organisations will have their own specific practices. However, the table does give an indication of the types of methods available to the practitioner and information sources within the organisation which can be utilised.

We can see that it has been suggested that training needs can exist at three levels (Boydell, 1983) and that a variety of methods are appropriate in identifying

Table 9.5 Identifying training needs

Level of training need	Methods/documentation available
Organisational level	Policy statements Organisation objectives Vision statements Mission statements Legislation
Job/occupational level	Job description Job analysis Interview with line managers Performance objectives Analysis of competency requirements Person specification
Individual employee	Personal profiles Performance appraisal Self-assessment Assessment centres Training audits

Source: Adapted from Beardwell and Holden (1994) and Boydell (1983)

Activity 9.8

1 Considering an organisation with which you are familiar, what methods are used to identify training needs?

2 What is your analysis of the appropriateness of a three-level approach to training as described by Boydell (1983)?

the varying needs. However, what questions should the practitioner consider to identify the specific nature of the need?

Stewart (1999) suggests a method which follows a staged approach to considering various areas for investigation when establishing training needs (see Figure 9.7 on page 206).

Stewart (1999) points out that it can be quite difficult to distinguish the nature of the cause at Stage 3 and whether this cause is training or non-training related. To help with this issue, Stewart identifies some common training and non-training causes (see Table 9.6).

Table 9.6 Nature of training and non-training causes

	Training causes	Non-training causes	
Performance	• Inadequate training • Inappropriate training • Skills/knowledge gaps • Inadequate recruitment and selection	• Lack of feedback/motivation • Job design faults • Organisation structure • Recruitment and selection procedures • Poor equipment/tools etc.	**Problems**

Source: Stewart (1999: 153)

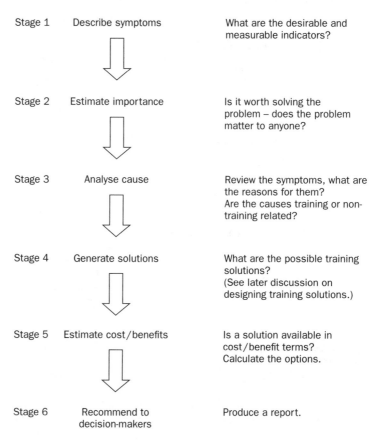

Stage 1	Describe symptoms	What are the desirable and measurable indicators?
Stage 2	Estimate importance	Is it worth solving the problem – does the problem matter to anyone?
Stage 3	Analyse cause	Review the symptoms, what are the reasons for them? Are the causes training or non-training related?
Stage 4	Generate solutions	What are the possible training solutions? (See later discussion on designing training solutions.)
Stage 5	Estimate cost/benefits	Is a solution available in cost/benefit terms? Calculate the options.
Stage 6	Recommend to decision-makers	Produce a report.

Figure 9.7 Staged approach for establishing training needs
Source: Adapted from Stewart (1999: 153)

It can be seen from this brief discussion on the first stage of the systematic approach to training that this stage is crucial to gain an informed understanding of the exact nature of the training need. Answers generated at this stage should link to the second stage of the model as presented which considers the design of training solutions.

It is interesting to consider what is actually happening in practice at the identification stage of training needs. For information relating to current practice we can consider the 2000 *IPD Training and Development Survey* (IPD 2000c). In order to gain information relating to whether the analysis of training needs are linked to business objectives the following topics were posed:

- Which of the following methods do you use in your establishment to analyse training needs?
- Rank the relative importance of the various methods you use for determining training needs.

The results of the survey suggested the following (see Table 9.7).

Line manager requests appears to be the most frequently used method of analysing training needs, with 95.7 per cent of respondents using this method,

Table 9.7 Ranking of methods most often used to analyse training needs as against those considered most important by training managers

	Method used to analyse training needs	Method considered most important
Line manager request	1	3
Employee requests	2	4
Performance appraisal	3	2
Training audit	4	5
Analysis of business plan	5	1
Project analysis	6	7
Cost/benefit analysis	7	6

Source: IPD Training and development survey (2000c)

followed by 93.2 per cent of respondents using employee requests and 89.2 per cent using performance appraisal.

Cost/benefit analysis appears to be the least utilised method, however, a significant difference occurs by sector. While approximately 40 per cent of establishments use cost/benefit analysis to identify needs, when the respondents were considered in sectors, figures suggested that 60 per cent of the private sector used the method as compared to 36.7 per cent of the public sector.

A review of this table suggests that although the training managers identified an analysis of business plan as the most important method, suggesting an awareness of the importance of linking training to business strategy, in practice this was only the fifth ranked method in use. This suggests a gap between principle and current practice.

Design and implementation of training

It is intended to discuss the next two stages of the systematic approach simultaneously as it can be argued that issues relating to design will have direct links to implementation and these links need to be considered at the design stage to aid integration between the two.

The first key stage of the design process is to develop specific aims and objectives for the training event. These should be influenced by the information generated at the identification stage of the systematic model. While it is not our intention to explore the writing of objectives in any detail, a full discussion can be found in Stewart (1999).

When designing training and development activities, an understanding of learning theories and processes is important. Different types of learning will require different types of process. Downs (1995) used the mnemonic MUD to categorise different types of learning, suggesting that all learning objectives will link to one or more of the following:

M – Memorising
U – Understanding
D – Doing

Downs suggests that, dependent on the nature of the learning objectives, different methods are appropriate to different types of learning event. For example, methods relating to memorising could be repetition, comparing and concentrating could aid understanding and doing could be developed by practice and feedback. This is a very simplistic categorisation and it is more likely that learning objectives will encompass different types of learning requirement.

As different methods appear to be appropriate to different learning objectives we can also consider at design stage the learning requirements of the individual. In Chapter 8 the Honey and Mumford learning styles classification was discussed. This suggests that individuals will respond better to certain methods dependent on their preferred learning style. For example, it could be suggested that an activist would respond well to role-play, and a theorist may enjoy the use of case studies.

Using this as a starting point consider the following.

Activity 9.9

1 Review your understanding of Honey and Mumford's learning styles in Chapter 8.

2 Generate a list for the *most* preferred and *least* preferred learning and training method in relation to each style.

It can be seen that the design of training solutions needs to take into account the type of learning objectives and the individual learning styles of the learner. The range of different training methods are vast, however. Reid and Barrington (1997: 231) present a summarised list of methods which can aid the decision relating to what type of training solution to implement:

- *On-the-job training* This type of training will include the traditional 'sitting by Nellie' approach which simply means watching and training a trainee while they are undertaking their normal routine (for example, watching a teacher teach a class).
- *Planned organisation experience* Training designed to be an integral part of the job-holder's position, for example, secondments to other departments, involvement in new projects or new systems. Mentoring is another example of this type of training – whereby the mentor assists the mentee with their development both personally and within the organisation.
- *In-house courses* These courses are held in-house (where the organisation takes responsibility for all aspects of the event) and may include a regular programme of generic-type training alongside events arranged for specific needs; for example, a change in work practice/legislation.
- *Planned experience outside the organisation* Encompassing activities such as visits and secondments to clients/competitors.
- *External courses* These will be run by external providers, e.g. consultants, universities, etc., and may lead to formal accreditation and qualifications.

- *Self-management learning* The individual will be involved in identifying their self-development needs and will be encouraged to reflect on their learning requirements and be involved in sourcing appropriate opportunities.

Activity 9.10

1 Consider the list of methods as classified by Reid and Barrington. What are the relative advantages and disadvantages of each type of training?

2 Reflecting on an organisation with which you are familiar, what evidence is there of different types of training being delivered in relation to Reid and Barrington's summary?

To review the types of training methods used by UK establishments, the Training and Development Survey conducted by the IPD is outlined (see Figure 9.8).

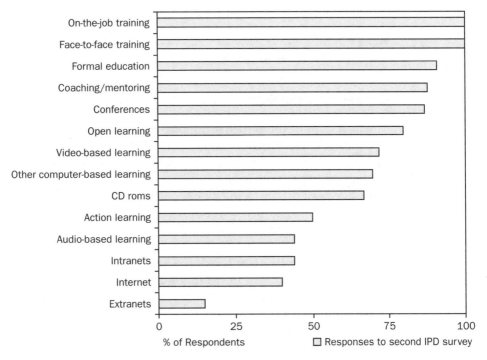

Figure 9.8 Which of the following training methods and facilities are used by your establishment?
Source: *IPD Training and Development Survey Report* (2000c: 10)

It is evident from this survey that traditional methods of training, i.e. face-to-face training and on-the-job training, continue to be a popular choice. However, if we consider further results from the same survey which considered net changes in percentage over a one-year period we can start to see the increasing influence of technology on training delivery in the UK (see Figure 9.9).

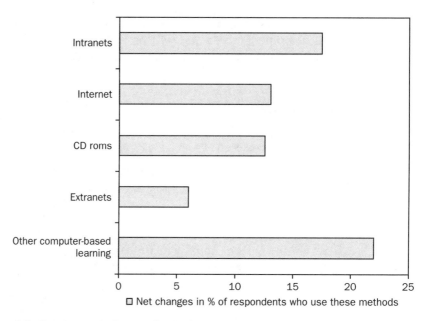

Figure 9.9 Net changes in the use of technological training methods over the 1999 to 2000 period

Source: *IPD Training and Development Survey Report* (2000c: 10)

Evaluation of training

The final stage of the systematic approach to training provision is the evaluation of training. This is defined by Bolton (1997: 125) as 'Any attempt to gain information on the effects of a training programme, and to assess the value of training in the light of that information.'

As discussed earlier in the chapter, it is very difficult for the employee development specialist to demonstrate the cost/benefit of training provision to the organisation. Difficulties relate to the long-term benefits derived from training provision which would necessitate costly ongoing evaluation. Additionally, unless a pre-test were to be undertaken, it would be difficult to attribute any improvement in knowledge/skills to the training course.

However, despite these difficulties it is important to evaluate training provision to aid continual improvement.

Reid and Barrington (1994: 291) suggest that the following key questions should be posed in evaluating training programmes:

1 Why is evaluation required?
2 Who should do it?
3 What aspects should be evaluated and when should this be done?
4 What kinds of measurement will be used?

It is not intended to provide a comprehensive answer to each of the above questions; detailed discussion can be found in Reid and Barrington (1997), Easterby-Smith (1986) and Stewart (1999).

Table 9.8 Reid and Barrington's approach to the evaluation process

Why is evaluation needed?
- To enable the effectiveness of an investment in training to be evaluated
- To inform the trainer of the relevance and level of the learning experience
- To provide feedback to the trainer in relation to the methods used in the training delivery
- To aid the individual evaluate their own learning process
- To provide feedback to inform any improvements which could be made

Who should carry out the evaluation?
- Involve those who could learn from it most, e.g. line manager, trainers, learners
- Avoid bias
- Ensure credibility, expertise and knowledge

What aspects of training should be evaluated and when?
- Reid and Barrington (1994: 293) present the framework based on the ideas of Hamlin (1974) and Whitelaw (1972) who outline how training can be evaluated at different levels.

Level 1	Reactions of trainees to the content and methods of training, to the trainer and to any other factors perceived as relevant. What did the trainer think about the training?
Level 2	Learning attained during the training period. Did the trainees learn what was intended?
Level 3	Job behaviour in the work environment at the end of the training period. Did the learning transfer to the job?
Level 4	Effect on the trainees' department. Has the training helped departmental performance?
Level 5	The ultimate level. Has the training affected the ultimate well-being of the organisation, for example, in terms of profitability or survival?

What kind of measurement will be used?
- A variety of different methods are appropriate to each level

Level 1	Questionnaires, interviews, group discussion
Level 2	Tests, examinations, projects, case studies
Level 3	On-the-job performance and improvement, increasingly difficult at more senior levels
Level 4/5	Very difficult to evaluate due to short-term/long-term issues, difficult to monitor behavioural change. However, organisational health indicators may be used, i.e. profitability, staff turnover, customer feedback

Source: Adapted from Reid and Barrington (1994)

However, a summary of issues worthy of consideration in relation to the key questions posed by Reid and Barrington (1997) are presented in Table 9.8.

It should be noted from the above summarised table that as evaluation progresses through the levels, measurement becomes more difficult. Additionally Beardwell and Holden (1994: 351) point out that 'While it is relatively easy to evaluate a formal off-the-job course, much on-the-job training often takes place in an informal way, which is usually subjective and open to wide interpretation.'

These issues demonstrate the relative difficulty of the task of the trainer in evaluating training provision, particularly at the higher levels where it is difficult to link improvement purely to training due to other external influences.

These difficulties also link to earlier discussions in the chapter in relation to the challenges facing the role of the employee development specialist and the credibility of the training and development function in organisations.

Discussion

We have explored throughout this chapter a number of key issues in relation to the context and practice of employee development.

While we have established the links to human resourcing strategies in organisations, and suggested that an organisation which professes to be practising the concept of 'human resource management' must pay serious attention to the integration of training and development strategies, we have seen through surveys, statistics and evidence presented by writers in this field that:

> The available evidence institutionally and in practice suggests that HRM policies and practices associated with training have taken root in only a few British companies, falling short of that which would be required in order to fuel an HRM revolution.
>
> (Ashton and Felstead, 1995: 250)

A number of issues can be associated with this evidence. We have explored the influence that British politics has in the types and levels of training undertaken in the United Kingdom and explored a number of survey results pointing to the types and amounts of training undertaken in organisations.

Challenges facing the profession have been indicated particularly in relation to demonstrating the cost/benefit of training to the organisation.

In relation to the role of the practitioner in this field we have considered different roles and approaches taken to the profession and the implications of such on the organisation. A traditional approach to training provision (the systematic approach) has been outlined and a summary of key issues to take into account at each stage of this cyclical approach have been identified.

To conclude, it is worth considering a suggestion by Keep (1992: 335) when reviewing an organisation's training and development practices:

> It can be suggested that training effort is one useful litmus test of the reality of HRM/HRD policies within British firms. If the training and development of its employees is not afforded high priority, if training is not seen as a vital component in the realisation of business plans, then it is hard to accept that such a company has committed itself to HRM.

Case Study 9.1

Sure Bet Insurance Group

Sure Bet Insurance Group (SBIG) is the result of a merger of two large, well-established and household-name insurance companies. The purpose of the merger included a declared intention to provide a strong basis to achieve growth in international business. The group operates in more than 70 countries, conducts business in most classes of insurance and delivers its products to individual and commercial customers through a complex set of distribution channels. The first year's operation of the new group achieved a turnover of

Case Study continued

£12 billion and the merger resulted in a market capitalisation of £10 billion. There have also been significant changes at the top of the organisation following the merger. A new Chief Executive has been appointed, along with a further three new directors. These appointments reflect the intention to internationalise the company as two, including the Chief Executive, came from a non-UK European country: one is American and the other is an Australian. The new board has introduced a matrix structure for the newly created SBIG which emphasises global, geographic regions as one of the two axes.

Angela Bland had worked as management development manager for one of the merged companies for 12 years. In SBIG, Angela has been appointed as a management development consultant working for a group HR manager with special responsibility for 'internationalising' the HR policies and processes in the new organisation. Angela's first task in her new role is to produce a development programme for middle managers across the group which will focus on raising their awareness of the aims and ambitions of the group and enable the managers to begin to analyse the implications and opportunities for them. In particular, the intention is that the programme will result in middle managers adopting a wider vision of their role to support the international ambitions of the group.

Angela has spent six months conducting research to inform design of the programme and to help plan its implementation. The focus of her research has been internal, to identify the nature and size of the target population and to establish the expectations of key stakeholders, including middle mangers, through a questionnaire survey of a representative sample; and external, to establish methods adopted by organisations of a similar size. Angela's external research has consisted of a review and analysis of published material and, where possible, visits to and discussions with relevant development staff in other, non-competitor businesses. The results of the internal research include a finding that the potential target population totalled nearly 5000 across the world, a typical profile of a middle-aged male who is professionally qualified but with little if any experience outside the insurance industry or country of origin and who demonstrates a high level of company loyalty. External research on practices in other organisations suggests that formal development events will be insufficient by themselves to achieve the intended aims of the programme. Direct experience and exposure to different cultural influences, both national and organisational (e.g. divisional and functional), are likely to be required. Angela's research has enabled her to produce the following principles to inform design and implementation of the programme:

- use division and country/region-based HRD staff in implementation
- involve senior managers at division/regional level in delivery of the programme
- participant groups to represent a mix of nationality, function, age and experience
- a varied number of methods, with a formal event forming the 'launch' and 'heart' of the programme
- involvement of participants' line managers, especially in pre- and post-event briefings
- an element of self-managed learning supported by appropriate materials
- production of personal development plans by participants related to and used throughout and after the programme. PDPs to be agreed with line managers

Angela is now in a position to produce more detailed proposals. These will be discussed with her manager before being presented to the group director of human resources. Angela has no concerns over necessary resources being allocated since internationalisation is high priority in SBIG. She is also confident that her research will support her arguments. It is now just a matter of working out the details.

1 What objectives should Angela present for the programme as being relevant and achievable?

2 What methods other than a formal development event would you suggest to Angela to include in the programme, and why?

3 Given the importance of the formal development event, what design features should Angela adopt? For example, objectives, duration, content and methods?

4 What arrangements should Angela consider for implementation? What factors should she take into account in deciding these arrangements?

5 How should Angela present her proposals to her manager and what advice would you give her on handling the meeting?

SUMMARY

In this chapter the following key points have been made:

- Key definitions which focus on education, training and development help us to develop an understanding of their implications for the practice of employee development.

- Organisations which profess to be practising the concept of 'human resource management' must pay serious attention to the integration of training and development strategies.

- Organisations taking a short-term view on training and development activities might view them as a cost rather than an investment.

- The government play a key role in the type of vocational training and development which is undertaken in the UK.

- There are a number of internal and external factors which influence the role of employee development in organisations.

- Organisations adopt different approaches to the practice of employee development.

- There are a number of methods available to the training specialist within the organisation to identify training needs.

- The design of training needs to take into account a number of variables including different types of learning and individual styles of learner.

- The evaluation of training is a complex activity.

FURTHER READING

For further details on the issues covered in this chapter, please consult Harrison (1997) and Stewart (1999).

Part **5** **Employee relations**

Chapter 10

Management strategic options for managing the employment relationship

John Leopold

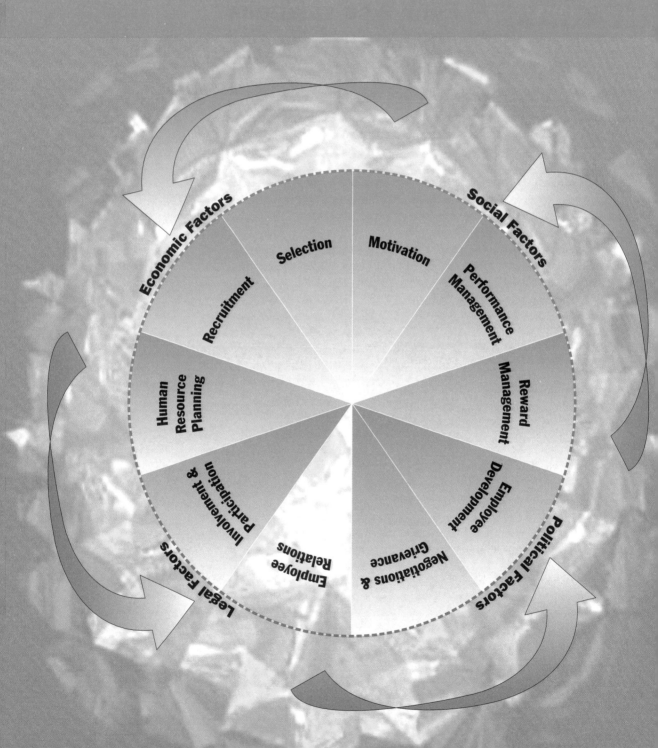

Having completed this chapter and its associated activities, readers should be able to:

- understand the concept of a frame of reference
- differentiate between the unitarist, pluralist and Marxist frame of reference
- differentiate between individualism and collectivism in the employment relationship
- appreciate the differentiation of management styles
- understand why individual workers may seek to join a trade union
- understand the strategic choices open to management around being or remaining non-union, or being unionised
- appreciate the state of union organisation in the United Kingdom and how this has changed over the past 25 years
- understand a number of reasons that have been put forward to explain union decline
- understand current legislation in the area of union recognition and appreciate its potential impact
- appreciate the employment relationship in non-union contexts

INTRODUCTION

In Chapter 1 we argued that the rise of trade union power in the 1970s was one of the reasons why personnel managers and personnel management came to be seen as more significant during that period. Personnel and, more specifically, industrial relations managers demonstrated expertise in conducting collective bargaining and in dealing with unions in the workplace. The steady decline of union membership and influence in the 1980s and 1990s seemed to obviate that requirement. Indeed it was seen by many management writers to have been a reactive, 'firefighting' approach to managing the employment relationship and advocates of human resource management sought a more strategic approach.

In this chapter we will examine the strategic options management may seek to pursue in their relationship with employees and the question of union recognition. In order to fully appreciate that, we must also understand different possible approaches to understanding the employment relationship and also what motivates employees to join a union or not. We then outline the state of union membership in Britain over the past 25 years and seek to understand the reasons for the extensive decline, but possible recent revival. This understanding may assist in shaping management decisions about how to manage the employment relationship.

Frames of reference

Participants in the employment relationship, managers, owners, employees, trade union leaders, come into the relationship with particular ways of viewing the world, especially the world of work, and the relationships that take place within that sphere. Fox (1966), drawing on the work of Thelen and Whithall, calls this way of viewing the world a frame of reference and defines it as

> the way in which each person perceives and interprets events by means of a conceptual structure of generalisations or contexts, postulates about what is essential, assumptions as to what is valuable, attitudes about what is possible, and ideas about what will work effectively. This conceptual structure constitutes the frame of reference of that person.
>
> (Fox, 1966: 2)

Fox translated this general concept into the sphere of employment relations when he outlined the unitarist and pluralist frames of reference. Both Fox (1974) and later writers have refined and developed this and added the radical frame of reference. The radical frame can include both those operating in a radical pluralist/Weberian mode and Marxists (Hyman, 1975).

The essence of the unitarist view of the employment relationship is that the organisation is seen as a team in which each team member has their place and part to play. The organisation has a common purpose that flows from the leadership of senior management. These managers are the one source of authority in the organisation and are also the sole focus of loyalty for all team members. It flows from this thinking that there is no place for trade unions in the organisation as these would be a competing source of loyalty and potentially a challenger to management as the sole source of authority, or opposition to management's 'right to manage'. Where management is forced to deal with unions they would seek to confine this to determining pay and conditions and not desire unions to have any say on decision-making within the organisation on managerial relations.

For the unitarist manager, conflict is seen as a pathological occurrence that needs to be removed, or cut out like a cancer, from the organisation. Thus industrial disputes would be blamed on militants or troublemakers and managers would seek to sack such people rather than examine any underlying cause of the conflict.

The pluralist view, on the other hand, sees the organisation as a coalition of individuals and groups. It is therefore accepted that different levels of management, or workers in different departments, might have different objectives and loyalties. Moreover it is accepted that it is legitimate for these differences to be articulated and expressed through trade unions. In the pluralist view it is management's job to manage the differences between these interest groups in such a way as to create and maintain balance or equilibrium which allows the organisation to move forward. Conflict between interest groups may well break out from time to time but it is expected that equilibrium can be restored through negotiation and agreement.

From the Marxist perspective, conflict is neither seen as pathological, nor something that can readily be brought back into balance, but as something that is endemic in the capitalist system of production. Management prerogatives, or 'management's right to manage' are not accepted and workers are constantly encouraged to challenge them. However, as there is a tension between trade union consciousness, where trade unions fight to improve workers' conditions within the confines of capitalist society, and class consciousness, where workers realise the need to overthrow capitalist society, then different Marxist writers have different expectations about the role of trade unions in capitalist society. Nonetheless, the Marxist perspective on industrial relations encompasses a wider social, political and economic analysis of capitalist society and is not confined to issues of job regulation or labour markets.

It is suggested that all participants in the employment relationship, managers, employees and, even, academic writers on the topic, view the world through one or other of these perspectives. The Marxist analysis informs the control of the labour process approach (Braverman, 1974; Thompson, 1989). One can also see the close link between the unitarist frame of reference and a human resource management approach with its emphasis on commitment, loyalty and strategic direction. But perhaps in recent years if trade unions have turned the corner in terms of membership decline, there may be scope for the ideas associated with the pluralist view to have a resurgence. In other words there may be more joint regulation of the employment relationship.

However, it is too simplistic to characterise attitudes towards the employment relationship as being either unitarist or pluralist, either harmony or conflict. Some aspects of the employment relationship are based on co-operation – to maintain earnings and the viability of the firm, but others are potentially divergent – the employer is likely to seek to buy labour at the lowest possible price, whereas employees seek the highest pay attainable in the economic and political circumstances. So the employment relationship is simultaneously a conflictual and a co-operative one.

The frames of reference approach applies to individuals and later writers have attempted to categorise organisations and develop the idea of a management style in industrial relations which can be applied to organisations. Purcell (1987) is one of the main advocates of this approach. He attempted to go beyond unitarism and pluralism by suggesting that the two key dimensions of management style are individualism and collectivism. Management style is defined as 'the existence of a distinctive set of guiding principles, written or otherwise, which set parameters to and signposts for managerial action in the way employees are treated and particular events are handled' (Purcell, 1987: 535).

Individualism is 'the extent to which the firm gives credence to the feelings and sentiments of each employee and seeks to develop and encourage each employee's capacity and role at work' (Purcell, 1987: 536). Collectivism, on the other hand, is 'the extent to which the organisation recognises the right of employees to have a say in those aspects of management decision-making which concern them' (Purcell, 1987: 538). Both of these dimensions are further subdivided into high and low. High individualism emphasises the *resource status* of employees whom employers seek to develop and nurture. Parallels may be seen here with high commitment, high performance work systems. Low individualism, however, stresses the *commodity status* of employees who are therefore a cost to be minimised and controlled. Paternalism is midway on this axis and is where the employer accepts some responsibility for the employee, but in a way that suggests that the employer knows best, not unlike the way some parents might treat teenagers.

Collectivism can be said to be high where management willingly *co-operate* with trade unions as representatives of employees and where participation through these representatives is about business-level decisions such as co-determination and collective bargaining for all employees. Low collectivism is where acceptance of employee representatives is grudging and *adversarial* and where participation is confined to lower-level job decision such as allocation of work in workgroups. A unitary style on this dimension would imply that management opposes collective relationships either openly or by covert means.

We can combine these two dimensions to create a range of possible management styles:

- *Sophisticated Human Relations* – high individualism, no collectivism, e.g. IBM or Hewlett-Packard
- *Paternalist* – medium individualism, no collectivism, e.g. John Lewis Partnership
- *Traditional* – low individualism, no collectivism, e.g. many owner-managed firms
- *Sophisticated Consultative* – high individualism, co-operative, e.g. Nissan
- *Modern Paternalist* – medium individualism, co-operative, e.g. BP, Shell
- *Bargained Constitutional* – low or medium individualism, adversarial, e.g. many public sector organisations

Two points can be seen from this. First, in general, collectivist styles tend to lead to union recognition, whereas individualist styles are more likely to lead to non-unionism. However, secondly, the dimensions are not clear cut and elements of individualism and collectivism may be combined rather than being incompatible with each other. Moreover, in recent years we can detect a clear shift in management policy away from collectivism towards individualism. However, the complexity of the situation means that management may have a range of decisions to make in determining its preferred strategic direction and we turn to this now.

Activity 10.1

Gather as much information as you can about any company you are familiar with. This could be a company you have worked for on a part-time basis, or a company you have done your placement in, or one you have read about in the quality press or other textbooks, or from the Internet.

1 From the information you have gathered see if you can place the company into one of the six management style categories outlined above.

2 What difficulties did you encounter in doing this?

3 What does this tell us about the concept of management style?

Strategic human resourcing options in management–union relations

A key human resourcing strategic decision for the managers of any employing organisation is one of whether or not they are going to recognise, or continue to recognise, a trade union (or several unions) as a legitimate vehicle for the expression of employee interests. While the preferred management style of the organisation, or of key managers within it, may help to shape this decision, it will be done so in the light of a range of contingent factors influencing human resourcing strategy decisions. These include external factors such as legislation, other employers' policies including an understanding of what constitutes good practice, and knowledge about union power. It also includes internal contingencies such as the size of the organisation, its ownership and location, as well as management's understanding of the links between business strategy and human resourcing strategy.

We now examine two of the key external factors – union power and legislation. On the one hand, managers will be aware of the decline of union membership and representation in the two decades since the peak of union density in 1979, and of the consequent decline in the proportion of employees having their pay and conditions determined through collective bargaining. On the other they need to operate in the context of statutory support given to union recognition in the Employment Relations Act 1999 and the possibility of some degree of union revival. We shall examine each of these contexts in turn.

Patterns of change in union membership and collective bargaining

Salamon (1998: 85) defines a trade union as 'any organisation whose membership consists of employees, which seeks to organise and represent their interest both in the workplace and society and, in particular, seeks to regulate the employment relationship through the direct process of collective bargaining with management'.

Before we outline the current state of union membership in Britain and analyse changes in the levels of membership over the past half-century, let us first consider the issue of union membership from the viewpoint of the individual worker.

Kochan (1980) has provided a useful model through which we may consider the line of thinking that most employees may go through in considering whether to join a trade union or not. This is presented in Figure 10.1.

The first stage in the employee's consideration is how they perceive the work environment. If it is a well-paid job, in excellent working conditions, with supportive managers and prospects of career advancement, then it may be the case that individual employees may not feel any need to seek to change this state of affairs. On the other hand if pay is absolutely or relatively poor, if physical working conditions are poor, if line managers are authoritarian and oppressive, and future prospects are limited then the employee may see a need to do something about the situation. However, it is not automatic that this will lead to joining a union and seeking a collective solution to collective problems. In some circumstances the employer may be known to be aggressively anti-union, or the situation

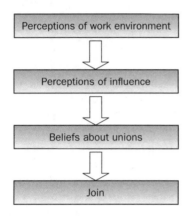

Figure 10.1 Why individuals join unions
Source: Adapted from Kochan (1980: 144)

may seem so desperate that a more immediate solution is sought. This is likely to be the individual one of seeking employment elsewhere rather than collectively seeking to improve the present employment.

However, in some cases it may be perceived that unions might be able to negotiate changes, and certainly this combined with union attempts at recruitment may lead to workers joining and seeking recognition. But even at this stage some employees may not support the principle of collective action and seek alternative solutions. At all of these stages in the process employers may seek to intervene by unilaterally altering pay and conditions of employment, by changing management style, or by making senior management views about unions known. Similarly unions may seek to influence this process by emphasising the areas where they believe they can positively influence outcomes.

Activity 10.2

You have a part-time job in a local bar. The hours are long, the manager often requires you to stay on beyond the agreed finishing time to clear up and you don't get paid any overtime. On top of this the basic pay is only just above the minimum wage level. You are unhappy with this situation, but are not sure what to do. You have often heard the manager commenting about lazy workers and blaming trade unions for all sorts of things he feels are wrong. You need the money to help you through your studies.

Using the Kochan model, what decisions would you take?

The thought processes outlined in the Kochan model may be looked at from the perspective of what unions have to offer potential members. Essentially there are three key points: collective strength, individual insurance and protection, and consumer-based services. Above all, if unions cannot be seen to deliver benefits to their members or potential members, then they are likely to have difficulty in retaining or winning members. Traditionally trade unions have delivered on improved pay and other terms and conditions of work through collective bargaining. This is premised on the belief that collectively workers can be a countervailing power against the strength of employers, whereas the individual worker has limited power.

But effective trade unionism is not just about pay, it is also about protecting the individual worker against arbitrary or capricious decisions of managers. We take out car insurance to protect us in the event of an accident, although we do not expect to be involved in accidents. In a similar way workers may join a union as a kind of insurance policy against management decisions, even though they do not anticipate difficulties, but so that the representational and legal support of the union can be brought into play in the event of any arising. Finally, in recent years unions have sought to attract and retain members by offering services such as reduced price insurance or holidays.

Activity 10.3

Assume that you are a union recruitment officer. Prepare a five-minute presentation setting out the case for joining your union.

Having considered union membership decisions from the point of view of the individual worker we now need to examine recent information about levels of union membership in Britain. The overall position of union membership is set out in Table 10.1.

The overall picture is that union membership has fallen dramatically since the peak in 1979, both in absolute terms and as a percentage of the working population. However, in 1998 there was an increase of 50,000 in the absolute number of union members, the first increase since 1979, but there was still a decline in the percentage of union members among employees in employment. The current position can be summed up by a few figures from the 1998 Workplace Employment Relations Survey (WERS98) (Cully, Woodland, O'Reilly and Dix, 1999).

Nearly half (47 per cent) of all workplaces have no union members at all, a figure which has risen from 36 per cent in 1990. The number of workplaces with unions recognised by employers has declined from 66 per cent in 1984, through 53 per cent in 1990 to 45 per cent in 1998.

Union recognition is less likely in workplaces that have been open for less than ten years compared with older workplaces (28 per cent, compared to 53 per cent).

Table 10.1 Changing levels of union membership

Year	Unions	Number	Working population %	Employees in employment %
1979	453	13,289	50	57
1982	408	11,593	44	54
1987	330	10,475	37	49
1989	309	10,158	39	34
1992	268	9,048	36	32
1995	247	8,031	32	29
1997	234	7,801	31	28
1998	238	7,851	X	27

Source: *Employment Gazette* and *Labour Force Trends* (various)

Significantly for our discussion about employer strategy and management style, in those workplaces whose management favour unions, there is a 62 per cent density figure and an 84 per cent level of actual recognition. However, in the 17 per cent of workplaces where managers oppose unions this is reflected in practice, as density levels are only 7 per cent and recognition 9 per cent. Union recognition is more likely in public sector workplaces than private (95 per cent, compared to 25 per cent), in workplaces that are part of a wider organisation rather than stand-alone (54 per cent, compared to 19 per cent) and in larger rather than smaller workplaces (Cully *et al.*, 1998: 92).

A number of competing explanations have been put forward to account for the decline:

- the impact of the business cycle
- the changing composition of employment
- changes in the legislation governing unions and their relations with employers
- the ways in which employers responded to the changed context
- ways in which unions sought to respond to continuing decline

The business cycle explanation focuses on the overall state of the economy and develops the general view that unions find it easier to recruit during upswings in the economy that during a recession. Disney (1990) argued that 'the "explanation" of the decline in trade union membership in the 1980s in Britain is straightforward. A period of rising unemployment, high real wage growth and a Conservative government is sufficient to explain the decline in density.' In other words, union members were losing their jobs in the recession, but those remaining in employment saw their real wages growing and saw less need for union membership. These economic changes took place while a Conservative government was changing the legislation governing trade unions which we shall consider below.

In the early 1980s there was also structural change in the economy with the loss of jobs in traditionally heavily unionised sectors of the economy and the growth of new jobs in traditionally less well-organised sectors (Millward and Stevens, 1986; Booth, 1989). However, by the time of the third Workplace Industrial Relations Survey in 1990, its authors argued that:

> In the first half of the decade it appeared that changes in the population of workplaces – particularly the demise of large highly unionised manufacturing plants – played a key role in the decline of union membership. In the second half, the explanations for the continuing decline were more likely to be a weakening of support for unionism among employees, various government measures constraining it and antipathy amongst a growing number of employers. (Millward, Stevens, Smart and Hawes, 1992: 201/2)

Freeman and Pelletier (1990) went as far as to attribute most of the decline to the series of laws passed by the Conservative government which among other things made it harder for unions to organise, to take effective industrial action, or to form a closed shop. The process of privatisation and breaking-up of public sector monopolies and other labour market changes also made things more difficult for unions. While the direct impact of each law may be difficult to measure exactly, there is no doubt that the cumulative effect of all the measures weakened unions and sent a clear signal to employers that unions were out of favour.

Employers wishing to minimise the impact of unions could respond to this situation by either pursing high commitment policies or operating in an aggressive anti-union manner (Blyton and Turnbull, 1998). We shall explore these options later.

While the above factors set the context and constraints within which unions have had to operate in the last two decades, they were not totally powerless and some unions have been more successful than others in adapting to changed circumstances. Among strategies adopted were revising trade union purposes, recruitment campaigns among hitherto weakly organised areas, mergers to create more viable organisations, and working for a Labour government in the hope that it would reverse some of the legislation which was believed to have been so harmful to unions (Bassett, 1986; Mason and Bain, 1991; Willman, 1996). For example, the three main unions recruiting in local government, the NHS and the utilities joined together to form UNISON in 1992. In the same year the electricians' union and the engineering union merged to form the Amalgamated Engineering and Electrical Union (AEEU). These various measures met with varying degrees of success and failure but probably served more to adjust the distribution of members rather than stem the decline.

Two important points need to be made about this analysis. First, the decline should not be attributed to any single cause, but rather the interplay and interaction of all five (Metcalf, 1991). Second, in changed economic and political circumstances it may be possible for unions to exert greater influence on their position and therefore employers may need to assess the circumstances and context in which they respond to employee and union demands differently from those which might have prevailed in the 1980s and early 1990s. After all, 44 of the UK's largest firms continue to recognise and operate with trade unions. Moreover, the overall decline in trade union membership masks some continuing pockets of strength, notably in the public sector, in banking and among professional employees. Of course the corollary of this is that there are areas of trade union weakness such as in small firms, in private services and among young workers.

Comparative note

Britain is not unique in the decline of union density in the last two decades. However, in some countries there has been an increase.

Table 10.2 Trade union membership by selected country as a percentage of all employees 1980–1995

Country	1980	1990	1995
Australia	48	40	33
Canada	36	36	34
Denmark	76	71	82
France	17	10	9
Italy	49	39	38
Japan	31	25	24
Netherlands	35	25	26
New Zealand	56	45	22
Sweden	80	82	83
UK	50	39	32
USA	22	16	15

Source: Brown, Deaken and Ryan (1997)

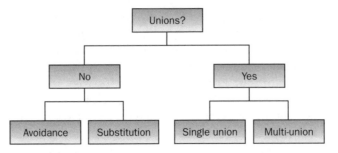

Figure 10.2 Key management decisions in employee relations

Operating within the context of these macro-changes in British industrial relations, employers, faced with demands from a trade union for recognition, may adopt one of three broad strategies.

1 They could *agree* to the principle of *recognition* and seek to negotiate a recognition agreement with the trade union or trade unions which would establish the procedural parameters of the relationship.
2 They could seek to *substitute* employee demands for recognition by managing the employment relationship in such a way that employees feel no desire or need to seek union representation but believe that the way the organisation is managed takes account of employee views and offers satisfactory rewards and working conditions that compare well in any comparison that may be made with similar organisations whether unionised or not.
3 They could seek to *avoid* recognition at all costs and may operate in what has become known as the 'black hole' of neither high commitment work practices nor traditional pluralist industrial relations.

These options may be expressed diagramatically, as in Figure 10.2. Let us examine each of these possibilities in turn.

Union recognition strategic option

Recognition of one or more trade unions for collective bargaining infers that the employer is willing to reach joint agreements over certain areas of decision-making about the employment relationship and that consequently these will no longer be areas of unilateral management decision-making. Some might see this as a loss of management prerogative, others that joint decision-making is more likely to be acceptable to employees and therefore more likely to be adhered to and operated in practice than decisions solely made by managers. We have already discussed various ways in which employees can resist management decisions that are perceived as being contrary to their interests. Although employers may be faced with demands for union recognition, the process of reaching agreement with the union(s) is likely to lead to a clarification and codification of a number of key issues.

First would be the establishment of the bargaining unit – which group of employees is to be covered. Management may be willing to bargain over the pay and conditions of production workers, but not for supervisors or support staff. The union may only have organised production workers and therefore only seek recognition for that group, or it may seek a wider recognition covering all employees up to managerial grades.

Negotiations over recognition are also likely to confront a key issue that is seen by many managers to be at the heart of policy on union recognition. That is whether there will be more than one union or just a single union covering all the employees in the agreed bargaining unit. Traditionally *trade* unions in Britain developed representing workers in different trades and sought to bargain up the price of their labour by differentiating their skills and experience from other groups of workers. Thus a situation developed where a multiplicity of unions were present in most workplaces each representing different trades or groups of workers. Employers found this situation difficult to deal with, having to reach agreement with many separate trade unions. In the 1960s and 1970s in particular it was alleged that the multi-union nature of unionised workplaces caused particular difficulties for British managers, especially over demarcation disputes, that were not faced by managers in West Germany where a smaller number of industry-based unions had been created after the Second World War. In subsequent years inward investing companies which were prepared to recognise unions preferred to do so on a single union basis or not at all. In effect they said, 'One union, or no unions.'

In a similar manner, employers who already had a multi-union situation sought to minimise the effects of this by moving towards single table bargaining whereby a number of unions continued to be recognised, but negotiations took place round a single table with all unions present together, rather than sequentially with each union trying to outbid the outcomes of the previous one. This meant that unions had to find ways of reconciling their differences and establishing common ground before meeting with management. This development occurred in the NHS and in many manufacturing environments (Gall, 1994). The WERS98 survey revealed that single table bargaining was found in 77 per cent of workplaces where collective bargaining was the dominant form of pay setting (Millward, Bryson and Forth, 2000: 203).

The final area of decision-making in a recognition agreement is over which issues are to be part of the substantive agreements, that is, which areas of decision-making are to be subject to joint decision-making. These are likely to include basic pay and conditions of employment such as hours of work and pensions, but when unions are strong they seek to extend the scope of collective bargaining into other areas such as pensions or training, whereas management might seek to restrict the areas covered when they feel that bargaining power is in their favour. The agreement would state how workplace trade union representatives or shop stewards are appointed and what support they might receive from management in doing their duties. Finally, a recognition agreement would also contain provisions for the resolution of disputes through conciliation or arbitration.

Substitution strategic option

Beaumont (1987) distinguishes between approaches based on union substitution and union avoidance as approaches to staying or becoming non-union. In considering union substitution approaches it might be useful to consider what unions have to offer employees and relate this to the chain of thought that employees might go through in deciding whether to join or not which was discussed above. The implication is that if management can intervene to influence any of these decisions then the outcome may be that employees do not perceive any need to join a union as they do not believe that it would be able to improve and affect terms and conditions of employment or the nature of the employment relationship.

The vulnerabilities of unions with employers who are the leading payers and providers of good working conditions in an industry or geographical area is that employees do not think that these can be improved upon substantially through collective bargaining. Employers could seek to provide alternative channels of 'employee voice' through such devices as open door systems, employee-based works councils and individual-based employee participation mechanisms (see Chapter 11) so that again employees do not feel that union channels of representation would significantly improve their situation at work. Finally, so many alternative providers of membership services exist through other membership and commercial organisations that this is not likely to be the prime route into union membership for non-members (Whitston and Waddington, 1994).

The essence of Beaumont's argument is therefore that employers can seek to substitute policies and practices that substitute for those which might follow from union membership and recognition. Employers can actively pursue such policies and in Chapter 1 we have characterised such an approach as being a high commitment – indirect control one. Beaumont (1987) refers to 'household name' non-union companies such as IBM, Marks & Spencer and Hewlett-Packard and they are presented as being distinctive from the traditional, sweatshop non-union employer which we consider next. However, subsequent to Beaumont's analysis even the employment relations practices of his 'household name' companies have come under fire as they have reduced employment levels and evidence has emerged that their purchasing power forces poor employment practices on to their small suppliers (Blyton and Turnbull, 1998: Chapter 9, Marchington and Wilkinson, 1996: 242–4).

Union substitution strategies are also apparent in the new dot.com sector of the economy where large salaries and share options make employee desire for unions less likely (*Guardian*, 9 September 2000).

A 'black hole' strategic option?

To the above categories of employer–employee relationships may be added the 'black hole' approach of operating with neither high commitment-indirect control approach, nor industrial relations. The location of such an approach can be seen in Guest's (1995) four-fold classification of options for managing the employment relationship, as displayed in Figure 10.3.

Beardwell (1997) has researched the characteristics of companies operating in this sphere. While there is no direct union recognition and consequent collective bargaining, there is evidence of a wide variety of pay determination mechanisms being used. The largest single category in his study was non-bargained collective pay rather than an emphasis on individualised pay, which being non-union might

		HIGH	LOW
IR Priority	HIGH	**New realism** High emphasis on HRM and IR	**Traditional collectivism** Priority to IR without HRM
	LOW	**Individualised HRM** High priority to HRM No IR	**The black hole** No HRM No IR

Figure 10.3 Guest's model of options for managing the employment relationship

at first sight imply. Moreover, there were companies in his study that derived their pay structures, either wholly or in part, from collective bargaining mechanisms in the industry the firm belonged to. The main conclusion was that pay settlement mechanisms were often unsystematic and this in turn reflected the absence of a clear overall strategy towards the management of the employment relationship. It is therefore no surprise to learn that not only did these firms lack unions, they also lacked personnel specialists, had patchy information flows and weak information channels. Or as Brown (1994) put it, 'We are not witnessing the emergence of a brave new world of non-union HRM but a tired old world of unrepresented labour.'

This picture is confirmed by WERS98 (Cully *et al.*, 1999: 107–11) where it was found that nearly half of all workplaces had no union members and two-thirds had no worker representatives. In around a third of all workplaces there was no formal structure to represent employee interests. These were mostly small organisations operating on stand-alone sites, particularly in the construction, hotel and restaurant and other business services sectors.

Statutory recognition

From 6 June 2000 applications for statutory recognition under the Employment Relations Act 1999 could be submitted to the Central Arbitration Committee. The existence of this legislation is now something that employers will have to take account of, as well as their assessment of the extent or likelihood of unionisation in their particular firm. Employers facing requests for union recognition may now respond to them through one of three ways – voluntary, automatic or balloting. The latter two involve statutory rights, but in the White Paper *Fairness at Work* (Department of Trade and Industry, 1998), which preceded the legislation, the government made clear that the voluntary route was the preferred one especially if it promoted partnership which could reconcile fairness with competitiveness.

In the event of the employer not agreeing voluntarily to union recognition, unions will be able to seek the support of the legislative provisions. Recognition will *automatically* be granted where the union can demonstrate 50 per cent plus one membership among the proposed bargaining unit. Recognition may also follow if, *following a ballot*, 40 per cent of employees eligible to vote, vote for recognition. Recognition through either of the statutory routes would cover pay, hours and conditions but would not, as the TUC wished, cover training. Significantly the statutory provisions do not apply to firms with 20 or fewer employees; yet union membership and recognition is lower in small workplaces. From evidence on recent union successes in achieving recognition it would appear that unions prefer to seek voluntary deals, but can threaten employers with the statutory procedures if they are unwilling to negotiate (Gall, 2000).

Another aspect of the new legislation which employers will have to take account of is the right of employees who are union members to be accompanied by a trade union representative or fellow employee during discipline and grievance procedures for serious issues even where a company does not recognise a union. Employers will also have to comply with the provision that there should be no discrimination on grounds of membership or non-membership of unions by acts of omission as well as positive acts. So even if an employer seeks to maintain a non-union situation, they may still have to deal with union representatives for individual grievance and discipline cases. The tactics used in seeking to achieve a union substitution or avoidance position will have to be lawful.

Partnership as a way forward?

In this chapter we have sought to emphasise that managing the employment relationship involves both conflict and co-operation. Recently there has been a resurgence of the use of 'partnership' to characterise the employment relationship. In this section of the chapter we analyse the use of this phrase. Partnership may relate to three sets of relationships within employment – between employer and employee, between employer and trade union, and between union and employee. *Fairness at Work*, for example, was heralded by Ian McCartney, the Trade and Industry Minister responsible for the legislation, as encouraging 'partnership between employer and employees', but at the same time he presented unions as 'partners in the workplace' (Unions 21, Newsletter, 1998). But the emphasis in the government's partnership approach is on the relationship between workers and employers, rather than between unions and employers. Indeed the Unions 21 interpretation of the White Paper is that unions are not seen as a collective countervailing force against employers' power, but as the friends for individual workers to help them gain their individual rights (Unions 21, 1998).

A different notion of partnership is put forward by the Trades Union Congress (TUC), which draws heavily on the continental European model of 'social partnership' based on agreement rather than legal prescription. This offers a legitimate role by both government and employers to trade unions as representatives of employees and their involvement in various institutional forums at the economy and workplace levels. Thus in a document tellingly entitled *Partnership for Progress* the TUC argues that 'many British companies have recognised the full potential of this EU approach, for example, by reaching voluntary agreements on information and consultation bodies in companies operating in this country and other Member States' (TUC, 1997: 21). The TUC's proposed partnership approach has four main prongs:

- employment security and new working practices
- giving employees a voice in how the company is run
- fair financial rewards
- investment in training (Monks, 1998: 176)

Claydon (1998) has traced the origins of this approach by the TUC to the 'New Bargaining Agenda' of the late 1980s and early 1990s. But he has also demonstrated that by and large this approach was not successful and rather than entice employers into partnership agreements the reality of this period was 'an acceleration in the pace of union derecognition since 1988 and its spread across a wider range of employment' (1998: 183). The partnership approach presumes that a bargaining agenda round areas of common concern can be found. The TUC believes that this will be over issues such as training, health and safety and equal opportunities. But Kelly (1996) believes that these three areas are also areas with 'serious conflicts of interest'. This was confirmed by the CBI's insistence that training should not be an automatic subject for collective bargaining following union recognition under the statutory procedures. Moreover the partnership approach implies that less weight is given to traditional adversarial approaches and issues. Yet, significant survey research (Heery, 1996; Kelly and Kelly, 1991) reveals the continued existence of 'us and them' attitudes among employees and their expectations that their trade unions will challenge management on issues that concern them. If instead they move down the path of co-operative issues and agendas, then the membership may react against the incorporation that they fear may take place. Moreover, one of the common areas, health and safety, has been found by Waddington and Whitston (1996) to be the second most frequent area of grievance that members expected unions to pursue. Gall (2000) has recorded 748 new union recognition agreements between 1995 and 2000, but no more than 150 of these describe themselves as 'partnership agreements'. Even here the term remains vague and does not comply with the TUC's four prongs.

The notion of partnership need not necessarily be mediated through trade unions and employers. The concept is also used to characterise the employer–employee relationship whether or not any unions are recognised in the workplace at all. Or as Beardwell (1998: 202) puts it, this notion of partnership is one 'constructed around the internal relationship within the firm without an external representative agency'. Such an approach has been discussed in Chapter 1 as the high commitment one, and the ways in which managers have attempted to use forms of employee involvement to enhance employee integration, co-operation and contribution have been explored in Chapter 13. In Kochan's version of this model (1986, 1995) employees must give commitment, flexibility and loyalty to the organisation in order for it to gain and sustain the economic performance of the firm. Kochan presents the relationship as one of mutual commitment but Beardwell (1998) shows that in effect this turns out to be unity on terms defined by the employing firm. Co-operation and partnership masks the potential tensions and conflict of the employment relationship. By contrast, the approach adopted in this book emphasises the dual nature of the employment relationship, that it involves both co-operation and conflict, not in a polarised alternative way but intertwined and interrelated. Thus attempts to deny conflict and assert co-operation would appear destined to failure.

Frames of reference

Read the following extracts from newspaper articles about strikes or union recognition situations.

The Guardian Friday January 29 1999

Danish firm's UK staff await equal treatment

Seumas Milne
Labour Editor

In a draughty industrial estate canteen in Wembley, north London, a group of mainly Asian factory workers pour out a list of grievances against their Danish employer: over health and safety, grading, their treatment at the hands of white supervisors, equal opportunities and sick pay.

The workers are employed by a firm called Rosti, which makes plastic casings for the electronics industry. Rosti is owned by Denmark's leading multinational, A.P. Møller. In Denmark, Møller is obliged to negotiate pay and conditions with its workers' trade unions – but not in Britain.

That will change when the Government's Employment Relations Bill, published yesterday, which gives a legal right to union recognition when more than half a workforce wants it, becomes law later this year.

Two years ago, Rosti tried to introduce a new shift pattern at the Wembley plant – which currently employs about 450 – of four 12-hour days on, four days off.

Several workers went to the local Citizens Advice Bureau, who referred them to the Transport and General Workers' Union. Within a few months, most shopfloor workers had joined the union, but Rosti management refused to negotiate with the TGWU.

The firm dropped the new shift pattern and tried to deal with the discontent with a consultative works committee.

But buoyed up by the promise of a right to union recognition under government legislation, the Rosti workers – who take home between £180 and £240 for a 40-hour week – stuck with the TGWU.

In November, the conciliation service Acas confirmed that the union had more than 55 per cent membership, which would entitle them to union recognition under the forthcoming law. Now Rosti has announced plans for 74 redundancies, which the TGWU's Steve Hart says appear to be targeted at the most effective organisers inside the factory.

Rosti insists a drop in orders is to blame and refuses to discuss its industrial relations problems.

Manjit Sahota, one of the factory activists, is exasperated. 'We're not troublemakers.

'We would like to co-operate with the company. We only want respect, dignity and equal opportunities.'

Case Study continued

Tesco embrace of union opens way to 'new era'

Seumas Milne
Labour Editor

A PARTNERSHIP agreement between supermarket group Tesco and shopworkers' union Usdaw aimed at creating a 'new era' of employee consultation and involvement was yesterday hailed by the government as a milestone in its drive for greater co-operation in the workplace.

The deal, which will replace traditional union bargaining with a hierarchy of interlocking staff forums, covers all 150,000 employees at Tesco, the country's leading supermarket chain and the largest private employer of unionised labour.

The new arrangements, which were unveiled yesterday to Tesco staff and shop stewards, were seized on by TUC general secretary John Monks as 'nailing the myths' about trade unionism and signalling to employers that they have nothing to fear from the planned legal right to union recognition.

Ian McCartney, the trade and industry minister negotiating his way through

Sign here

Recent partnership agreements – trading flexibility for job security

Blue Circle: 3 year deal in 1997
United Distillers: extended to 1999
Rover: 3 year deal in 1997
Hyder: Welsh Water and Swalec
Legal and General: signed 1997

CBI and TUC demands over how that right should be implemented, said he was delighted with the Tesco-Usdaw deal, which showed that partnership was 'at the heart of a successful and competitive business'.

The goal of European-style 'social partnership' is at the heart of TUC strategy, but most private sector partnership agreements have effectively boiled down to trading flexibility for job security.

The Usdaw deal with Tesco – and expanding business where redundancy is not an issue – is different. For the company, Tesco's retail Human Resources director,

Catherine Glickman, says it is about replacing adversarial and inflexible structures with better 'two-way communication' to manage change.

The advantage for Usdaw, its general secretary Bill Connor believes, is that the union will be 'at the centre of the business, rather that on the sidelines raising grievances'. Usdaw will also get company co-operation with recruitment.

Formalised bargaining will be replaced with a system of consultative staff forums at the 588 Tesco stores, elected by all employees, which will send union representatives to three regional forums.

They will elect a national negotiating forum, but the three 30-strong regional forums will have the final say on the company's annual pay offer.

The agreement is likely to come under fire from some Usdaw activists, who have in the past criticised the relationship between the union leadership and Tesco management as excessively cosy.

Case Study continued

Management strategic options for managing the employment relationship ● **233**

The Guardian Monday December 14 1998

Work for millionaire David Dimbleby and you may have to buy your own notepad and pens. **Seumas Milne** lifts the lid on the treatment of his employees and reveals the wider fear of the proprietors: the return of the unions

Question time for press barons

David Dimbleby was at his most genial, holding forth on the unsung glories of local publishing at a glittering party to celebrate the 125th anniversary of his flagship newspaper, the Richmond and Twickenham Times. It was a big night out for the family firm, owned by the Dimblebys for more than a century, and the Peacock Room in Isleworth's Syon Park had been chosen for the reception for local bigwigs, staff and advertisers. 'I'm really grateful to all of you,' he told them a fortnight ago, 'who put your faith and confidence in what we do.'

But barely an hour earlier, as the BBC Question Time presenter and millionaire media grandee put the finishing touches to his chairman's speech, his employees had been at a Wandsworth pub holding a gathering of their own, with a rather less celebratory theme. Before turning up to the Syon Park extravaganza, discontented staff working on the south-west London group's eight titles voted to set up a National Union of Journalists 'chapel' – or office-based branch – at the profitable Dimbleby papers to tackle longstanding problems of low pay and poor working conditions. In the union-phobic newspaper world of the 1990s, what might elsewhere be an unremarkable event could very well be regarded as verging on an act of industrial war.

At the Richmond paper's glass-fronted Victorian offices, which have been 'union free' for many years, the 31-year-old sports editor is expected to work evenings and weekends on top of his basic 75-hour fortnight for a standard reporter's salary of £7,800 a year, after a recent increase. On a strict contractual basis, that works out just above the Government's forthcoming minimum wage of £3.60. In terms of hours actually worked, it falls below it.

Staff get three weeks' holiday a year and sick pay is discretionary. The newspapers may have helped make their proprietor of more than 30 years' standing a wealthy man, but cheese-paring at the group is still taken to remarkable lengths. Journalists say they often have to buy their own note-pads and pens and have just been banned from making calls to mobile phones. At Richmond, the news editor, Sarah Griffin, was sacked last year while on maternity leave, but reinstated with £4,000 compensation after the NUJ took her case to an industrial tribunal.

Along the River Thames at the Wandsworth Borough News, the Dimbleby group's other editorial base, one reporter covering last May's local elections for the Putney and Wimbledon Times was refused and expenses refund for a £15 taxi ride he took home from the count at 4am after public transport had closed down – he works in an off-licence in the evening to make ends meet. Until the Inland Revenue caught up with the BBC broadcaster's business last year, most journalists were paid £23.10 a day as self-employed freelancers, but have now been taken on staff.

'I love the job and take pride in it, but I hate the company because they're taking the mickey,' one Wandsworth-based journalist says of Dimbleby & Sons, which describes itself as a 'forward-looking company'. None wants to be quoted by name for fear of inviting the sack or harming their chances of finding a job elsewhere.

Both the 60-year-old scion of a broadcasting dynasty – who fought a prolonged battle with unions in the early 1980s and has refused to recognise them at his papers ever since – and his managing director, Harry Lorraine, declined requests to discuss the firm's working conditions, which the NUJ says are not the worst among local papers. But last year Dimbleby insisted his employees were 'extremely happy and get very good training', though staff say there is no training at all.

Now however, the Government's imminent Fairness at Work bill, which will create a legal right to union recognition where the majority of a workforce wants it, means that the liberal broadcaster and his newspapers' managers may soon be obliged to discuss pay and conditions with the journalists' union. Nor is Dimbleby the only media proprietor who looks likely to have to drop his resistance to talking to his employees' chosen representatives. Many are extremely unhappy about it and are doing whatever they can to avoid the return of trade unions to their editorial strongholds.

Activity 10.4

1 Adopting first a unitarist perspective, and then a pluralist one, how would you interpret the scenarios depicted?

2 Which perspective, unitarist or pluralist, seems to you to offer a view which assists our understanding of the situation most?

SUMMARY

In this chapter the following key points have been made:

- Actors in employment relations may seek to understand their world though a frame of reference.

- The essence of the unitarist, pluralist and Marxist frames of reference have been outlined.

- Following Purcell, individualism and collectivism have been identified as the two key dimensions of management style.

- A number of possible management styles were identified.

- Kochan's model for considering why individual employees might join a trade union was outlined.

- Trade union membership has decline markedly since 1979, but for an interplay of reasons rather than a single prime cause.

- Union decline is not peculiar to Britain, but in some countries union membership has remained stable, or even grown.

- A range of strategic options face employers on whether or not to institutionalise conflict through union recognition and collective bargaining.

- These include union recognition, substitution of unions, and the avoidance, or 'black hole', strategic options.

- 'Partnership' as a model of the employment relation is shown to have a variety of meanings and be problematic.

DISCUSSION QUESTIONS

1 Outline the approaches that management may take in their relationship with trade unions.

2 Why did trade union membership decline in Britain in the last twenty years?

3 What are the prospects for trade union recovery in the next few years?

R   FURTHER READING

There are a number of other undergraduate texts available that explore the issues introduced here in more detail. These include Beardwell and Holden (2001), Bratton and Gold (1999) and Hollingshead, Nicholls and Tailby (1999). Students wishing a more advanced discussion of the issues raised should consult Leopold, Harris and Watson (1999), Marchington and Wilkinson (2000) and Salamon (1998).

Chapter 11

Employee involvement and participation

John Leopold

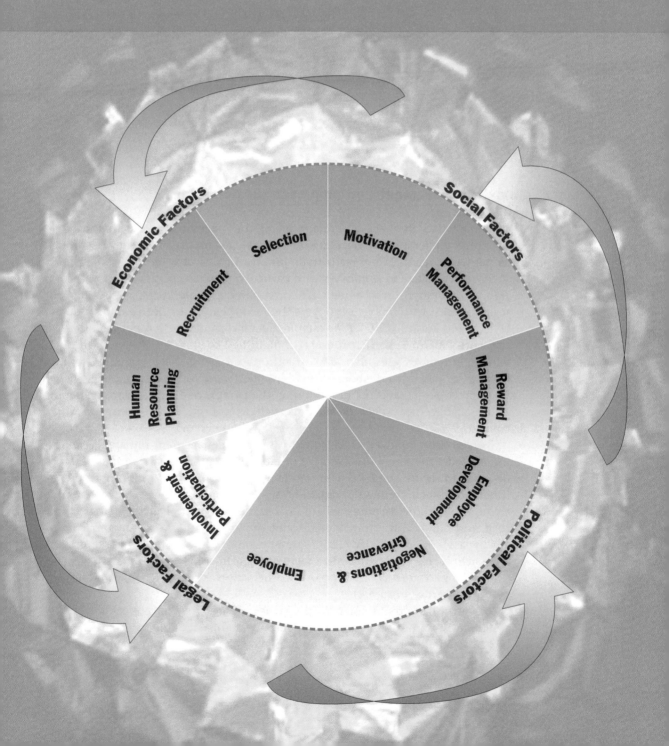

Having completed this chapter and its associated activities, readers should be able to:

- differentiate between employee participation and employee involvement
- explore different objectives held by managers, employees and trade unions, in terms of employee involvement and participation
- consider these in terms of a participation continuum
- examine forms of representative participation
- review a number of forms of employee involvement
- show, through a case study, ways in which potentially conflicting objectives of participation and involvement schemes might be related to an organisation's overall human resourcing strategy

Employee involvement and employee participation

In the previous chapter we have considered the range of strategies that management may contemplate in deciding how to relate to employees. We have examined in particular relationships with trade unions. In this chapter we examine how management relate to employees with particular emphasis on employee participation and employee involvement. The first point to make is that we should not regard these two terms as synonyms, but see them quite clearly differentiated. Hyman and Mason (1995), for example, offer a clear distinction between the two concepts. Employee participation is distinguished by state involvement, through which procedures are advocated or introduced to regulate potential conflict between employers and labour. It is state supported, union initiated, usually based on indirect participation of union (rather than employee) representatives in joint union management decision-making such as collective bargaining or works councils.

By contrast, employee involvement is seen as management initiated, attempting to secure the direct involvement of individual employees in various schemes designed to secure employee commitment, motivation and loyalty so as to contribute to the achievement of organisational goals and objectives. Management is trying to overcome situations where workers are poorly motivated, alienated from their work and poorly rewarded materially. Unitarist in essence, this approach usually bypasses or ignores trade union presence, and, while becoming the dominant approach in the 1980s and into the 1990s, can in some organisations be found sitting alongside forms of the employee participation approach (Hyman and Mason, 1995; Millward *et al.*, 1992).

We can also see that these two approaches relate to the concept of the pluralist and unitarist frame of reference introduced in Chapter 10. Employee participation is clearly pluralist in conception and recognises that unions have a role to play in representing worker interests and that these interests are legitimate. The pluralist notion of balance and equilibrium also permits management to argue for a distinction between joint decision-making, or collectively bargained, issues and consultative issues where management will listen to the employee point of view but reserve the right to decide otherwise. Students may, for example, have representatives on Faculty Boards of Study, but the academics, at the end of the day, reserve the right to take a course of action contrary to student opinion even though they are perfectly willing to listen to representations of behalf of students. Employee involvement, on the other hand, is clearly unitarist in outlook and assumes a common sense of purpose and the involvement mechanisms are designed principally to win employee commitment to that purpose.

The key points of contrast between employee involvement and employee participation are summarised in Table 11.1. We will draw upon these points of distinction as we examine in detail some of the possible institutional forms of employee participation and involvement. The essential point to establish is that the two approaches are distinct in their origin, advocacy and intended outcomes, and therefore we must avoid using the terms interdependently. The distinctions may be highlighted by considering the potential range of form of employee participation and involvement in terms of a participation continuum as in Table 11.2.

Table 11.1 Employee involvement and participation compared

Employee involvement	Employee participation
Individualistic	Collective
Direct	Indirect via employee representatives, usually but not always, union based
Championed by management	Championed by trade unions
Purpose – to elicit employee identification and commitment	Purpose – to exercise employment rights
Grown without specific legislative support	Often supported by legislation
Assumes common interest between employees and management	Based on assumption of reconciling a plurality of interests

Table 11.2 Employee participation and involvement continuum

Management inspired and controlled schemes			←————————————————→			Worker/union inspired and controlled schemes	
No participation	Financial involvement	Communications	Employee involvement	Consultation	Collective bargaining	Worker representation on final decision-taking bodies	Self-management
Job roles	Profit sharing	Team briefing	Job enlargement quality circles	Joint consultative committee Joint health and safety committee	Joint negotiating committee	Worker directors	Worker co-operatives

By use of this continuum we can differentiate clearly between those institutional forms of participation and involvement that are management inspired or controlled, such as financial involvement or communication schemes, and those that are more likely to be workers' and/or trade union inspired and controlled, such as collective bargaining or the election of worker directors.

Within the continuum there is an area where management and union aspirations overlap so that there are possibilities of areas of joint consultation and decision-making. On the other hand, managers are unlikely to advocate or actively support worker self-management, while unions are unlikely to be comfortable with a management which insists that the organisation has no participation, or only forms that are totally management controlled.

Two other points of distinction will be explored throughout this chapter. First, the distinctions between the *direct* involvement/participation of individual employees and of employees being represented *indirectly* by elected representatives. The other is the distinction between participation/involvement on task- or job-related issues, such as through quality circles, and business-related levels of decision-making, as might take place at board level. Let us now look at a number of examples of both employee participation and employee involvement.

Representative participation

Representative participation is an indirect form of employee participation, and joint consultative committees (JCCs) are the most commonly found form of representative participation where management and employees' representatives, usually but not always trade union based, meet on a regular basis to discuss issues of mutual concern. JCCs have waxed and waned in terms of popularity, which can be interpreted in terms of cycles (Ramsey, 1977). For example, JCCs went through a resurgence in the 1970s, before declining to being present in only 29 per cent of workplaces by the end of the 1980s (Millward *et al.*, 1992). This can be partially attributed to the fall in the number of larger workplaces where they were more likely to be found. WERS98, however, found that the same proportion of workplaces had a formally constituted workplace JCC (Cully, Woodlands, O'Reilly, Dix,

1999: 244). However, like other surveys, the WERS98 study showed that formal JCCs were more likely in unionised than non-union companies, in larger companies and in the public sector. Or, as Cully *et al.* (1999) put it, 'Union representation and indirect employee participation go hand-in-hand rather than being substitutes for one another' (100). This also appears to confirm the duality of representative participation identified by Hyman and Mason (1995: 127), of formal approaches in large manufacturing companies and the public sector, but informal and loose structures in smaller organisations and the service sector.

Beyond the debate on the rise and fall of JCCs in practice is the question of the significance of those committees where they continue to exist. Millward *et al.* (2000) found that there had been a decline in functioning committees – that is, meeting at least once every three months. Moreover, it was clear that it was management rather than employees or unions who decided whether to discontinue or introduce consultative committees. The WERS98 (Cully *et al.*, 1999: 101) survey found that the most commonly discussed topics were:

- working practices (88 per cent)
- health and safety (86 per cent)
- welfare services and facilities (83 per cent)
- future workplace plans (83 per cent)

The focus is on job-related issues and management regarded committees as being very influential where the members were appointed by management and they met at least monthly. Where unions appointed the representatives, the committees only met quarterly or less and managers regarded them as less effective. Pay was only a topic in 50 per cent of committees, which suggests that this was more likely to be considered a negotiating rather than a consultative issue.

Activity 11.2

Find out about joint consultative committees in any organisation you are familiar with.

1 What range of topics is dealt with?

2 How are employee representatives chosen?

3 What levels of management are involved in the committee?

4 What do these three factors indicate to you about the nature of the committee?

Employee representation on workplace health and safety

Employee representation on health and safety at work issues is underpinned by statute. The Health and Safety at Work Act 1974 laid down various duties that employers and employees and others had to fulfil towards health and safety in all workplaces. (For more information on the wider aspects of health and safety at work, see Bratton and Gold, 1999; Foot and Hook, 1999; Stredwick, 2000).

Subsequently the Safety Representatives and Safety Committees Regulations 1977 laid down the detailed rights and responsibilities of these two elements in health and safety management. Under these regulations safety representatives are appointed by recognised trade unions. Subsequently, due to concerns and objections about the representation of employees in non-union workplaces, the Health and Safety (Consultation with Employees) Regulations 1996 provided for management to consult either with elected representatives of employees or directly with employees. Safety representatives have rights to

- inspect the workplace
- investigate accidents
- have paid time off to perform their duties
- be provided with equipment and support to fulfil their function

A further right that safety representatives have is if two or more request that the employer set up a health and safety committee, then the employer has to comply with this request and consult them about it. Joint health and safety committees are therefore another vehicle for indirect employee participation. When the Regulations were first implemented in 1978, there was an increase in the number of committees in non-unionised workplaces and in workplaces where the operations were not considered to be high risk from a health and safety point of view. The WERS98 survey (Cully *et al.*, 1999: 96) revealed that 39 per cent of workplaces had a joint health and safety committee and that these were more likely in unionised workplaces. However, this survey also showed that a joint committee existed in 31 per cent of non-unionised workplaces. So participation on health and safety can exist in both union and non-union contexts, and overall, in 1998, 68 per cent of workplaces had some form of employee representation on health and safety matters. Moreover, this is one area of the employment relationship where the overall incidence of representation has remained stable over the past twenty years (Millward *et al.*, 2000: 117).

European works councils

Employee participation has in part been defined as emanating from the state. The European Union has sought to enact a number of pieces of legislation that would have the effect of enhancing employee representative rights within firms, especially those operating on a pan-European basis. One of these rights is the right to establish a European works council in companies with more than 1000 employees in the European Economic Area (the EU states plus Iceland, Liechtenstein and Norway), and where there are at least 150 employees in two member states. The European Works Council Directive was agreed in 1993 and was due to be implemented in 1996. However, in the UK the previous Conservative government was hostile to any such extension of collective employee rights and secured an opt-out from the Social Chapter and any provisions under it at the Maastricht Treaty in 1991. In 1997, however, the newly elected Labour government reversed these policies and the Directive was implemented in Britain on 15 December 1999.

Affected companies had until 22 September 1996 (15 December 1999 in the UK) to agree a customised system under Article 13 before the Special Negotiating Body procedure laid down in the directive took effect. Some 130 British companies and a further 170 non-UK owned, but UK-based, companies were covered by the legislation.

Comparative note

As can be seen from the table below, the Directive is likely to lead to the establishment of EWCs across the whole of the European Union, but most significantly in Germany and Britain. As the Directive also applies to all eligible companies, no matter the country of origin, then a significant number of American companies are covered.

Table 11.3 Number and country of origin of European Works Councils at June 2000

Country	Eligible firms	Actual EWCs
Australia	9	3
Austria	42	15
Belgium	66	28
Canada	16	3
Denmark	58	26
Finland	49	22
France	148	50
Germany	414	102
Italy	53	17
Ireland	38	5
Japan	46	20
Luxembourg	4	2
Netherlands	112	42
Norway	22	15
South Africa	1	1
Spain	32	1
Sweden	99	37
Switzerland	94	33
UK	237	91
US	287	83

Source: Adapted from European Trade Union Institute (2000)

If eligible companies did not set up a voluntary-based EWC, then the statutory rights would apply. These are:

- to meet central management annually to receive information on progress of the organisation's business and its prospects
- to be informed and consulted by central management about any proposal likely to have serious consequences for employees' interests
- EWC members to inform employee representatives of the outcome of information and consultation
- management to pay expenses

Many British companies, such as BT, ICI and United Biscuits, had established voluntary agreements at an early stage (Cressey, 1998). By negotiating voluntary agreements companies were able to influence the tone, approach and constitution of the European Works Council. Management could seek to use it as a vehicle to project management plans, demonstrate management expertise and seek to elicit trade union and employee commitment for the espoused strategy. Moreover, through early agreement management could seek to influence whether worker representation would be employee, or trade union based, and whether any trade union representation would include full-time officials or be confined to lay representatives working in the company (Cressey, 1998; IDS 1997b). From the experience of the establishment of EWCs involving British firms Marchington and Wilkinson (1996: 266) concluded that 'despite the generally negative response from employers and the Conservative government to these proposals, organisations which already have workable structures for multi-level consultative committees have little to fear from EWCs'.

Employee involvement

While we have begun by considering three forms of employee participation, a central theme of this chapter is the marked shift along the participation continuum from worker/trade union inspired and controlled schemes towards management inspired and controlled schemes over the period from the 1970s to the 1990s. The dominance of involvement mechanisms in the 1980s and 1990s has been assisted by enabling legislation (such as that for financial involvement); government exhortation (on flexibility and efficiency); through the example of inward investing industry, particularly Japanese and American; and because of the focus on competitive advantage through efficiency and quality. WERS98 provides us with a summary of the shift from representative to indirect forms of employee voice – 'There was a major shift from channels involving representatives, usually able to call upon the information and resources of independent trade unions, to channels where employees communicated directly with management, largely on occasions and on terms set by management themselves' (Millward et al., 2000: 135).

As Hyman and Mason (1995) argue (see Table 11.1 on page 239), there are different supporting mechanisms, trajectories and objectives underpinning employee participation and employee involvement. The objectives of management initiated employee involvement includes educating employees about the realities of the business; gaining employee commitment to corporate goals; developing employee contributions to increased efficiency; and improving productivity and customer service. The term 'empowerment' is sometimes used interchangeably with 'involvement'. Wilkinson (1998) argues that empowerment should be applied properly to information sharing, upward problem-solving, task autonomy, attitudinal shaping and self-management. What all these schemes have in common is that they are based on the unitarist frame of reference and 'take place within the context of a strict management agenda' (40). Marchington and Wilkinson (1996) identify four categories of employee involvement:

- downward communication
- upward problem-solving
- task participation
- financial involvement

Each of these will be considered in turn.

Downward communication

The principal objective of such schemes is for managers to inform and educate employees directly so that they accept management plans. A variety of techniques are available that vary in their degree of formality/informality, their regularity and in whether they rely on oral or written communication, and whether they are face-to-face or indirect. They include formal written communication such as employee reports, house journals or company newspapers; videos and, increasingly, e-mail; informal and non-routinised communications between managers and their staff; and formal team briefings based on a cascade system, and larger meetings of groups of employees, representing all of the employees in the organisation (IDS, 1997c). Many of these schemes require the active involvement of line managers and are not the preserve of human resources or communications specialists.

WERS98 found that 60 per cent of workplaces systematically used the management chain for communicating with all employees, a figure that was consistent since the 1984 survey (Cully *et al.*, 1999, Chapter 4). Increased use of newsletters, suggestion schemes and regular face-to-face meetings between management and workforce were reported. Only 5 per cent of workplaces used none of these forms of downward communication and many of these had the characteristics of 'black hole' workplaces – neither union nor personnel specialists and often stand-alone sites.

We can consider one of these forms in a little more depth. Team briefings are a system of communication operated by line management based upon the principle of cascading information down the line. The aim is to provide employees with a greater sense of belonging, common purpose and improved moral. Through this method management hope to achieve a number of specific goals:

- reinforce the role of line managers as providers of knowledge and information
- control the grapevine
- reduce misunderstandings
- assist in the acceptance of change
- increase workforce commitment to primary task
- improve upward communication

Team briefings, in particular, remained popular, being used in 61 per cent of workplaces, and had increased during the 1990s especially in private sector workplaces with neither union representation nor a functioning consultative committee (Millward *et al.*, 2000: 120). The method was used more in large establishments and in foreign-owned establishments of all sizes. Moreover, use of multiple channels of communication was more common in unionised than non-unionised workplaces which suggests that unionised workers have greater opportunities to explore their views with management than do non-unionised workers (Gennard and Judge, 1997: 128).

So this method of employee involvement is prevalent but by no means universal. Perhaps this is because of the range of problems found in operating team briefing in practice. These include difficulties in tailoring the principle of reaching all levels of the organisation in four days due to the problems of shift work, continuous process work and of reaching workers whose job takes them away from the main place of work, such as health visitors or sales representatives. There have also been reported problems in achieving the goal of reinforcing the role of line managers in situations where mangers have difficulty in clearly passing down complex messages or in controlling meetings. Finally, the information cascaded down must be relevant and comprehensive and this is not always the case.

Upward problem-solving

The principal objective of involvement schemes that come under this sub-heading is to permit management to draw upon employees' knowledge of their jobs. This can be either at an individual level through attitude surveys or suggestion schemes, or at a group level through quality circles or total quality management (TQM). Marchington and Wilkinson (1996: 262) argue that through these schemes managers wish 'to increase the stock of ideas within the organisation, to encourage co-operative relations at work, and to legitimate change'. Increasingly such schemes are part of an overall continuous improvement approach.

WERS98 evidence reveals that two-way communication systems are used in a minority of companies. In terms of upward problem-solving, 38 per cent of workplaces had examples of a group set up to solve specific problems or discuss aspects of performance or quality, 45 per cent use staff attitude surveys, and 33 per cent of workplaces operated a suggestion scheme. With a few exceptions all three schemes were more likely to be found in large rather than small workplaces, in workplaces which were part of a larger organisation rather than stand-alone companies, in the public sector rather than the private, and in foreign-owned rather than British-owned workplaces. For example, the NHS Executive has required all NHS Trusts to conduct an employee attitude survey on an annual basis from April 2000. While we have considered three types of upward problem-solving schemes here, and the notion of having an integrated set of human resource policies and practices would suggest the use of interlocking and overlapping schemes, the reality is that 35 per cent of workplaces only used one of these forms, while 30 per cent used none at all, again predominately small organisations.

At first sight this low usage of attitude surveys and suggestion schemes seems puzzling. There are a number of high-profile accounts of companies saving large sums of money from suggestions made and of employees receiving financial rewards for their suggestions. A UK Association of Suggestion Schemes survey found savings to companies of almost £40million, including as much as £2.75 million at British Airways, and payments to employees of nearly £2 million (IDS, 1997c). The IPM (1988) believe that in addition to the financial returns, there are also benefits in that the climate of employee relations can improve, as can two-way communications, because employees feel that management is prepared to ask for their views. Finally, some organisations believe that knowledge of a successful suggestion scheme enhances their position with both customers and potential employees.

These schemes may not be so universal because in practice such formality may not be necessary in smaller organisations. But Marchington (1992: 185) has pointed out three drawbacks which may make organisations wary of adopting them. First, while some employees may feel good about the pay-out from the scheme, others may be resentful of the amount, or of the amount relative to the size of savings made. Second, supervisors may feel that their position is threatened or undermined by senior management going directly to employees rather than through the line. Lastly, and this relates to other upward problem-solving approaches such as quality circles and TQM, why should some staff be specifically rewarded for good suggestions, when the alternative approach requires a constant search for continuous improvement by all staff?

Quality circles and Total Quality Management

Quality circles and Total Quality Management (TQM) may be considered together. Quality circles in practice are groups of volunteers, usually between four and eight in number, who meet regularly to identify, analyse and solve job-related problems generally under the guidance of a supervisor. They present their solutions for management to decide whether to implement them or not. Researchers (Collard and Dale, 1989; Hill, 1991) have identified two distinct, although related, management objectives for quality circles – to enhance organisational performance and to improve employee relations. Other benefits that management hope for include communication, problem-solving, employee development, improved moral and improved quality. While around two-fifths of organisations operate such schemes, the actual number of workers involved is often less that 10 per cent of those eligible to join and there is often a high failure rate with them (Bradley and Hill, 1987: 73).

A number of reasons have been put forward to account for this lack of success of quality circles. One major area concerns the position of management. Quality circles can threaten the position of middle managers and supervisors, partly because they are tackling problems which they might have been expected to identify and solve, partly because they change the relationship between the managers and the workforce in ways in which managers perceive as being 'soft', and because quality circles add to their workloads for comparatively small returns (Bradley and Hill, 1987: 75–6).

The evidence on the impact of quality circles on employees is mixed. Evidence from the US suggests that involvement in them can have a positive impact on attitudes and performance (Griffin, 1988). This is supported by research in the UK (Webb, 1989: 23), but this and other research (Bradley and Hill, 1983: 303; Marchington and Parker, 1990: 199) suggests that any such improvement may not be sustained over time and that there can be differences between members and non-members of circles which can have an overall disadvantageous impact.

Quality circles can be perceived by unions as being a threat to their position in that established working practices and agreements may be undermined by decisions of quality circles without reference to established procedures, or that employees will come to identify more closely with the employer to the detriment of the relationship with the union.

Tuckman's (1994) analysis of the situation following the fizzling out of quality circles was that management turned to TQM because it appeared to offer a solution based on the notion of a *total* management system. TQM was to become everyone's concern and responsibility, not just the small minority who volunteered to participate; it would be company-wide rather than confined to departments which opted in, and be led by senior management. The aim of approach shifted from improving employee relations to improving quality in order for the organisation to remain competitive. In the later 1980s these concepts spread from manufacturing to the service sector in the guise of customer care (Tuckman, 1995). In approaching this, however, TQM necessitated a workforce willingly co-operating in continuous improvement rather than merely complying with existing approaches and methods.

Marchington (1992: 93–5) distinguishes a 'hard' and 'soft' approach to TQM in practice. On the one hand are those advocates, following the 'excellence school of management', who call for open management styles, delegated responsibility and increased autonomy to staff. This 'soft' approach is contrasted with the 'hard' operations management view which stresses measurement and arguably leads to less discretion for employees. The third, 'mixed' approach borrows from both the other approaches but in a unitarist fashion. Putting TQM into practice means balancing the production-oriented and employee relations-oriented elements which, as, Marchington clearly identifies, means managing 'the tensions between, on the one hand, following clearly laid-down instructions while, on the other, encouraging employee influence over the management process' (94).

Work by Wilkinson, Redman, Snape and Marchington (1998) allows us to assess how these tensions have been played out in the 1990s, as the authors put it, between the promise of TQM and its principles of continuous improvement, or TQM as a slightly longer-lived management fad. The evidence appears to be mixed. Wilkinson *et al.* review a number of studies from the UK and the US as well as presenting their own survey and case study results. They conclude that TQM has become more widespread in both countries, is usually implemented in response to perceived competition and represents an attempt to win and sustain competitive advantage. But 'whilst there is evidence of successful implementation with a significant impact an organisational performance, the results are disappointing for the proponents of TQM in a large number of cases' (86). Problems in implementing TQM included severe resource limitations, costs constraints, an emphasis on short-term goals, the impact of the reduction on staff morale and difficulties in the measurement of quality and lack of commitment within the organisation, including top management (181). There was, however, little evidence of union resistance to quality management despite the suspicions unions may have about the implicit unitarism of TQM.

However, the unitarism can give rise to contradictions. For example, TQM is based on high trust, building employee commitment to the need for service quality and continuous improvement, but in their food retailing case 'mystery shoppers' were used to check that predicted norms of customer care behaviour were being implemented. This low-trust compliance approach could backfire when set aside the commitment approach. The fundamental unresolved tension is between 'the call for empowerment and individual innovation on the one hand and the requirement for conformance to tight behavioural specifications on the other' (179).

Wilkinson *et al.* examine the views expressed by some (Hammer and Champy, 1994) that TQM is not capable of effecting the transformational change which is believed necessary to regain competitive advantage because it is too much based on incremental change. Thus TQM is seen as a fad whose time is gone and is being replaced by business process re-engineering and stretch management. Wilkinson *et al.* dispute this view and suggest that 'while the high tide of the TQM movement may have receded, this does not mean that its impact has been negligible or insignificant; it has left its mark on British management' (188). But they do concede that TQM is often re-interpreted by managers who are reluctant to give up power and are driven by short-term considerations. Thus they suggest that what exists in the UK is Partial Quality Management.

Task participation

Task participation is a form of direct employee involvement in which employees are encouraged or expected to extend the range and type of tasks undertaken at work (Marchington and Wilkinson, 1996: 262). In Chapter 5 we looked at two examples of task participation – job enrichment and job redesign. Here we focus on a third – teamworking. Marchington (1992) identifies three separate, but potentially overlapping, reasons why employers may introduce task participation – as a counter to work alienation, as an attempt to increase employee commitment and as a contribution to competitive advantage.

Teamworking

The concern about flexibility is reflected in the use of teamworking as the 1990s manifestation of job redesign. In its ultimate form it has been labelled high performance work design (Buchanan, 1994) and involves a group of multi-capable workers who switch between tasks, organise and allocate work, and are responsible for all aspects of production, including quality. Buchanan (1994: 100) sees this approach as being quite different from the QWL approaches of earlier decades in that 'management motives are therefore strategic rather than operational, concerned with competition and customer satisfaction rather than with employment costs'. Yet the word 'teamworking' is used loosely and in WERS98 it was found that 65 per cent of workplaces claimed to be engaged in it. Yet when a strict definition of teamworking, like Buchanan's, is applied then this figure slumps to only 3 per cent.

Geary (1994: 441) finds that 'teamworking' is a term used in a variety of different ways, a unitarist rousing cry for all employees to work together, not least as forms of teamworking range from groups of individuals simply sharing skills and knowledge to more or less self-managing work units. He suggests that this latter, more sophisticated form is largely confined to a small number of well-publicised companies, many of which were originally established on greenfield sites, and, indeed were often incoming Japanese companies (642). Marchington (1992: 116) suggests that the chemicals and vehicle production industries are the predominant location of teamworking in practice and cites a number of examples. These approaches require a heavy involvement in training, rotation of tasks, delegated responsibility for meeting production targets and a markedly changed role for supervisors. Buchanan (1994: 101–3) cites the example of Digital Equipment Corporation plant in Ayr, where 'the high performance teams were clearly seen as fundamental to the plant's competitive strategy, and they were supported by extensive training, a redefinition and eventual elimination of the role of first-line supervision, and changes to management structure and style'.

Teamworking, however, can face similar problems to those experienced with job-restructuring programmes. It can be stressful (Berggren, 1989; Black and Ackers, 1990) for workers and managers alike. In addition, it can be viewed by the workforce as an attempt to increase control over the labour process and intensify work (Parker and Slaughter, 1988).

Financial involvement

A number of different schemes aimed at linking part of an individual employee's rewards to the success of the unit and/or of the organisation as a whole exist. These include profit sharing, employee save-as-you-earn or sharesave schemes, and all employee share plans. These schemes have been encouraged by successive governments since 1978 and most recently in the 2000 budget. Although there have been many changes in the detail, the essence of state support is through tax relief that benefits both the individual employee and the organisation offering the scheme.

Management have a number of objectives behind their introduction and while these may be overlapping, they can also be competing and contradictory. Baddon *et al.* (1989) discovered from a survey of 1000 companies and detailed case study work in five organisations four main management objectives behind the introduction of profit-sharing and employee share ownership schemes:

- encouraging the co-operation and involvement of all employees in improving the performance of the business
- giving employees a sense of identification with the company
- rewarding employees for past performance
- generating a sense of business awareness among employees

Once again WERS98 helps us to understand the extent to which such schemes are in use. The use of profit-sharing schemes, which had increased markedly in the 1980s, remained high at 46 per cent of workplaces, but the use of share ownership schemes which had also risen in the 1980s fell between 1990 and 1998 to only 24 per cent of workplaces (Cully *et al.*, 1999: 233). Nonetheless, this means that just under half of all workplaces (48 per cent) had no form of financial involvement and those that had were again more likely to be in larger workplaces, in workplaces with a personnel specialist and with an integrated employee development plan (Cully *et al.*, 1999: 69). There were, however, signs here of integration, both of different types of scheme being in the same organisation rather than as alternatives, and more significantly of financial participation being associated with other forms of employee involvement such as downward and upward communication (71).

Impact of financial involvement

A number of studies have been conducted which have tried to assess the impact that the various forms of financial involvement have had. An early attempt, admittedly from two strong advocates of such schemes, was from Bell and Hanson (1984) who argued that financial involvement schemes are warmly welcomed by employees and that it is seen as 'good for the company and its employees'. While their research might suggest that such schemes do have an impact on employee commitment and loyalty, a number of other more detailed research studies cast doubt on this. Work by Baddon *et al.* (1989) reveals that profit sharing and employee share ownership is seen by employees in very instrumental ways. They conclude that

> The benefits of most schemes are generally too small to have much prospect of marking the kind of impact management would wish. The benefits tend not to be seen by employees as an essential element of pay which would generate commitment but are more typically regarded as 'just another kind of bonus'. (1989: 274)

Moreover, this study suggested that rather than share schemes being a vehicle for eliciting employee commitment, it was only already committed and loyal employees, whose personal finances permitted, who took up share schemes. Furthermore, this was more likely to be white-collar workers and managers than blue-collar workers. In other words, those employees management would most like to build a commitment relationship with are the very ones who are least likely to take up financial involvement.

A long-standing trade union objection to share ownership is that of 'double jeopardy', i.e. that employees should not have both their jobs and their capital tied up in the same company, because redundancies would lead to a loss of income and of savings simultaneously. From the employees' perspective, two further potential drawbacks about financial participation exist. First, none of these schemes, with the exception perhaps of ESOPs, offer employees any increased participation in decision-making. At best they may elicit an orientation towards an appreciation of the marketplace and an understanding of business priorities as seen by top management, but they do not permit employees to exercise a voice in decision-making even in their role as share owners. Nor with many of the schemes is there a direct link between the schemes and the effort expected of the employee on a day-to-day basis, nor is the pay-out regular enough to act as a motivator. Other payment and motivation systems would be necessary to provide such links. Moreover, the existence of share ownership schemes which focus on the parent company may not sit comfortably with other involvement schemes which focus on the work team or the subsidiary company.

Conclusion

In this chapter we have stressed the differences between employee participation and employee involvement (EI) and demonstrated the prevalence of employee involvement forms in the last 20 years. We have related this to a concern by management to elicit employee commitment and identification as part of an overall strategy to gain and retain competitive advantage. At the same time we have shown that although employee involvement approaches may be dominant over employee participation ones, neither are majority practices and in one in six workplaces in Britain in 1998 there was no employee voice (Millward *et al.*, 2000: 122). In many cases employee involvement initiatives are more likely to be found in foreign-owned companies and in large organisations.

We now turn to consider the extent to which the various forms of employee involvement and participation which we have identified and considered fit together, either with each other or with the overall human resourcing strategy of the organisations. Here we need to consider the extent to which various forms of EI are merely management fads and fashions which come and go. We have already suggested that some approaches might be contradictory. For example, a share ownership scheme that focuses on the parent company might not sit comfortably with a teamworking initiative which focuses on the immediate work group. Similarly, a communications approach which emphasises line management's position and authority might not be compatible with a task participation approach that seeks to eliminate immediate supervision and emphasise autonomous work groups. At a higher level there is a tension between the current emphasis on an employee involvement approach with earlier approaches based on employee participation. This is often common in public sector organisations where union-based joint consultative committees operate alongside team briefing and other communication schemes based on direct involvement between management and employees.

Marchington, Wilkinson, Ackers and Goodman (1993) provided a useful device which allows us to make sense of the dynamics of schemes and their interrelationship which we have explored in detail earlier (see Figure 11.1).

In this the dynamics of EI are graphically represented as a series of waves, thus capturing the ebbs and flows of a particular technique over time and in comparison with each other, in this case a large private sector firm. This diagram can be replicated for any firm. Some evidence for this understanding of the dynamics of forms of employee participation and involvement comes from comparisons in the panel sample in the WIRS surveys (Millward *et al.*, 2000: 110): 'Between 1990 and 1998 12 per cent of continuing workplaces discontinued their functioning consultative committee whilst 17 per cent established one.' A further 18 per cent had one at both surveys, but it is not known what happened in the intervening years.

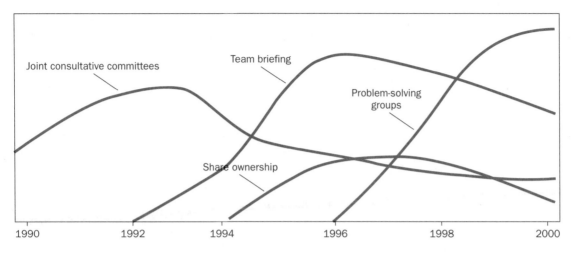

1990   1992   1994   1996   1998   2000

Figure 11.1 Movements of employee involvement and participation schemes within an organisation over time

Source: Adapted from Marchington *et al.* (1993)

Activity 11.3

Find out information about any company, either through personal experience, from other reading or from the Internet and draw the equivalent diagram for an organisation you are familiar with.

Consider the trajectories of each form and why they declined or continue to (co)exist.

It is also suggested that the confused and confusing pattern which emerges can be further complicated by inter-departmental rivalries over the ownership and objectives of particular initiatives. This diagram suggests that there is no guarantee of success for EI initiatives. We have stressed that one of the distinguishing features of EI is that it is management led. Yet the practices we have examined here suggest that it can fail or move into decline because of the action of managers. The messages can be contradictory and competing, the penetration of the initiatives can be weak; and first-line managers, on whom much depends, can feel threatened or bypassed by initiatives and may not actually implement them. Moreover, there is evidence that the training of managers to implement schemes is often inadequate and that when faced with the dilemma of spending time and money on developing initiatives and the rigours of meeting production or service demands, the latter take priority.

We have stressed that employee involvement is based on a unitarist view of the organisation; that there is an identity of interest between employee and employer. Yet many of the initiatives we have examined are designed to create the very commitment and identity which is presumed to exist. Marchington (1995: 290) on the basis of a review of survey evidence, concludes that employees are attracted to the general concept of involvement and participation but somewhat cynically points out that this is unremarkable since the alternative is an autocratic and non-communicative management style. But often, as we have shown above, their support is based on instrumentalism, a share bonus or time off monotonous work, rather than signs of commitment and loyalty. Many schemes, such as team briefing and quality circles, only involve a minority of employees for a minority of their working time and therefore their potential to transform the total employment relationship must be limited.

The final point of contrast between participation and involvement is to consider the role and position of trade unionism. Participation is seen as being union led, whereas not only is involvement management led, it is often designed to undermine or bypass union organisation (Kelly, 1988; Smith and Morton, 1993). The biggest threat to unions is that management may attempt to weaken collective bargaining, where unions effectively have a right of veto, to channel more issues through joint consultation and to increase direct communication to employees so as to reinforce the management message. On the other hand, union responses to some specific involvement initiatives have tended to be more in the 'bored hostility' camp than outright opposition.

While there is some evidence of non-union firms using a combination of EI techniques to maintain a non-union presence, the survey evidence indicates that non-union firms as a whole are less likely than their union counterparts to operate them (Sisson, 1993). In many cases EI and collective bargaining run in parallel (Storey, 1992). A more recent trade union approach (Monks, 1998) is to take the rhetoric of employee involvement and to turn it into a trade union demand for greater involvement in the management operation of the workplace. Combined with the window of opportunity offered by the European Works Council Directive, this may allow unions in the workplaces they are still strong in to put the employee participation approach back on the agenda. But for many employers operating in the 'black hole' of neither traditional industrial relations nor HRM, employee involvement is alien. Here we might let Marchington have the final say by repeating his words of 1995 (302).

> It could be argued that the haphazard, uneven and piecemeal way in which EI has been introduced into most employing organisations so far many not provide a fair indication of what it can achieve under a regime of 'soft' HRM.

Case Study 11.1

Quickcure NHS Trust

Quickcure NHS Trust is a large general hospital operating in an urban conurbation. It employs 5000 staff across all the range of medical, nursing and professions allied to medicine disciplines and appropriate support staff. About 40 per cent of these staff are members of a trade union or professional association. While pay is still based on national pay negotiating and pay review outcomes, for a long number of years a local joint consultative committee has existed. It meets bi-monthly and is a large body with some 18 employee representatives meeting with up to a dozen managers. Eight years ago the practice of having a separate meeting with TUC and non-TUC affiliated organisations was ended, and now the committee is dominated by UNISON, representing nursing, administrative, portering and lower grades of management staff. The doctors' organisation, the BMA, remains aloof from this arrangement. The committee

Case Study continued

discusses a range of topics and a perusal of the minutes of the previous years shows that staff car parking, allocation of holidays and the state of the nurses' homes are the issues that come up most frequently. They also appear never to get resolved at the meetings.

Recently, a new Director of Human Resources has been appointed. This person has extensive experience in private sector organisations in the telecommunications and information technology industries. She is appalled to discover that very little direct communication between managers and subordinates takes place. Managers seem to rely on communication to staff representatives through the JCC. This stands in contrast with her experience where a range of employee involvement techniques were in place. She is also concerned that there is no local pay determination.

Activity 11.4

1 Put yourself in the place of the Director of Human Resources. What form(s) of employee involvement would you suggest introducing to Quickcure NHS Trust?

a) What would you do about the JCC?

b) What opposition would you anticipate towards your plan?

2 You are a department manager in Quickcure NHS Trust. What suggestions about employee involvement might you expect the new Director of Human Resources to make? Which would you accept and why?

3 You are a UNISON employee representative in Quickcure NHS Trust. How would you respond to proposals to have the JCC meet less frequently and for more direct forms of employee involvement to be introduced?

SUMMARY

In this chapter the following key points have been made:

- A differentiation can be made between employee participation and employee involvement.

- An employee participation and involvement continuum can be used to distinguish between those initiatives that are management led as opposed to those that are worker/union controlled.

- From the 1980s to the 2000s, the dominant approaches in organisations have largely been management inspired and controlled.

- Managers have sought to use employee involvement techniques in an attempt to gain employee commitment to organisational goals.

- Four main approaches of involvement can be seen: downward communication, upward problem-solving, task participation and financial involvement.

- A framework can be utilised to understand the movement of particular forms of employee participation and involvement within an organisation over time, the relationship between different forms, and between these and HR strategy.

DISCUSSION QUESTIONS

1 How would you differentiate between employee participation and employee involvement?

2 Examine ways in which European Union policy and practice has influenced the policies of UK governments and/or the practices of UK companies.

3 Why might line managers feel threatened by the introduction of employee involvement or participation measures?

FURTHER READING

Employee participation, involvement and communications issues appear in most HRM and industrial relations textbooks. Appropriate references for specific topics have appeared in the text and are listed in the bibliography. Two key texts that address all the issues covered in this chapter are Hyman and Mason (1995) and Marchington (1992).

Chapter 12

Regulating the employment relationship: unilateral, joint and third-party decisions

John Leopold

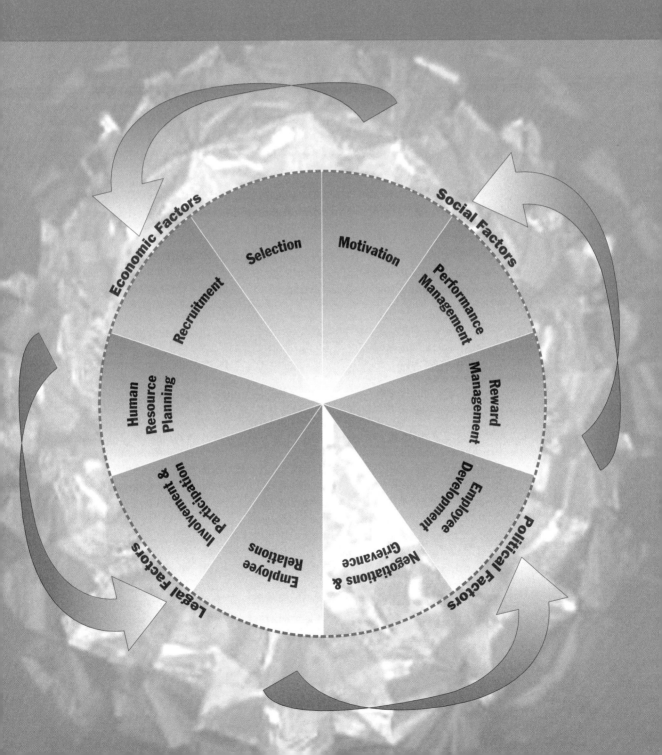

Having completed this chapter and its associated activities, readers should be able to:

- understand the sources of rules in the workplace
- appreciate the difference between substantive and procedural rules and agreements
- define collective bargaining
- appreciate the advantages and disadvantages of collective bargaining
- outline a recognition agreement
- understand differences in the levels of collective bargaining
- appreciate the advantages and disadvantages to employers of decentralised collective bargaining
- understand the advantages of having grievance, discipline and dismissal procedures
- appreciate the role of managers in operating these
- understand the thrust and direction of labour law in the UK in recent years
- understand the application of legislative rules in the workplace in a limited number of areas
- appreciate that British governments, employers and trade unions are bound by European-wide rules in some aspects of the employment relationship

INTRODUCTION

Consider for a minute your position as students in the institution you are studying in. When you registered you would have signed a declaration agreeing to abide by the rules of the university. These may have been laid down by the institution's governing body, but in some cases the students' union may have been involved in agreeing the regulations. In the module you are studying the tutor may have laid down rules about deadlines for coursework submission, or behaviour in seminars. You and your fellow students may have had some say in the establishment of these rules through student representatives on the staff–student committee. On the other hand, there may be a general understanding that coursework due on a Friday can be handed in on a Monday without penalty. If you fail the module there may be rules for appealing against the outcome, perhaps on the grounds of mitigating circumstances, or of transcripts containing errors. Failing this you may consider taking legal action against the university on grounds of failing to deliver what seemed like contractual promises. In extreme cases you may have recourse to the 'visitor' or some other 'third party' source of appeal.

Using this scenario of student life we can show how 'rules' in the workplace may be derived from a number of sources:

- *Unilateral action* – by either management or trade unions – as in the case of statement of rules decreed by the university.
- *Joint decisions* – through negotiations and bargaining between management and representatives of employees or students, as in the case of the students' union agreeing rules with the institution's governing body, or through custom and practice as in the example of no penalty for handing in Friday coursework on a Monday.
- *Third-party intervention* – either through an attempt to reconcile differences through an independent party as in the case of the 'visitor' system, or by legal enactment.

One other difference in the type of rules has also been introduced – that between procedural and substantive rules. *Procedural rules* concern the establishment of processes by which cases are dealt with, as, for example, the rules governing appeals against exam board decisions, or in a workplace context the procedures to investigate employee grievances, or to carry out decisions to dismiss employees in a fair manner. *Substantive rules* refer to matters such as the penalty for late submission of coursework or the changing level of student fees. Procedural rules, once established, are expected to be in existence for some years, although they will include provision for being altered. Substantive rules, on the other hand, are more likely to be changed on a regular basis, in the case of student fees and wages, usually annually. In the world of work we may take substantive rules as shorthand for economic rules and procedural for managerial rules.

Let us now translate these initial concepts into the workplace situation. Rules about the way work is to be done and the conditions for rewarding people doing it may be made unilaterally by management. In certain situations strong unions may be able to impose a unilateral decision on management. On the other hand, usually where unions are recognised by management for collective bargaining, both the procedural and substantive rules are made jointly. We shall consider these circumstances in more depth below. The world of employment relations also has procedures and facilities to settle disputes by third-party intervention. In the UK the main body for this is ACAS – the Advisory, Conciliation and Arbitration Service. Although set up by government, ACAS is required to act impartially in seeking to promote good industrial relations. As its name suggests ACAS officers can offer *advice*. They can *conciliate* whereby they endeavour to get the disputing parties back together again to talk through their problems and reach agreement. Lastly, they can *arbitrate by* appointing an independent third person or persons to make a final decision which both parties agree in advance to accept (Tower and Brown, 2000).

Finally, there are a number of areas of the employment relationship where governments have chosen to intervene and lay down substantive rules, such as on the minimum wage, or maximum hours of work. They have also set out procedures governing the relationship between employers and trade unions as in the conduct of strikes or picketing. There are also procedures for employers and managers to follow in their relationship with individual employees, such as in dealing with discipline and dismissal or granting parental leave. We shall consider these legal aspects later in the chapter.

Collective bargaining

In this chapter we shall, by and large, assume that, in considering the issues outlined in Chapter 10, management has decided on a strategic option that involves recognising one or more trade unions for the purpose of collective bargaining. We shall therefore concentrate on the implications and consequences of this decision. However, it should be noted that the individual aspects of managing the employment relationship, grievance, discipline and dismissal, also apply in non-union situations.

Goodman (1984: 145) has defined collective bargaining as:

> A process through which representatives of employers and of employee organisations act as the joint creators of the substantive and procedural rules regulating employment. In addition they frequently accept the main responsibility for interpreting, applying and enforcing these rules.

The key elements of this definition may be represented diagramatically as follows (see Figure 12.1):

Figure 12.1 Model of collective bargaining

The essence of establishing collective bargaining is that the employer has agreed to recognise a trade union or trade unions to represent employees in negotiations over pay and conditions and procedural rules such as discipline and dismissal. In so doing, a recognition agreement will have been signed and this will have spelled out important issues such as which group of employees are covered by the agreement in the 'bargaining unit'. It would also have been agreed at this stage which union or unions would represent the groups of workers covered by the agreement. (Refer back to Chapter 10 for detail on these points.)

Recognition agreements

Having decided which union or unions to recognise, employers then have to decide on their policy towards the *scope*, or extent, of bargaining. A fundamental point about determining rules through joint collective bargaining is that the decision-making is no longer unilateral. Management therefore has to be clear about which areas of decision-making it is prepared to relinquish control over and share with trade unions. Unions, for their part, seek to extend joint decision-making as far as possible, covering both conditions of employment and the ways in which work is organised and managed. There is therefore a tension and potential conflict of interest over the scope of bargaining; a tension that is sometimes called 'the frontier of control'. The scope of bargaining usually includes pay, hours of work and holidays, but where unions are stronger can extend into pensions, rules on promotion, additional leave and training provision.

The recognition agreement would also usually include a set of rules, or procedures, on how to resolve disputes. These may well involve bringing in a third-party body, such as ACAS, to assist in bringing the negotiating parties back together to reach their own agreement, or of having the third party determine the outcomes for the negotiators through arbitration. Clauses would probably exclude the use of strikes or lockouts until these procedures had been exhausted. This provides one of the key benefits to management of formal recognition – the avoidance of informal or 'wildcat' strikes while disputes are considered through the formal procedures.

Two broad reasons are put forward to explain why managements are willing to agree to collective bargaining. These relate to disadvantages in the alternative unilateral or third-party methods of determining rules. Bargaining, unlike unilateral management action, is participative in that it involves joint agreements with representatives of workers. The outcomes therefore have, it is argued, more chance of being accepted because they are a joint decision and the union will be involved in explaining and selling these outcomes to its members. Bargaining is also centred on the industry, or, more likely in recent years, on the organisation, and is therefore seen by managers as being more adaptable than having substantive outcomes determined by statute, which is likely to be applied in a blanket way across the whole economy. However, even where collective bargaining does take place it is only likely to involve human resource specialists and a limited number of senior managers, so that some line managers may feel that they have no say in the process but still have to abide by and operate the outcomes.

Collective bargaining also has disadvantages from a management perspective. As has already been argued, it is a limitation on management freedom or the notion of 'management prerogative'. That is why some managements refuse to recognise unions and engage in collective bargaining, and why those that do seek to limit the scope of bargaining. On the other hand, management freedom may not be worthwhile if employees refuse to accept their decisions and leave the firm in search of better pay and working conditions. The second argument against collective bargaining is a macro-economic one. It is argued by some that bargaining creates monopolistic or oligopolistic situations for the supply of labour and therefore forces up wage rates. Such people therefore advocate the weakening of trade union power and the removal of state controls on the labour market to allow market forces to operate freely. Such views were dominant in government policy in the period of the 1979–97 Conservative administration.

Bargaining structure

We have already touched upon some of the analytical features of the structure of collective bargaining. In Table 12.1 we show the key dimensions, indicate the possible categories and give examples.

Table 12.1 Bargaining structure

Dimension	Categories	Examples
Level	High	Economy
	Medium	Industry
	Low	Workplace
Unit	Broad	All worker
	Narrow	Workplace sub-group
Form	Formal	Written
	Informal	Oral
Scope	Comprehensive	Terms and conditions plus conditions of work
	Restricted	Basic terms and conditions

We have examined the arguments around the scope of bargaining, and also seen that management will have to take account of the size and shape of the bargaining unit in the recognition agreement. Furthermore, ever since the report of the Donovan Commission in 1968, there has been a clear preference for formal written agreements over informal oral ones. It is argued that greater procedural formality in the conduct of industrial relations will help avoid the potential for disputes over ill-defined informal agreements. This leaves us to consider the level at which collective bargaining is conducted.

In this there has been a marked shift of policy and practice in Britain over the last thirty years or so. While WERS98 revealed that collective bargaining is now the method of determining pay and conditions in a *minority* of UK organisations, it also confirmed that where it does still exist, it is conducted at the level of the organisation, or of a unit within it. This stands in contrast to the situation that prevailed in Britain from roughly the end of the First World War to the 1970s, when bargaining was conducted at the industry level. Where unions were recognised, employers through employers' associations representing an entire industry would bargain at the national level to set pay and conditions for that industry. In this arrangement, the scope of bargaining was somewhat limited to the basics of pay and basic working conditions and significantly did not extend to detailed issues of the organisation of work. The associated procedural agreements would also contain dispute resolution clauses designed to quickly take disputes out of the workplace and back to the national negotiators to resolve.

In this way employers were able on the one hand, to say that they recognised unions as was the public policy wish, but on the other hand, minimised their influence within the workplace, and meant that most line managers did not have day-to-day involvement with trade union representatives. Employers were also able to set uniform wages rates for the industry. This made it impossible for unions to bargain up wage rates through picking on weaker firms. It also made it difficult for new entrants to the industry to compete on the basis of lower wages, as the unions would combine with the existing employers to prevent this. In effect, wages were taken out of competition.

Unions also found such national bargaining arrangements beneficial, as it was easier to maintain pay rates within the same industry than to maintain a geographical labour market rate across industries. National bargaining also helped build national union cohesion and enhance the power and influence of national as opposed to local union leaders.

Multi-employer bargaining was the dominant system for some fifty years from the end of the First World War until the 1950s and 1960s. However, the locus of bargaining then shifted to single-employer bargaining as well-organised shop stewards sought to supplement formal multi-employer agreements with informal plant-level ones. This meant that managers at all levels had to deal with union representatives within the workplace on a day-to-day basis. The 1968 Donovan Commission described this situation as 'two systems of industrial relations' and it was then that succeeding governments sought to formalise plant-level bargaining. As a consequence, workplace shop stewards emerged as powerful and influential actors in industrial relations.

However, since the 1970s the marked decline in the existence of national industry level bargaining has seen a trend towards no bargaining at all, with pay and conditions of work being determined unilaterally by management. Where bargaining continued, it was decentralised. This change began in the private sector but followed into the public sector especially after the wave of privatisation of large public sector employers in the 1980s and 1990s. Although for much of the period Conservative governments were in power and pursued a policy of weakening trade unions and of loosening state controls over the labour market, this was not a principal reason motivating employers to change. Four main reasons have been put forward to explain this change, all deriving from company managements' desire to change their arrangements (Jackson, Leopold and Tuck, 1993).

Research evidence shows that employers wanted to *relate bargaining strategy to business strategy*. An example of this is Tesco who had been members of the employers' association for the retail food industry. In the 1980s Tesco pursued a business strategy of moving its image upmarket in order to compete with the leading retailer J. Sainsbury. This meant offering better customer service and better value added for customers. Tesco management believed that this meant being able to employ the best staff in any geographical area and that would be best achieved by paying more than other retailers. However, as they were party to bargaining arrangements that paid the same to all employees in the industry this could not be achieved without withdrawing from the industry arrangements and setting up Tesco based alternatives.

Another reason cited by employers is the desire *not to be constrained by competitors* who are in the same bargaining arrangement. This partly applied in the Tesco example above, but also applied to Coats Viyella and Courtaulds in the hosiery and knitwear industry. These two firms dominated the industry with 30 per cent market share whereas the rest of the industry comprised a large number of small firms. The two giants wanted to introduce new working practices to utilise capital investment in new equipment but felt that their competitors held them back. Both firms broke away from the industry arrangements and set up their own alternatives. This example relates to the third reason for change – the desire to establish *something for something* bargaining. Coats Viyella wanted to offer improved pay and conditions in return for changed working practices rather than just going along with the rate of inflation or rises in average wages or some such national indicator.

The fourth and final reason for decentralising bargaining is perhaps a more philosophical one. With the growth in importance of ideas associated with human resource management, especially the notions of identity and commitment to the organisation, companies wanted to find ways of *binding their employees to them*. Many managers believed that this was not possible if pay was determined outside the organisation in national industry-wide bargaining arrangements. Also, they believed that such arrangements made it more difficult to link pay to performance in ways discussed in Chapters 6 and 7. Therefore, employers wanted to bring bargaining within the company and even to decentralise it down to business units in some cases. Linked to this has been a reduction in the scope of bargaining, particularly issues to do with staffing levels (Millward, Bryson and Forth, 2000).

In spite of such persuasive reasons, these changes were not without problems for employers. If bargaining was to be conducted in company and particularly within divisions of companies, then line managers would have to add negotiating to their range of responsibilities. Also they would have to be trained to take on the role, and for new managers the ability to negotiate would have to be part of the selection criteria. Finally, the existence of decentralised bargaining opened up to unions, in favourable labour market conditions, the possibility of playing one employer off against another and engaging in leapfrog bargaining tactics.

Comparative note

The decentralisation of bargaining structures has not been confined to Britain. By contrast, in the USA, bargaining was always very decentralised and took place at the workplace level. On the other hand, in Sweden, bargaining was extremely centralised and took place at the national level with wage agreements between the employers federation and the equivalent of the TUC. However, in the past decade, led by management, bargaining has moved down to industry and company level.

In Holland bargaining continues at the industry or sector level, but many of the agreements now require further decisions in the workplace and these are taken in the works council rather than with trade union representatives, even though many of the works council members are also active trade unionists. An example of this has been the broad decision in industry negotiations to reduce working time, but with the detail of implementation being left to works councils. This has resulted in common hours of work for an industry, but variations between firms in how this is achieved.

Grievance handling, discipline and dismissal

Grievance procedures

While the decentralisation of collective bargaining has expanded the range and number of managers likely to have a responsibility in this area, there are two aspects of managing the employment relationship that nearly every line manager will have to deal with at some point in their careers. These concern handling employees' grievances and dealing with disciplinary cases, sometimes leading to dismissal. Both grievances and discipline and dismissal cases are best dealt with through a formal procedure. These procedures may be determined by unilateral management action, or through agreement with recognised trade unions, but in both cases are overlaid with statutory requirements. While human resource specialists will be involved in designing and agreeing these procedures, their day-to-day operation will largely be the responsibility of line managers with support and advice from HR.

Employees may be dissatisfied about various aspects of their relationships at work, perhaps concerning substantive conditions like pay, or the temperature in the workplace, or about the way in which a particular manager or other employee has treated them. Some grievances may at first sight appear trivial, others much more serious, but the essential point is that they are the employee's grievance and as such must be resolved. These expressions of dissatisfaction may not always surface, but when they do, and are raised formally with managers, they become grievances and managers need to know how to respond to them. Here we confine ourselves to individual grievances, but it should be noted that some grievances might have a wider impact and become collective disputes.

In smaller companies, especially non-union ones, managers may still deal with any grievance on an informal *ad hoc* basis. However, it is recognised that it is better if grievances can be dealt with through a formal procedure agreed in advance and known by employees and managers alike. The WERS98 survey revealed that 92 per cent of establishments had formal procedures for grievance and discipline, a marked change on the mere 8 per cent found in a government survey in 1969 (Cully *et al.*, 1999). In this way, employees can have some confidence that their grievances will be dealt with in a fair and impartial manner and expeditiously. Timing is of the essence, for if the grievance is not resolved quickly it may develop into something more serious. Most grievance procedures therefore lay down time limits for dealing with each stage and moving on to the next level. However, it is generally recognised that it is best to resolve grievances as close to their source as possible. The procedure would also spell out the rights an employee has to be accompanied by a fellow worker or trade union representative. Such rights are, since September 2000, enshrined in law under the Employment Relations Act 1999. An example of such a procedure is shown in the combined grievance/discipline procedure in Table 12.2. In summary, the three key principles that should be in all grievance procedures are that they should be simple to understand, be speedy in their application with clear time limits at each stage and ensure employees are treated equitably.

Table 12.2 Grievance and disciplinary procedure stages

	Grievance procedure	Disciplinary procedure
Stage 1	Employee raises grievance informally with immediate supervisor.	Manager raises issue informally with employee. The issue could be settled with a mild rebuke, or advice or an formal oral warning, the latter being recorded.
Stage 2	If the employee is not satisfied with the response, a meeting is convened between the employee and line manager with the supervisor present. The employee may be represented.	If the issue is more serious, or minor problems continue, a meeting is convened with the employee with his or her representative or colleague. The line manager may have an HR officer present. The matter will be formally investigated and if proven is likely to result in a first written warning, which is recorded.
Stage 3	If the employee is still not satisfied, he or she can take the grievance to senior manager or director level in the presence of the line manager and employee representative if available. A final decision will be taken within a set number of working days, say five or seven.	In the event of continued problems, a further meeting will be convened by the manager with the employee and his or her representative/colleague. A member of HR will also be present. The outcome can be a final written warning which makes it clear that the employee will be dismissed if the offence is repeated or improvement not made. This is recorded.
Stage 4		If the issue is one of gross misconduct, or if there has been no improvement since the final written warning within the agreed lapsed time, then a further meeting will be convened. A senior member of management may be present together with all the parties from the previous meeting. After investigation, if the offence is proven, the employee may be dismissed. The employee has a right of appeal.
Stage 5		At the appeal, which usually takes place within a specified time, say three to five days from the dismissal decision, a senior manager or director listens to the evidence and may decide to uphold the appeal, to reduce the severity of the sanction, or to uphold the original decision.

Source: Adapted from Stredwick (2000: 216)

Management may chose not to have a procedure, or where one exists not all operational managers may treat it seriously. There are, however, at least two constraints to this position. First, there is a legal requirement for employers who have at least 20 employees to supply a copy of their grievance procedure to all employees within two months of the start of their employment. Second, there are consequences of *not* dealing with grievances. As we have already indicated the issue may flare up in to a collective dispute. Alternatively an employee may respond by leaving, which may well prove to be a loss to the organisation. This also has possible legal implications for the organisation and its management should the employee then claim constructive dismissal at an employment tribunal on the grounds that a serious grievance had not been dealt with. Finally, a grievance can turn into a discipline issue against the aggrieved employee who expresses his/her exasperation at management's inactivity in a way that transgresses the rules. It is to discipline and dismissal that we now turn.

Discipline and dismissal

If grievances are employee initiated, then discipline is initiated by management. Just as at university there are specific rules about late submission of essays, attendance at classes or academic plagiarism, so in the workplace there are rules on time-keeping, absenteeism, theft and violence towards fellow employees. Management will have laid down most of these rules, and some may be statutory requirements. Offences against the rules are usually placed into two categories – misconduct and gross misconduct. As its name suggests, gross misconduct is more serious, and it often can lead to summary dismissal as a punishment. We shall return to the question of dismissal later.

Issues of fairness and justice come to the fore in considering disciplinary procedures. While each case may be dealt with on an individual *ad hoc* basis it is considered better if organisations have a clear disciplinary procedure and that their managers follow this carefully. While trade unions are generally reluctant to jointly determine rules and offences for which employees may be punished, they do seek to establish jointly agreed procedures to deal with cases that may arise. Even in non-union situations management do not have a free hand as ACAS has published a revised *Code of Practice on Disciplinary and Grievance Procedures* (ACAS, 2000). While employers are not obliged to follow this to the letter, in the event of an unfair dismissal case at an employment tribunal, the employer would have to show very good reason for not doing so.

The ACAS code sets out that disciplinary procedures should:

- be in writing
- specify to whom they apply
- be non-discriminatory
- provide for matters to be dealt with without undue delay
- provide for proceedings, witness statements and records to be kept confidential
- indicate the disciplinary actions which may be taken
- specify the levels of management which have the authority to take the various forms of disciplinary action
- provide for individuals to be informed of the complaints against them and where possible all relevant evidence before any hearing
- provide workers with an opportunity to state their case before decisions are reached

- provide workers with the right to be accompanied (under statute this is by a fellow worker or trade union official of their choice)
- ensure that, except for cases of gross misconduct, no worker is dismissed for a first breach of discipline
- ensure that disciplinary action is not taken until the case has been carefully investigated
- ensure that individuals are given an explanation for any penalty imposed
- provide a right of appeal – normally to a more senior manager – and specify the procedure to be followed

Many of the clauses in this code follow the rules of 'natural justice', such as the right to know the charge against you, and having situations fully investigated before any action is taken. Employers of more than 20 people are required to provide them with a copy of the discipline procedure within two months of the commencement of their employment. The value of clear procedures is that both employer and employee know what standards of conduct are expected, what may happen if these standards are not adhered to, and how cases will be dealt with. The intention here is to overcome problems of uneven treatment of employees by managers in different departments adopting different standards and approaches. But even with clear procedures that are likely to have been drawn up by the personnel or HR department, and in unionised workplaces agreed with the trade unions, the operation of the procedures are dependent on line managers and there may be inconsistency in practice. Indeed, some line managers may resent having to operate through red tape and bureaucracy and wish to move more quickly to dismiss employees they regard as unsatisfactory. This can be overcome in part through training so that managers are aware of why the procedures are there and what is expected of them. HR specialists can also provide support and guidance to line managers in implementing the procedure.

In the event of a breach of rules, the employer may seek to punish the employee for the offence. The ultimate punishment in this case is dismissal, but actions short of that could include suspension for a period, or issuing oral or written warnings. The warning would stay on the person's record for a specified period of time and if the offence is repeated, then a second or third breach may warrant dismissal. However, if a set period of time elapses with no repetition, then the procedures usually allow for the warning to be struck from the employee's record. In cases of gross misconduct the employer may have the right under the procedure and in law to dismiss instantly.

Perhaps understandably discipline tends to be associated with punishment. A more constructive alternative, or complementary, approach would be to focus on improved performance rather than punishment, and for the manager to try to find ways to assist the employee to reach the required standards for timekeeping, performance or behaviour that has led to the disciplinary action in the first place. Indeed, the revised ACAS code (2000: 7) states, 'Disciplinary procedures should not be viewed primarily as a means of imposing sanctions. Rather they should be seen as a way of helping and encouraging improvement amongst workers whose conduct or standard of work is unsatisfactory.'

Dismissal – fair and unfair

Ultimately there will be cases where an employer dismisses an employee. In law this dismissal may be fair or unfair. In determining this, the notion of substantive and procedural fairness comes into play. In law (to be found in the Employment Rights Act 1996) there are only five potentially fair reasons to justify dismissal:

- a reason related to the *capability* (including health) or qualifications of the employee for performing work of the kind he or she was employed to do
- reasons related to the employee's *conduct*
- that the employee was *redundant*
- that the employee could not continue to work in the position that he or she held without contravention (either on his or her part or on that of the employer) of a duty or restriction imposed under or by a *legal enactment*
- *some other substantial reason* of a kind to justify the dismissal of an employee holding the position which that employee held (e.g. reorganisation of the business)

In addition to this list of potential fair reasons for dismissal there are also a number of reasons that are automatically unfair. These are:

- pregnancy or maternity
- refusing to work on a Sunday
- trade union membership or activity
- reasonable actions by an employee representative for health and safety, pensions, or consultations on redundancy or business transfer
- unfair selection for redundancy
- transfer of undertakings
- asserting a statutory right

Activity 12.1

You work in a supermarket. Consider the reasons for which employees might be disciplined but not dismissed. Make a list of these and discuss them with a colleague.
  Now, consider reasons for which employees might be dismissed.

1 Would you consider these reasons to be potentially fair?

2 Can you fit them in to the categories for fair dismissal given above?

Currently an employee, both full and part-time, with one year's service may claim unfair dismissal at an employment tribunal and must do so within three months of losing their job. They do so by completing an IT1 form and submitting it through ACAS. Another form of third-party intervention comes into play here as an ACAS Conciliation Officer would try to get the employer and employee to settle the case before it actually reaches a tribunal. They have some success in this. For example, in 1999/2000, of the 42,791 unfair dismissal cases cleared during that year, 48 per cent were settled (ACAS, 2000). The first line of defence for the employer is to demonstrate that the reason for dismissal fell into one of the five categories above. If it does not, then the employee would win the case. However, even if it does, the employer would not necessarily win the case as they would also have to demonstrate that the procedure used was also fair. The ACAS Code of Practice may be used in an attempt to demonstrate this. In law, the employer must demonstrate that they acted reasonably in reaching the decision to dismiss.

Third-party intervention – governments and industrial relations

We turn now to the third route by which rules in the workplace may be created – through legal enactment by the government. In Britain trade unions have long campaigned for legislation to protect their members' interests. This might include laws on health and safety at work, or for the provision of state pensions. In effect, unions have sought legislation to cover those areas where collective bargaining did not reach. Despite such attempts to influence governments to pass legislation favourable to employees, the British system of industrial relations was for fifty or sixty years after the end of the First World War characterised as being a voluntarist one. That is, the state by and large left the two parties to the employment relationship, employers and trade unions, to reach voluntary agreements without state intervention. This did not mean, however, that there was no state involvement in the system. Governments laid down the rules of conduct in dispute situations through legislation defining and limiting industrial disputes. There was also statutory provision of conciliation and arbitration services to enable bargaining to get back on the rails where agreements could not be reached, and there was legislation governing some aspects of the employment relationship such as health and safety and minimum pay in certain industries. This approach stood in marked contrast to that in continental European countries. Here most aspects of the employment relationship, including trade union rights and the right to strike, were legislated for, and statutory control over labour market issues such as minimum pay and hours of work was the norm.

The pace of legislation governing industrial relations increased during the 1960s and 1970s, casting doubt over the notion of Britain having a voluntarist system. The detail need not detain us, but we do need to understand the significance of the changes made by the Conservative governments in the period 1979–97 and the differences made by the Labour government that followed.

Dickens and Hall (1995: 256) succinctly summed up the major thrust of the Conservative governments' legislation. It was 'To weaken trade union power, to assert individualist rather than collective values and to reassert employer prerogative.'

In terms of weakening trade union power, in a series of step-by-step Acts, under the Conservatives:

- trade unions' rights to take industrial action were severely constrained
- secondary actions and secondary picketing were made unlawful
- industrial action could not be taken without a prior individual secret postal ballot

- unofficial strikers could be selectively dismissed
- union chief officers and national executive members were made subject to secret individual ballots and to obligatory re-election
- the closed shop was made unlawful and unenforceable
- unions as organisations were made subject to financial penalties and their funds subject to sequestration, so that potentially they could be made ineffective and indeed bankrupt

At the same time measures were taken to reduce statutory control over the labour market and the employment relationship:

- Rights of groups of employees to claim pay comparability with other similar groups were abolished.
- The qualifying period of employment for individuals claiming unfair dismissal was extended from six months to two years.
- Controls over minimum pay for certain industries were reduced and eventually abolished in 1993.
- An opt-out clause from the Social Protocol of the Treaty on European Union (Maastricht Treaty) was negotiated in 1990. This meant that Britain did not have to comply with labour market measures that the other member states subsequently agreed to.

Low pay and long hours

Since the election of a Labour government in 1997, some changes in these policies have been made. We have already considered the new legislation on statutory union recognition through the Employment Rights Act 1999 in Chapter 10 and the ending of the Maastricht opt-out and the introduction of European Works Councils for firms in Britain in Chapter 11. We will now consider changes in two specific aspects of labour market policy – low pay and the minimum wage and hours of work and controls over maximum working time.

Figure 12.2 shows the distribution of low pay on a comparative basis. The countries with the highest percentage of employees earning less than two-thirds of median earnings, US, UK and New Zealand, are countries with deregulated labour markets. By contrast those European countries with lower percentages of low-paid workers have long been economies where many aspects of the labour market were regulated. The extent of low pay in the British context is illustrated by the fact that in 1996 over 1 million employees earned less than £2.50 per hour and of these nearly 60 per cent were women. Almost 25 per cent of all employees in the same year earned less than £4 per hour, and of these 25 per cent were aged 16 to 20. Low pay therefore particularly affects women and younger workers.

In the deregulated economy run by the Conservative government, all statutory protection for low-paid workers was ended in 1993 with the abolition of the Wages Councils. Pay levels were left to find their market rate and employers had no legal constraint on what they paid as a minimum. Supporters of this situation claimed that leaving wage setting to the market would result in lower unemployment, as people would be able to get jobs that would otherwise be prevented by

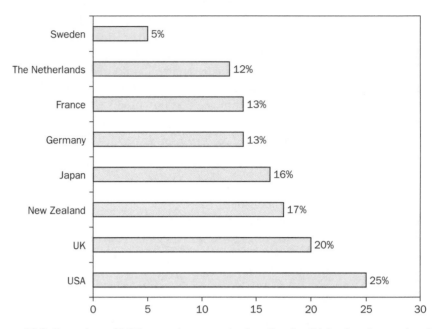

Figure 12.2 Percentage of full-time employees earning less than two-thirds of median earnings in selected countries

Source: OECD (1996)

a minimum standard. It was argued that raising pay to a statutory minimum would be inflationary and would damage the international competitive position of British firms.

On the other hand, the incoming Labour government, with trade union support, argued that social justice would be served by eliminating low pay and its associated poverty. Moreover, there would also be economic advantages. There would be savings on social security benefits paid to low income families, and a minimum standard would enhance competitiveness by requiring more investment in training and more efficient ways of working. Finally, the supporters of the statutory national minimum wage were able to point to the experiences of continental European counties and indeed the US to demonstrate the beneficial effects.

Following a period of research and consultation by the Low Pay Commission, the government introduced a statutory national minimum wage of £3.60 from April 1999, rising to £3.70 in October 2000 and £4.10 from October 2001. A youth rate of £3 (£3.20 from 1 June 2000, £3.50 from 1 October 2001 and £3.60 from October 2002) for workers aged 18 to 21 was also introduced, alongside a development rate of £3.20 for all workers starting a new job with a new employer and who receive accredited training for six months. The issue of the different rate for young workers has been raised in Chapter 6 and you should refer to the activity there.

The evidence about the impact of the statutory minimum wage appears to be that it has benefited 1.5 million workers, has not led to demands from other workers to restore wage differentials, has not led to increased unemployment, and has been easily absorbed into a growing economy. In addition, research by

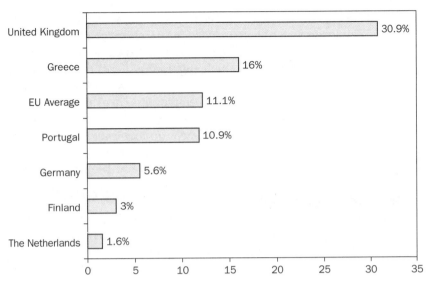

Figure 12.3 Percentage of full-time employees working 46+ hours in 1996

the Cambridge University Centre for Business Research found that the national minimum wage acted as a spur to competition and efficiency (Kitson and Wikinson, 2000). On the other hand, the level at which the rates were set has irked trade union activists and they continue to campaign for a significant increase in the rates and the abolition of the young workers differential. At the same time most employers seem to have adjusted to having this aspect of the employment relationship determined by statute rather than by unilateral management decision or jointly bargained agreements.

A second aspect of the employment relationship that has been brought under statutory control is that of working time. Here we also find the influence of the European Union. While most EU member states have minimum wage legislation, these all precede the European Social Chapter and are not directly attributed to it. On the other hand when the Labour government ended the Social Chapter opt-out, the European Working Time Directive was one of the first pieces of legislation that impacted on British employers and employees. We can again set the issue in a comparative and international context by considering the information in Figure 12.3.

From these figures we can see clearly that prior to the Working Time Directive British workers worked the longest hours in Europe. In the context of deregulation and employer prerogative these hours had not been controlled through collective bargaining. The Directive was introduced into Britain from October 1998 and laid down the following basic provisions:

- maximum working week of 48 hours including overtime
- minimum daily rest period of 11 consecutive hours per 24 hours
- minimum annual paid holiday of three weeks, rising to four from 23 November 1999.

It was estimated that the introduction of these provision immediately benefited 1.7 million workers and the holiday pay entitlement benefited a further

2.5 million. Research into the introduction of the directive showed that by and large employers were able to manage the necessary changes and there were relatively few legal cases about non-implementation. However, one aspect of the British directive was the ability to vary the regulations either through a collective agreement with a trade union, a workforce agreement where there is no recognised trade union, or by individual agreement with employees. There are signs that individual employees were forced to agree to variations in working hours or else they would lose their job. There is also evidence of a continuing long-hours culture by managers and as managers are not covered by the legislation, the introduction of the Directive has not helped them greatly (Blair, Karsten and Leopold, 1999).

Comparative note

While the introduction of the Working Time Directive in Britain was to some extent controversial, other European governments have been forging ahead with even more radical laws on working time. The most obvious example here is France where in 1999 the government legislated for a 35-hour week. Employer opposition to this measure was so fierce that demonstrations were organised. The government believed that the measure was necessary to help reduce unemployment.

Activity 12.2

1 Prepare a list of those aspects of the employment relationship that you consider legitimate for governments to intervene in.

2 Draw up a similar list of areas you believe that the state should *not* intervene in.

3 Give reasons for your list in both cases.

Case Study 12.1

Discipline and dismissal

Read the following three scenarios of grievance, discipline, or dismissal cases and then be prepared to answer the questions that follow.

Sara's story

Sara had been a machine operator with the organisation for ten years and had been regarded as a good employee. She had an exemplary attendance record and her work was of high quality. Over the past three months, however, Sara had frequently been late for work and had not turned up at all on some occasions.

- As her department manager what steps would you take to investigate this situation and what would be the likely outcomes?
- If you were Sara's union representative what action would you take?

In both cases justify your answers.

Case Study continued

Michael's story

Michael works for a family-owned and -run garden centre as a gardener/sales assistant. His immediate manager is Bob, one of two partners who own the centre. Bob and Michael have a good working relationship and a number of informal understandings have grown up between the two of them. These include a custom and practice that has developed where Michael comes in late on a Friday morning, but stays later on Saturdays in the busy summer months. This allows Bob to leave sharp on a Saturday and travel to visit a relative in a nearby hospital.

Bob unexpectedly dies and the remaining partner takes on a new manager, Jean, who had held a management position with a large chain of DIY and garden centres. This organisation had a range of formal policies and procedures and Jean was used to operating in such an environment. After a couple of weeks Jean notices Michael coming in late on a Friday. She takes him aside and challenges him, and then warns him that if he continues to come in late he will face dismissal.

● If you were Michael, what action would you take next and why?

Amanda's story

Jim is an IT specialist working for a call centre. His work is fundamental to the development of a new phase of the company's business. Amanda, a manager from another section, came to meet him at his workstation, but as she was early and he had not returned from another appointment she was alone at his workstation. Accidentally she touched his computer to reveal pornographic images. This was against company policy. She immediately reported this to the department manager, who tried to play down her concerns and insisted that Jim was such a key member of his development team that he could not countenance taking any action against him for such a 'trivial' matter.

● You are Amanda. What do you do next and why?

SUMMARY

In this chapter the following key points have been made:

- Rules in the workplace may be made either through unilateral decisions of management, or strong trade unions; joint decision-making in collective bargaining, or custom and practice; or third-party intervention through conciliation or arbitration, or legislation.
- Rules may be either about substantive conditions such as pay or hours of work; or procedural, about the general principles governing the way things are done.
- Collective bargaining is 'a process through which representatives of employers and of employee organisations act as the joint creators of the substantive and procedural rules regulating employment' (Goodman, 1984).
- Collective bargaining implies prior union recognition and a lessening of managerial prerogative in those areas that become subject to joint decision-making.
- Managers may accept this reduction because they believe that joint decision-making will lead to better acceptance of the decision by employees, but are only

willing to concede this over a limited number of areas. Unions on the other hand seek to extend the areas of joint decision-making.

- Collective bargaining now exists in a minority of workplaces and where it continues has been decentralised in recent years.

- The moves to decentralise bargaining have been led by management, rather than by government or unions.

- Managers need to consider how to deal with employee grievances and any decision to discipline and dismiss workers in a fair and consistent manner.

- Most organisations use formal procedures to try to ensure this.

- Line managers will usually deal with grievance and discipline and dismissal cases, but there are various ways in which HR specialists can support them.

- Employers must comply with legislation on unfair dismissal.

- During the period of the previous Conservative governments the thrust of legislation was to deregulate the labour market and to weaken trade union power. This also included hostility to regulation via the European Union.

- The 1997 Labour government has reversed some of these policies and in particular has introduced a statutory national minimum wage and controls over maximum working time.

DISCUSSION QUESTIONS

1 What are the implications of an employer agreeing to bargain collectively with a union over pay and working conditions?

2 What are the advantages and disadvantages to employers of decentralising their collective bargaining arrangements?

3 What are the advantages to managers and employees of dealing with grievances and disciplinary cases through formal procedures?

4 What should line managers expect from HR specialists in order to be confident of conducting discipline and dismissal cases fairly?

5 To what extent should governments intervene in labour market and employment relationship rule making?

FURTHER READING

Readers interested in the detail of employment law are advised to consult Lewis and Sargeant (2000). Issues of grievance, discipline and dismissal are covered in other introductory text books such as Foot and Hook (1999), Marchington and Wilkinson (2000) and Stredwick (2000). Collective bargaining is covered in Hollingshead, Nicholls and Tailby (1999) and Salamon (1998).

Bibliography

ACAS (1999), *Annual Report*, London: HMSO.

ACAS (2000), *Code of Practice on Disciplinary and Grievance Procedures*, London: HMSO.

Adams, J.S. (1965), 'Inequity in social exchange', *Advances in Experimental Social Psychology*, Berkowitz, L. (ed.), New York: Academic Press.

Alderfer, C.P. (1972), *Existence, Relatedness and Growth: Human Needs in Organisational Settings*, New York: Free Press.

Allen, N.J. and Meyer, J.P. (1990), 'The measurement and antecedents of affective, continuance and normative commitment to the organisation', *Journal of Occupational Psychology*, 63, 11–18.

Anthony, P. (1994), *Managing Culture*, Buckingham: Open University.

Aranya, N. and Ferris, K.R. (1984), 'A re-examination of accountants' organisational–professional conflict', *The Accounting Review*, 59, 1–15.

Argyle, M. (1972), *The Psychology of Interpersonal Behaviour* (2nd edn), Harmondsworth: Penguin.

Armstrong, M. (1987), 'Human Resource Management: a case of the emperor's new clothes?', *Personnel Management*, 31 (4), 27–9.

Armstrong, M. (1992), *Human Resource Management: Strategy and Action*, London: Kogan Page.

Armstrong, M. (1994), *Using the HR Consultant*, London: Institute of Personnel and Development.

Armstrong, M. (1996), *Employee Reward*, London: Institute of Personnel and Development.

Armstrong, M. (2000), *Performance Management*, London: Kogan Page.

Armstrong, M. and Brown, D. (1998), 'Relating competencies to pay: the UK experience', *Compensation and Benefits Review*, 30 (3), 28–39.

Armstrong, P. (1995), 'Accountancy and HRM', *Human Resource Management: A Critical Text*, Storey, J. (ed.), London: Routledge.

Arnold, J., Cooper, C. and Robertson, I. (1998), *Work Psychology: Understanding Human Behaviour in the Workplace* (2nd edn), London: Pitman Publishing.

Ashton, D. and Felstead, A. (1995), 'Training and development', in Storey, J. (ed.), *Human Resource Management: A Critical Text*, London: Routledge.

Atkinson, J. (1984), 'Manpower strategies for flexible organisations', *Personnel Management*, 16 (8): 28 (24), 28–31.

Atkinson, J. (1985), 'Flexibility – planning for an uncertain future', *Manpower Policy and Practice* (Spring), 13–24.

Atkinson, J. and Meager, N. (1986), *New Forms of Work Organisations*, IMS Report 121, Brighton.

Baddon, L., Hunter, L., Hyman, J., Leopold, J. and Ramsay, H. (1989), *People's Capitalism? A Critical Analysis of Profit Sharing and Employee Share Ownership*, London: Routledge.

Barham, K. Fraser and Heath, I. (1987), *Management for the Future*, Ashridge: Ashridge Management College/FMC.

Barling, J., Wade, B. and Fullagar, C. (1990), 'Predicting employee commitment to company and union: divergent models', *Journal of Occupational Psychology*, 63, 49–61.

Barlow, G. (1989), 'Deficiencies and the perpetuation of power: latent functions in management appraisal', *Journal of Management Studies*, 26 (5), 499–517.

Bartlett, F.C. (1932), *Remembering: An Experimental and Social Study*, Cambridge: Cambridge University Press.

Bartol, K. and Durham, C. (2000), 'Incentives: theory and practice', Cooper, C. and Locke, E. (eds), *Industrial and Organisational Psychology: Linking Theory with Practice*, Oxford: Blackwell.

Bassett, P. (1986), *Strike Free*, London: Macmillan.

Beardwell, I. (1997), 'Into the "black hole"? An examination of the personnel management of non-unionism', *New Zealand Journal of Industrial Relations*, 22 (1), 37–49.

Beardwell, I. (1998), 'Bridging the gap? Employee voice, representation and HRM', in P. Sparrow and M. Marchington, *Human Resource Management: The new agenda*, London: Financial Times/Pitman Publishing.

Beardwell, I. and Holden, L. (1994), *Human Resource Management: A Contemporary Perspective* (1st edn), London: Pitman Publishing.

Beardwell, I. and Holden, L. (1997), *Human Resource Management: A Contemporary Perspective* (2nd edn), London: Pitman Publishing.

Beardwell, I. and Holden, L. (2001), *Human Resource Management: A Contemporary Approach* (3rd edition), London: Financial Times/Prentice Hall.

Beaumont, P.B. (1987), *The Decline of Trade Union Organisation*, London: Croom Helm.

Bechtold, S.E. (1988), 'Implicit optimal and heuristic labour staffing in a multiobjective', *Multilocation Environment Decision Sciences*, 19 (2), 353–72.

Beer, M., Spector, R., Lawrence, P., Mills, Q. and Walton, R. (1984), *Managing Human Assets*, New York: Free Press.

Bell, W. and Hanson, C. (1984), *Profit Sharing and Employee Share Owning Attitude Survey*, London: Industrial Participation Association.

Bennett, R. and Leduchowicz, T. (1983), 'What makes for an effective trainer?', *Journal of European Industrial Training*, 17 (2), 1.

Berggren, C. (1989), 'New production concepts in final assembly in the Swedish experience', in S. Wood (ed.), *The Transformation of Work?*, London: Unwin Hyman.

Black, J. and Ackers, P. (1990), 'Voting for employee involvement at General Motors', paper presented to the 8th Labour Process Conference, University of Aston, March.

Blair, A., Karsten, L. and Leopold, J. (1999), 'The European Working Time Directive and its effect on flexibility within organisations in a British–Dutch comparative analysis'. Paper presented at ISIDA conference on Time and Management, Palermo, 2000.

Blinkhorn, S. and Johnson, C. (1991), 'Personality Tests: the great debate', *Personnel Management*, September, pp. 38–43, cited in Corbridge and Pilbeam (1998), p. 111.

Blyton, P. and Turnbull, P. (1998), *The Dynamics of Employment Relations*, 2nd edn, London: Macmillan.

Bolton, T. (1997), *Human Resource Management: An Introduction*, Oxford: Blackwell.

Booth, A. (1989), 'The bargaining structure of British establishments', *British Journal of Industrial Relations*, 27 (2), 225–34.

Boydell, T.H. (1983), *A Guide to the Identification of Training Needs*, London: British Association for Commercial and Industrial Education.

Bradley, K. and Hill, S. (1987), 'Quality circles and managerial interests', *Industrial Relations*, 26 (1), 68–82.

Bramham, J. (1994), *Human Resource Planning*, London: Institute of Personnel and Development.

Brannen, P. (1983), *Authority and Participation in Industry*, London: Batsford.

Bratton, J. and Gold, J. (1999), *Human Resource Management: Theory and Practice* (2nd edn), Basingstoke: Macmillan Business.

Braverman, H. (1974), *Labour and Monopoly Capital*, New York: Monthly Review Press.

Brewster, C., Hegewisch, A. and Mayne, L. (1994), 'Flexible working practices: the controversy and the evidence', *Policy and Practice in European Human Resource Management*, Price Waterhouse Cranfield Survey (eds), London: Routledge.

Brewster, C., Mayne, L., Tregaskis, O., Parsons, D., Atterbury, S., Hegewisch, A., Solaer, S., Aparicio-Valverde, M., Picq, T., Weber, W., Kabst, R., Waglund, M. and Lindström, K. (1997), *Working Time and Contract Flexibility in the EU: Main report*, Directorate General for Employment, Industrial Relations and Social Affairs of the European Commission, Cranfield: Centre for European Human Resource Management.

Bristow, E. (1974), 'Profit-sharing, socialism and labour unrest', *Essays in Anti-Labour History*, Brown, K.D. (ed.), London: Macmillan.

Broderick, R. and Boudreau, J.W. (1992), 'Human Resource Management Information technology, and the competitive edge', *Academy of Management Executive*, 6 (2), 7–17.

Brown, R.K. (1990), 'A flexible future in Europe? Changing patterns of employment in the United Kingdom', *British Journal of Sociology*, 41 (3), 301–27.

Brown, W. (1994), 'The consequences of dismantling British collective bargaining', *Review of Employment Topics*, 2 (1), 1–11.

Brown, W., Deakin, S. and Ryan, P. (1997), 'The effect of British industrial relations legislation 1979–1997', *National Institute Economic Review*, 161, 69–83.

Buchanan, D. (1994), 'Principles and practice in work design', *Personnel Management*, Sisson, K. (ed.), Oxford: Blackwell.

Buchanan, D. and Huczynski, A. (1997), *Organisation Behaviour: An Introductory Text* (3rd edn), Hemel Hempstead: Prentice Hall.

Buckley, R. and Caple, T. (2000), *The Theory and Practice of Training* (4th edn), London: Kogan Page.

Buller, P.F. (1988), 'Successful partnerships: HR and strategic planning at eight top firms', *Organisational Dynamics*, 17 (2), 27.

Bullock Report (1977), *Report of the Committee of Inquiry in Industrial Democracy*, Chairman Lord Bullock, Cmnd, London: HMSO.

Burchill, F. (1997), *Labour Relations*, Basingstoke: Macmillan.

Claydon, T. (1998), 'Problematising partnership: the prospects for a co-operative bargaining agenda', in Sparrow, P. and Marchington, M., (eds) *Human Resource Management: The New Agenda*, London: Financial Times/Pitman Publishing.

Clegg, H. (1985), 'Trade unions as an opposition which can never become a government', *Trade Unions* (2nd edn), McCarthy, W.E.J. (ed.), Harmondsworth: Pelican.

Clifford, N., Morley, M. and Gunnigle, P. (1997), 'Part-time work in Europe', *Employee Relations*, 19 (6), 555–67.

Collard, R. and Dale, B. (1989), 'Quality circles', *Personnel Management in Britain*, Sisson, K. (ed.), Oxford: Blackwell.

Coopers & Lybrand Associates (1985), *A Challenge to Complacency: Changing Attitudes to Training: A Report to the Manpower Services Commission and the National Economic Development Office*, Sheffield: MSC.

Corbridge, M. and Pilbeam, S. (1998), *Employment Resourcing*, London: Financial Times/Pitman Publishing.

Cressey, P. (1998), 'European works councils in practice', *Human Resource Management Journal*, 8 (1), 67–79.

Cully, M., O'Reilley, A., Woodland, S. and Dix, G. (1998), *The 1998 Workplace Employee Relations Survey: First findings*, London: DTI.

Cully, M., Woodland, S., O'Reilly, A. and Dix, G. (1999), *Britain at Work as Depicted by the 1998 Workplace Employee Relations Survey*, London: Routledge.

Curry, A. and Stancich, L. (2000), 'The intranet: an intrinsic component of strategic information management?', *International Journal of Information Management*, 20, 249–68.

De Grip, A., Hoevenberg, J. and Willems, E. (1997), 'A-typical employment in the European Union', *International Labour Review*, vol. 13, no. 1, 49–71.

Department for Education and Employment (2000a), *Towards a National Skills Agenda: Third report of the National Skills Task Force. Tackling the adult skills gap: Upskilling adults and the role of workplace learning*, Sheffield.

Department for Education and Employment (2000b), *Labour Market Quarterly Report, February 2000*, Sheffield: A Skills and Enterprise Network Publication.

Department for Education and Employment (2000c), *Labour Market Quarterly Report, May 2000*, Sheffield: A Skills and Enterprise Network Publications.

Department for Education and Employment (2000d), *Labour Market and Skills Trends*, Sheffield: A Skills and Enterprise Network Publication.

Department of Employment (1974), *Company Manpower Planning HMSO Report*.

Dickens, L. and Hall, M. (1995), 'The State: Labour law and industrial relations', *Industrial Relations: Theory and Practice in Britain*, Edwards, P. (ed.), Oxford: Blackwell, 255–303.

Disney, R. (1990), 'Explanations of the decline in trade unions density in Britain', *British Journal of Industrial Relations*, 28 (2), April, 165–76.

Downs, S. (1995), *Learning at Work*, London: Kogan Page.

Drucker, P. (1974), *Management*, Oxford: Butterworth-Heinemann.

DTI (1998), *Fairness At Work*, Cm 3968, London: Department of Trade and Industry.

Duncan, C. (1988), 'Why profit-related pay will fail', *Industrial Relations Journal*, 19 (3), 186–200.

Easterby-Smith, M. (1986), *Evaluation of Management Education, Training and Development*, Aldershot: Gower Publishing.

Eisenhardt, K. (1989), 'Agency theory: an assessment and review', *Academy of Management Review*, 14 (1), 57–74.

European Trade Union Institute (2000), http://www.etuc.org/ETUI/ visited 30 June 2000.

Fincham, R. and Rhodes, P. (1999), *Principles of Organisational Behaviour* (3rd edn), Oxford: OUP.

Finn, W. (2000), 'Screen test', *Personnel Management*, 6 (13), 38–43.

Fisher, C. (1999), 'Performance management and performing management', *Strategic Human Resourcing: Principles, Perspectives and Practices*, Leopold, J., Harris, L. and Watson, T. (eds), London: Financial Times/Pitman Publishing.

Fletcher, C. (2000), 'Performance appraisal: assessing and developing performance potential', *Work and Organizational Psychology: A European Perspective*, Chmiel, N. (ed.), Oxford: Blackwell.

Fombrum, C.J., Tichy, N. and Devanna, M.A. (1984), *Strategic Human Resource Management*, New York: John Wiley.

Foot, M. and Hook, C. (1999), *Introducing Human Resource Management* (2nd edn), Harlow: Longman.

Ford, R.N. (1969), *Maturation Through the Work Itself*, New York: American Management Association.

Fowler, A. (1996), *Employee Induction: A Good Start* (3rd edn), London: IPD.

Fox, A. (1966), *Industrial Sociology and Industrial Relations*, London: HMSO.

Fox, A. (1974), *Beyond Contract: Work Power and Trust Relations*, London: Faber.

Freeman, R. and Pelletier, J. (1990), 'The impact of industrial relations legislation on British union density', *British Journal of Industrial Relations*, vol. 28 no. 2, 141–64.

Gagne, R.M. (1974), *The Essentials of Learning for Instruction*, Illinois: University of Illinois Press.

Gall, G. (1994), 'The rise of single table bargaining in Britain', *Employee Relations*, 16 (4), 62–71.

Gall, G. (2000), 'In place of strife?', *People Management*, 6 (18), (September), 26–30.

Geary, J. (1994), 'Task participation: employees' participation enabled or constrained', *Personnel Management*, Sisson, K. (ed.), Oxford: Blackwell.

Gennard, J. and Judge, G. (1997), *Employee Relations*, London: IPD.

Goodman, J. (1984), *Employment Relations in Industrial Society*, Oxford: Philip Allan.

Graham, H. and Bennet, R. (1995), *Human Resources Management*, London: Pitman Publishing.

Greenberg, J. and Lind, E. (2000), 'The pursuit of organizational justice: from conceptualization to implication to application', *Industrial and Organizational Psychology*, Cooper, C. and Locke, E. (eds), Oxford: Blackwell.

Griffin, R. (1988), 'Consequences of quality circles in an industrial setting', *Academy of Management Journal*, 31, 338–58.

Guest, D. (1987), 'Human resource management and industrial relations', *Journal of Management Studies*, 24 (5), 503–21.

Guest, D. (1989), 'Human resource management: its implications for industrial relations and trade unions', *New Perspectives on Human Resource Management*, Storey, J. (ed.), London: Routledge.

Guest, D. (1992), 'Employee commitment and control', *Employment Relations: The Psychology of Influence and Control at Work*, Hartley, J. and Stevenson, G. (eds), Oxford: Blackwell.

Guest, D. (1995), 'Human Resource Management, trade unions and industrial relations', *Human Resource Management: A Critical Text*, Storey, J. (ed.), London: Routledge.

Hackett, T. and McDermott, D. (1999), 'Integrating compensation strategies: a holistic approach to compensation design', *Compensation and Benefits Review*, 31 (5), 36–43.

Hackman, J.R. and Oldham, G.R. (1975), 'Development of the job diagnostic survey', *Journal of Applied Psychology*, 60 (2), 159–70.

Hackman, J.R., Oldham, G.R., Janson, R. and Purdy, K. (1975), 'A new strategy for job enrichment', *California Management Review*, 17 (4), 57–71.

Hall, C. (1998), 'Most of Britain's new doctors are recruited abroad', *Daily Telegraph* [online] 24 July. Available from Electronic Telegraph [accessed 4 January 2001] http://www.telegraph.co.uk/et?ac=003369858810515&rtmo=wense00b&atmo=ttttttttd&pg=/et/98/7/24/ndoc24.html

Hall, D.T. and Nougaim, K.E. (1968), 'An examination of Maslow's Need Hierarchy in an organisational setting', *Organisational Behaviour and Human Performance*, 3 (1), 12–35.

Hall, L. and Torrington, D. (1989), 'How personnel managers come to terms with the computer', *Personnel Review*, 18 (6), 26–31.

Hall, M. (1992), 'Behind the European works councils directives: the European Commission's legislative strategy', *British Journal of Industrial Relations*, 30 (4), 547–61.

Hamblin, A.C. (1974), *Evaluation and Control of Training*, McGraw Hill: Maidenhead.

Hamlin, B. (1999), 'The national context', *Employee Development Practice*, Stewart, J. (ed.), London: Financial Times/Pitman Publishing.

Hammer, M. and Champy, J. (1994), *Re-engineering the Corporation: A Manifesto for a Business Revolution*, New York: Hager Business.

Harris, D.M. and De Simone, R.L. (1994), *Human Resource Development*, Orlando: Dryden Press.

Harris, L. (1999), 'Performance pay and performing for pay', *Strategic Human Resourcing: Principles, Perspectives and Practices*, Leopold, J., Harris, L. and Watson, T. (eds), London: Financial Times/Pitman Publishing.

Harrison, R. (1993), *Employee Development*, London: IPD.

Harrison, R. (1997), *Employee Development*, London: IPD.

Heery, E. (1996), 'Risk, representation and the new pay', *Personnel Review*, 25 (6), 54–65.

Hendry, C. (1995), *Human Resource Management: A Strategic Approach to Employment*, Oxford: Butterworth-Heinemann.

Hendry, C., Woodward, S., Bradley, P. and Perkins, S. (2000), 'Performance and rewards: cleaning out the stables', *Human Resource Management Journal*, 10 (3), 46–62.

Hercus, T. (1992), 'Human resource planning in eight British organisations: a Canadian perspective', *The Handbook of Human Resource Management*, Towers, B. (ed.), Oxford: Blackwell.

Herzberg, F. (1968), 'One more time: how do you motivate employees?', *Harvard Business Review*, 46 (1), 53–62.

Herzberg, F. (1987), 'Workers' needs the same around the world', *Industry Week*, 21, September, 29–30.

Herzberg, F., Mausner, B. and Snydeman, B.B. (1959), *The Motivation to Work*, New York: Wiley.

Hickson, D. and Pugh, D. (1995), *Management Worldwide: The Impact of Societal Culture on Organisations Around the Globe*, London: Penguin.

Hilgard, E.R., Atkinson, R.C. and Atkinson, R.L. (1971), *Hilgard's Introduction to Psychology* (5th edn), New York: Harcourt Brace Jovanovich.

Hill, S. (1991), 'Why quality circles failed but total quality might succeed', *British Journal of Industrial Relations*, 29 (4), 541–69.

Hollingshead, G., Nicholls, P. and Tailby, S. (1999), *Employee Relations*, London: Financial Times/Pitman Publishing.

Honey, P. and Mumford, A. (1986), *The Manual of Learning Styles*, Maidenhead: Peter Honey.

HRIS software suppliers http://www.softwaresource.co.uk/SupplierList.asp Accessed 18 October 2000.

Huczynski, A. and Buchanan, D. (1991), *Organisational Behaviour*, Hemel Hempstead: Prentice Hall.

Hunter, L., Mcgregor, A., McInnes, J. and Sproull, A. (1993), 'The "flexible firm": strategy and segmentation', *British Journal of Industrial Relations*, 31 (3), 383–408.

Huselid, M. (1995), 'The impact of human resource management practices on turn-over, productivity and corporate financial performance', *Academy of Management Journal*, 38 (3), 635–72.

Hyman, R. (1975), *Industrial Relations: A Marxist Introduction*, London: Longman.

Hyman, J. and Mason, B. (1995), *Managing Employee Involvement and Participation*, London: Sage.

Idris, A. and Eldridge, J. (1998), 'Reconceptualising human resource planning in response to institutional change', *International Journal of Manpower*, 19 (5), 343–57.

IDS (1997a), *Community Personnel Policies*, IDS Study 631, London: Income Data Services.

IDS (1997b), *European Works Councils*, IDS Study 637, London: Income Data Services.

IDS (1997c), *Suggestion Schemes*, IDS Study 638, London: Income Data Services.

IDS (1998), *Profit Sharing*, IDS Study 641, London: Income Data Services.

IDS (2000), *Temporary Workers*, IDS Report 689, London: Income Data Services.

IES/IPD (2000), *Computers in Personnel: Annual Survey Results*, London: Institute for Employment Studies and the Institute for Personnel and Development Report.

Iles, P. and Salaman, G. (1995), 'Recruitment, selection and assessment', *Human Resource Management: A Critical Text*, Storey, J. (ed.), London: Routledge.

Institute of Personnel Management (1988), 'Suggestion schemes', *Personnel Management*, Factsheet 11, November.

IPD (1995), *The IPD Codes of Practice*, London: Institute of Personnel and Development.

IPD (1999a), *The IPD Guide on Managing Diversity: Evidence from Case Studies*, London: Institute of Personnel and Development.

IPD (1999b), 'Performance pay trends in the UK', *IPD Survey Report No. 9*, London: Institute of Personnel and Development, September.

IPD (2000a), 'Study of broad-banded and job family pay structures', *IPD Survey Report No. 11*, London: Institute of Personnel and Development, January.

IPD (2000b), *IPD Survey Report No. 14: Recruitment*, London: Institute of Personnel and Development.

IPD (2000c), *Training and Development, IPD Survey Report*, London: IPD.

Iverson, R.D. (1996), 'Employee acceptance of organisational change in the role of organisational commitment', *International Journal of Human Resource Management*, 7 (1), 123–49.

Iverson, R.D., Deery, S. and Erwin, P.J. (1994), 'Absenteeism among health care workers – causes and intervention strategies'. Paper presented at the 54th Academy of Management, Dallas, Texas.

Jackson, M.P., Leopold, J.W. and Tuck, K. (1993), *Decentralisation of Collective Bargaining: An Analysis of Recent Experience in the UK*, Basingstoke: Macmillan.

Kahneman, D. and Tversky, A. (1979), 'Prospect theory: an analysis of decisions under risk', *Econometrica*, 47, 262–91.

Kaplan, R. and Norton, D. (1992), 'The balanced scorecard: measures that drive performance', *Harvard Business Review*, January/February, 71–9.

Kaplan, R. and Norton, D. (1993), 'Begin by linking measurements to strategy', *Harvard Business Review*, September/October, 134–42.

Keep, E. (1992), 'Corporate training strategies: the vital component?', *Human Resource Strategy*, Saloman, G. (ed.), London: Open University/Sage.

Kelly, G.A. (1955), *The Psychology of Personal Constructs*, New York: Norton.

Kelly, J. (1982), *Scientific Management, Job Redesign and Work Performance*, London: Academic Press.

Kelly, J. (1988), *Trade Unions and Socialist Politics*, London: Verso.

Kelly, J. (1996), 'Union militancy and social partnership', *The New Workplace and Trade Unionism: Critical Perspectives on Work and Organisation*, Ackers, P., Smith, C. and Smith, P. (eds), London: Routledge.

Kelly, J. and Kelly, C. (1991), '"Them and us": social psychology and "The new industrial relations"', *British Journal of Industrial Relations*, 29 (1), 25–48.

Kinnie, N.J. and Arthurs, A.J. (1993), 'Will personnel people ever learn to love the computer?', *Personnel Management*, (June), 46–51.

Kinnie, N.J. and Arthurs, A.J. (1996), 'Personnel specialists' advanced use of information technology: evidence and explanations', *Personnel Review*, 25 (3), 13–19.

Kitson, M. and Wilkinson, F. (2000), 'How paying the minimum wage raises the stakes', *Guardian*, 25 September, 23.

Kochan, T. (1980), *Collective Bargaining and Industrial Relations*, Homewood, Illinois: Irwin.

Kochan, T., Katz, H.C. and McKersie, R.B. (1986), *The Transformation of American Industrial Relations*, New York: Basic Books.

Kohn, A. (1993), 'Why incentive plans cannot work', *Harvard Business Review*, September/October, 54–63.

Kolb, D. (1983), *Experiential Learning: Experience as the Source of Learning and Development*, Hemel Hempstead: Prentice Hall.

Kolb, D., Rubin, M.I. and McIntyre, J.M. (1984), *Organisation Psychology* (4th edn), Hemel Hempstead: Prentice Hall.

Lamb, J. (2000), 'Recruiters turn to India for IT expertise as skills crisis bites', *People Management*, 6 (17), 12–15.

Lashley, C. (1997), *Empowering Service Excellence: Beyond the Quick Fix*, London: Cassell.

Latham, G. and Wexley, K. (1981), *Increasing Productivity through Performance Appraisal*, Addison-Wesley: Reading, Mass.

Lawler, E.E. (1973), *Motivation in Work Organisations*, New York: Brooks Cole Publishing.

Lawler, E. (1995), 'The new pay: a strategic approach', *Compensation and Benefits Review*, July/August, 46–54.

Lawler, E.E. and Suttle, J.L. (1972), 'A causal correlational test of the need Hierarchy Concept', *Organisational Behaviour and Human Performance*, 7 (2), 265–87.

Layard, R., Mayhew, K. and Owen, B. (1994), *Britain's Training Deficit*, Aldershot Avebury: MSC.

Legge, K. (1995), *Human Resource Management: Rhetoric and Realities*, London: Macmillan.

Leighton, P. (2000), 'Don't ask, don't tell', *People Management*, 6 (10), 42–4.

Leopold, J. (1997), 'BellSouth', *Human Resource Management in Action. Contemporary New Zealand Cases*, Vol. 1, Elkin, G., Palmerston North, New Zealand: The Dunmore Press.

Leopold, J. and Hallier, J. (1997), 'Start-up and ageing in greenfield sites', *Human Resource Management Journal*, 7 (2), 72–88.

Leopold, J., Harris, L. and Watson, T. (1999), *Strategic Human Resourcing: Principles, Perspectives and Practices*, London: Financial Times/Pitman Publishing.

Lewis C. (1985), *Employee Selection*, London: Hutchinson.

Lewis, D. and Sargeant, M. (2000), *Essentials of Employment Law* (6th edn), London: CIPD.

Locke, E.A. (1976), 'The nature and causes of job satisfaction', *Handbook of Industrial and Organisational Psychology*, Dunnette, M.D. (ed.), Chicago: Rand McNally.

Locke, E.A. and Latham, G.P. (1990), *A Theory of Goal Setting and Task Performance*, Englewood Cliffs, NJ: Prentice-Hall.

MacInnes, J. (1987), *Thatcherism at Work*, Milton Keynes: Open University Press.

MacInnes, J. (1988), 'The question of flexibility', *Personnel Review*, 17 (3), 12–15.

Manpower Services Commission (1981), *A New Training Initiation*, Sheffield: MSC.

Mansell-Lewis, E. (1997), 'Intranet essentials', *Computer Weekly*, October, 44.

Marchington, M. and Wilkinson, A. (2000), *Core Personnel and Development* (Annotated 2000 Edition), London: CIPD.

Marchington, M. (1988), 'The four faces of employee consultation', *Personnel Management*, May.

Marchington, M. (1992), *Managing the Team*, Oxford: Blackwell.

Marchington, M. (1994), 'The dynamics of joint consultation', *Personnel Management*, Sisson, K. (ed.), Oxford: Blackwell.

Marchington, M. (1995), 'Employee relations', *Strategic Prospects for HRM*, Tyson, S. (ed.), London: IPD.

Marchington, M., Goodman, J., Wilkinson, A. and Ackers, P. (1992), *New Developments in Employee Involvement*, London: Employment Department, Research Series No. 2.

Marchington, M. and Parker, P. (1990), *Changing Patterns of Employee Relations*, Hemel Hempstead: Harvester Wheatsheaf.

Marchington, M. and Wilkinson, A. (1996), *Core Personnel and Development*, London: Institute of Personnel and Development.

Marchington, M. and Wilkinson, A. (2001), *Core Personnel and Development*, 2nd edn, London: Institute of Personnel and Development.

Marchington, M., Wilkinson, A., Ackers, P. and Goodman, J. (1993), 'The influence of managerial relations on waves of employee involvement', *British Journal of Industrial Relations*, 31 (4), 553–76.

Marginson, P. (1989), 'Employment flexibility in large companies: change and continuity', *Industrial Relations Journal*, 29 (2), 101–8.

Marston, P. (1997), 'BA offers a £2000 recruitment fee', *Daily Telegraph* [online] 10 June. Available from Electronic Telegraph [accessed 4 January 2001] http://www.telegraph.co.uk/et?ac=003369858810515&rtmo=lvPSQkzt&atmo=tttttttd&pg=/et/97/6/10/nba10.html

Maslow, A. (1943), 'A theory of human motivation', *Psychological Review*, (50) 4, 370–96.

Maslow, A.H. (1959), *Motivation and Personality*, New York: Harper & Rowe.

Mason, R. and Bain, P. (1991), 'Trade union recruitment strategies: facing the 1990s', *Industrial Relations Journal*, 22 (1), 36–45.

Matthieu, J. and Zajac, D.M. (1990), 'A review and meta analysis of the antecendents, correlates and consequences of organisational commitment', *Psychological Bulletin*, 108 (2), 171–94.

Mayne, L., Tregaskis, O. and Brewster, C. (1996), 'A comparative analysis of the link between flexibility and HRM strategy', *Employee Relations*, 18 (3), 5–24.

McClelland, D.C. (1999), *Human Motivation*, Cambridge: Cambridge University Press.

McCole, D. and Wilkinson, A. (1998), 'The rise and fall of TQM: the vision, meaning and operation of change', *Industrial Relations Journal*, 29 (1), 18–29.

McConville, T. and Holden, L. (1999), 'The filling in the sandwich: HRM and middle managers in the health sector', *Personnel Review*, 28 (5/6), 406–24.

McGregor, A. and Sproull, A. (1991), *Employers' Labour use Strategies: Analysis of an employer survey*, London: Department of Employment Report, Research Paper No. 83.

McKenna, E. (2000), *Business Psychology and Organisational Behaviour* (3rd edn), Hove: Psychology Press.

Mento, A.J., Steel, R.P. and Karren, R.J. (1987), 'A meta-analytic study of the effects of goal setting on task performance: 1966–1984', *Organisational Behaviour and Human Decision Processes*, 39, 52–83.

Metcalf, D. (1991), 'British unions: dissolution or resurgence?', *Oxford Review of Economic Policy*, 7 (1), 18–32.

Meulders, D., Plasman, O. and Plasman, R. (1996), 'A typical work in the European experience', *Transfer*, vol. 2, no. 4, 574–601.

Meyer, J.P., Allen, N.J. and Smith, C.A. (1993), 'Commitment to organisations and occupations: extension and test of a three component conceptualisation', *Journal of Applied Psychology*, 78, 538–51.

Midgley, S. (1999), 'Work of fiction', *People Management*, 5 (11), 58.

Miller, G.A. (1966), *Psychology: The Science of Mental Life*, Harmondsworth: Penguin Books.

Millward, N., Bryson, A. and Forth, J. (2000), *All Change at Work: British Employment Relations 1980–1988, as Portrayed by the Workplace Industrial Relations Survey Series*, London: Routledge.

Millward, N. and Stevens, M. (1986), *British Workplace Industrial Relations 1980–1984*, The DE/ESRC/PSI/ACAS Survey, London: Gower.

Millward, N., Stevens, M., Smart, D. and Hawes, W.R. (1992), *Workplace Industrial Relations in Transition*, Aldershot: Dartmouth.

Mohapatra, P.K.J., Mandal, P. and Saha, B.K. (1990), 'Modelling age and retirement in manpower planning', *International Journal of Manpower*, 11 (6), 27–31.

Monks, J. (1998), 'Trade unions, enterprise and the future', *Human Resource Management: The New Agenda*, Sparrow, P. and Marchington, M. (eds), London: Financial Times/Pitman.

Mullins, L. (1999), *Management and Organisational Behaviour*, London: Pitman Publishing.

Mumford, E. (1976), 'A strategy for the redesign of work', *Personnel Review*, 5, 33–9.

Munro Fraser, J. (1971), *Psychology: General, Industrial, Social*, London: Pitman.

Myers, D.G. (1995), *Psychology* (4th edn), New York: Worth.

Parker, B. and Caine, D. (1996), 'Holonic modelling: human resource planning and the two faces of Janus', *International Journal of Manpower*, 17 (8), 30–45.

Parker, M. and Slaughter, J. (1988), *Choosing Sites: Union and the Team Concept*, Boston: South End Press.

Paul, W.J. and Robertson, K.B. (1970), *Job Enrichment and Employee Motivation*, Aldershot: Gower.

Peltu, M. (1996), 'Death to cuts', *Computing*, 9, May, 34.

Penn, R. (1992), 'Flexibility in Britain during the 1980s: recent empirical evidence', *Fordism and Flexibility*, Burrows, R., Gilbert, N. and Pollert, A. (eds), Basingstoke: Macmillan, pp. 66–86.

Pettigrew, A., Jones, E. and Reason, P. (1982), *Training and Development Roles in their Organisational Setting*, Sheffield Training Division: MSC.

Pfeffer, J. (1994), *Competitive Advantage through People*, Boston: HBS Press.

Piore, M.J. and Sable, C. (1984), *The Second Industrial Divide: Prospects for Prosperity*, New York: Basic Books.

Pollert, A. (1988a), 'Dismantling flexibility', *Capital and Class*, 34 (Spring), 42–75.

Pollert, A. (1998b), 'The "flexible firm": fiction or fact?', *Work, Employment and Society*, 2 (3), 281–316.

Pollert, A. (ed.) (1991), *Farewell to Flexibility*, Oxford: Blackwell.

Pontusson, J. (1990), 'The politics of new technology and job redesign: a comparison of Volvo and British Leyland', *Economic and Industrial Democracy*, 11, 311–36.

Poole, M. (1986), *Towards a New Industrial Democracy*, London: Routledge.

Poole, M. and Jenkins, G. (1990), *The Impact of Economic Democracy: Profit Sharing and Employee Shareholding Schemes*, London: Routledge.

Porter, L.W. and Lawler, E.E. (1968), *Managerial Attitudes and Performance*, Homewood, Illinois: Irwin.

Prais, S.J. (1985), 'What can we learn from the German system of education and vocational training?', *Education and Economic Performance*, Worswick, G.O.N. (ed.), London: IPD.

PricewaterhouseCoopers (2000), *East Midlands Business Survey*, PricewaterhouseCoopers in association with Warwick Business School and The Nottingham Trent University Report.

Proctor, S., Rowlinson, M., Mcardle, L., Hassard, J. and Forrester, P. (1994), 'Flexibility, politics and strategy: in defence of the model of the flexible firm', *Work, Employment and Society*, 8 (2), 221–42.

Purcell, J. (1987), 'Mapping management styles in employee relations', *Journal of Management Studies*, 24 (5), 533–48.

Purcell, J. (1989), 'The impact of corporate strategy on human resource management', *New Perspectives on Human Resource Management*, Storey, J. (ed.), London: Routledge, pp. 63–86.

Ramsey, H. (1977), 'Cycles of control: worker participation in sociological and historical perspectives', *Sociology*, 11 (3), 481–506.

Ramsey, H. (1983), 'Evolution or cycle? Worker participation in the 1970s and 1980s', *Organisational Democracy and Political Processes*, Crouch, C. and Heller, F. (ed.), International Yearbook of Industrial Democracy, Yearbook, London: Wiley.

Ramsey, H. (1990), *The Joint Consultation Debate: Soft Soap and Hard Cases*, Discussion Paper No. 17, Glasgow, Centre for Research in Industrial Democracy and Participation.

Redman, T. and Snape, E. (1992), 'Upward and onward: can staff appraise their managers?', *Personnel Review*, 27 (7), 32–46.

Reid, M. and Barrington, H. (1994), *Training Interventions*, 4th edn, London: IPD.

Reid, M. and Barrington, H. (1997), *Training Interventions*, 5th edn, London: IPD.

Reilly, P. (1996), *Human Resource Planning: An Introduction*, Brighton: The Institute for Employment Studies, Report 312.

Ribeaux, P. and Poppleton, S.E. (1978), *Psychology and Work*, London: Macmillan Education.

Richards-Carpenter, C. (1989), 'Manpower planning makes a comeback', *Personnel Management*, 21 (7), 55–65.

Roberts, K.H. and Glick, W. (1981), 'The job characteristics approach to task design: a critical review', *Journal of Applied Psychology*, 66, 193–217.

Robinson, D. (1997), *HR Information Systems: Stand and Deliver*, Brighton: Institute for Employment Studies Report 335.

Roger, A. (1970), *The Seven Point Plan*, 3rd edn, London: NFER.

Rogers, C. (1965), *Client-centred Therapy*, Boston: Houghton Mifflin.

Rogers, C. (1969), *Freedom to Learn*, Ohio: Merrill.

Rollinson, D., Broadfield, A. and Edwards, D.J. (1998), *Organisation Behaviour and Analysis*, Harlow: Addison Wesley Longman.

Ross, R. and Schneider, R. (1992), *From Equality to Diversity: A Business Case for Equal Opportunities*, London: Financial Times/Pitman Publishing.

Rowe, H. (2000), 'Part-time hopefuls find few flexible friends in finance', *Personnel Today*, 67.

Rudman, R. (1995), *Performance Planning and Review*, Melbourne: Pitman Publishing.

Salamon, M. (1998), *Industrial Relations theory and practice*, 3rd edn, Hemel Hempstead: Prentice Hall.

Schein, E. (1985), *Organisational Culture and Leadership*, San Francisco: Josey-Bass.

Schein, E. (1988), *Organisational Psychology*, New Jersey: Prentice Hall.

Schmitt, N. and Chan, D. (1998), *Personnel Selection: A Theoretical Approach*, London: Sage.

Schruijer, S. (1992), 'Recruitment and integration of women in the Dutch Royal Air Force', *Human Resource Management in Europe: Text and Cases*, Vickerstaff, S. (ed.), London: Chapman and Hall.

Sisson, K. (1993), 'In search of HRM', *British Journal of Industrial Relations*, 31 (2), 201–10.

Sisson, K. and Storey, J. (2000), *The Realities of Human Resource Management: Managing the Employment Relationship*, Buckingham: Open University Press.

Smith, P. and Morton, G. (1993), 'Union exclusion and the decollectivisation of industrial relations in contemporary Britain', *British Journal of Industrial Relations*, 31 (1), 97–114.

Stainer, G. (1971), *Manpower Planning*, London: Heinemann.

Stewart, J. (1996), *Managing Change through Training and Development*, 2nd edn, London: Kogan Page.

Stewart, J. (1998), 'The psychology of decision making', Jennings, D. and Wattam, S. (eds), *Decision Making: An Integrated Approach*, 2nd edn, London: Financial Times/ Pitman Publishing.

Stewart, J. (1999), *Employee Development Practice*, London: Financial Times/Pitman Publishing.

Stewart, J., Manhire, E. and Hall, R. (1999), 'Employee training and development', *Strategic Human Resourcing: Principles, Perspectives and Practices*, Leopold, J., Harris, L. and Watson, T. (eds), London: Financial Times/Pitman Publishing, pp. 217–38.

Stewart, R. (1963), *The Reality of Management*, London: Pan.

Storey, J. (1992), *Developments in the Management of Human Resources*, Oxford: Blackwell.

Storey, J. (ed.) (1995), *Human Resource Management: A Critical Text*, London: Routledge.

Straw, J. (1989), 'Equal Opportunities', *Employment Resourcing*, Corbridge, M. and Pilbeam, S. (eds), London: Financial Times/Pitman Publishing

Stredwick, J. (2000), *An Introduction to Human Resource Management*, Oxford: Butterworth-Heinemann.

Tailby, S. and Pearson, E. (1998), 'Employee relations in the south-west', *Work and Employment*, 6 (Spring).

Tansley, C. (1999), 'Human Resource Planning: Strategies, systems and processes', *Strategic Human Resourcing: Principles, Perspectives and Practices*, Leopold, J., Harris, L. and Watson, T. (eds), London: Pitman Publishing, pp. 39–62.

Tansley, C., Newell, S. and Williams, H. (2001), 'Effecting HRM-style practices through an integrated Human Resource information system: an e-greenfield site?', *Personnel Review* (Special Issue: Managing the Employment Relationship in Greenfield Sites), 30 (3), 351–70.

Taylor, F.W. (1947), *Scientific Management*, New York: Harper and Row.

Taylor, S. (1998), *Employee Resourcing*, London: Institute of Personnel and Development.

Thompson, P. (1989), *The Nature of Work: An Introduction to Debates on the Labour Process*, London: Macmillan.

Torrington, D. and Hall, L. (1998), *Human Resource Management*, Hemel Hempstead: Prentice Hall.

Towers, B. and W. Brown (eds) (2000), *Employment Relations in Britain: 25 years of the Advisory, Conciliation and Arbitration Service*, Oxford: Blackwell.

Townley, B. (1994), 'Communicating with employees', *Personnel Management*, Sisson, K. (ed.), Oxford: Blackwell.

Trades Union Congress (1994), *Human Resource Management: A Trade Union Response*, London: TUC.

Trades Union Congress (1997), *Partners for Progress: Next Steps for New Unionism*, London: Trades Union Congress.

Tuckman, A. (1994), 'The yellow brick road: total quality management and the restructuring of organisational culture', *Organisation Studies*, 15 (5), 727–51.

Tuckman, A. (1995), 'Ideology, quality and TQM', *Making Quality Critical: Studies in Organisational Change*, Wilkinson, A. and Willmott, H. (eds), London: Routledge.

Turnow, W. (1993), 'Introduction to special issue on 360-degree feedback', *Human Resource Management*, Summer/Fall, 311–16.

Tyson, S. and Fell, A. (1992), *Evaluating the Personnel Function*, Cheltenham: Thornes.

Ulrich, D. (1987), 'Strategic human resource planning: why and how?', *Human Resource Planning*, 10 (1), 37–56.

Unions 21 (1998), *Fairness at Work White Paper: Preparing a Response*, London: Unions 21.

Unknown (2000), *Labour Market Spotlight*, Labour Market Trends Report.

Valentine, R. and Knights, E. (1998), 'TQM and BPR – can you spot the difference?', *Personnel Review*, 27 (1), 78–85.

Vickerstaff, S. (1992), *Human Resource Management in Europe: Text and Cases*, London: Chapman and Hall.

Vroom, V.H. (1964), *Work and Motivation*, Chichester: Wiley.

Waddington, J. and Whitston, C. (1996), 'Empowerment versus intensification: union perspectives of change in the workplace', Ackers, P., Smith, C. and Smith, P. (eds), *The New Workplace and Trade Unionism: Critical Perspectives on Work and Organisation*, London: Routledge.

Walker, J.W. (1980), *Human Resource Planning*, London: McGraw-Hill.

Walsh, J. (1999), 'HR: slow to gain input at board level', *People Management*, 5 (15), 15–29.

Walsh, T. (1991), 'The reshaping of flexible labour? European policy perspectives', *Flexible Future*, Blyton, P. and Morris, J.A. (eds), Berlin: Walter De Gruyter, pp. 349–64.

Walters, M. (ed.) (1995), *The Performance Management Handbook*, London: Institute of Personnel and Development.

Walton, J. (1999), *Strategic Human Resource Development*, Harlow: Pearson Education.

Wanous, J.P. and Zwany, A. (1977), 'A cross-sectional test of need hierarchy', *Organisational Behaviour and Human Performance*, 18, 78–97.

Watson, T. (1994), 'Recruitment and Selection', *Personnel Management: A Comprehensive Guide to Theory and Practice in Britain*, Sisson, K. (ed.), Oxford: Blackwell.

Watson T. (1995), *Sociology, Work and Industry*, Routledge: London.

Watson, T. (1999), 'Human resourcing strategies: choice chance and circumstance', Leopold, J., Harris, L. and Watson, T. (eds), *Strategic Human Resourcing Principles, Perspectives and Practices*, London: Financial Times/Pitman Publishing.

Webb, S. (1989), *Blueprint for Success: A Report on Involving Employees in Britain*, London: Industrial Society.

Weitzman, M. (1984), *The Share Economy*, Cambridge, Mass: Harvard University Press.

Whiddett, K. and Kandola, B. (2000), 'Fit for the job?', *People Management*, 6 (11), 30–4.

Whitehead, M. (1999), 'Churning questions', *People Management*, London: IPD, 5 (19) 46–8, September.

Whitelaw, M. (1972), *The Evaluation of Management Training: A Review*, London: Institute of Personnel Management.

Whitston, C. and Waddington, J. (1994), 'Why join a union?', *New Statesman and Society*, 18 November, 36–8.

Wilkinson, A. (1998), 'Empowerment: theory and practice', *Personnel Review*, 27 (1), 40–56.

Wilkinson, A., Marchington, M., Goodman, J. and Ackers, P. (1992), 'Total quality management and employee involvement', *Human Resource Management Journal*, 2 (4), 1–20.

Wilkinson, A., Redman, T., Snape, E. and Marchington, M. (1998), *Managing with Total Quality Management*, London: Macmillan.

Williams, H. (2000), 'How can human resource information systems inform and enable strategy making?', Human Resource Management Nottingham: Nottingham Business School, Nottingham Trent University (MA in Strategic Human Resource Management).

Willman, P. (1996), 'Merger propensity and merger outcomes among British unions 1986–1995', *Industrial Relations Journal*, 27 (4), 331–8.

Wilson, B. (1987), 'Manpower planning of future requirements', *International Journal of Manpower*, 8 (3), 3–8.

Wilson, J.P. (ed.) (1999), *Human Resource Development*, London: Kogan Page.

Winstanley, D. (2000), 'Conditions of worth and the performance management paradox', *Ethical Issues in Contemporary Human Resource Management*, Winstanley, D. and Woodall, J. (eds), Oxford: Macmillan.

Winstanley, D. and Stuart-Smith, K. (1996), 'Policing performance: the ethics of performance management', *Personnel Review*, 25 (6), 66–84.

Index

and recruitment 54
and training benefits 190–1

hair stylists, recruitment procedures 59–60
half-life analysis 40
hard human resource management 12,
    26–7
head-hunters 67
health and safety, employee representation
    241–2
Health and Safety at Work Act (1974) 241
Health and Safety (Consultation with
    Employees) Regulations (1996) 242
Herzberg's two-factor theory 112–14
Hislop Brewery, individual learning case
    study 184–5
Honey and Mumford's learning styles 181,
    208
hours of work 273–4
Human Resource Information Systems
    (HRIS) 27, 44–9
Human Resource Management (HRM)
  and employee training 190–1
  hard and soft 12, 26–7
  meanings of 8–9
  models of 9–13
  personnel management comparison
    9–10
  policy goals 9, 190–1
  see also personnel management
Human Resource planning (HRP)
  analysis and investigation 31–8
  and business planning 25–7
  definitions 29–30
  forecasting labour supply and demand
    38–42
  framework 31
  implementation and control 44–9
  and manpower planning 28–30
  planning and resourcing 43–4
Human Rights Act (1999) 45, 58
humanist learning theory 181–2
humanist psychology 172–3

image, problem of 3–4, 8
individual learning 169–86
  case study 184–5
  psychology of 170–3
  theories of 173–83
individualism 219–20

induction 100
ineffective performance
  case study 144
  management 143–4
insight, humanist learning theory 181–2
Institute of Personnel and Development
    (IPD)
  Training and Development Survey (2000)
    205–6, 209–10
  see also Chartered Institute of Personnel
    and Development
Institute of Personnel Management 5–6
institutional theory, reward systems 153
integrated reward systems 164
internal labour market 36
internal labour supply, forecasting 39–41
Internet
  and human resource planning 48
  recruitment and selection 99
interviewing, as selection method 92–4,
    97, 99
intranets, human resource planning 47–8
Islamic approaches
  recruitment methods 56
  selection methods 82

job analysis 62–6
job description 63
job enrichment 119–23
job evaluation, pay structures 156
job satisfaction see motivation
joint consultative committees (JCCs)
    240–1
joint decisions, employment relationship
    259
just in time approach, recruitment 57

kaleidoscope model 10–11
Knowledge, Abilities, Skills, and Other
    characteristics (KASO) 62
Kochan model of union membership
    221–2
Kolb's experiential learning cycle 180–1

labour demand, forecasting 38–9
Labour Force Survey, training 194–7
labour market
  external 32–5
  internal 36
labour supply, forecasting 39–41

labour turnover analysis 40
learning
  behaviourist learning theory 174–6
  case study 184–5
  cognitive learning theory 178–9
  definitions 174
  experiential learning theory 180–1
  humanist learning theory 181–2
  social learning theory 177–8
  theories of 173–83
  training methods 207–9
Learning Styles Questionnaire (LSQ)
  180–1
line managers
  and human resource planning 37, 41–2,
    43, 49
  personnel role 7
  and selection process 80
low pay, government legislation 271–3

Maastricht Treaty 271
management
  employment relationship options
    217–36
  partnership with employees 230–1
  and trade unions 221–30
Management by Objectives (MBO) 138
management consultants, reward systems
  163
managerial judgement 39
manpower planning, and human resource
  planning (HRP) 28–30
Marxist frame of reference, employment
  relationship 218–19
Maslow's hierarchy of needs theory 110–12
Megginson Model, employee development
  202–3
mentoring 178
minimum wage 155, 272–3
motivation 109–27
  case study 124–6
  and commitment 123–4
  content theories 110–14
  process theories 114–23
  and reward 151–4
  scientific management approach
    109–10
motivational potential score 120
MUD, learning objectives 207–8
Munro Fraser's five-point plan 63–4

National Minimum Wage (NMW) 155,
  272–3
National Skills Task Force 194
nominal group technique 39

objective-based methods, performance
  management 138–40
OKI, greenfield site case study 18–19
operant conditioning 175–6
organisational approaches, employee
  development 200–11
organisational assessment, and human
  resource planning 36
organisational commitment 123–4
organisational justice theory of motivation
  117–18
organisational performance pay system
  161

part-time work 35–6
partnership, employment relationship
  230–1
paternalism, employment relationship
  220
Pavlov's dogs 175
pay
  competency-based methods 158–9
  external pay relationships 155–6
  government legislation 271–3
  internal pay relationships 156–8
  'new pay' 149, 159
  organisational performance 161
  performance-related pay (PRP) 159–61
  reward systems 150, 155–61
  skill-based 158–9
  structures 155–8
  systems 158–61
  time-based 158
pay curves 157–8
performance management 129–46
  and appraisal 135–6
  case study 134
  competency-based methods 140
  conflicts 131–2
  and ethics 145
  formal and informal 132–4
  ineffective performance 143–4
  methods 136–42
  objective-based methods 138–40
  system or process 131